American Furniture

AMERICAN FURNITURE

1996

Edited by Luke Beckerdite

Published by the CHIPSTONE FOUNDATION

Distributed by University Press of New England

Hanover and London

EDITOR
Luke Beckerdite

BOOK AND EXHIBITION REVIEW EDITOR
Gerald W. R. Ward

ASSOCIATE EDITOR
Catherine E. Hutchins

EDITORIAL ADVISORY BOARD
Luke Beckerdite, *Executive Director, Chipstone Foundation*
John Bivins, Jr., *Conservator and Decorative Arts Consultant*
Edward S. Cooke, Jr., *Associate Professor, Department of the History of Art, Yale University*
Wallace Gusler, *Master of the Shop–Gunsmith, Colonial Williamsburg Foundation*
Morrison H. Heckscher, *Curator of American Decorative Arts, Metropolitan Museum of Art*
Brock Jobe, *Deputy Director of Collections, Conservation, and Interpretation, H. F. du Pont Winterthur Museum*
Robert F. Trent, *Conservator and Decorative Arts Consultant*
Gerald W. R. Ward, *Associate Curator, American Decorative Arts & Sculpture, Museum of Fine Arts, Boston*
Gregory R. Weidman, *Assistant Director for Special Projects, Maryland Historical Society*
Philip D. Zimmerman, *Museum and Decorative Arts Consultant*

Cover Illustration: Detail of the support of a card table attributed to Deming and Bulkley, New York City, ca. 1825. (Courtesy, Charleston Museum.)

Design: Wynne Patterson, Pittsfield, Vermont
Photography: Gavin Ashworth, New York, New York

Published by the Chipstone Foundation
Distributed by University Press of New England, Hanover, NH 03755
© 1996 by the Chipstone Foundation
All rights reserved
Printed in the United States of America 5 4 3 2 1
ISSN 1069–4188
ISBN 0–87451–793–1

Contents

Editorial Statement

American Furniture is an interdisciplinary journal dedicated to advancing knowledge of furniture made or used in the Americas from the seventeenth century to the present. Authors are encouraged to submit articles on any aspect of furniture history, essays on conservation and historic technology, reproductions or transcripts of documents, such as account books and inventories, annotated photographs of new furniture discoveries, and book and exhibition reviews. References for compiling an annual bibliography also are welcome.

Manuscripts must be typed, double-spaced, illustrated with 8" × 10" black-and-white prints or transparencies, and prepared in accordance with the *Chicago Manual of Style*. Computer disk copy is requested but not required. The Chipstone Foundation will offer significant honoraria for manuscripts accepted for publication and reimburse authors for all photography approved in writing by the editor.

Luke Beckerdite

Preface

The Chipstone Foundation was organized in 1965 by Stanley Stone and Polly Mariner Stone of Fox Point, Wisconsin. Representing the culmination of their shared experiences in collecting American furniture, American historical prints, and early English pottery, the foundation was created with the dual purpose of preserving and interpreting their collection and stimulating research and education in the decorative arts.

The Stones began collecting American decorative arts in 1946, and by 1964 it became apparent to them that provisions should be made to deal with their collection. With the counsel of their friend Charles Montgomery, the Stones decided that their collection should be published and exhibited.

Following Stanley Stone's death in 1987, the foundation was activated by an initial endowment provided by Mrs. Stone. This generous donation allowed the foundation to institute its research and grant programs, begin work on three collection catalogues, and launch an important new journal, *American Furniture*.

Allen M. Taylor

Introduction

Luke Beckerdite

American Furniture 1996 presents exciting new research on a wide variety of subjects. In their article on seventeenth-century joinery from Braintree, Massachusetts, Peter Follansbee and John D. Alexander attribute a remarkable group of carved furniture to the shop established by William Savell, Sr. Years of making furniture out of green wood have given the authors unique insights into seventeenth-century woodworking technology and enabled them to separate the products of the Savell shop from those of contemporary New England joiners. Deborah Dependahl Waters's article "Is It Phyfe?" explores the continuing problem of differentiating the work of New York cabinetmaker Duncan Phyfe from that of his early nineteenth-century competitors and from later copies and adaptations. The South Carolina Low Country was an important market for New York cabinetmakers during the early to mid-nineteenth century. In "Beautiful Specimens, Elegant Patterns: New York Furniture for the Charleston Market 1810–1840," Maurie D. McInnis and Robert A. Leath show how New York artisans such as Phyfe, Charles Honoré Lannuier, and Deming & Bulkley marketed their wares in Charleston and how they accommodated wealthy patrons with a taste for the latest European fashions. Although previously unpublished, the furniture that the authors attribute to Deming & Bulkley ranks among the finest American work in the classical style.

Few American designers have attained the status of Louis Comfort Tiffany. His participation in the furniture reform movement is documented in Milo M. Naeve's article on a unique suite of breakfast room furniture designed by Tiffany and made by New York cabinetmakers J. Matthew Meier and Ernest Hagen. Naeve's analysis of this suite and contemporary articles encouraged by Tiffany sheds light on the designer's artistic philosophy during this period. Reform designers admired the simplicity and practicality of earlier vernacular furniture, particularly seating forms. In "Frog Backs and Turkey Legs: The Nomenclature of Vernacular Seating Furniture, 1740–1850," Nancy Goyne Evans explores the variety and vocabulary of vernacular seating. Because terminology changed over time and varied from one area to another, Evans's study will be an invaluable reference for future researchers.

By showing alternative sources for rococo imagery, Richard Randall's article "Designs for Philadelphia Carvers" builds on Morrison H. Heckscher's "English Furniture Pattern Books in Eighteenth-Century America" in *American Furniture* 1994. Luke Beckerdite's article on immigrant carvers and the development of the rococo style in New York also expands on earlier research by attributing several examples of architectural carving to an apprentice trained by Henry Hardcastle. Other articles in this volume challenge previous attributions. In "Boston and New York Leather Chairs: A Reappraisal," Roger Gonzales and Daniel Putnam Brown contend that many of the early eighteenth-century leather chairs that curator Benno M. Forman and historian Neil D. Kamil attributed to New York were actually made in Boston. Similarly, Leigh Keno, Joan Barzilay Freund, and Alan Miller's article, "The Very Pink of the Mode: Boston Georgian Chairs, Their Export, and Their Influence," is a compelling argument for attributing to Boston an enormous body of seating furniture thought to have been made in New York and Newport. The authors tie several chairs directly to Boston carver John Welch and indirectly to merchant-upholsterer Samuel Grant, who purchased chair frames from members of the Perkins family and distributed them through a clientele network that included merchants, professionals, and ship captains in New York and Rhode Island. Their exhaustive research also reveals that Boston merchants and artisans like Grant dominated the coastal chair trade by "making style a commodity."

American Furniture is all about new ideas and new ways of looking at furniture. Carey Howlett's "Admitted into the Mysteries: The Benjamin Bucktrout Masonic Master's Chair" shows how symbols connected Masons to ancient traditions and served as instructional devices that promoted Enlightenment ideals of tolerance and individual responsibility. In "The Rococo, the Grotto, and the Philadelphia High Chest," Jonathan Prown and Richard Miller argue that contemporary interpretations of American rococo objects are more rooted in nineteenth- and twentieth-century perceptions of the world than in the cultural ideas that the style expressed. Prown and Miller urge the reader to "*think* rococo"—to see the Philadelphia high chest through the eyes and minds of educated eighteenth-century patrons.

In establishing *American Furniture,* the Chipstone Foundation sought to provide a forum for new research, to forge a link between American studies, social history, and the decorative arts, and to create a dialogue between academics, curators, conservators, collectors, and individuals in the trade. Response to the first three volumes has exceeded our expectations. Only a few copies of the 1993 and 1994 issues remain, and our last publication, comprised of papers presented at the symposium "Diversity and Innovation in American Regional Furniture," has received very favorable reviews. The 1997 volume will include papers presented at "A Region of Regions: Cultural Diversity and the Furniture Trade in the Early South," a symposium co-sponsored by the Chipstone Foundation and the Colonial Williamsburg Foundation and scheduled to be held November 13 to 16, 1997. For information on registration, please contact: Deborah Chapman, Program Manager, Williamsburg Institute, Colonial Williamsburg Foundation, P.O. Box 1776, Williamsburg, Virginia 23187-1776.

American Furniture

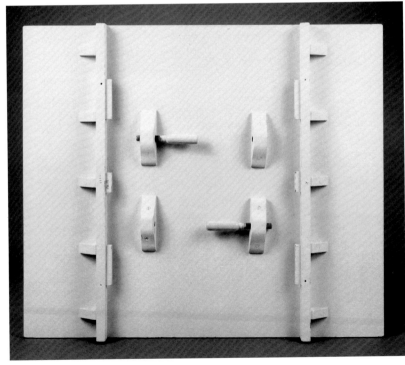

Figure 1 Table designed by Louis Comfort Tiffany and made by J. Matthew Meier and Ernest Hagen, New York City, 1882–1885. Pine; white enamel paint. H. 28", W. 39", D. 48". (Courtesy, Art Institute of Chicago, anonymous gift.)

Figure 2 Detail of the bottom of the table illustrated in fig. 1.

Milo M. Naeve

Louis Comfort Tiffany and the Reform Movement in Furniture Design: The J. Matthew Meier and Ernest Hagen Commission of 1882–1885

▼ DOCUMENTARY EVIDENCE now reveals that innovative furniture design must be included in the diverse interests of Louis Comfort Tiffany (1848–1933). Personal papers of this major presence in the American arts remain tragically elusive, if they survive, but his interest in furniture design fortunately can be shifted from speculation to documentation by linking contemporary evidence to a remarkable breakfast suite that has survived intact and recently become publicly known (see figs. 1, 3, 5). Tiffany commissioned the suite from Manhattan cabinetmakers J. Matthew Meier (1830–1913) and Ernest Hagen (1822–1889) for his apartment in the Tiffany family building, completed in 1885 at the northwest corner of Madison Avenue and 72d Street in New York City (fig. 7).

The suite documents Tiffany's participation in the furniture reform movement, which originated in England and stressed practicality, simplicity, and economy. The two tables are the same width and height but different lengths so they could be used separately or placed together, and their tops are independent of the bases for convenient cleaning, moving, and storage (see figs. 1, 2). The two armchairs and ten side chairs (see figs. 3–6) are sturdy and comfortably large. All are made of cheap pine and maple, upholstered in leather, and painted with white enamel for cleaning ease. Construction details are intentionally conspicuous. For example, black paint accentuates the heads of the screws securing the table bases together and the tacks securing the leather to the chair backs. Parallels to these tables and chairs are unknown in contemporary and historic European or American domestic furniture.[1]

Tiffany's suite survives in good condition. Donors requesting anonymity gave half of the furniture to the Mark Twain Memorial in Hartford, Connecticut, in 1976 and half to the Art Institute of Chicago in 1981 and 1982. Use of the suite by Tiffany and his descendants required repainting and reupholstering about a generation ago; the original appearance is not evident from the furniture, but illustrations and descriptions of it during Tiffany's lifetime reveal that the present painted surfaces and brown leather upholstery are accurate. In 1988, the Art Institute restored black paint to the heads of screws and upholstery tacks.

Tiffany's furniture has long survived the home for which it was designed. His order for the suite coincided with the architect's submission of designs for the Tiffany family residence on April 9, 1882, and delivery of the suite coincided with the building's completion on October 1, 1885. Tiffany's father, Charles Lewis (1812–1902), commissioned the three-apartment structure:

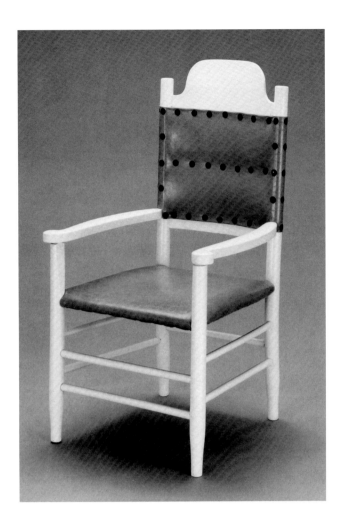

Figure 3 Armchair designed by Louis Comfort Tiffany and made by Barnes Brothers for J. Matthew Meier and Ernest Hagen, New York City, 1882–1885. Maple; white enamel paint, leather upholstery. H. 42", W. (seat) 22", D. (seat) 21". (Courtesy, Art Institute of Chicago, anonymous gift.)

Figure 4 Rear view of the armchair illustrated in fig. 3.

the first two floors above the street were intended for the elder Tiffany (but leased to a tenant); the level above it was for an unmarried daughter, Louise; and the two levels at the top—within a steeply pitched and gabled roof— were for Louis Comfort Tiffany's family (fig. 7). The breakfast room was adjacent to the windows at the top of the projecting cylindrical turret on the southeast corner of the building overlooking Madison Avenue. Tiffany may have removed the furniture, perhaps without reinstallation, when he renovated the building and added three stories in 1909—seven years after buying it from his father's estate. Tiffany could have continued using the furniture in the building until his death in 1933. Heirs would then have removed the furnishings before a later owner razed the building in 1939.[2]

The architectural design of the Tiffany residence was as carefully conceived as the breakfast suite to make an innovative aesthetic statement. Stanford White, of the architectural firm McKim, Mead and White, was undoubtedly responsible for many elements of the building. Louis Comfort Tiffany's role in the design is problematical. He was assuredly the architectural liaison for his family in developing the unusual plan, and he probably originated features of the design that are eccentric in buildings by McKim, Mead and White. On the basis of interviews with Tiffany three decades after the building's completion, Charles de Kay asserts that Tiffany designed the

Figure 5 Side chair designed by Louis Comfort Tiffany and made by Barnes Brothers for J. Matthew Meier and Ernest Hagen, New York City, 1882–1885. Maple; white enamel paint, leather upholstery. H. 40", W. (seat) 17", D. (seat) 19". (Courtesy, Art Institute of Chicago, anonymous gift.)

Figure 6 Rear view of the side chair illustrated in fig. 5.

roof area and infers his responsibility for the architectural style—unusual among buildings by McKim, Mead and White in suggesting Henry Hobson Richardson's then new and vaguely Romanesque aesthetic. In an article about his American travels for the January 24, 1885, issue of *The Critic*, Sir Edmond Gosse expressed typical enthusiasm for Tiffany's effort: "I think it the most beautiful modern domestic building I have almost ever seen." In this setting, Tiffany frequently entertained acquaintances among artists, musicians, actors, writers, and the socially prominent. He may have entertained guests informally in the breakfast room; however, normally the widower and his three children probably received most of their meals there.[3]

By 1900 Tiffany may have been concerned that the exotic and lavish rooms of his apartment soon would be dismantled by his aging father's heirs, or he may have been considering remodeling them. In either case, Tiffany wanted the public to know their original appearance. In October of that year, the *Architectural Record* abruptly published the interiors—fifteen years after their completion—in a well-illustrated article. The date of the photographs for the illustrations is uncertain, but one of the three views of the breakfast room includes the complete suite of furniture (fig. 8). In November, the *Ladies Home Journal* republished the illustrations in an article titled "The Most Artistic House in New York City." The *Architectural*

Record did not include text about the building or its interiors, but the *Ladies Home Journal* did. A caption titled "Enamel Furniture in Breakfast-Room" stated: "Nothing could be more simple, and yet striking, than the furniture in Mr. Tiffany's breakfast-room. It is white enamel studded with black nails."

Tiffany surely reviewed the articles prior to publication, if he did not actually implement them, and it is significant that the furniture received particular emphasis. The breakfast suite offered the only major opportunity in the apartment for his designs, because the articles reveal that Tiffany furnished the other rooms with his collection of furniture from India, the Near East, England, and America. The English and American objects expressed the new vogue for "antiques" of the seventeenth, eighteenth, and early nineteenth centuries.[4]

Tiffany commissioned the practical breakfast furniture from Meier and Hagen, a small firm with about ten employees. The better-known principal, Ernest Hagen, emigrated from Hamburg in 1844 and trained in New York City in the shop of Krieg and Dohrmann. He formed his partnership with J. Matthew Meier, another German immigrant, in 1858 and continued it until Meier retired in 1888. Hagen and Meier moved to a shop at 213 East 26th Street in 1867 and were still at that address when Tiffany commissioned the suite. During the early 1880s, they mostly made furniture and altered unfashionable furniture into current styles for clients of substantial but not extraordinary means. They also sold and reconditioned furniture of the eighteenth and early nineteenth centuries for customers interested in antiques. Hagen retired about 1905, and the firm continued under two sons.[5]

The only known shop records for Meier and Hagen are in an order book for the years 1880–1886. This book reveals that Tiffany was in contact with the firm about the breakfast suite (specified for the Madison Avenue and 72d Street building) on three occasions. The first reference to the furniture is an undated order in 1882 (fig. 9); the second reference is an order dated May 7, 1885 (fig. 10); and the third reference is the following July 18, when he paid for the work as well as for miscellaneous furniture in a bill with a revised date that may be June 5 (figs. 11, 12). The sequence of orders and the detailed specifications document Tiffany's approach to the project. He initiated his designs almost concurrently with White's, deferred delivery of the suite until completion of the building about three years later, and experimented with the furniture designs during the interval.

The surviving tables (figs. 1, 2) generally relate to the 1882 order (fig. 9) and closely conform to the 1885 bill (figs. 11, 12). The two Tiffany requested, each supported by two sawhorses made independently of the tops, are identical in measurements to the surviving tables. Both are 4' deep and 2'4" high; one is 5' wide (Twain Memorial), and the other is 3'6" wide (Art Institute of Chicago). On the 1882 order, the lower braces of the sawhorses are marked out. Although this deletion could have corrected an error by Meier and Hagen, it more likely expresses Tiffany's opinion that supports were unnecessary. The 1885 bill includes an additional feature of "8 wooden Screws" for engaging each sawhorse to a cleat on the bottom of the table tops (fig. 2). The "large iron nails" specified for the sawhorses in 1885, and

Figure 7 Stanford White for McKim, Mead and White, Charles L. Tiffany family residence, 19 East 72d Street (Madison Avenue at 72d Street), New York City, designed 1882, built 1882–1885. Photograph, 6⅝" × 8⅝". (Collection of the New-York Historical Society.)

Figure 8 Breakfast room designed by Louis Comfort Tiffany for his apartment in the Charles L. Tiffany residence as it appeared ca. 1885–1900. Illustrated in the *Architectural Record* 10, no. 2 (October 1900): 195. Illustration, 4⅝" × 5¾". (Courtesy, Ryerson-Burnham Library, Art Institute of Chicago.)

described as "black nails" in the *Ladies Home Journal* article, were probably replaced with screws when the tables and chairs were repainted and fitted with new leather. The leather on the table legs (fig. 1), first specified on the 1885 bill (fig. 11) and illustrated in the *Architectural Record* (fig. 8), had been removed before the furniture was donated to the Twain Memorial and Art Institute. The trim has not been restored for lack of evidence about it. A curious omission in the 1885 bill is a charge for paint; however, the *Ladies Home Journal* considered it a major feature of the suite. If not an oversight in the bill, that cost may have been included in unspecified general charges. A small table, not mentioned in the surviving order book yet illustrated in the *Architectural Record* beside the cabinet on the right side of the breakfast room (fig. 8), supplemented the suite. This table (Twain Memorial) is the same height and width as the others but 2'6" long.

Tiffany's ingenious and practical approach in designing the chairs is also well documented in the order book. The first reference to the chairs in 1882 reveals that Meier and Hagen subcontracted them, because the firm ordered a "straight back splint chair" from Barnes Brothers for what was termed a "sample to experiment" (fig. 9). The Manhattan firm specialized in chairs, and Ambrose E. Barnes was the principal. In the 1885 bill, the chairs are identified as "Maple Kitchen Chairs" (fig. 11). Tiffany's radical change of the Barnes Brothers' design, after analysis of it, is also recorded in the "Made to order" bill of 1885. It specified that the backs be canted instead of upright, that the seats be upholstered in leather instead of being woven from thin wooden strips (splints), and that the back slats be covered in leather (fig. 10). Dimensions written on this order also imply that Tiffany changed them from the "sample." [6]

Tiffany's final designs boldly express the reform principles that evolved in English furniture design during the mid-nineteenth century. The revolt

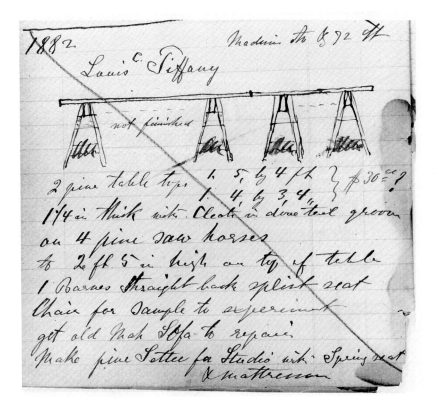

against shoddy construction and "sham" imitations of historic furniture crystallized in Augustus Welby Pugin's *The True Principles of Pointed or Christian Architecture* (London, 1841). Publishers reprinted the book frequently, and it became one of the most influential tracts of the time. Pugin states his two "great rules for design" on the first page and discusses them throughout the book for furniture as well as architecture: *"1st, that there should be no features about a building which are not necessary for convenience, construction, or propriety; 2nd, that all ornament should consist of enrichment of the essential construction of the building."* These principles were variously reduced to "function," "simplicity," and "order" by Christopher Dresser in *The Art of Decorative Design* (London, 1862) and by William Morris in *Hopes and Fears for Art* (Boston, 1882). Morris and others appealed to English nationalism by echoing Pugin's remark: "In short, national feelings and national architecture are at so low an ebb, that it becomes an absolute duty in every Englishman to attempt their revival."[7]

Circumstantial evidence reveals that Tiffany was familiar with another book influenced by Pugin—Charles Locke Eastlake's *Hints on Household Taste in Furniture, Upholstery and other Details* (London, 1868). Eastlake's book greatly influenced American furniture reform design. The first American edition appeared in Boston in 1872 with an introduction by Charles C. Perkins. Americans published six editions by 1881, the year before Tiffany initiated his designs with Meier and Hagen. Tiffany's brother-in-law, Donald G. Mitchell, referred to Eastlake's concepts in essays about Tiffany's setting and furnishings for his apartment in New York City on the top floor of the Bella Apartment House at 48 East 26th Street, written for *Our*

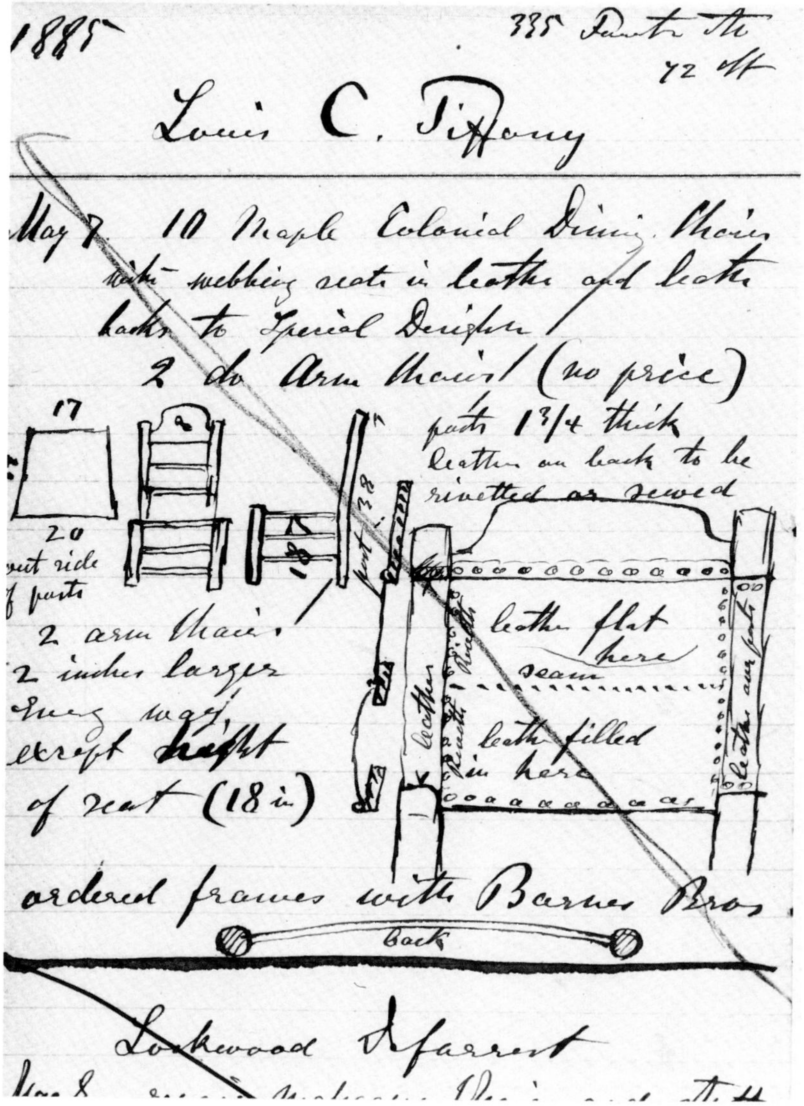

Figure 10 J. Matthew Meier and Ernest Hagen Order Book, entry for chairs in the breakfast suite designed by Louis Comfort Tiffany, May 7, 1885. (Collection of the New-York Historical Society, gift of *The Magazine Antiques*.)

Continent in 1882. If Mitchell had not previously known of Eastlake's book and of Morris's *Hopes and Fears for Art*, he learned of them from Tiffany, for Mitchell's letter to Tiffany on November 25, 1881, reveals that Tiffany supervised his articles and recommended books as background for them.[8]

Tiffany's furniture offers remarkable parallels to Eastlake's general philosophy and his specific ideas for furniture given in the 1878 Boston edition of *Hints on Household Taste*. Eastlake's endorsement of "the spirit and principles of early manufacturers" and "not the absolute forms in which they found embodiment" continued one of Pugin's principles. Eastlake, however, ranged far beyond Pugin's medieval precedents in English furniture. Tiffany's specification that his chairs have "bridle leather with large iron hollow nails on the flat back" (figs. 3, 5, 10) relates to Eastlake's endorsement of the tacked leather upholstery on seventeenth-century chairs. Tiffany could have studied examples in Eastlake's illustrations, old or new English versions imported since the 1870s, or American interpretations of the form (fig. 13). Tiffany's unusual concept of small tables, conveniently placed together

335. Fourth Stree
Had it and
72 off?

Louis C. Tiffany

1885

June

+ Webster "Kitchen Chair +

2 pine tables and saw horses with
leather trimmed legs and large iron nails

1 table 5 ft by 4 ft
1 table 4 ft by 3.6.

100 ft lumber	7.	7.00
1/2 hide leather	5.25
large nails	but	1.50
8 wooden screws	2
Cab maker (studio)	1 week	15

1 1/2 tops made like drawing
barrels with wooden screws
cost 39.20

2 extra horses		3.75
1 1/2 day labor		70
lumber for them	11	
putting on leather		2.50
500 fellow nails		2

charge 50 00

8 fin
2 mas 10 Maple Kitchen Chairs and
2 do Arm Chairs for Barnes Bros
made to order and upholstered with flat
all hair seats in natural Columbia bridle
leather with large iron hollow nails on the
flat back 12 frames cost 24.00

altering and sandpapering them
and new arms on arm chairs

4 days Cabinet maker cost 10.00

12 00

2
in maple
96
cost
a 4.50

7 July 1 40 lb leather a 23 (flower) 32.20
6.00 nails restoretools & trim filing 9.40
13 lbs hair 42 3.46
60 yd webb 2
18 yd burlaps, Muslin & tacks 8 - 1.44
trim & tacks 36
72 2 hours upholster 18.00
3 cartage & health cost 108.00

oval tinned
(100)
8 hair
a 12 1/2
108
a 140.00

4.00

2 arm chairs finished 14 28 00

1 large pine back Sofa
7 ft by 26 inches to fit over steam pipes
with wood bottom & flat Spring seat like Spring Box
a hair Mattress on top

50 ft lumber	5	2.50
Cabinet maker	1 1/4 day	3.13
29 x 2 1/2 Springs	4	1.16
7 1/2 g hair new & stuff	60	
2 1/2 lbs hair 42	1.05	
t + t	15	
upholster 5 hours	1.25
box cost	10.84

3.96 in

charge 14 00

Mattress for it

6 1/2 yd thick	16	99
10 lbs hair 42	4.20
twine	10
cover button	25
upholster 11 hours	2.75

Mattress cost
8.29
charge
cover found 12 00

216

1885

Louis C. Tiffany

Carried 216 00

1 Single Spring Mattress done over
with new ticking

84 2 1/2 new Springs	4	32
4 1/2 y burlaps	8	36
9 a C a thick	14	98	228
1 lbs hair	20	42
t + t	500
upholster 18 hours	c 9.28

charge 9 00

1 Childs Crib Mattress done up (partly augm)
with 2 lbs new hair 42 1.36
3 hours labor 75
211
charge 3 00

1 bamboo Settee
covered in Mattress found
upholster 8 1/2 hours 2.50
cover 75 leather 50
charge 4.60

2 large Ottomans recovered
and old cover washed

upholster 6 hours	1.50
2 1/2 yd Libre	13	33
t + t	15
wash cover	75
	2.73

charge 6 00

1 turkish iron back chair new seat put
oak altered & covered in Mattress found

8 1/2 webb	16
1 yd cambric	8
3 1/2 yd cord	8	28
2 1/2 yd gimp	15	38
t + t	10
cover 75 leather	98
upholster 18 hours	4.75
c	6.13

100

charge 9 00

1 antique Mahog Sofa, in Muslin
(cover found) including price of covering

1 7/6 yd plush Libre 65 4
extra for bronze nails 5

Credit by old Sofa in exchange 748

per Contract due 56 00

1/2 yd Copper red plush
furnished for cushion 1 50

452 Louis Tiffany old Sword 308 00
18 15

320 00

Figure 11 J. Matthew Meier and Ernest Hagen Order Book, bill (first page) for the breakfast suite designed by Louis Comfort Tiffany, June 5(?), 1885. (Collection of the New-York Historical Society, gift of *The Magazine Antiques*.)

Figure 12 J. Matthew Meier and Ernest Hagen Order Book, bill (second page) for the breakfast suite designed by Louis Comfort Tiffany, June 5(?), 1885. (Collection of the New-York Historical Society, gift of *The Magazine Antiques*.)

Figure 13 Side chair, Boston, 1665–1695. Soft maple and red oak. H. 36", W. (seat) 18", D. (seat) 15¼". (Courtesy, Winterthur Museum.)

Figure 14 Drafting room of Hugh Garden (standing), Chicago, ca. 1895. Photograph, 4³/₈" × 4¹/₂". (Collection of Mrs. William Dorr.)

or dismantled when not needed, parallels Eastlake's recommendation for small tables with the same objectives, though Tiffany's tables differ in form and lack the hinged flaps proposed by Eastlake. Like Eastlake, Tiffany eschewed carving and moldings, accepted the use of screws or nails (unusual in the reform movement, which advocated "honest" construction by joints), favored painted or stained surfaces on cheap woods lacking decorative grain, and preferred rectilinear forms that were rigid and cheaper—and therefore assumed to be better—than curved ones because they required less labor or material. Many of these recommendations appear later in Robert W. Edis's *Decoration & Furniture of Town Houses* (London, 1881) and in publications by other disciples of the reform movement, but currently there is no evidence that Tiffany knew of them or Edis's book.

Other features of Tiffany's furniture express the reform movement's admiration of vernacular forms that were simple, practical, and economical. The sawhorses with "tops made like drawing boards with wooden Screws" (fig. 11) repeat the form of contemporary architectural drafting tables, which would have been quite familiar to Tiffany (fig. 14). Precedents for the shaped top slat of the chairs, exaggerated in height by Tiffany, and the general form of the legs and stretchers are well represented in American vernacular furniture from the seventeenth through the nineteenth centuries (fig. 15). Tiffany also would have found precedent for the enamel finish of the chairs and tables, in addition to Eastlake's recommendation, in the durable and cheap bedroom furniture, known for a generation in the United States as "cottage furniture." The back posts of Tiffany's chairs are an exception to tradition. Like contemporary American versions in the aes-

Figure 15 Great chair, Norwich or Lebanon, Connecticut, 1661–1715. Soft maple and black ash. H. 44½", W. (seat) 23½", D. (seat) 17". (Courtesy, Art Institute of Chicago, Wesley M. Dixon, Jr., Fund.)

thetic movement, they are stripped of historical reference by the absence of finials in the manner popularized, if not invented, by English designer Edward William Godwin (fig. 16).[9]

Identification of Tiffany's chairs as "colonial" in Meier and Hagen's order book (fig. 10) may be the assessment of the cabinetmakers or Tiffany. All three men were familiar with American colonial furniture. The craftsmen were selling and reconditioning it at the time of the order, and Tiffany's interest is documented by descriptions and photographs of his collection in publications about his residences in the Bella Apartment House and in the family building at Madison Avenue and 72d street. Regardless of who was

Figure 16 Side chair by Herter Brothers, New York City, ca. 1877–ca. 1879. Cherry (stained black) with unidentified inlay woods. H. 37³/₄", W. (seat) 17³/₈", D. (seat) 16³/₄". (Courtesy, Art Institute of Chicago, Mrs. Alfred J. Burdick Fund.)

responsible for the term "colonial," it clearly designated general principles instead of specific prototypes. The word "colonial" held particular importance at the time, for Americans had just marked the centennial of the American Revolution and were as imbued with a nationalistic celebration of their past and future as Pugin or Morris in England. Charles C. Perkins typically expressed it in his preface to the 1878 edition of Eastlake's *Hints* by writing that "we may hope that the national mind [of Americans reading the book] will reveal hitherto unsuspected artistic faculties."[10]

Tiffany was notably reticent in discussing his theories in the arts, but basic principles in the design of the breakfast suite can be deduced from fragmentary contemporary information published about his related projects and concepts. The persistent theme of "simplicity" in Tiffany's brief article, "The Gospel of Good Taste," in the November 1910 issue of *Country Life in America*, is summarized in his caption for an illustration of a "colonial kitchen": "Poverty compelled our ancestors to choose simple furnishings, and in that simplicity, softened and beautified by a strong home feeling, lies their charm. All art that is genuine is essentially simple." Tiffany reiterated his concern for function and appropriate materials or mediums in a lecture published in the April 1916 issue of the *International Studio*: "I have always striven to fix beauty in wood or stone or glass or pottery, in oil or water colour, by using whatever seemed fittest for the expression of beauty." In a December 1917 article for *Harper's Bazaar* titled "The Quest for Beauty," he urged Americans to invent their own "furniture and decorations," because "very few" imported objects were "consistent with our own civilization, ideals, mode of living." [11]

Donald G. Mitchell, Tiffany's "voice" in publishing his 1879 residence in the Bella Apartment House, identified the designer's requirements for furniture for a breakfast room, or family dining room, in an article titled "An Early Breakfast" in the March 15, 1882, issue of *Our Continent*. Tiffany felt that chairs, particularly for children, should be "of good, honest structural development" and that tables should present a "sober, solid aspect, not to be overset by an over-weighted platter or an over-careless servant easily." The furniture should be of "such strong work and such staunchness" that it "will make the young people cherish it when the dishes which we old folks eat from are forever shattered." Designs must meet "present, positive, actual needs" and be inspired by "noble old traditions" while founding "new traditions to blend at some future time with still older ones, and so contribute its quota toward the rounding out of the great cycle of art development." Mitchell's article, which appeared the year Tiffany began planning the larger and more elaborate breakfast room in his apartment at Madison Avenue and 72d Street, discusses the designer's program for planning furniture in it. Tiffany's emphasis on breakfast room furniture, as a significant feature of a residence, explains the exceptional care he gave to designing the new suite. His pride in it is revealed by the articles he evidently encouraged to be written for the *Architectural Record* and *Ladies Home Journal* in 1900. [12]

Tiffany's breakfast suite of 1882 to 1885 differs significantly from contemporary innovative furniture, and it has no parallels among known commissions for the Associated Artists in which Tiffany participated from its founding in 1879 to its dissolution in 1883. Although his involvement in domestic interior design was limited, after 1883 he may have been responsible for much of the furniture in his two country houses, The Briars (ca. 1886) and Laurelton Hall (1904). Available photographs of the now destroyed interiors do not, however, show furniture comparable to the breakfast suite. It is equally singular among the known "art furniture" designed by Tiffany's contemporaries, inspired by Eastlake, Japanese art, and other sources (fig. 16). The closest parallel to Tiffany's general approach in the breakfast furniture occurs in 1884 and 1885 projects from the architectural office of Henry Hobson Richardson. Current evidence suggests that these designs were influenced by Richardson's staff member, Francis H. Bacon, but they reveal a greater reliance on specific motifs from eighteenth-century American furniture than the furniture of Tiffany. His designs are unprecedented in our knowledge of the English and American search for rational furniture with minimal decoration, obvious construction, practical surfaces, and functional forms.[13]

1. Martin P. Levy to Milo M. Naeve, May 13, 1996; Simon Jervis to Milo M. Naeve, May 23, 1996; Alan Crawford to Milo M. Naeve, July 1, 1996; and Frances Collard to Milo M. Naeve, August 20, 1996, confirm the lack of comparable English furniture.

2. Dates for the building are variously reported in the literature on McKim, Mead and White, but papers of the firm at the New-York Historical Society (hereinafter cited as NYHS) include a bill dated April 9, 1882, for the design that is annotated as paid (McKim, Mead and White Bill Book 1, p. 212) and several bills and payments leading to the final bill on October 1, 1885, for which the payment date is not recorded (McKim, Mead and White Bill Book 2, p. 222). The house has not been studied. For comment about it, see Robert Koch, "The Stained Glass Decades: A Study of Louis Comfort Tiffany (1848–1933) and the Art Nouveau in America" (Ph.D. dissertation, Yale University, 1957), pp. 121–24. For recent comment, see Lawrence Wodehouse, *White of McKim, Mead and White* (New York and London: Garland Publishing, Inc., 1988), pp. 130, 131, 139 n. 37. For excellent published illustrations of the exterior, a measured drawing of the facade, and a plan of the "First Floor," see Architectural Book Publishing Company and McKim, Mead and White, *A Monograph of the Works of McKim, Mead and White, 1879–1915*, 2d ed. with introductory essay by Leland Roth (New York: Benjamin Blom, 1973), pls. 5, 5A. Incomplete records for the building in the archives of McKim, Mead and White at the NYHS include a blueprint for a measured drawing of the facade before changes were made to accommodate Tiffany's apartment and a blueprint for the plan of the first floor only. Photographs of the house in the Prints and Photographs Department of the NYHS include an exterior view from the George P. Hall Files, five snapshots of architectural details in the vertical files under "T," and another exterior photograph evidently taken at the conclusion of construction in the McKim, Mead and White archives. Charles de Kay, *The Art Work of Louis C. Tiffany* (Garden City, N.Y.: Doubleday, Page, & Co., 1914), as published in facsimile with an introduction by J. Alastair Duncan (Poughkeepsie, N.Y.: Apollo, 1987), p. 59. George F. Heydt, "Louis Comfort Tiffany Scrapbook" (New York, 1919), p. 42 (Archives of American Art microfilm of the original owned by Henry B. Platt). Tiffany's purchase of the property and renovation of it are reported in clippings from several newspapers; most of the clippings include a dateline and part of the newspaper title, but they lack a page number; significant among the clippings are the *New York American*, December 8, 1902, and March 7, 1909; and the *New York Times*, March 28, 1909. For the later history of the building, see Koch, "The Stained Glass Decades," pp. 121–22.

3. See de Kay, *The Art Work of Louis C. Tiffany*, pp. 57–58. Koch, "The Stained Glass Decades," p. 122, considers Tiffany's responsibility for the architectural style an unresolved issue: Tiffany could have drawn the sketch illustrated by de Kay (p. 57) after White completed the initial design for the building, and de Kay and Tiffany did not meet until 1911. Robert Koch states, however, in *Louis C. Tiffany, Rebel in Glass* (New York: Crown Publishers, Inc., 1964), p. 63, that Tiffany "selected a Richardsonian style." Sir Edmond Gosse, "Mr. Gosse's Notes on America," *The Critic* 3, no. 56 (January 24, 1885): 38.

4. *Architectural Record* 10, no. 2 (October 1900): 191–202. "The Most Artistic House in America," *Ladies Home Journal* 17 (November 1900): 12–13. For the collecting of American furniture, see Rodris Roth, "The Colonial Revival and 'Centennial Furniture,'" *Art Quarterly* 27, no. 1 (1964): 57–81; Marilynn Johnson, "Art Furniture: Wedding the Beautiful to the Useful," in *In Pursuit of Beauty: Americans and the Aesthetic Movement* (New York: Metropolitan Museum of Art, 1986), pp. 162–64.

5. Information about Meier and Hagen is from Elizabeth Stillinger, "Ernest Hagen—Furniture Maker," *Maine Antique Digest* (November 1988): 8D–16D.

6. *Trow's New York City Directory* listed Barnes Brothers at various addresses on Pearl and Elizabeth Streets during the 1880s. It also noted that they specialized in chairs and listed Ambrose E. Barnes as the principal.

7. Augustus Welby Pugin, *The True Principles of Pointed or Christian Architecture* (London:

John Weale, 1841), p. 66. Mansell Belcher, *A. W. N. Pugin: An Annotated Critical Bibliography* (London and New York: Marshall Publishing, Ltd., 1987), No. A 29, pp. 56–67. Christopher Dresser, *The Art of Decorative Design* (London: Day and Son, 1862), pp. 1–2. William Morris, *Hopes and Fears for Art* (Boston: Roberts Brothers , 1882), pp. 109–10, 180–82, 66.

8. Charles Locke Eastlake, *Hints on Household Taste in Furniture, Upholstery and other Details* (London: Longmons, Greene & Co., 1868). For an analytical biography and comment on Eastlake's book, see Charles L. Eastlake, *A History of the Gothic Revival*, edited and with an introduction by J. Mordaunt Crook, 2d ed. (England and New York: Leicester University Press, and Humanities Press, 1978), especially pp. 19–20. For Eastlake's influence in the United States, see Mary Jean Smith Madigan, "The Influence of Charles Locke Eastlake on American Furniture Manufacture, 1870–90," *Winterthur Portfolio* 10 (Charlottesville: University Press of Virginia for the Winterthur Museum, 1975), pp. 1–22. For American editions of Eastlake's *Hints on Household Taste*, see Henry-Russell Hitchcock, *American Architectural Books*, 2d ed. with introduction by Adolf K. Placzek and appendix by William H. Jordy (New York: DaCapo Press, 1976), p. 36. For direct references to Eastlake's concepts and to Morris's book, see Donald G. Mitchell, "From Lobby to Peak," *Our Continent*, May 17, 1882, p. 217. Mitchell's series "From Lobby to Peak" includes numerous allusions to Eastlake's concepts. See February 15, 1882, p. 5; February 22, 1882, p. 21; March 1, 1882, p. 37; March 15, 1882, p. 69; March 22, 1882, p. 85; March 29, 1882, p. 101; April 12, 1882, p. 132; April 19, 1882, p. 148; and May 3, 1882, p. 185. For Tiffany's association with Mitchell on the articles, see Mitchell-Tiffany Family Papers, Sterling Memorial Library, Manuscripts and Archives, Yale University, New Haven, Connecticut.

9. For cheap furniture with an enamel paint finish, see E. C. Woodbridge's advertisement for "Cottage and Enamel Furniture" made in his shop in New York City in the unpaginated advertising section of the *Cosmopolitan Art Journal* 4, no. 1 (March 1860). For the chair finials, see Edward William Godwin, *Art Furniture and Artistic Conservatories* (1877; reprint ed., New York and London: Garland Publishing, 1978), pl. 11, "Chair" in "Library Furniture." Tiffany could have known Godwin's design by visits abroad, publication of it, exhibitions in the United States, versions by Herter Brothers, or a version by Associated Artists in which Tiffany was a partner. For dissemination of the design and the date of the chair shown in fig. 16, see Catherine Hoover Voorsanger, "Side Chair," no. 33, in Katherine S. Howe, Alice Cooney Frelinghusen, Catherine Hoover Voorsanger, et al., *Herter Brothers: Furniture and Interiors for a Gilded Age* (New York: Harry N. Abrams, 1994), pp. 193–94, 256 n. 6.

10. Stillinger, "Ernest Hagen—Furniture Maker," p. 10 D. For the Bella Apartment House, see "Mr. Louis C. Tiffany's Rooms," *Artistic Houses, Being a Series of Interior Views of A Number of the Most Beautiful and Celebrated Homes in the United States*, 2 vols. in 4 parts (1883–1884; reprint ed., New York: Benjamin Blom, 1971), 1:1–6. For The Briars, see Koch, *Louis C. Tiffany, Rebel in Glass*, p. 183. Charles Locke Eastlake, *Hints on Household Taste in Furniture, Upholstery and Other Details* (1868; reprint ed., Boston: James R. Osgood & Co., 1878), p. xiv.

11. Louis Comfort Tiffany, "The Gospel of Good Taste," *Country Life in America* 19, no. 2 (November 1910): 105. "Louis Comfort Tiffany," *International Studio* 58, no. 230 (April 1916): LVIII. Louis Comfort Tiffany, "The Quest for Beauty," *Harper's Bazaar* 52, no. 12 (December 1917): 43.

12. Donald G. Mitchell, "An Early Breakfast," *Our Continent* 1, no. 5 (March 15, 1882): 69.

13. Wilson H. Faude, "Associated Artists and the American Renaissance in the Decorative Arts," *Winterthur Portfolio* 10 (Charlottesville: University Press of Virginia for the Winterthur Museum, 1975), pp. 101–30. For The Briars, see Koch, "The Stained Glass Decades," pp. 299–303; and Koch, *Louis C. Tiffany, Rebel in Glass*, pp. 131, 132, 183. For Laurelton Hall, see Koch, "The Stained Glass Decades," pp. 302–11; and Koch, *Louis C. Tiffany, Rebel in Glass*, pp. 142–44, 196–202. Anne Farnam, "H. H. Richardson and A. H. Davenport: Architecture and Furniture as Big Business in America's Gilded Age," in *Tools and Technologies: America's Wooden Age*, edited by Paul B. Kebabian and William C. Lipke (Burlington, Vt.: Robert Hull Fleming Museum, University of Vermont, 1979), p. 84.

Nancy Goyne Evans

Frog Backs and Turkey Legs: The Nomenclature of Vernacular Seating Furniture, 1740–1850

▼ T E R M I N O L O G Y associated with vernacular seating furniture in the eighteenth and nineteenth centuries can be variable, obscure, misleading, and above all confusing. Nomenclature changed with time, distance, and document. This study, based on an analysis of more than two hundred documents—account books and sheets, estate and insolvency records, family papers, shipping records, court records, and advertisements—explores the vocabulary of vernacular seating furniture in four categories: common woven-bottom chairs, Windsor chairs, fancy chairs, and chair stock. A certain amount of overlap occurs between and within the groups. During the period covered by this study, vernacular seating furniture was part of every American household as well as many businesses and institutions.

Common woven-bottom chairs were already a market fixture when colonial artisans at Philadelphia introduced the Windsor chair during the mid-1740s. By the 1780s the new form was on its way to dominating the vernacular market. The same decade marked the introduction of another seating form, the fancy chair. This elegant seat, which offered the customer variety in surface color and decoration, soon occupied a position at the high end of the trade and had a marked impact on the Windsor. Until then, verdigris green surfaces prevailed in Windsor seating. The fancy chair provided new directions in market appeal to which the Windsor chairmakers quickly responded. As a rule of thumb in identifying vernacular seating furniture in middle-class households of the 1790s, common chairs furnished the kitchen, Windsors occupied the dining room, and fancy chairs brightened the parlor.

This study draws heavily on New England craft records, because they survive in greater number than those of other regions. Samplings from Middle Atlantic locations, although fewer, adequately represent the work of craftsmen from New York to Maryland. Craft documents produced by southern craftsmen are uncommon.

Common Woven-Bottom Chairs

Common, kitchen, and *slat-back chairs* generally had similar elements (fig. 1). The difference lay in structure—number of back slats, extent of turned work—and surface embellishment, which ranged from the absence of finish to stained, colored (pigment in resin), and painted surfaces. A limited number of great chairs, or chairs with arms, and children's chairs were also constructed with slats. The cross members in the back, often graduated in size from top to bottom, varied in profile from straight to arched, double-arched, elliptic, and truncated form. For purposes of reference and pricing,

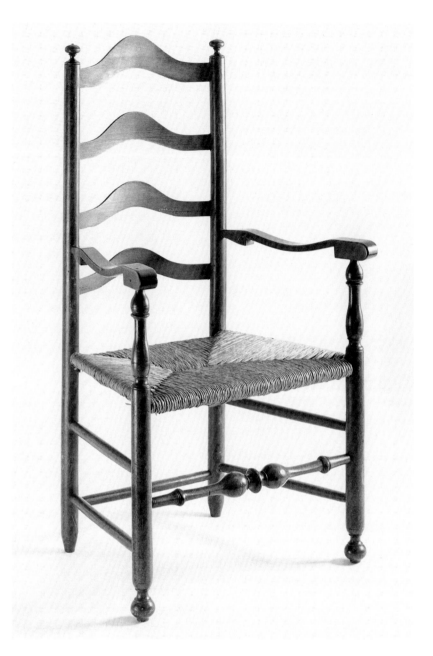

Figure 1 Slat-back armchair, Delaware Valley, 1750–1780. Maple and hickory (microanalysis). H. 43", W. 24⁷/₈", D. 20¹/₂". (Courtesy, Winterthur Museum.)

Figure 2 Banister-back side chair, attributed to Andrew Durand, probably Milford, Connecticut, 1740–1760. Maple and ash. H. 45⁵/₈", W. 19¹/₈", D. 14". (Courtesy, New Haven Colony Historical Society, New Haven, Connecticut; photo, Winterthur Museum.)

craftsmen frequently identified slat-back chairs by the number of cross members in the back. The price increased with the number of slats.

Solomon Fussell (d. 1762), a Philadelphia chairmaker, charged 4s apiece for "half doz 3 Slat Coloured Chairs" in 1738. His "best Six Slat Chairs" were priced at 6s 6d (1745). Armchairs cost more. The example illustrated in figure 1 has another feature that would have added to the price, a "turnd frunt," or fancy stretcher. Fussell frequently purchased ready-formed chair parts from turning specialists. Itemized among this stock are chair *lists,* the shaved sticks that form the framework for weaving the rush seat. The chairmaker also recorded "Checkt bottoms" on occasion, identifying a woven material referred to today as splint.[1]

John Gaines II (1677–1748) and his son Thomas (1712–1761) of Ipswich, Massachusetts, were in business earlier than Fussell. They also made "slat-

Figure 3 Fiddle-back armchair, eastern Connecticut, possibly New London County, 1765–1795. Maple and ash. H. 43¹/₈", W. 23", D. 17". (Courtesy, Museum of Our National Heritage, Lexington, Massachusetts; photo, Winterthur Museum.)

ted" chairs, which they sometimes referred to as "splatted" chairs. Color choices included black and brown. Another common term describing the slat-back chair appears in the accounts of David Haven (d. 1800/1801), who made and sold "three Back" and "Common 4 Back" chairs at Framingham, Massachusetts, at the end of the eighteenth century. Haven sold some of his chairs without the woven seats. Many chairs were stained or stained and varnished. References to "White Chairs" identify seating that was unpainted, or "in the wood" as they were often described in the trade. The "Chair stuff" Haven received from suppliers to frame his chairs consisted of "Long Posts" (vertical back members), "short Posts" (front legs with or without arm supports), "Backs" (slats), "Rounds" (stretchers), and "seatlists."[2]

Banister-back chairs, like those with slat backs, were in the American furniture market early in the eighteenth century. Considerably more work marked their construction, and the price was proportionally higher. A number of New England examples have uncarved, intricately sawed *crown tops.* The example illustrated in figure 2 has been attributed to Andrew Durand (1702–1791) of Milford, Connecticut, whose sons John (1735–1780) and Samuel I (1738–1829) followed him in business. A chair attributed to the sons is close in form, aside from substituting an embowed slat for a crown. From an analysis of John's accounts, it appears that this frame is what he described as a "black" chair. References to seating furniture by color rather than pattern are reasonably common in craftsmen's records. The banister-back chair was a popular style in Connecticut and Rhode Island; but it was also made as far north as New Hampshire, where James Chase (1737–1812) of Gilmanton had a few lingering calls for the pattern at the turn of the century.[3]

The terms *york chair* and *fiddle-back chair* seem in most instances to have identified the same pattern in the records of producers and consumers (fig. 3). When both words appear in the same record, as they do in the memorandum (order) book of Amos Denison Allen (1774–1855) and the account book of Samuel Durand I (both craftsmen from eastern Connecticut), they represent different periods of recordkeeping by each man. Because Durand's entries record furniture sales, they are priced. The cost of york chairs and fiddle-back chairs was the same—6s apiece, or $1 in the new currency of the post-revolutionary period. Other records show that within either category the price could fluctuate, indicating that options were available in terms of structural and surface embellishment. At the shop of Elisha Hawley (1759–1850) in Ridgefield, Connecticut, "fiddle Back Chairs" cost anywhere from 5s to 7s 10d apiece. One group of 7s chairs identified as "green" appears to have been painted instead of colored, stained, or coated with cheaper paint colors, such as black or brown. Half a dozen chairs constituted a *set.*[4]

Although the term *york chair* is found in coastal Connecticut and Rhode Island records, its use there is less frequent than *fiddle-back chair.* A distinctive rush-seat chair, framed with a yoke crest, splat back, and front legs of conical form ending in pad feet, was popular in New York City and its satel-

Figure 4 High-back Windsor armchair, Philadelphia, ca. 1765. Yellow poplar (seat) with maple, oak, and hickory. H. 44⅝", W. 25⅜", D. 16". (Mr. and Mrs. James Palmer Flowers collection; photo, Winterthur Museum.)

lite regions (northern New Jersey, Long Island, and the Hudson Valley) from the 1750s through the end of the century. Several are documented with makers' stamps. This New York pattern seems to have given rise to the sobriquet *york chair* along the northern coast of Long Island Sound. A few yoke-top Connecticut chairs are made with heavy New York pad-foot legs, but more are turned with embellished cylindrical legs (fig. 3). In New York *fiddle-back* is presumed to have been the common term for yoke-top, splat-back seating, in view of James Chestney's (d. 1862) use of this term in 1797 at Albany in a newspaper advertisement that illustrates this type of chair.[5]

Windsor Chairs: The 1740s to 1799
The nomenclature of eighteenth-century Windsor furniture is relatively straightforward, because the number of patterns introduced to the market was limited in contrast to the activity in the nineteenth century. *Windsor*

Figure 5 Low-back Windsor armchair, Philadelphia, ca. 1755–1762. Yellow poplar (seat) with maple, oak, and hickory. H. 28 1/8", W. 28", D. 16 5/8". (Mr. and Mrs. Joseph A. McFalls collection; photo, Winterthur Museum.)

chair was the generic name for all patterns of this construction, although the term often specifically distinguished the armchair from the side chair in references itemizing mixed forms.

The first pattern in the market was designated a *high-back chair* because of its tall structure (fig. 4). Today that term has been obscured by the popularity of the late nineteenth-century appellation *comb-back chair,* which refers to the top piece. The high-back Windsor was anything but a poor man's chair. Priced between 14*s* and 18*s* at Philadelphia in the quarter century before the Revolution, the cost equaled that of about three-days' wages for an average tradesman. Many of the purchasers were merchants who retained some chairs for personal use and shipped others to clients. An important coastal market was Charleston, South Carolina, where merchants Sheed and White advertised "high backed" Windsors among their stock in 1766. New York was another prewar market. When the wealthy Quaker merchant Walter Franklin died about 1780, his executors listed five high-back Windsors in the household.[6]

Newport, Rhode Island, chairmakers also produced tall Windsor chairs before and after the Revolution. Some were for domestic use; others furnished public institutions, such as the green chairs purchased for the Newport County courthouse in 1784, among which was one described as "Large

Figure 6 Sack-back Windsor armchair, Amos Denison Allen, South Windham, Connecticut, ca. 1796–1800. Chestnut (seat) with maple and oak (microanalysis). H. 36 1/8", W. 22 3/4", D. 15 1/4". (Courtesy, Winterthur Museum.)

with high back." Green high-back Windsors comprised part of the furniture cargoes that Aaron Lopez, a Newport merchant, shipped regularly to southern coastal and tropical markets during the 1760s. Verdigris green was, in fact, the common color of all American Windsor seating until after the Revolution, giving rise everywhere to the appellation *green chairs*. Stephen Girard, a merchant prince of Philadelphia, included a category in his accounting system for "Green Chairs" as late as 1787. *Philadelphia chair* was a term that recognized the principal center of Windsor production in the eighteenth century. The estate of Isaac Smith, a Boston merchant, contained a "large Philadelphia Chair" in 1787.[7]

By the 1780s the high-back chair had been in the market for three decades. A slimmer version with a circular seat introduced at Philadelphia in the 1760s is sometimes referred to in documents as a *small high-back chair*. After the Revolution, chairmakers substituted an oval seat and exchanged the ball feet for tapered legs. By then tall chairs were being made in New England. A type particularly sought today by collectors is one associated with

Nantucket Island that has a decided cant to the back and is frequently fitted with *braces*—a pair of spindles mounted in an extension at the seat back. Island inventories describe the nomenclature: "Large Green Chair," "high Back Green Chair," "Great Green Chair," "Mans high Back Chair," and "high wooden bottom Chair." The last phrase focuses on the critical unit of construction in the Windsor, the plank seat.[8]

Sheed and White also offered Philadelphia *low-back chairs* for sale at Charleston in 1766 (fig. 5). A rare document dated in 1762 and acknowledging the receipt of £4.10 for six chairs of this pattern from Philadelphia businessman Garrett Meade is signed by Thomas Gilpin (fl. 1752–1767). Gilpin, who first made Windsor chairs in the 1750s, produced the earliest known documented examples (branded). Aaron Lopez of Newport recorded an alternative term for the low-back Windsor when he shipped "12 Round Green Chairs" to a tropical port in 1767. The term *round* is significant yet ambiguous. Clarification occurs a year later in an invoice regarding furniture shipped to Maryland, which lists "10 round back straw bottom'd Chairs" and "4 round back wooden bottom Green Chairs." The straw- or rush-bottom chairs were roundabouts, produced as either vernacular or joined seating in the eighteenth century. The low Windsor duplicates the circular profile of the arm rail.[9]

Although the low-back chair is the rarest of all Windsor patterns, probate records identify its broad distribution in households of Boston, Nantucket, Newport, New York, and Philadelphia. In 1779 appraisers at Newport identified "green round about Chairs" in Nicholas Lechmere's confiscated Tory estate. Six low-back Windsors complemented the five high ones in Walter Franklin's household at New York, and at Philadelphia, widow Rebecca Seaton enjoyed the comfort of a cushion with her low-back Windsor.[10]

Philadelphia chairmakers introduced the *sack-back chair* to the market during the early 1760s. Although craftsmen eventually made this chair in greater numbers than high-back and low-back chairs, the pattern never achieved the popularity in Philadelphia or the Middle Atlantic region that it attained in New England (fig. 6).

The first mention of the pattern appears to be in a notice by Andrew Gautier, a New York shopkeeper who imported and sold Philadelphia Windsor chairs as early as 1765. By the 1770s several terms supplemented *sack-back* to identify the armchair framed with a bow enclosing the spindle tops.[11]

Francis Trumble (ca. 1716–1798) of Philadelphia described "arch top" chairs in 1770 priced at 15s apiece. A year later he delivered a dozen similarly priced chairs to John Cadwalader, identifying them as "round top" Windsors. The term appeared again a few years later when Uriah Woolman shipped twenty-four chairs and other cargo to Charleston, South Carolina, where dealers were already advertising chairs of this description. Trumble provided further insights into nomenclature when he billed Isaac Hazlehurst and Company in 1789 for a large order of eight dozen chairs, placed on board the ship *Canton* bound for the Far East. Among the patterns listed are "Scroled Arm [Chairs]" and "Plain Armed D[itt]o." The prices were somewhat lower than earlier. A sack-back, or round-top, chair with plain

Figure 7 Fan-back Windsor side chair, Francis Trumble, Philadelphia, ca. 1778–1785. Yellow poplar (seat) with maple, black walnut, oak, and hickory (microanalysis). H. 35³/₄", W. 23¹/₂", D. 19¹/₄". (Courtesy, Winterthur Museum.)

Figure 8 Detail of right crest terminal of the chair illustrated in fig. 7.

arms is illustrated in figure 6. The scroll arms are terminated by small, carved knuckles, formed by attaching extra pieces of shaped wood to the lower surface of the tips.[12]

The nomenclature for the sack-back chair took a different turn in eastern Connecticut, where the work of Amos Denison Allen is identified by branded examples (fig. 6) and by orders recorded in his memorandum book. Only careful analysis of the orders and prior knowledge of Allen's production, however, identify his "armed Chairs @ 9/4 each" as sack-back Windsors. The term *Windsor* never appears in his records. In neighboring Scotland, Connecticut, Judge Ebenezer Devotion acquired "arm Chairs" from nearby chairmakers Theodosius Parsons (fl. 1784–1799) and Ebenezer Tracy, Sr. (1744–1803). The records of Solomon Cole (1772–1870), who worked in Glastonbury, south of Hartford, are somewhat more comprehensive than those of Allen. The price range for his "arm d Chair," which he produced from 1795 to 1807, was broad, ranging from 6s to 10s 6d. Cole framed one chair with rockers and charged 11s. Yellow and green are mentioned as finish colors.[13]

Production of the *fan-back* Windsor, the first side chair in the market, reached its stride following the Revolution (fig. 7). Market acceptance of the chair can be measured in the proliferation of Windsor records in the postwar period and their initial focus on this pattern. The Windsor side chair offered consumers greater flexibility in furnishing and more attractive prices. Philadelphia customers had two options: a "plain" (also "common") pattern or a "Scrowl top" one. Carved crest terminals embellished the second pattern (fig. 8), and about one shilling separated the two in price. Fan-back Windsors were available from the leading Philadelphia chairmakers —William Cox (d. 1811), Joseph Henzey, Sr. (1743–1796), and Francis Trumble—as well as from "workmen whose names [were] less up." At his untimely death in 1793, John Lambert owned a supply of chair parts used in constructing fan-back Windsors: "Chair Bottoms made" (finished seats), "Stretchers," "Sticks" (spindles), and "30 Fan Back top Rails bent." A decade later, "50 fan back Chairs partly finished" stood in the shop of Ansel Goodrich (ca. 1773–1803) at Northampton, Massachusetts, when the chairmaker died suddenly at age thirty.[14]

The fan-back Windsor was the first in a long line of plank-seat side chairs employed for dining. In 1785 when a member of the Coates family of Philadelphia purchased "Six Scrowl Top Dining Chairs" from Joseph Henzey, the practice was already established. The word *dining* serves a dual role here as a synonym for *Windsor* and as a window on function. Outside the dining room, fan-back chairs furnished ships' cabins, inns, resort hotels, a theater in Boston, and the premises of a dancing master in Portland, Maine. The chair remained a salable product well into the nineteenth century, especially in New England. In 1811 appraisers itemized seven fan-back chairs with the contents of Ebenezer Knowlton's (ca. 1769–1810) woodworking shop in Boston. Connecticut chairmakers Oliver Avery (1757–1842) of North Stonington and Samuel Douglas (d. 1845) of Canton recorded sales of fan-back chairs in 1813 and 1816, respectively.[15]

Figure 9 Bow-back Windsor armchair and side chair, Joseph Henzey, Philadelphia, 1785–1790. Yellow poplar (seat) with maple, oak, hickory, and ash (microanalysis). (Left to right) H. 37⅝", 36⅞"; W. 20½", 17⅝"; D. 17¾", 16". (Courtesy, Winterthur Museum.)

About 1785 the chairmaking community at Philadelphia introduced a second Windsor side chair to the American furniture market, this one with a rounded back (fig. 9). Evidence of its early fabrication in city shops occurs in the receipt book of Robert Blackwell, who purchased "8 ovel-back Chairs" for £4 from John Letchworth (1759–1843) in 1787. Outside Philadelphia the chair was better known as a *bow-back* Windsor. For the first time a Windsor side chair and a companion armchair were designed en suite. A substantial change in the turned work of the base introduced simulated *bamboo* elements at Philadelphia (the baluster leg was retained some years longer in other locations). The average local price of the side chair at 11s 3d, up several shillings from the cost of the fan-back chair, reflected the newly fashionable status of the pattern in the urban center.[16]

The redesigned turnings of the bow-back Windsor gave rise to another name frequently associated with this pattern, that of *bamboo chair,* although the term was more common after 1800 to describe a later style. One of the popular painted surfaces for the bow-back chair was pale yellow, or "straw" color, one that simulated the natural material. White, green, and mahogany were other color choices, and purchasers of armchairs had the option of choosing real or painted mahogany arms, as indicated in Stephen Girard's order to Joseph Henzey for "Bamboo windsor Chairs with mohogny arms" priced at 18*s* 9*d* apiece. Short resting pieces attached to the back frame of the chair were referred to as "elbows." Thirty-three were enumerated in John Lambert's shop inventory (1793), along with modish "Turned Bamboo Feet" and "Turnd Bamboo Sticks." Together the Lambert and Trumble (1798) inventories describe the primary element of the rounded chair back in three stages of production: "Bowes for Chairs (in the Ruff)" (Trumble), "Long Bows cleaned up," and "Long Bows bent" (Lambert).[17]

Other variations in nomenclature relative to the bow-back chair can be noted outside Pennsylvania. Amos Denison Allen of Connecticut consistently identified the bow-back form as a "Dining Chair" in his memorandum book, again providing a focus on function rather than form. Of the two styles of eighteenth-century Windsor side chairs, the bow-back chair was the more satisfactory design for use around a table because it had no protruding top piece.[18]

Given the profile of the bow-back Windsor, the word *round* again figures in descriptions, although records do not always distinguish clearly between this chair and the sack-back chair. Cost and numbers can provide clues. The unit price of six "Round Chairs" (bow-backs) framed in 1790 at Salem, Massachusetts, by Josiah Austin (1746–1825) was 7*s* 6*d*. Another local shop priced two "round top," or sack-back, armchairs at 10*s* a few years later. In upstate New York, Elihu Alvord (1775–1863) of Ballston Springs supplied "101 round back windsor Chairs" for Nicholas Low's Sans Souci Hotel in 1804, charging 7*s* 6*d* apiece, the same as Austin. A year later Hector Sanford (1780–1837) offered round-back chairs and newer eastern styles to customers in Chillicothe, Ohio.[19]

The most elusive Windsor pattern to track in records is the one developed about 1790 in New York City and known today as a continuous-bow chair (fig. 10). Although New York moved rapidly during the 1790s toward premier status among American seaports, and her chairmakers engaged in a productive commerce in seating furniture, few local craft records exist for this period. A 1792 bill from chairmaker Peter Tillou (fl. 1765-1798) to a Mrs. Montgomery lists "12 New Fashion Painted chairs" priced at 9*s* 6*d* apiece. The price may identify armchairs, but the bow-back chair was also a relatively new pattern in the market at this date. More positive evidence of the chair exists outside the city.[20]

Following New York's lead, craftsmen in Connecticut and Rhode Island also produced continuous-bow chairs. A notation dated 1793 in the account book of Elisha Hawley of Ridgefield, Connecticut, appears to identify this pattern: "To Winsor Chair three boss [bows]." An uncommon triple-back chair seems implied, but in fact the bows probably were bends—one at the

Figure 10   Continuous-bow Windsor armchair, Walter MacBride, New York City, ca. 1792–1796. Yellow poplar (seat) with maple and oak (microanalysis). H. 37 5/8", W. 25 1/2", D. 17 3/8". (Courtesy, Winterthur Museum.)

top and two forming the arms. The price was *9s.* Continuous-bow chairs with family histories are still owned locally.[21]

The best information about production of the continuous-bow chair comes from the shop records of Amos Denison Allen of South Windham, Connecticut. Again, only careful analysis of Allen's memorandum book and knowledge of his documented Windsor work permits identification of his "fancy" chair as the pattern in question. The price was about the same as that for his sack-back chair; Windsor side chairs were one to two shillings cheaper. When Allen started making continuous-bow chairs in 1797, the backs were strengthened with a pair of extra spindles anchored in a rear extension of the seat, as illustrated in figure 10. Only later did the craftsman make special note of "Fancy Chs without braces." Customers chose green, yellow, blue, or red (brownish) painted surfaces. A few chairs, probably those in the bamboo style only, were ornamented with narrow stripes. Based on recorded orders, Allen's customers paired their continuous-bow chairs with both fan-back and bow-back side chairs.[22]

Windsor Chairs: 1800 to 1850

When Robert Taylor and Daniel King (fl. 1799–1800) of Philadelphia billed Stephen Girard for "1 Doz Newfashiond Wite Dining Chairs" at $2 apiece on May 21, 1799, the chairmakers identified a second bamboo-framed Windsor pattern introduced to the American chairmaking community at Philadelphia (fig. 11). Local artisans fitted the new chair with a squared back in place of the round one that had been in the market for over a decade. The new design was commonly referred to everywhere as a *bamboo* Windsor, and it was still a marketable product in 1810 when Joseph Burden (fl. 1791–1837) supplied a dozen chairs to Girard for his flourishing export trade. At Wilmington, Delaware, a short distance down the Delaware River from Philadelphia, merchant James Brobson shipped "Six doz'n Bamboo Chairs" to Barbados in 1804. Jared Chesnut (fl. 1800–1837), a local chairmaker, could have been the supplier (fig. 11).[23]

As early as 1801 David Alling (1773–1855) purchased "Bamboo Stuff" from suppliers for his nascent, although already flourishing, chairmaking enterprise at Newark, New Jersey, across the bay from New York City. He finished some chair seats with rush, and others with cane, but his wood-seat "Windsor Bamboo" was also a viable product for more than a decade. Allen Holcomb (1782–1860), a New Englander who migrated to upstate New York via Troy in the early nineteenth century, produced sets of "Bamboo Dining Chairs," a reminder that the Windsor side chair in its successive patterns through the mid-nineteenth century occupied a principal position in the American dining room.[24]

Craftsmen throughout New England framed bamboo chairs, a term that remained common into the 1820s, although alternative names describe similar products. *Square-back,* or *square-top,* chair is a generic appellation that identifies most Windsor styles from 1800 to 1850. When used by Solomon Cole of Connecticut in 1806–1807, "square top" described chairs "with double bows" much like that in figure 12. The pattern is a variation of figure 11,

Figure 11 Square-back Windsor side chair with double bows, Jared Chesnut, Wilmington, Delaware, ca. 1804–1810. Yellow poplar (seat) with maple, walnut, oak, and hickory (microanalysis). H. 33⅞", W. 18¼", D. 16¼". (Courtesy, Winterthur Museum.)

with alternate spindles piercing the lower cross rod ("bow") of the crest. Cole's side chairs were priced at 9s equaling $1.50. Silas E. Cheney's (1776–1821) comparable "square Back Chairs" cost $1.33 if "plain" and $1.50 when "ornimented." He also framed a companion armchair at his shop in Litchfield, Connecticut.[25]

The identification of slim top pieces as "bows" was also common practice outside New England. Charles C. Robinson (d. 1825) of Philadelphia made chairs with "Double Bows" and "Single Bows." The word *bow* derives from the lateral bend of the cross rods, which complements the curve at the back of the seat. When distinguishing between back pieces for square-back chairs and oval-back chairs, appraisers of Henry Prall's (d. 1802) estate identified "Longe Bows" and "short Bows." Thomas Adams's (fl. 1797–1855) bill for furniture made for the U.S. War Department at Washington in 1814 lists a variant of the term as "1 Dozen Chairs Single Tops" priced at $1.50 apiece.[26]

Early nineteenth-century craftsmen also distinguished between chairs with *straight backs* (fig. 11) and *bent backs* (fig. 12), a practice that continued well into the century. The nomenclature differentiates straight back posts socketed into the seat at a slight cant from posts steamed and bent before socketing, although neither term identifies the actual crest pattern. Both back forms had a broad geographic distribution. Straight-back chairs appear in the records of craftsmen as widely separated as Thomas Boynton (1786–1849) of Windsor, Vermont, William Beesley (1797–1842) of Salem, New Jersey, and Caleb Gallup (d. 1827) of Norwalk, Ohio.[27]

Bent-back chairs are mentioned more frequently in records than straight-back chairs, probably because they represent a variation from standard framing practice. The added labor of bending the backs also made them more costly. In 1819 David Alling of Newark, New Jersey, shipped two dozen each of yellow and green "winsor bent backs" to New Orleans. In upstate New York bent-back chairs and bedstead posts were part of a barter arrangement in which Allen Holcomb of Otsego County received a clock case in exchange. In New England Thomas Boynton made bent-back chairs in Boston before he relocated to Hartland–Windsor, Vermont, in 1811–1812. In Vermont his bent-back production included, appropriately, "single top" and "Double top" Windsors. Elizur Barnes (1780–1825) of Middletown, Connecticut, framed "Bent Back Wood Seat" chairs a few years later. Eastern patterns were available at many "western" locations shortly after their introduction. In 1816 Henry May and Thomas S. Renshaw (fl. 1816 to ca. 1818) advertised bent-back chairs at Chillicothe, Ohio.[28]

Other terms also describe the bent-back chair. *Spring-back* (or "sprung-back") was used by Bernard Foot (fl. 1813–1818) at Newburyport, Massachusetts, and by David Pritchard (1775–1838) and Silas Cheney in Connecticut. A receipted bill signed by Isaac Stone (b. 1767) at Salem, Massachusetts, in 1811 identifies "Fallback Bamboo Chairs." The records of David Pritchard focus on a term that describes another feature of the early nineteenth-century bamboo chair. Between 1804 and 1807 he sold sets of "miter-top" chairs from his Waterbury, Connecticut, shop. The side chair shown in figure 12 has the "miter," or diagonal groove, at the junctures of the top rail and back

Figure 12 Square-back Windsor side chair with double bows, Daniel Abbot and Company, Newburyport, Massachusetts, ca. 1809–1811. White pine (seat). H. 33", W. 19 3/8", D. 17 3/8". (Courtesy, Society for the Preservation of New England Antiquities, gift of Mrs. Arthur M. Merriam.)

posts. The joints are actually round tenons and mortises located below the miters. The grooves in bamboo-style chairs are aptly described as "creases" in the shop inventory of Anthony Steel (d. 1817) of Philadelphia. The 1817 document lists "creased" stock consisting of "sticks" (spindles), "elbows" (arms), "feet" (legs), and "stretchers."[29]

A crest pattern that was extraordinarily popular in New England during the 1810s is difficult to track in contemporary records (fig. 13). The profile of the top piece imitates that of joined chairs introduced by cabinetmakers in Boston about the turn of the century. A paucity of records by local craftsmen during this period may account for the lack of good information, and the pattern also may have been known by more than one name.

A document that appears to throw light on the subject is the probate inventory of cabinetmaker Benjamin Bass (fl. 1798–1819), who died at Boston in 1819. The enumeration, which lists both formal and vernacular seating furniture, names several patterns, among them "Tablet Chairs wooden bottoms." Prices are in the same range as Bass's "Bamboo Chairs" at $1.25 to $1.50 apiece. Tablet-top chairs were framed with the crest tenoned to the top of the back posts. With its bulging uprights flanking the spindles, the chair illustrated in figure 13 may be a variant type that Henry Beck (1787–1837) of Portsmouth, New Hampshire, called a "swell back;" or, that term may simply describe a bent-back chair. Between 1812 and 1814, Thomas Boynton, who had only recently removed from Boston to Vermont, identified one of the chairs he produced at his "manufactory" at Hartland-Windsor as a "fancy top Bb [bent back] Chair." He priced it at $2. The term "fancy" was a general one used throughout the early nineteenth century to describe several top pieces, each uncommon, or special, in its pattern or variation.[30]

The alternative in nineteenth-century Windsor construction to framing the crest on top of the back posts was to place the back piece between the posts (fig. 14). The basic pattern is referred to as a *slat-back* Windsor in period documents. The style, introduced in New York and New England before 1810 and slightly later in other areas, remained popular into the 1840s. Both straight and bent profiles were available. In the earliest patterns, creased cylindrical spindles accompany a plain rectangular slat. Slats were also referred to as *benders* because of their lateral curve. David Alling paid a journeyman $4.50 in 1816 to paint and ornament "24 Windsor Slat Backs" whose upper structure was framed in the general pattern of the chair shown in figure 14. Alling was a considerable supplier of the New York furniture market.[31]

During the 1820s the spindle count in slat-back chairs was reduced from six or seven to four or five, and the terms *four-rod* and *five-rod* chair came into use (fig. 15). Thomas Walter Ward II stocked both styles at his store in Pomfret, Connecticut, in the 1830s. Jacob Felton (1787–1864) of Fitzwilliam, New Hampshire, supplied the Boston market, and Elbridge Gerry Reed (1800–1870) of Sterling, Massachusetts, framed hundreds of rod-style slat backs for fellow chairmakers in Worcester County. At Hartford, Connecticut, Philemon Robbins (fl. 1833–1870s) acquired his four-

Figure 13 Tablet-top Windsor side chair, southern New Hampshire, 1810–1822. White pine (seat). H. 35³⁄₈", W. 18", D. 15³⁄₄". (Courtesy, Shelburne Museum, Shelburne, Vermont; photo, Winterthur Museum.)

Figure 14 Slat-back Windsor side chair, New York City, ca. 1809–1815. Yellow poplar (seat). H. 34³/₄", W. 16³/₈", D. 14¹/₄". (Private collection; photo, Winterthur Museum.)

and five-rod chair stock from Sullivan Hill (b. 1808), a supplier in Spencer, Massachusetts. The wholesale price of five-rod chairs was 12¹/₂ percent higher than that of four-rod chairs because of the extra labor. When Robbins retailed the chairs, the markup was 40 to 47 percent greater than the wholesale cost.[32]

Many four- and five-rod chairs were framed with ball-turned spindles, which gave rise to the term *ball-back* chair (fig. 15). The choice of pattern

Figure 15 Slat-back Windsor side chair, eastern Massachusetts, possibly Worcester County, 1820–1830. White pine (seat). H. 34", W. 17½", D. 16¼". (Courtesy, New Hampshire Historical Society, Concord; photo, Heritage Plantation of Sandwich, Sandwich, Massachusetts.)

name was a matter of local preference. A word of caution is in order, how-ever. A ball-back chair could be framed with horizontal sticks and balls rather than vertical members. Many chairs of the second type had rush or cane seats instead of wooden bottoms. Crossover terminology between Windsor and fancy seating is thus a factor to be reckoned with in interpre-tation. In 1825 Elizur Barnes of Middletown, Connecticut, specifically identified stock framed in his shop as "Ball Back Wood Seet Cheirs." Another time he described the same seating as "ballback winsor." Ball-back chairs with vertical sticks were produced for several decades. In 1842 at a sale disposing of part of the estate of chairmaker Peter A. Willard (fl. 1824–1842) of Sterling, Massachusetts, quantities of "Balld Rods" were sold at 20¢ and 25¢ per hundred. Similar stock was offered the same year at Philadelphia in the estate of Charles Riley (fl. 1813–1842).[33]

Figure 16 Slat-back Windsor side chair, eastern Massachusetts, possibly Worcester County, 1820–1830. White pine (seat). H. 34$^{1}/_{8}$", W. 17$^{3}/_{8}$", D. 15$^{1}/_{4}$". (Courtesy, John Tarrant Kenny Hitchcock Museum, Riverton, Connecticut; photo, Winterthur Museum.)

The method of framing a slat-style crest piece between the back posts produced yet another term identifying a Windsor: *mortise-top*. "6 Yellow mortised-top Chairs" stood in the "West Chamber" of the home of Peter A. Willard at Sterling, Massachusetts, in 1842. The shop records of fellow Worcester County chairmaker Elbridge Gerry Reed indicate that he framed thousands of mortise-top chairs for area entrepreneurs. Sometimes Reed had to bend "the stuff" first. His pay for framing mortise-top chairs ranged from under 10¢ per chair to as much as 25¢, an indication that patterns more complicated than the simple spindle styles were involved.[34]

A variant pattern in mortise-top construction introduced a loaf-shape slat and arrow-shape spindles to the Windsor chair back (fig. 16). Neither term is contemporary with the period, however. Windsors with this crest may have been referred to as "Round Top Chairs," a term used at Waterbury, Connecticut, in 1839 by appraisers of the estate of chairmaker David Pritchard. Another candidate is *fancy-top,* a term mentioned in the correspondence of Joel Pratt, Jr. (1789–1868), of Sterling, Massachusetts. During the mid-1840s, Calvin Stetson (d. ca. 1860) of Barnstable on Cape Cod retailed fancy-top chairs received from his Boston supplier, William P. Haley (fl. 1837–1859). Some are described as painted a dark color.[35]

Appraisers who inventoried Anthony Steel's estate at Philadelphia in 1817 identified broad spindles of the type shown in figure 16 as "flat Sticks." The profile is actually a slimmed down neoclassical urn, adapted first for use in fancy seating. During the 1810s the shaped stick became a feature in some high-quality Windsors. The Steel inventory also lists "chair stumps," or posts, along with "elbows" (arms). The records of Joel Pratt, Jr., and Elbridge Gerry Reed of Massachusetts introduce substitute terms for the heavy uprights in chair backs and arms. The preferred name in Worcester County was *pillar,* although on occasion Reed referred to *standards.* Armchairs are uncommon in nineteenth-century Windsor work, however. The bread-and-butter seating form of the trade was the side chair.[36]

The chair illustrated in figure 16 is notable for another feature. Its surface is painted to resemble maple. Both the random striping and raw sienna color, varying from light yellowish brown for the ground to medium shades for the streaking, reinforce that image. Chairs with surfaces "which are imitations of various kinds of Wood, such as Rose Wood, Sattin Wood, Hair [*sic*] Wood, Maple Wood, &c." were advertised in 1815 by William Haydon (fl. 1799–1833) of Philadelphia, although the period of their greatest popularity came later. W. A. and D. M. Coggeshall (fl. 1835–1845) of Newport, Rhode Island, retailed "Imitation Maple" chairs of various patterns in 1835, several years before A. and J. B. Mathiot (fl. 1840–1851) offered chairs in "a variety of imitation wood colors" at their "GAY STREET CHAIR WARE ROOMS" in Baltimore.[37]

Double-back and triple-back Windsors were other staples of the eastern Massachusetts chair trade that fall into the general category of mortise-top chairs (fig. 17). The extra work of preparing mortise holes in the posts to receive the crosspieces at midback would have placed the chairs, especially the triple-back pattern, toward the upper range of Elbridge Gerry Reed's labor charge for framing mortise-top chairs. Collectively, the crosspieces of the upper structure, whether narrow or broad, were referred to as "Backs" in the account book of Joel Pratt, Jr., of Sterling. That record lists thousands of chair parts, including "Rods," received from suppliers. Although sizes are omitted, short, ball-turned sticks, such as those illustrated in figure 17, would have been included with the rods.[38]

By the second quarter of the nineteenth century the chair trade in eastern Massachusetts and adjacent areas provided employment for hundreds of individuals—suppliers of chair stock, framers, ornamental painters, and retailers. Many more found jobs in support capacities as teamsters and suppliers of raw materials. Vast quantities of framed chairs were retailed and

Figure 17 Triple-back Windsor side chair, Joel Pratt, Jr., Sterling, Massachusetts, 1820–1835. White pine (seat). H. 33 3/8", W. 17", D. 15 7/8". (Courtesy, Old Sturbridge Village, Sturbridge Massachusetts; photo, Winterthur Museum.)

wholesaled throughout the region and funneled into Boston and other urban centers for broader distribution. Josiah Prescott Wilder (1801–1873) and Jacob Felton produced chairs in southern New Hampshire. Wilder's principal market was Lowell, a rising textile manufacturing center on the Merrimack River northwest of Boston. Felton sent chairs east to Boston and west to Brattleboro, Vermont, on the Connecticut River. One of his products was the "square front [seat] Doubl back" chair. Elbridge Gerry Reed and Samuel Stuart (d. 1829) were substantial chairmakers in Worcester County. In 1829 "1 hundred triple back chairs" stood in Stuart's shop ready to be transported to a large market such as Boston in his "one horse wagon & chair rack."[39]

Luke Houghton (d. 1877) of Barre, Massachusetts, purchased his stock and distributed his "duble back chairs" in a localized market that encompassed about a dozen towns in Worcester County. Other central Massachusetts craftsmen supplied chairs for Philemon Robbins's retail establishment in Hartford. At Norwich near the coast in 1830, the partners Congdon and Tracy (fl. 1830–1831) advertised "1000 CHAIRS Just received from one of the best manufactories in New England." Their stock included both "double back" and "five rodded" chairs in "light and dark" colors.[40]

For three decades, from the 1820s through the 1840s, New York City and adjacent areas (upstate New York, Newark, New Jersey, and Connecticut) were strongholds of the *roll-top* pattern in wooden- and woven-bottom seating. Modest production of the roll-top Windsor also can be noted in eastern Pennsylvania, eastern Massachusetts (fig. 18), and other locations. New York chairmakers probably introduced the roll-top chair during the late 1810s, although most evidence supporting the prominence of the pattern appears later. The distinctive, turned top piece was already current abroad in 1802 when illustrated and described as a "roller" in *The London Chair-Makers' and Carvers' Book of Prices for Workmanship*. The pattern probably was fashionable in New York in 1819 when John K. Cowperthwaite (fl. 1807–1833) used a woodcut of a roll-top, cane-seat fancy chair to illustrate an advertisement. That chair was not a stock cut but appears to have been designed for Cowperthwaite's personal use: the front legs are terminated by typical New York, carved paw feet and the midback crosspiece is a pattern that appeared in the 1817 *New York Book of Prices for Manufacturing Cabinet and Chair Work* (see fig. 31).[41]

David Alling of Newark, New Jersey, whose chairmaking accounts provide a window on the New York trade in the absence of comprehensive records for that city, constructed roll-top seating between 1827 and 1839 (and perhaps earlier, since his records for the early 1820s are incomplete). Fellow chairmakers Benjamin W. Branson (d. 1835) and Richard D. Blauvelt (fl. 1824–1852) made roll-top chairs in New York during the 1830s. Records for craftsmen residing upstate in Otsego County document an active trade in roll-top (also called roll-back) seating from the mid-1820s until the early 1850s and probably reflect activity throughout the region.[42]

In neighboring Connecticut, where many more records survive, trade was brisk. Levi Stillman (1791–1871) of New Haven first recorded the roll-

Figure 18 Roll-top Windsor side chair with raised seat, John D. Pratt, Lunenburg, Massachusetts, ca. 1835–1840. White pine (seat). H. 34⅝", W. 16⅞", D. 15½". (Carrie and Raymond Ruggles collection; photo, Winterthur Museum.)

top pattern in 1822. Two years later he sold "6 doz roll top Windsors" for export priced at $90. Roll-top chairs were also in demand in the central part of the state, as corroborated in the records of Elizur Barnes (Middletown), David Pritchard (Waterbury), and Philemon Robbins (Hartford). James Gere (b. 1783) had many requests for roll-top Windsors at his coastal shop in Groton. Some customers ordered suites of side chairs and armchairs.[43]

A lesser-known roll-top chair of eastern Massachusetts origin is illustrated in figure 18. Its extra embellishment placed it at the top of the market in the Lunenburg shop of John D. Pratt (1792–1863). *Fancy* front legs and stretchers, which reflect considerable influence from New York vernacular design, replace the usual bamboo-type supports. The most prominent and unusual feature of the chair is, however, the seat—a design referred to dur-

Figure 19 Tablet-top Windsor side chair with scroll seat, central Vermont, 1840–1850. White pine (seat). H. 33", W. 17⁷⁄₈", D. 14⁵⁄₈". (Courtesy, State of Vermont, Division for Historic Preservation, Old Constitution House, Windsor; photo, Winterthur Museum.)

ing the period as a *raised seat* and a type more common on rocking chairs than on stationary chairs. The curves are achieved by adding a half scroll at the lower front edge and gluing up the back extension, or "rise," from one or more stacked pieces of wood. Elbridge Gerry Reed of Sterling, Massachusetts, first mentioned a raised seat in 1834. Jacob Felton and Josiah Prescott Wilder of New Hampshire and Thomas Boynton of Vermont also made chairs with this seat in the mid-1830s. On one occasion Philemon Robbins of Hartford identified the seat by its profile, calling it an "ogee seat."[44]

During the 1820s when the slat-back styles (figs. 15, 16) rose to popularity, tablet-framed patterns (fig. 13) were less prominent than in the 1810s;

however, renewed interest at the end of the decade brought both squared- and rounded-end examples into the market. Craftsmen continued to frame many tablets on round tenons. In an alternative construction, they attached the crest to the flattened faces of the back posts at shallow ledges, or rabbets, and secured them from the back with screws (fig. 19). This assembly method gave rise to the term *screwed-back* (or *screwed-top*) *chair,* although the crest piece itself varied in profile. Elbridge Gerry Reed of Sterling, Massachusetts, framed chairs of this design by 1829.[45]

The side chair illustrated in figure 19 has an unusual feature—a *scroll seat,* formed by attaching a half scroll to the seat front. Unlike the raised seat (fig. 18), there is no elevated back structure. Chairmakers, including Philemon Robbins of Hartford, Connecticut, used this construction for rocking chairs and top-of-the-line stationary seating. Thomas Walter Ward II stocked scroll-seat chairs at his store in Pomfret, Connecticut, in 1838, and Josiah Prescott Wilder still framed chairs of this description two decades later at New Ipswich, New Hampshire.[46]

A tablet with an extension at the center and large rounded ends, frequently shouldered as illustrated in figure 20, was popular in Pennsylvania, Maryland, and adjacent areas from the late 1830s. Preceding this pattern was a large, rectangular tablet with a generous overhang at the ends, which originated in Baltimore (see fig. 32). That city gave its name to the general style. Chairmakers used either round tenons or rabbets to frame the top piece. Frederick Fox (fl. ca. 1840–1877) offered "Baltimore Chairs" for sale in 1845 at the sign of the "Red Chair" in Reading, Pennsylvania. Three years earlier, appraisers itemized sets of Baltimore-style chairs in the estate of Charles Riley at Philadelphia; a few were painted in imitation maple. Loose top pieces in the shop were referred to as "Baltimore Bows."[47]

The popularity of Baltimore-style chairs extended to New York and New England, where imitations were of a general nature only. In 1835 Benjamin Branson of New York supplied local chairmakers with Baltimore chairs: in July Tweed and Bonnell (fl. 1823–1843) bought "two Bondls of Boltimore Stuff" for framing. On August 29, Branson credited James Vanderbilt (fl. 1830–1835), a painter and chairmaker, for painting and ornamenting twenty-five dozen Baltimore chairs. The same day he sold the chairs to the firm of Benjamin and Elijah Farrington (fl. 1826–1835) for $7.50 a dozen, a price that allowed the partners to make a profit. At Sterling, Massachusetts, Elbridge Gerry Reed contracted with Benjamin Stuart (1793–1868), a fellow chairmaker, from November 1837 to February 1838 to frame a total of 360 Baltimore chairs for regional distribution. The presence of "36 Baltimore Chairs unfinished" in the shop of Daniel W. Badger (1779–1847) at Bolton, Connecticut, a decade later underscores the longevity of the style.[48]

A new feature of the Windsor chair during the 1840s was a bold vertical back splat, or *banister,* adapted from contemporary formal furniture and based generally on eighteenth-century design (fig. 20). By midcentury Pennsylvania chairmakers had introduced the pierced banister. Outside Pennsylvania the banister-back support is found most often in wood-seat chairs made in Maryland, northern New England, and the Midwest.

Figure 20   Tablet-top Windsor side chair with banister, central Pennsylvania, 1850–1860. Yellow poplar (seat). H. 34$\frac{1}{8}$", W. 18$\frac{1}{4}$", D. 15$\frac{1}{8}$". (Private collection; photo, Winterthur Museum.)

Figure 21 Tablet-top fancy side chair, Baltimore, Maryland, 1804–1814. Maple, yellow poplar, and mahogany (microanalysis). H. 33³/₄", W. 19", D. 15". (Courtesy, Winterthur Museum.)

Fancy Chairs

The earliest evidence of *fancy chair* making in America dates to the mid-1780s. Samuel Claphamson (d. 1808), cabinetmaker and chairmaker "late from London," settled in Philadelphia and advertised modish furniture, from commode sideboards to fancy chairs. During the 1790s several New York craftsmen became associated with fancy chair making. William Palmer (fl. 1787–1841), who began as a painter and gilder, advertised fancy seating furniture in 1796. He was followed by John Mitchell (fl. 1796) and William Challen (fl. 1796–1833), both chairmakers from London. Challen advertised "every article in the fancy chair line . . . after the newest and most approved London patterns," which pinpoints the origin of the new painted form. The fancy chair differs from the Windsor in its basic construction. The seat is an open frame fastened to long, continuous back members and finished with a woven bottom.[49]

The earliest identifiable American fancy chairs date from the start of the nineteenth century and originated in Baltimore, a center that quickly achieved prominence as a producer of painted furniture (fig. 21). Here, the principal feature of the chair back is an urn-shape banister flanked by slim, flat sticks of complementary profile, possibly the "Urn spindles" of William Haydon's and William H. Stewart's (fl. ca. 1809–1818) black and gold chairs made in 1818 at Philadelphia. Both elements are included in George Hepplewhite's *The Cabinet-Maker and Upholsterer's Guide* in engraved plates dated 1787. The slim crest with a modest overhang at the posts is of slightly later date. A prototype is illustrated in the 1802 *London Book of Prices,* where it is called a "tablet top." That volume also includes posts with a backward bend, or "sweep." The fancy chair profile served as a model for the later introduction of bent backs to Windsor seating.[50]

A feature of note at the center of the crest in the Baltimore chair is the painted ornament symbolic of music. Brothers John and Hugh Finlay (fl. 1803–1816), who in the early nineteenth century rose to prominence as chairmakers in Baltimore, described this and other ornaments suitable for crest pieces in an 1805 advertisement: "real Views, Fancy Landscapes, Flowers, Trophies of Music, War, Husbandry, Love, &c." This description, in turn, leads to another that further expands on the nomenclature of the chair back. Henry May and Thomas S. Renshaw (fl. ca. 1816–1818), newly in business as chairmakers in Chillicothe, Ohio, in February 1816, identified part of their output as "Broad Tops with landscapes." Renshaw had recently worked for several years in Baltimore. Three years later at Norfolk, Virginia, Humberston Skipwith purchased "12 Broad top Chairs" from the shop of Joshua Moore (fl. 1804–1819) for his home in Mecklenberg County. This second reference reinforces the supposition that *broad-top* commonly described the rectangular tablet that was a trademark of the Baltimore style in fancy and Windsor seating for four decades.[51]

One of the two seating materials of the fancy chair was cane, a woven, open material particularly suited to warm climates. An 1804 schedule of property in the Boston shop of William Seaver (fl. 1793–1837) lists "82 India Cane Bottoms." Further insight on this item occurs a few years later in an advertisement by Asa Holden (1762–1854) of New York, who, while speaking of his fancy chairs with cane or rush seats, noted: "The cane seats are warranted to be American made, which are known to be much superior to any imported from India."[52]

Were it not for the records of David Alling of Newark, New Jersey, two distinctive turned-spindle patterns would be anonymous today, and the chairs they embellish would be known simply by the generic term *spindle-back* (figs. 22, 23). In records dating from 1801 to 1804, Alling described the double-baluster turning of the first pattern as a "Cumberland Spindle" (fig. 22). Complementing the spindles in the chair back (and under the arms when present, see fig. 23) were "Cumberland front rounds," or stretchers. If Alling's records were more complete, they would likely show that the

Figure 22 Spindle-back fancy side chair with Cumberland spindles, New York City, 1800–1815. Maple, birch, and yellow poplar (microanalysis). H. 35", W. 19", D. 15¾". (Courtesy, Winterthur Museum.)

pattern remained current through the decade and beyond. Allen Holcomb of Otsego County in upstate New York used the term occasionally into the 1820s, principally to describe sticks in wagon chairs. The source of the word *Cumberland* is obscure.[53]

Some chairs framed with Cumberland spindles have a slim slat, or bender, for a crest piece. Others are constructed with cross rods at the top (see fig. 23). The tapered front legs of the chair in figure 22, rounded at the top and marked by an inset cuff near the bottom, are sometimes found on other fancy chairs associated with New York. The long posts of the back, although based on those used in eighteenth-century vernacular seating (see fig. 1), are reduced in diameter, tapered top and bottom, and bent and framed to flare outward and backward slightly.

The woven rush used to seat this chair was more common than cane and less expensive. Rush was often referred to in the trade as *flag*. It was purchased and stored in bundles. David Alling sometimes acquired as many as five hundred bundles at a time, much of it obtained in New York where it was brought in on sloops and often sold at the dock. In his records for 1828–1829, Elisha Harlow Holmes (b. 1799) of Essex, Connecticut, identified both "dry flags" and "green flags" and noted that he had paid to have flag cut at waterside and ferried to a pickup point. Rush had to be properly cured, or dried, before it was bundled and stored; otherwise it rotted and became unfit for use.[54]

Gaps in Alling's records make it impossible to know the exact length of time he produced the *organ-spindle* chair, another spindle-back pattern (fig. 23). The period from 1815 to 1820 is highlighted in his records, but the chair probably was available commercially as early as 1810. Alling framed both top-of-the-line Windsors and fancy chairs with organ spindles in a range of

Figure 23 Spindle-back fancy armchair and side chair with organ spindles, New York City, 1810–1822. Woods and dimensions unknown. (Courtesy, Old Sturbridge Village; photo, Henry E. Peach.)

colors. Organ spindles are named for their resemblance to the pipes of the musical instrument. The creased sticks of this pattern complement the framework that supports them. An almost identical side chair, which bears the label of New York chairmaker George W. Skellorn (b. ca. 1775), is accompanied by a printed billhead inscribed in 1819 that identifies it as a "Bamboo chair."[55]

Imitation bamboowork was popular for several decades in New York City and surrounding areas. Alling produced chairs of this type with rush or cane seats between 1801 and 1822. On Manhattan Island, bamboo chairs usually sold for $2 to $2.50. William Palmer's cane-seat chairs were priced at the higher figure, as were William Buttre's (1782–1864) "bamboo fancy and gold Cheirs." Evidence from across Connecticut—from New Haven and Groton to Middletown, Waterbury, and Litchfield—supports the popularity of the fancy bamboo chair in a region heavily influenced by the New York furniture market. Prices were comparable. As far north as central Vermont "gilt fancy bamboo chairs" were *de rigueur* in stylish public houses. Frederick Pettes ordered half a dozen chairs from Thomas Boynton in 1815 at a cost of $3 apiece for his inn at Windsor.[56]

Rush seats in quality fancy chairs were frequently painted, both for durability and decorative effect. Elizur Barnes of Middletown, Connecticut, sold "white Paint for Cheir Seets" to a customer in 1824. When working for Silas Cheney of Litchfield, Connecticut, in 1808, William Butler (fl. 1807–1809) put seats in six fancy chair frames and then painted them "2 Cots." A parallel reference in the Alling accounts provides additional information: "To matting, moulding & ptg seat 2 coats." *Matting* described the process of weaving a rush seat. In *moulding* a matted seat the chairmaker took strips of wood (the "moulding") and nailed them around the outside edges to form a casing that could be painted and ornamented. The seats of the chairs in figure 23 have been finished in this manner.[57]

Closely associated with the bamboo style in period records are chairs whose framework is secured with ornamental cross sticks and turned *balls* (fig. 24). Sometimes the horizontal pieces are squared; here they are turned with small hollows, or spools, that add significantly to the ornamental effect and complement the hollows and bands of rings in the vertical members. Variant patterns employ a slat or roll at the crest and multiple cross sticks and balls at midback.

Both David Alling of Newark, New Jersey, and Silas Cheney of Litchfield, Connecticut, made *ball-back bamboo* fancy chairs by the mid-1810s and probably earlier. Both acquired much of their stuff for framing from suppliers. Alling's sources were local; Cheney carted his prepared materials from as far away as Lee, Massachusetts, located due north in Berkshire County. Retail prices realized for ball-back chairs were about the same as those for organ-spindle chairs. On two occasions in 1819–1820, however, Alling described high-end market products: "ball back bamboe, Gilt balls, rush seats" and "ball back, green & Gilt, bronsed, rush [seats]," priced at $3.34 and $4.17 apiece, respectively. The higher-priced chair was also available in yellow; *bronzing* was the period term for stenciling. In later years the

Figure 24 Ball-back bamboo fancy armchair, New York City, 1810–1820. Woods and dimensions unknown. (Courtesy, Old Sturbridge Village; photo, Henry E. Peach.)

name *ball-back* was also applied to Windsor chairs with ball-turned vertical spindles, although a few Windsors were made during the 1810s in the fancy style of the chair in figure 24.[58]

An optional feature of ball-back bamboo chairs (fig. 24) and organ-spindle chairs (fig. 23), as noted by Alling, was the outward, forward flare of the lower front legs. When shipping chairs with similar legs to New Orleans in 1819, the chairmaker identified the supports as "bent front feet." Legs without this feature were described simply as "Strait front feet," when such differentiation was necessary. The 1802 *London Book of Prices* illustrates a closely related leg and describes it in a section titled "Sweeping, Toeing, and Rounding Front Legs." There, however, the bend, or "sweep," of the lower leg was produced on the lathe. Tiny, beadlike toes of the type illustrated in figure 24 remained popular for several decades.[59]

A diverse selection of early nineteenth-century documents provides insights on a fancy chair introduced just before 1810 that was framed with either a *single-cross* or a *double-cross* "splat" in the back (fig. 25). The top half

Figure 25 Detail of tradecard, William Buttre, New York City, ca. 1813. Engraving. 5⅞" × 4¼" (overall image). (Courtesy, Winterthur Museum Library, Joseph Downs Collection of Manuscripts and Printed Ephemera.)

of William Buttre's two-scene tradecard, which depicts the painting room at his New York manufactory, shows workmen adding decoration and applying a finish coat of varnish to cross-back chairs in the two styles. Buttre's auxiliary location on Crane Wharf is first cited in the city directory for 1813.[60]

The 1802 *London Book of Prices* illustrates three designs for chair backs with single "angular splats." London influence in fancy chair design was also transferred to America in another way. Samuel J. Tuck (1767–1855), a chairmaker and importer of painters' materials at Boston, expanded his business soon after the turn of the century to include imported furniture. His October 15, 1803 advertisement describes "London made Chairs, newest fashion viz. . . . black and [gold] cross back chairs." Circulation of the London price book and the availability of London-made cross-back chairs eventually influenced fancy chair production in several coastal American cities, although interaction between the Atlantic seaports also remained strong. On December 12, 1810, Boston chair dealers Nolen and Gridley (fl. 1810–1813) announced that they had just received "from one of the first Manufactories at New-York—300 Fancy CHAIRS, of different patterns, some elegant . . . viz . . . green and gold double Cross Backs . . . white and gold double cross d[itt]o."[61]

Prior to commissioning his pictorial tradecard, Buttre used a printed bill-head with the address and text accompanied by a woodcut of a single-cross fancy chair. An inscribed copy is dated 1810, the year the same text and cut appeared in the advertising section of the New York City directory. David Alling probably already produced the cross-back pattern at Newark, although a hiatus in his accounts from 1807 to 1815 (and during the late 1810s) precludes knowing this fact for certain. The chair manufacturer framed both single- and double-cross chairs in 1815–1816. Ground colors of green and white are mentioned; the decoration was "Bronzed," gilt, or striped. Alling's records also mention "dimond front rounds," braces similar in design to that at the front of the single-cross chair. Allen Holcomb in his migratory travels from Connecticut to Otsego County, New York, constructed cross-back chairs about 1809–1810 in the shop of Simon Smith (d. 1837), at Troy on the upper Hudson River. The chairs probably were little different from those manufactured at New York and Newark. During the 1810s, Baltimore, Boston, and Philadelphia chairmakers produced their own cross-back chairs; subtle differences distinguish one from the other. A few Windsors also were made in the cross-back style.[62]

A Boston fancy chair of modest popularity in its several variations is identified by a single, one-line reference in the probate inventory of Benjamin Bass, a cabinetmaker and chairmaker of the city who died in 1819 (fig. 26). The nine "3 Stick" chairs standing "In Price's Store" had wooden bottoms, although the pattern is better known as a fancy chair than as a Windsor. Three-stick backs apparently had their genesis at the start of the 1810s, a time when Samuel Gragg (1772–1855) of Boston used similar two-stick and three-stick braces as stretchers in the front of some of his "elastic," or bentwood, chairs. With its tablet-centered crest, the side chair illustrated in

Figure 26 Three-stick fancy side chair, Boston, Massachusetts, 1810–1822. Woods unknown. H. 33¹/₄", W. 18¹/₄", D. 16¹/₈". (Courtesy, Museum of American Folk Art, New York, gift of the Historical Society of Early American Decoration; photo, Winterthur Museum.)

Figure 27 Advertisement, Thomas Cotton Hayward, *New England Palladium and Commercial Advertiser,* Boston, Massachusetts, July 11, 1819. (Courtesy, Massachusetts Historical Society, Boston; photo, Winterthur Museum.)

figure 26 appears to be an early cross-stick design. The visual rhythm of the crest, the three-stick lower back, and the two-stick front brace appears to owe a considerable debt to the New York ball-back chair (fig. 24) or a related pattern. Nolen and Gridley's importation of New York chairs in 1810 opens the door to this possibility. There is also a remarkable similarity in the ringed, bent, and toed "feet" of the Boston and New York chairs, a pattern that, by the end of the decade, had broad distribution.[63]

Sweep (bent) back posts, with their surfaces shaved to provide a convenient surface for ornamentation, all but replaced round (cylindrical) posts (figs. 21–23) by the late 1810s. Open-stick and tablet-centered crests also gave way to solid slat styles (fig. 27) in the pursuit of painted decoration. The chair in Thomas Cotton Hayward's (1774–1845) advertisement appears to have swelled and reeded legs, a pattern that may have been another New York importation. The front stretcher, consisting of an oval tablet flanked by tiny, flat-faced beads, is a Boston feature, however, and appears in chairs of several patterns. A Windsor chair with a back similar to that in figure 26 has a front stretcher of this design. Tablet tops replaced slats as crest pieces in three-stick chairs by the 1820s, and, the pattern was carried into the late 1830s. Three designs are common: a rectangle with hollow corners, a flared rectangle with an upper-back roll, and rounded-end tablets.[64]

A *fret* can be defined as a panel or a panel-like form that is pierced through or shaped around the outside, or both, to create a decorative pattern. Cabinetmakers and chairmakers alike used frets to good advantage in the backs of formal and vernacular chairs. The use of frets in seating furniture was already current in London when a lattice-type example with diamond-shape piercings appeared in the 1802 *London Book of Prices*.[65]

Figure 28 Billhead and bill, John Knox Cowperthwaite, New York City, printed ca. 1810–1812, inscribed 1816. (Courtesy, Winterthur Museum Library, Joseph Downs Collection of Manuscripts and Printed Ephemera.)

Like many fancy chair patterns, the *fret-back* style may have originated in New York. Asa Holden of that city used a woodcut of a fret-back chair in an advertisement that began in 1812. John K. Cowperthwaite's pictorial billhead inscribed in 1816 but printed about 1810 to 1812 illustrates a similar fancy chair (fig. 28, left). The diamond-like fret is the same pattern as that in the London price book. Indeed, "dimond fret back" fancy chairs are itemized in the accounts of David Alling of Newark, New Jersey, in 1819 and Henry Wilder Miller (1800–1891) of Worcester, Massachusetts, in 1827. By then, diamond-fret fancy chairs had been illustrated in advertisements by Thomas Sill (1776–1826) of Middletown, Connecticut (1814), and by Caleb(?) Davis and John Bussey (fl. 1819) of Albany, New York.[66]

A highly ornamental pattern in fretwork pairs leaf forms and small balls, or beads. The armchair shown in figure 29 illustrates a large set of fancy furniture comprised of twelve side chairs, two armchairs, and a settee that was purchased in New York through an agent in 1816 by a Portsmouth, New Hampshire, resident. The rounded-front seat, which is typical of New York production (see figs. 23–25, 28), is referred to as a "Bell seat" in the 1817 *New York Book of Prices*. Allen Holcomb framed "8 bell Seat Chairs" and "Cased" the seats when working for Simon Smith at Troy, New York, in 1810. The terms *casing* and *moulding* appear to have been interchangeable. Arms of the general type on this chair are illustrated in the 1802 *London Book of Prices*, which describes them as "scroll elbows" on "turn'd stumps." The pattern apparently was common for seating furniture framed with leaf-and-bead frets, because armchairs from at least five different sets have elbows and supports of this design.[67]

The introduction of fretted panels to New York chairs had a substantial impact on fancy chair making in Connecticut because of the strong commercial interaction between the two areas. As previously mentioned, Thomas Sill of Middletown illustrated a diamond-back chair in an 1814 advertisement. Thomas West (1786–1828) of New London made "Fancy Chairs of the latest and most approved New York Fashions," and at Redding, James S. Chapman (fl. 1809–1810) sold his "warranted" chairs at "New-York prices." Levi Stillman, a furniture maker of neighboring New Haven, recorded the sale of both fancy and Windsor fret-back chairs during the 1820s. The cost of "getting out frets" by shop journeymen was recorded as 8¢ and 12½¢ by James Gere of Groton and Silas Cheney of Litchfield. The patterns probably were different; the cost reflects the intricacy of the profile, the number of piercings, or both.[68]

The fret of a fancy chair made in Connecticut has an intricate top profile (fig. 30). Seymour Watrous (fl. 1824–1825) of Hartford illustrated a comparable fret-back chair in 1824 when advertising his start in business. The front stretcher of the chair in the woodcut appears to duplicate the uncommon profile of the example illustrated here, with its central reel flanked by urn-shaped turnings. A square seat and turned crest are also features of both chairs. The roll-top is, in fact, more common than the slat-back with the scroll-type fret. Chair surfaces are about equally divided between painted finishes and natural maple. In 1819 David Alling of Newark, New Jersey, shipped "one doz fret back Curled maple [chairs] in good order" to New Orleans for sale on commission. If some of Alling's chairs had arms, they may have looked like these, which duplicate the posts and scrolls of a New York chair (see fig. 24).[69]

A chair fret of a different type than those in the previous examples was introduced to the New York furniture market in the late 1810s (fig. 31). The pattern is delineated in the 1817 *New York Book of Prices*, with an oval tablet at the center instead of a rectangular one. The price book describes the crosspiece as a chair banister "with double Prince of Wales feathers, tied with a gothic moulding." Chairmakers used the distinctive back piece in joined, fancy, and Windsor seating furniture. The pattern was exceedingly popular, particularly in curled maple and with the central element carved in an open leaf pattern. The general style appears to have remained fashionable

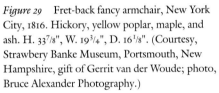

Figure 29   Fret-back fancy armchair, New York City, 1816. Hickory, yellow poplar, maple, and ash. H. 33⁷/₈", W. 19³/₄", D. 16¹/₈". (Courtesy, Strawbery Banke Museum, Portsmouth, New Hampshire, gift of Gerrit van der Woude; photo, Bruce Alexander Photography.)

Figure 30   Fret-back fancy armchair, Connecticut, 1815–1830. Woods unknown. H. 33¹/₂", W. 18³/₄", D. 15¹/₄". (Courtesy, Rhode Island Historical Society; photo, Winterthur Museum.)

throughout the 1820s. The fret may have been the one identified in 1829 at a furniture auction in Salem, Massachusetts, as a "N. York back." David Alling shipped chairs to New Orleans in 1820 described as "1 doz ovel fret backs, gilt and bronsed rose wood, rush seats." The term *oval* may refer to the central tablet of the back piece, as illustrated in the price book.[70]

Prince of Wales feathers as decorative elements had appeared earlier in New York chairs. One of the designs in Thomas Sheraton's *The Cabinet-Maker and Upholsterers' Drawing Book* (1793) was popular in joined seating at the turn of the century. The principal ornament of the center back is a tall urn, or vase, surmounted by plumes tied at the center with a knot, or "moulding." Redesigning the feather motif as a horizontal fret was an easy task in an innovative chair market such as existed at New York. The profile is repeated to good effect between the front legs, although braces of this design are rare. The moldings, or casings, enclosing the rush work of the seat differ from those in bell-seat chairs (see fig. 29). The back and side pieces are flat, shaped strips nailed in place. The front piece, which is half of a turned cylinder, is attached in the same manner to the corner leg blocks. Here, it coordinates in profile with the fret and front brace and is considerably more ornate than usual (see fig. 30).[71]

Figure 32 shows a later version of the Baltimore tablet-crested chair illustrated in figure 21, a seating form identified by May and Renshaw in 1816 as a *broad-top* chair. In some regions broad-top chairs fitted with a small rolled lip at the upper back edges of the crest were called *scroll-top* chairs. Baltimore residents knew this particular seating piece as a "Circle Chair" or "Single side piece" chair. The terminology, which was used by Bryson Gill (fl. 1822–1831) in an 1824 advertisement, focuses on the unusual seat frame with

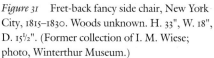

Figure 31 Fret-back fancy side chair, New York City, 1815–1830. Woods unknown. H. 33", W. 18", D. 15½". (Former collection of I. M. Wiese; photo, Winterthur Museum.)

Figure 32 Tablet-top fancy side chair (also "Circle Chair"), John R. Robinson, Baltimore, Maryland, 1829–1835. Woods unknown. H. 32⅛", W. 19½", D. 17". (Private collection; photo, Winterthur Museum.)

its rear cylinders. The following year John R. Robinson (fl. 1812–1845), the maker of this branded chair (fig. 32), emphasized his "SPLENDID ASSORT-MENT OF CHAIRS . . . made portable" for shipping. Baltimore in the 1820s was a flourishing center of the furniture export trade.[72]

Neoclassical design in Baltimore furniture was an adaptation of classical forms and decoration as interpreted in European centers, principally London and Paris. Baltimore craftsmen became acquainted with the style and its motifs through design books and imported furniture. Hugh Finlay (1781–1830), the leading painted furniture manufacturer in Baltimore, even traveled to Europe in 1810 to acquaint himself better with developments. The "circles," or cylinders, in the seat of this chair (fig. 32), accented by applied, pressed-metal rosettes, although an uncommon feature, suggest pivoting or movable joints, a theme that recurs in neoclassical design. Baltimore circle chairs usually have *Roman* (tapered cylindrical) front legs and baluster supports at the back, above and below the seat. All the terminals are accented at seat level with multiringed ball turnings, an element present at seat level with multiringed ball turnings, an element present at seat level with multiringed ball turnings, an element present at seat level. The ambitious floral decoration of the crest bears a strong resemblance in composition to ornament on furniture documented to the shop of John Hodgkinson (fl. 1822–1857) and, in finer form, to work attributed to Hugh Finlay.[73]

The *crown-top* was one of the two most popular fancy chair patterns in New England during the 1830s (fig. 33). Equally in demand was the roll-top chair (see fig. 30). The crown-style top piece, with its distinctive scroll ends and raised center, probably was introduced to the furniture market at the end of the 1820s, and Connecticut appears to have been the chief center of production. Like other nineteenth-century furniture designs, the crown profile originated in Europe and was transmitted to America through printed materials and exported furniture. One of the earliest representations of this top piece appears in the October 1815 issue of Rudolph Ackermann's *The Repository of Arts, Literature, Commerce, Manufactures, Fashions and Politics.* By the mid-1820s, design books by P. and M. A. Nicholson and George Smith illustrated similar patterns.[74]

An early reference to the American crown-top chair is in the accounts of David Pritchard of Waterbury, Connecticut, under the date 1832. Two years later Pritchard's brother-in-law, Lambert Hitchcock (1795–1852), signed and dated a receipt for "6 Crown top Rich g[il]t chairs" sold to a private customer at Hitchcocksville (now Riverton). Entrepreneur Hitchcock was also represented in Hartford. Isaac Wright (1798–1838) and Philemon Robbins stocked Hitchcock's crown-top chairs in their furniture stores. Both rush- and cane-bottom chairs were available to consumers, as itemized in the insolvency inventory of Frederick Parrott and Fenelon Hubbell (fl. 1835) of Bridgeport. The records of David Alling of Newark, New Jersey, indicate that crown-top chairs were also made and marketed in the greater New York area. Construction of the crown crest in rabbets on the faces of the back posts, the joints secured by screws, suggests other terms that may have identified this top piece and related round-end patterns. Elbridge Gerry Reed framed hundreds of "Screwd back" chairs in Sterling, Massachusetts, during the 1830s at a time when chairmakers in the southern market were constructing *stump-back* chairs, a term that refers to the blunt tips of the back posts.[75]

The "1 doz. crown top oval fret scroll front" chairs that David Alling delivered in 1833 to Joseph W. Meeks and Company in New York appear to have resembled the chair in figure 33. There are no other candidates in the 1830s for the "oval fret." Parrott and Hubbell's insolvency records at neighboring Bridgeport describe another term for this distinctive back piece: "frog fret." The curved elements that tenon the fret to the posts simulate the legs of the amphibian. Again, the pattern may have been inspired by a European source. The plate from Ackermann's *Repository* delineating the possible prototype for the crown top illustrates another chair with a fret remarkably similar to this one.[76]

Records relating to Philemon Robbins, Peter A. Willard, and Jacob Felton, chairmakers of Connecticut, Massachusetts, and New Hampshire,

Figure 33 Crown-top fancy side chair with frog back and turkey legs, Connecticut, 1830–1840. Woods unknown. H. 35³/₄", W. 17³/₄", D. 14⁷/₈". (Courtesy, Rhode Island Historical Society; photo, Winterthur Museum.)

Figure 34 Grecian (or scroll-back) fancy side chair with scalloped top, possibly John W. Patterson, Philadelphia, 1830–1840. Yellow poplar, maple, and basswood (microanalysis). H. 32½", W. 17⅞", D. 16⅜". (Courtesy, Winterthur Museum.)

respectively, describe "turkey legs" or chairs framed with these supports. The only obvious candidate is illustrated in figure 33. The joint above the bird's claw foot remains, and the multi-ring turnings simulate its fluffed feathers. Aside from serving as a brace between the front legs, the scroll-type stretcher, which is a rarity, serves to unite the upper and lower structures of the chair.[77]

Figure 34 shows one of several early nineteenth-century interpretations of classical seating furniture that falls under the general umbrella of *Grecian* furniture. Before that name became generally current in American furniture-making circles, the term *scroll-back* was in use. Characteristically, the structure of the chair above the seat exhibits an ogee curve in profile, the post tops scrolling backward and the lower ends sweeping forward to the roll at the seat front. The legs are usually of a hollow-curve, or *klismos,* form.

Elements of the Grecian style, as described, are delineated in the 1802 *London Book of Prices*. In 1807 Thomas Hope published a line-engraved side view of a scroll-back chair in *Household Furniture and Interior Decoration* (London), and drawings of relatively simple scroll-back chairs are included in the March 1809 and December 1811 issues of Ackermann's *Repository*, both publications known to have circulated in America.[78]

Chairs of the new form were exported to America by the start of the nineteenth century. Samuel J. Tuck, a Boston chairmaker, advertised "London made . . . japanned scrawl [scroll] back" chairs in 1803. A few years later Boston chair dealers Nolen and Gridley offered "cane color Scroll back" chairs made in New York. The term continued in use for several decades, as indicated by a bill inscribed in March 1839 by William Cunningham (fl. 1828–1851) of Wheeling, West Virginia, and by an advertisement dating to the following decade by Frederick Fox of Reading, Pennsylvania.[79]

The term *Grecian*, as it relates to seating furniture, first came into use in America during the 1810s. William Haydon (fl. 1799–1833), a chairmaker of Philadelphia, advertised "Grecian [chaise] Longues" in 1815. Three years later James J. Skerrett of the city purchased "Six Chairs Grecin Pat'n" from James Mitchell (fl. 1817–1840). The manufacture of Grecian chairs in fine or painted wood was widespread and of long duration. Curled maple and imitation maple, cane seats and rush seats, were all available. Special embellishment is described in the "Grecian Gilt chairs" purchased in 1834 at Albany, New York, by Peter Gansevoort. Calvin Stetson's "Harrison Grecian" chairs sold at Barnstable, Massachusetts, in the 1840s reflect both interest and opportunism in contemporary political events. At about the same date Benjamin F. Heywood (d. 1843) made "Grecian banister back chairs" in Gardner, Massachusetts.[80]

A banister and handsome gilt and polychrome decoration provide visual interest in the chair shown in figure 34, one of a set of eight chairs with a family history suggesting that John W. Patterson (fl. ca. 1817–1840) of Philadelphia may have been the maker. Patterson's apprenticeship in Baltimore perhaps explains the strong overtones in this chair of a design associated with that southern center, especially in the choice of thematic banister, front stretcher, and surface ornament. The crest also figures prominently in the discussion. It is described as a "Scallaped top" in a handwritten "Book of Prices for Making Cabinet & chair furnature" dated in 1838 by James C. Helme (fl. 1827–1841) of Plymouth, Luzerne County, Pennsylvania. Although the profile is an uncommon one, Windsor chairs also are known with this subtle feature at the crest top.[81]

In concluding this survey of the language of chair design, it is well to note current emphasis on historical accuracy in the study of period furniture. This interest extends to finishes, decorative treatments, stuffing and covering materials, and even the use and placement of objects in interior settings. Considerably less attention has been focused on nomenclature, although the assimilation of correct terminology is only another short step now that a framework exists upon which to build.

1. Solomon Fussell Account Book, 1738–1748, Stephen Collins Collection, Library of Congress (hereinafter cited as LC), Washington, D.C. (microfilm, Joseph Downs Collection of Manuscripts and Printed Ephemera, Winterthur Museum Library, Winterthur, Del. [hereinafter cited as DCM and WML]).

2. John Gaines II and Thomas Gaines Account Book, 1712–1762, DCM; David Haven Account Book, 1785–1800, DCM.

3. John Durand Account Book, 1760–1783, Milford Historical Society (hereinafter cited as Mfd HS), Milford, Connecticut (microfilm, DCM); James Chase Account Books, 1797–1812, private collection (transcription, Charles S. Parsons, New Hampshire Notes, Visual Resources Collection [hereinafter cited as VRC], WML).

4. Amos Denison Allen Memorandum Book, 1796–1803, and Elisha Hawley Account Book, 1781–1805, Connecticut Historical Society (hereinafter cited as CHS), Hartford; Samuel Durand Daybook, 1806–1838, Mfd HS.

5. "York" chairs with pad feet are documented by brand to the New York shops of David Coutant (collection of Historic Hudson Valley) and Jacob Smith (collection of New York State Museum, see John L. Scherer, *New York Furniture at the New York State Museum* [Alexandria, Va.: Highland House, 1984], cat. 22). Connecticut examples are in Robert F. Trent, *Hearts and Crowns: Folk Chairs of the Connecticut Coast, 1720–1840* (New Haven, Conn.: New Haven Colony Historical Society, 1977), figs. 34, 38, 39. James Chestney in *Albany Chronicle* (Albany, N.Y.), August 10, 1797, as illustrated in Dorothy Ellesin, "Collectors' Notes," *Antiques* 106, no. 6 (December 1974): 1033.

6. Francis Trumble Bills to Thomas Wharton, August 14, 1761, and to Hollingsworth and Rudolph, June 10, 1770, Harrold Gillingham Collection, Historical Society of Pennsylvania (hereinafter cited as HSP), Philadelphia, Pa.; Sheed and White in *South Carolina Gazette* (Charleston, S.C.), June 23, 1766, Prime Cards, WML; Walter Franklin Inventory, September 18, 1786, DCM.

7. William Davis Bill to State of Rhode Island, April 28, 1784, Rhode Island Colony Records, v. 12, p. 517, Rhode Island State Archives, Providence; Aaron Lopez Outward Bound Invoice Book, 1763–1768, Newport Historical Society, Newport, R.I.; Stephen Girard Journal, 1786–1790, Girard Papers, Girard College, Philadelphia, Pa.; Isaac Smith Inventory, December 4, 1787, Suffolk County Probate Court, Boston, Mass. (microfilm, DCM).

8. Inventories of Silvanus Coffin (September 25, 1784), Andrew Myrick (January 14, 1783), Henry Clark (August 30, 1792), Jonathan Burnell (May 1799), and Richard Bunker (January 6, 1794), Nantucket County Probate Court, Nantucket, Mass.

9. Sheed and White, *South Carolina Gazette;* Garrett Meade Receipt Book, 1759–1762, Dreer Collection, HSP; Lopez Invoice Book.

10. Nicholas Lechmere Confiscated Estate, 1779, Confiscated Loyalist Estates, DCM; Franklin Inventory; Rebecca Seaton Inventory, 1766, Register of Wills, Philadelphia, Pa. (microfilm, DCM).

11. Andrew Gautier in *New York Gazette* (New York), June 6, 1765.

12. Francis Trumble Bill to Hollingsworth and Rudolph, September 5, 1770, Gillingham Collection; Francis Trumble Bill to John Cadwalader, July 19, 1771, Cadwalader Papers, General John Cadwalader, HSP; Uriah Woolman Bills of Lading, 1772–1775, HSP; John James and Sykes and Lushington in *South Carolina Gazette,* December 7, 1771, and September 12, 1774; Isaac Hazlehurst and Company List of Disbursements and Invoice of Cargo for Ship *Canton,* December 1, 12, 1789, William Constable Shipping Papers, Constable-Pierrepont Papers, New York Public Library (hereinafter cited as NYPL), New York.

13. Allen Memorandum Book; Ebenezer Devotion Ledger, 1775–1799, New London County Historical Society, New London, Conn.; Solomon Cole Account Book, 1794–1809, CHS.

14. Hazlehurst Invoice of Cargo; William Cox Bill to Stephen Girard, September 5, 1787, Girard Papers; Joseph Henzey Bill to member of Coates family, November 25, 1785, Coates-Reynell Papers, HSP; Stephen Collins and Sons Letter to Joseph Blake, June 15, 1795, Letter Book, 1794–1801, Collins Collection; John Lambert Estate Records, 1793, Register of Wills, Philadelphia, Pa.; Ansel Goodrich Estate Records, 1803, Hampshire County Probate Court, Northampton, Mass.

15. Henzey Bill to Coates family; Owners of Schooner *Nancy* Account with Winslow Lewis, July 30, 1791, Greenough Papers, Massachusetts Historical Society, Boston; Thomas Beck vs. William Campbell and William Freeman vs. George Labottiere, Miscellaneous Legal Suits, 1808, Cumberland County, Massachusetts (Maine), DCM; Nicholas Low Account with Miles

Beach, June 7, 1805, Nicholas Low Papers, LC; William Seaver Bill to Joseph Russell, October 18, 1794, Boston Theatre Papers, Boston Public Library, Boston, Mass.; Ebenezer Knowlton Estate Records, 1811, Suffolk County Probate Court, Boston, Mass. (microfilm, DCM); Oliver Avery Account Book, 1789–1813, DCM; Samuel Douglas Account Book, 1810–1858, Connecticut State Library (hereinafter cited as CSL), Hartford.

16. Robert Blackwell Receipt Book, 1783–1792, HSP.

17. Jones and Clark in *Charleston City Gazette* (Charleston, S.C.), July 7, 1791, Prime Cards, WML; William Cox Bill, March 12, 1791, and Joseph Henzey Bill, September 20, 1792, to Stephen Girard, Girard Papers; John B. Ackley Bill to Samuel Coates, November 26, 1800, Reynell and Coates Collection, Baker Library, Harvard University, Cambridge, Mass.; Lambert Estate Records; Francis Trumble Estate Records, 1798, Register of Wills, Philadelphia, Pa.

18. Allen Memorandum Book.

19. Josiah Austin Bill to Waters and Sinclair, March 1, 1790, Waters Family Papers, Essex Institute (hereinafter cited as EI), Salem, Mass.; Elijah and Jacob Sanderson Account with Micaiah Johnson, 1794–1795, Papers of Elijah Sanderson, EI; Elihu Alford (Alvord) Bill to Nicholas Low, July 30, 1804, Low Papers; Hector Sanford in *Scioto Gazette* (Chillicothe, Oh.), December 11, 1805 (reference courtesy of John R. Grabb).

20. Peter Tillou Bill to Mrs. Montgomery, March 6, 1792, Robert R. Livingston Papers, New-York Historical Society (hereinafter cited as NYHS), New York.

21. Elisha Hawley Account Book, 1781–1805, CHS.

22. Allen Memorandum Book.

23. Taylor and King Bill, May 21, 1799, and Joseph Burden Bill, December 12, 1810, to Stephen Girard, Girard Papers; James Brobson, Shipping Record Book, 1790–1805, DCM.

24. David Alling Account Book, 1801–1839, and Ledger, 1815–1818, New Jersey Historical Society (hereinafter cited as NJHS) (microfilm, DCM); Allen Holcomb Account Book, 1809–ca. 1828, Metropolitan Museum of Art, New York.

25. Cole Account Book; Silas E. Cheney Account Book, 1807–1813, Litchfield Historical Society (hereinafter cited as LHS), Litchfield, Conn. (microfilm, DCM).

26. Charles C. Robinson Daybook, 1809–1825, HSP; Henry Prall Estate Records, 1802, Register of Wills, Philadelphia, Pa.; Thomas Adams Bill to U.S. War Department, November 9, 1814, Miscellaneous Treasury Accounts of the First Auditor, Treasury Records, National Archives, Washington, D.C.

27. Thomas Boynton Ledger, 1810–1817, Dartmouth College Library (hereinafter cited as DCL), Hanover, N.H. (microfilm, DCM); William G. Beesley Daybook, 1828–1836, Salem County Historical Society, Salem, N.J.; Caleb Gallup Inventory, November 28, 1827, in Jane Sikes Hageman and Edward M. Hageman, *Ohio Furniture Makers,* 2 vols. (Cincinnati, Ohio: by the authors, 1989), 2:23.

28. David Alling Invoice Book, 1819–1820, NJHS (microfilm, DCM); Holcomb Account Book; Boynton Ledger; Elizur Barnes Account Book, 1821–1825, Middlesex Historical Society, Middletown, Conn.; Henry May and Thomas S. Renshaw in *Scioto Gazette and Fredonian Chronicle* (Chillicothe, Ohio), February 29, 1816 (reference courtesy of John R. Grabb).

29. Bernard Foot Bill to Ebenezer Pearson, September 24, 1813, Pearson Family Papers, EI; David Pritchard, Jr., Account Books, 1800–1810 and 1827–1838, Mattatuck Museum, Waterbury, Conn.; Silas E. Cheney Account Books, 1816–1822 and 1813–1846, LHS (microfilm, DCM); Isaac Stone Bill to Ebenezer Fox, November 28, 1811, Papers of Ebenezer Fox and Family, EI; Anthony Steel Estate Records, 1817, Register of Wills, Philadelphia, Pa.

30. Benjamin Bass Inventory, 1819, Suffolk County Probate Court, Boston, Mass. (microfilm, DCM); Henry Beck in *New Hampshire Gazette* (Portsmouth), September 20, 1808, as quoted in Parsons, New Hampshire Notes; Boynton Ledger.

31. Alling Ledger.

32. Thomas Walter Ward II Inventory Book, ca. 1838–1845, DCM; Jacob Felton Daybook 1836–1838, Old Sturbridge Village (hereinafter cited as OSV), Sturbridge, Mass.; Elbridge Gerry Reed Daybook, 1829–1851, private collection (photocopy, OSV); Philemon Robbins Account Book, 1833–1836, CHS.

33. Barnes Account Book; Peter A. Willard Estate Records, 1842–1843, Worcester County Probate Court, Worcester, Mass.; Charles Riley Estate Records, 1842, Register of Wills, Philadelphia, Pa. (microfilm, DCM).

34. Willard Estate Records; Reed Daybook.

35. David Pritchard Estate Records, 1839, Genealogical Section, CSL; William Knights

Letter to Joel Pratt, Jr., September 21, 1837, private collection (microfilm, OSV); Calvin Stetson Account Book, 1843–1857, DCM.

36. Steel Estate Records; Joel Pratt, Jr., Account Book, 1822–1829, private collection (microfilm, OSV); Reed Daybook.

37. William Haydon in *United States Gazette* (Philadelphia, Pa.), June 20, 1815; W. A. and D. M. Coggeshall in *Rhode Island Republican* (Newport), July 15, 1835; A. and J. B. Mathiot in *Matchett's Baltimore Director[y], for 1840–1841* (Baltimore, Md.: Baltimore Director[y] Office, [1840]), n.p.

38. Reed Daybook; Pratt Account Book.

39. Josiah Prescott Wilder Daybook and Ledger, 1837–1861, Charles S. Parsons, Wilder Family Notes, VRC; Felton Daybook; Reed Daybook; Samuel Stuart Estate Records, 1829, Worcester County Probate Court, Worcester, Mass.

40. Luke Houghton Ledgers A to C, 1816–1851, Barre Historical Society, Barre, Mass. (microfilm, DCM); Robbins Account Book; Congdon and Tracy in *Norwich Courier* (Norwich, Conn.), October 27, 1830.

41. *The London Chair-Makers' and Carvers' Book of Prices for Workmanship* (London: T. Sorrell, 1802), pl. 3, fig. 6, and p. 41; John K. Cowperthwaite in *Longworth's Almanac, New-York Register, and City Directory* (New York: Jonathan Olmstead, 1819), p. 4; *The New-York Book of Prices for Manufacturing Cabinet and Chair Work* (New York: J. Seymour, 1817), pl. 6.

42. Alling Account Book; David Alling Receipt Book, 1824–1842, and Daybook, 1836–1854, NJHS (microfilm, DCM); Benjamin W. Branson Estate Records, 1835, DCM; Richard D. Blauvelt Bill to Mr. Shaler, April 10, 1833, Landaur Collection, NYHS; Robert C. Scadin Daybook, 1829–1831, Chauncey Strong Daybook, 1842–1852, and Miles Benjamin Daybook and Ledger, 1821–1829, all New York State Historical Association, Cooperstown, N.Y.

43. Levi Stillman Account Book, 1815–1834, Sterling Library, Yale University, New Haven, Conn.; Barnes Account Book; Pritchard Account Books; Robbins Account Book; James Gere Account Book, 1809–1839, and Ledger, 1822–1852, CSL.

44. Pratt Account Book; Reed Daybook; Felton Daybook; Wilder Daybook and Ledger; Thomas Boynton Ledger, 1817–1847, DCL (microfilm, DCM); Robbins Account Book.

45. Reed Daybook.

46. Robbins Account Book; Ward Inventory Book; Wilder Daybook and Ledger.

47. Frederick Fox in *Berks and Schuylkill Journal* (Reading, Pa.), April 26, 1845; Riley Estate Records.

48. Branson Estate Records; Reed Daybook; Daniel W. Badger Estate Records, 1847–1848, CSL.

49. Samuel Claphamson in *Pennsylvania Packet* (Philadelphia, Pa.), January 8, 1785, as quoted in Alfred Coxe Prime, comp., *The Arts and Crafts in Philadelphia, Maryland, and South Carolina, 1721–1785* (Philadelphia: Walpole Society, 1929), p. 162. William Palmer in *Weekly Museum* (New York), October 15, 1796, John Mitchell in *The Argus* (New York), March 4, 1796, and William Challen in *New-York Gazette and General Advertiser* (New York), February 22, 1797, all as quoted in Rita Susswein Gottesman, comp., *The Arts and Crafts in New York, 1777–1797* (New York: New-York Historical Society, 1954), pp. 113, 124, 140.

50. William Haydon and William H. Stewart Bill to James J. Skerrett, March 17, 1818, Loudonn Papers, HSP; George Hepplewhite, *The Cabinet-Maker and Upholsterer's Guide* (1794; reprint of 3d ed., New York: Dover, 1969), pls. 3 left, 6 left; *London Book of Prices*, pl. 3, fig. 1, and pl. 5, no. 13.

51. John and Hugh Finlay in *Federal Gazette and Baltimore Daily Advertiser* (Baltimore, Md.), November 8, 1805, as quoted in William Voss Elder III, *Baltimore Painted Furniture, 1800–1840* (Baltimore, Md.: Baltimore Museum of Art, 1972), p. 11; May and Renshaw in *Scioto Gazette and Fredonian Chronicle;* Joshua Moore Bill to Humberston Skipwith, July 12, 1819, Peyton Skipwith Papers, Swem Library, College of William and Mary, Williamsburg, Va.

52. David Tilden vs. William Seaver, 1804, Colonial Court Records Project, Social Law Library, Boston, Mass. (reference courtesy of Charles A. Hammond and John T. Kirk); Asa Holden in *New-York Evening Post* (New York), August 4, 1812.

53. Alling Account Book; Holcomb Account Book.

54. Alling Account Book, Receipt Book, and Daybook; Abijah Coon advertisement for rush in *Weekly Museum*, July 22, 1797, as quoted in Gottesman, comp., *Arts and Crafts,* pp. 136–37; Elisha H. Holmes Account Book, 1825–1830, CHS.

55. Alling Ledger and Invoice Book; photographs of Skellorn chair and billhead in VRC, no. 69.11.

56. Alling Account Book, Ledger, and Invoice Book; David Alling, Receipt Book, 1803–1824, and Ledger, 1803–1853, NJHS (microfilm, DCM); William Palmer Bill to Chancellor Robert R. Livingston, June 22, 1807, Robert R. Livingston Papers, NYHS; William Buttre Bill to Oliver Wolcott, December 8, 1810, CHS; Stillman Account Book; Gere Account Book; Barnes Account Book; Pritchard Account Book, 1800–1810; Cheney Account Books, 1816–1822, 1813–1846; Boynton Ledger, 1810–1817.

57. Barnes Account Book; Silas E. Cheney Account with William Butler, March 26, 1808, Superior Court Records, Litchfield County, Conn., CSL; Alling Daybook.

58. Alling Account Book; Cheney Account Books, 1816–1822, 1813–1846; Ebenezer West, Timothy West, and (?) Hatch Bill to Silas Cheney, December 26,1814, Superior Court Records, Litchfield County, Conn.

59. Alling Invoice Book, *London Book of Prices,* pl. 4, no. 13, and p. 24.

60. *Longworth's Almanac, New-York Register, and City Directory* (New York: David Longworth, 1813), p. 89.

61. *London Book of Prices,* pl. 3, figs. 1–3; Samuel J. Tuck in *Columbian Centinal* (Boston, Mass.), October 15,1803; (?) Nolen and William S. Gridley in *Columbian Centinel,* December 12, 1810.

62. Buttre Bill to Wolcott; Alling Ledger, 1815–1818; Holcomb Account Book.

63. Bass Inventory; Nolen and Gridley, *Columbian Centinel.*

64. The three-stick Windsor chair is illustrated in Nancy Goyne Evans, *American Windsor Chairs* (New York: Hudson Hills, 1996), fig. 7-29.

65. *London Book of Prices,* pl. 3, fig. 6.

66. Holden, *New-York Evening Post; London Book of Prices,* pl. 3, fig. 6; Alling Invoice Book; Henry Wilder Miller Account Book, 1827–1831, Worcester Historical Museum, Worcester, Mass.; Thomas Sill in *Middlesex Gazette* (Middletown, Conn.), December 22, 1814; Davis and Bussey in B. Pearce, *The Albany Directory* (Albany, N.Y.: E. and E. Hosford, 1819), n.p.

67. The family and purchase background of the chair in figure 29 is given in *Portsmouth Furniture: Masterworks from the New Hampshire Seacoast,* edited by Brock Jobe (Boston: Society for the Preservation of New England Antiquities, 1993), cat. 100; and Gerald W. R. Ward and Karin E. Cullity, "The Wendell Family Furniture at Strawbery Banke Museum," in *American Furniture,* edited by Luke Beckerdite (Hanover, N.H.: University Press of New England for the Chipstone Foundation, 1993), pp. 253–55. *New-York Book of Prices,* as excerpted in Charles F. Montgomery, *American Furniture: The Federal Period* (New York: Viking Press, 1966), p. 104; Holcomb Account Book; *London Book of Prices,* pl. 6, no. 9, and p. 46. Chairs with similar elbows and supports are in: *The Ornamented Chair,* edited by Zilla Rider Lea (Rutland, Vt.: Charles E. Tuttle, 1960), pp. 51–52, figs. 33, 35; Northeast Auctions, "New Hampshire Auction," August 3–4, 1991, lot 570; Sotheby's, "Fine American Furniture, Folk Art, Folk Paintings, and Silver," June 21, 1989, lot 346; Ronna L. Reynolds, *Images of Connecticut Life* (Hartford, Conn.: Antiquarian and Landmarks Society of Connecticut, 1978), p. 79.

68. Sill, *Middlesex Gazette;* Thomas West in *Connecticut Gazette* (New London, Conn.), February 10, 1810; James S. Chapman in *Connecticut Herald* (New Haven, Conn.), April 18, 1809; Stillman Account Book; Gere Ledger; Sidney Twidel Bill to Silas E. Cheney, December 3, 1819, Superior Court Records, Litchfield County, Conn.

69. Seymour Watrous in *Hartford Courant* (Hartford, Conn.), March 2, 1824, as illustrated in Lea, ed., *Ornamented Chair,* p. 90; Alling Invoice Book.

70. *New-York Book of Prices,* pl. 6, fig. D, as illustrated in Montgomery, *Federal Furniture,* p. 104; T. Deland Bill to Daniel W. Rogers, April 13, 1829, Papers of Daniel W. Rogers, EI; Alling Invoice Book.

71. Thomas Sheraton, *The Cabinet-Maker and Upholsterers' Drawing-Book* (1793; reprint ed., New York: Dover, 1972), pl. 36, no. 1. Federal-period chairs patterned after Sheraton's designs are in: Montgomery, *Federal Furniture,* cats. 58–60; Marshall B. Davidson, *The American Heritage History of American Antiques from the Revolution to the Civil War* ([New York]: American Heritage, 1968), p. 49, top; *19th-Century America* (New York: Metropolitan Museum of Art, 1970), cat. 5.

72. Bryson Gill and Company in *Matchett's Baltimore Directory for 1824* (Baltimore, Md.: R. J. Matchett, 1824), n.p.; John Robinson in *American and Commercial Daily Advertiser* (Baltimore, Md.), October 6, 1825.

73. Gregory R. Weidman, "The Furniture of Classical Maryland, 1815–1845," in *Classical Maryland, 1815–1845* (Baltimore, Md.: Maryland Historical Society, 1993), pp. 89–110, including figs. 124, 131. A nineteenth-century "Roman" chair with tapered legs is in Pauline Agius,

Ackermann's Regency Furniture and Interiors (Marlborough, England: Crowood Press, 1984), pl. 15.

74. Agius, *Ackermann's Regency Furniture*, pl. 78, left; designs by P. and M. A. Nicholson (H. Fisher, publisher) and George Smith in Edward Joy, *Pictorial Dictionary of British 19th-Century Furniture Design* (Woodbridge, England: Antique Collectors' Club, 1977), pp. 214–15.

75. Pritchard Account Book, 1827–1838; Lambert Hitchcock Bill to Gerral(?) Adams, December 12, 1834, as illustrated in John Tarrant Kenney, *The Hitchcock Chair* (New York: Clarkson N. Potter, 1971), p. 134; Isaac Wright Account Book, 1834–1837, CSL; Robbins Account Book; Frederick Parrott and Fenelon Hubbell Insolvency Inventory, 1835, CSL; Alling Account Book and Daybook; Reed Daybook; Anne Castrodale Golovin, "Cabinetmakers and Chairmakers of Washington, D.C., 1791–1840," *Antiques* 107, no. 5 (May 1975): 906–22.

76. Alling Account Book; Parrott and Hubbell Insolvency Inventory; Agius, *Ackermann's Regency Furniture*, pl. 78, right.

77. Robbins Account Book; Willard Estate Records; Felton Daybook.

78. *London Book of Prices*, pl. 4, no. 14, and pl. 5, no. 13; Thomas Hope, *Household Furniture and Interior Decoration* (1807; reprint ed., New York: Dover, 1971), pl. 40, no. 6; Agius, *Ackermann's Regency Furniture*, pls. 2, 34.

79. Tuck, and Nolen and Gridley, *Columbian Centinel;* William Cunningham Bill to Mr. A. Broadwell, March 23, 1839, W. Graham Arader III, New York; Fox, *Berks and Schuylkill Journal.*

80. William Haydon in *United States Gazette* (Philadelphia. Pa.), June 20, 1815; James Mitchell Bill to James J. Skerrett, April 10, 1818, Loudonn Papers; William Miller Bill to Peter Gansevoort, December 27, 1834, Gansevoort-Lansing Collection, NYPL; Stetson Account Book; Benjamin F. Heywood Estate Records, 1843, Worcester County Probate Court, Worcester, Mass.

81. James Helme Book of Prices, 1838, DCM.

Richard H. Randall, Jr.

Designs for
Philadelphia Carvers

▼ T H R O U G H O U T   T H E eighteenth century, the proverb, the adage, and the wise saying were popular daily fare. Franklin's *Poor Richard's Almanac* was read widely, both for entertainment and sage advice. In 1751 Poor Richard noted that "ambition often spends foolishly what avarice had wickedly collected." This observation might well have been the moral of the Aesop's fable "The Dog and the Meat," or "The Dog and His Shadow," as it is sometimes called, wherein a dog with a succulent piece of beef in his mouth sees his reflection in a stream. Thinking it is another dog with a fine morsel, he relinquishes what he has and jumps into the water to seize the other, only to end up with nothing.

Such fables were often depicted in architectural interiors. An early representation of "The Dog and the Meat" appears on a colored marble chimneypiece (fig. 1) originally installed in Woodcote Park, Lord Baltimore's house in Epsom, Surrey. The house was designed by Isaac Ware and completed about 1750. The chimneypiece is attributed to Sir Henry Cheere, who based his design on an engraving in Wencelaus Hollar's *Aesop Paraphras'd* (London, 1665) (fig. 2).

This particular Aesop fable appeared twice in Philadelphia, first on the front of a ten-plate stove cast by William Henry Stiegel at Elizabeth Furnace in 1769 (fig. 3), and again on the chimneypiece tablet that London-trained carver Hercules Courtenay furnished for Samuel Powel's townhouse in

1770 (fig. 4). Not only are the posture of the dog and the position and configuration of the mill in the background of the stove plate and tablet remarkably similar (despite the shift from a vertical to a horizontal format), but the techniques used to carve the casting pattern match those used on the tablet. Powel began renovating his house soon after purchasing it from Charles Stedman, Stiegel's partner in Elizabeth Furnace.[1]

Courtenay's design source was the illustration for "The Dog and the Meat" in one of Francis Barlow's London editions of *Aesop,* issued in 1666 and 1687 (fig. 5). Barlow brought his skill as an observer and a painter of animals into full play in his books, which depicted, in a new and original manner, the wild and tame creatures naturalistically involved in the actions of the stories. With its large etched plates and wide circulation, Barlow's *Aesop* had a profound impact on book illustration, affecting readers and artists for nearly two hundred years.[2]

Although no eighteenth-century Philadelphia library or estate inventory listed Barlow's book, Aesop's fables were popular there. James Logan owned Latin and French editions of *Aesop* (the former dated 1698); James Cox and Deborah Logan owned English versions; the Library Company of Philadelphia owned the third edition of Dr. Samuel Croxall's translation (London, 1731); and the Biddle family owned the first American edition of Croxall's translation (Philadelphia, 1777).[3]

Courtenay, Stiegel, or Powel may have owned a copy of Barlow's *Aesop,*

but there were other sources for the same Barlow design. Elisha Kirkall based many of his illustrations for Croxall's *Aesop's Fables* on those in Barlow's book, including "The Dog and the Shadow" (fig. 6). Barlow, who returned to animal painting after the second edition of the fables, lent or sold his plates for an Amsterdam edition of *Aesop,* printed in French in 1704. The previous year, London bookseller R. Newcomb sold Barlow's illustrations bound in various groups. There were, thus, a number of volumes of fables in which Hercules Courtenay or one of his patrons could have found the Barlow etching.[4]

Born in Ireland, Courtenay may have known that "The Dog and the Meat" was depicted on the mantel in the small dining room at Russborough (built 1741–1750) outside of Dublin. That design followed Barlow's print exactly. Alternatively, he may have become acquainted with Barlow's *Aesop* during his apprenticeship with London carver Thomas Johnson, whose *One Hundred and Fifty New Designs* (1758, 1761) included references to Aesop's fables. This design book and Johnson's *New Book of Ornaments* (London, 1762) influenced Philadelphia furniture and architectural carving from the mid-1760s to the Revolution.[5]

Another English design book available to Philadelphia carvers was Thomas Chippendale's *The Gentleman and Cabinet-Maker's Director* (1754). Plate 22 in the third edition (1762) includes designs for "French" chairs, one with upholstery taken from Barlow's illustrations for "The Nightingale and the Hawk" and "The Dog and the Meat" (fig. 7). In other plates, Chippendale featured chimney tablets representing "The Bear and the Bee Hive" and "The Leopard and the Fox" from Barlow's *Aesop* and a firescreen with needlework depicting "The Peacock's Complaint." Like other rococo designers, Chippendale appreciated Barlow's spritely, well-rendered animals. Courtenay was undoubtedly familiar with the *Director.* The Library

Figure 6 Elisha Kirkall, "The Dog and the Shadow," from Dr. Samuel Croxall, trans., *Aesop's Fables,* 1st ed. (London, 1722). Metal cut in white line. (Private collection.)

ÆSOP's FABLES. 9

FAB. V. *The Dog and the* Shadow.

A Dog, croffing a little Rivulet with a Piece of Flefh in his Mouth, faw his own Shadow reprefented in the clear Mirrour of the limpid Stream; and, believing it to be another Dog, who was carrying another real Piece of Flefh, he could not forbear catching at it: but was fo far from getting any thing by his greedy Defign, that he dropt the Piece he had in his Mouth, which immediately funk to the Bottom, and was irrecoverably loft.

The APPLICATION.

He that catches at more than belongs to him, juftly deferves to lofe what he has. Yet nothing is more common, and, at the fame time, more pernicious than this felfifh Principle. It prevails, from the King to the Peafant; and all Orders and Degrees of Men, are more or lefs infected with it. Great Monarchs have been drawn in, by this greedy Humour, to grafp at the Dominions of their Neighbours; not that they wanted any thing more to feed their Luxury, but to gratify their infatiable Appetite for Vain-Glory. If the Kings of *Perfia* could have been contented with their own vaft Territories, they had not loft all *Afia* for the fake of a little petty State of *Greece.* And *France,* with

Figure 7 Design for a "French" chair on plate 22 of Thomas Chippendale's *Gentleman and Cabinet-Maker's Director,* 3d. ed. (London, 1762).

Company of Philadelphia owned a copy of the third edition, and the estate inventory of Philadelphia cabinetmaker Thomas Affleck listed "Shippendale's [*sic*] designs."[6]

A more unusual source for Barlow's illustrations in Philadelphia was a deck of playing cards, published in London in 1759 (fig. 8). "The Dog and Piece of Flesh" appears on the Jack of Diamonds with the moral: "So Fancy'd Crowns led the young Warriour on/Till Loosing all, He Found himself undone." Several of the engravings on the cards are signed "I. Kirk" and bear the date 1759.[7]

Barlow's original etching of "The Dog and the Meat" was, therefore, available to Philadelphia artisans in 1666 and 1687 editions of his fables, in loose plates bound in 1703, and in the Amsterdam French edition of 1704. Variations of this illustration could also be found in the early editions of Croxall's *Aesop's Fables,* in the 1759 deck of cards, and in Chippendale's *Director.* It is difficult, however, to determine which of these sources inspired Courtenay and whether it was the carver, the Library Company, Samuel Powel, or William Henry Stiegel who supplied the design.

Aesop's fables also appear on contemporary Philadelphia furniture. The Howe family high chest and matching dressing table (at the Philadelphia Museum of Art), for example, have carved drawer appliqués representing "The Fox and the Grapes." The overall design was borrowed from an earlier illustration, but the fox was taken directly from Thomas Johnson's design for a mirror on plate 21 of *One Hundred and Fifty New Designs.* Barlow's illustrations, however, were not the source of any of the other animals depicted on Philadelphia case furniture, which include the phoenix on a ca. 1768 high chest base (in the Diplomatic Reception Rooms, U.S. Department of State), the swan on its accompanying dressing table (at the Museum of Fine Arts, Boston), and the lamb and ewe on a contemporary chest-on-chest (at the Winterthur Museum). The geese on the lower drawer appliqués of the "Pompadour" high chest and dressing table (at the Metropolitan Museum of Art) are based on the design for a chimneypiece tablet on plate 5 in Johnson's *New Book of Ornaments.*[8]

Several Pennsylvania and New Jersey iron foundries produced castings based on Aesop's fables. Two side plates for six-plate stoves cast at Batsto Furnace in Burlington, New Jersey, depict "The Fox and the Stork." A German variant of "The Tortoise and the Eagle" fable appears on a sideplate cast at Centre Furnace, Centre County, Pennsylvania. Aside from the aforementioned stove plate depicting "The Dog and Meat," only one other casting based on a Barlow image is known. A sideplate marked "17 BATSTO 70" was taken directly from his illustration for the "Ringdove and the Fowler," including the anachronistic, seventeenth-century costume of the hunter.[9]

The fables illustrated by Barlow and other artists provided a wealth of imagery for designers like Johnson and Chippendale and tradesmen like Courtenay. Whether depicted in prints or in three-dimensional form, these images also served as reminders of human virtue and frailty. For Powel and Stiegel, Courtenay's carved representations of "The Dog and the Meat" presented a daily warning of the sin of avarice.

Figure 8 I. Kirk, playing card depicting "The Dog and Piece of Flesh," London, 1759. Engraving. (Courtesy, United States Playing Card Collection.)

1. For more on Courtenay, see Luke Beckerdite, "Philadelphia Carving Shops, III," *Antiques* 131, no. 5 (May 1987): 1044–64. The Stiegel stove is illustrated and discussed in Morrison H. Heckscher and Leslie Greene Bowman, *American Rococo, 1750–1775: Elegance in Ornament* (New York: Harry N. Abrams, 1992), p. 227, no. 163.

2. Edward Hodnett, *Francis Barlow, First Master of English Book Illustration* (Berkeley: University of California Press, 1978), pp. 220–22. The book was initially printed in 1666.

3. Listed with donor's names in the card catalogue of the Library Company, Philadelphia.

4. The influence of Barlow's illustrations continued well after 1770, and they can be found in use by John Stockdale in London in 1793 and, more significantly, were the basis of the famous wood engravings of Thomas Bewick, published in 1784 and 1818. An edition of *La Fontaine,* printed in Paris in 1799, had plates by Augustin Legrand based on Barlow, and another collection of fables with cuts after Barlow was printed in French by Ramoissenet about 1790. A Berlin edition, *Hundert Fabeln,* was published in 1830 with color added to the illustrations.

5. *Georgian Society Records,* Dublin, 1913, pl. 64. The left frieze panel on the ca. 1770 chimneypiece from the Stamper-Blackwell Parlor (in the Winterthur Museum) features a stag being pursued by hounds. A similar scene appears in the background of Aesop's "Stag and Reflection."

6. Morrison H. Heckscher, "English Pattern Books in Eighteenth-Century America," in *American Furniture,* edited by Luke Beckerdite (Hanover, N.H.: University Press of New England for the Chipstone Foundation 1994), p. 188.

7. Catherine Hargrave, *A History of Playing Cards* (New York: Dover, 1966), fig. 203; H. T. Morley, *Old and Curious Playing Cards* (reprint; Secaucus, N. J.: Wellfleet Press, 1989), pp. 166–68. A complete set of these cards is housed in the museum of the United States Playing Card Company in Cincinnati and a second set has been noted in England.

8. David Stockwell, "Aesop's Fables on Philadelphia Furniture," *Antiques* 60, no. 6 (December 1951): 523. Helena Hayward, *Thomas Johnson and the English Rococo* (London: Alec Tiranti, 1964), fig. 15. The Howe high chest and Johnson design are illustrated in Philadelphia Museum of Art, *Philadelphia: Three Centuries of American Art* (Philadelphia: by the Museum, 1976), pp. 132–33, nos. 104a–b. For the phoenix high chest base and its matching dressing table, see Alexandra W. Rollins, ed., *Treasures of State: Fine and Decorative Arts in the Diplomatic Reception Rooms of the U.S. Department of State* (New York: Harry N. Abrams, 1991), pp. 150–51, fig. 66; and Edwin J. Hipkiss, *Eighteenth-Century American Arts, the M. and M. Karolik Collection* (Boston: Museum of Fine Arts, 1941), pp. 102–3, no. 55, respectively. The lamb and ewe chest is shown in Joseph Downs, *American Furniture: Queen Anne and Chippendale Periods* (New York: Macmillan, 1952), no. 184 and Gregory Landrey, "The Conservator as Curator: Combining Scientific Analysis and Traditional Connoisseurship," in *American Furniture,* edited by Luke Beckerdite (Hanover, N.H.: University Press of New England, 1993), pp. 147–59. For the "Pompadour" chest, see Heckscher and Bowman, *American Rococo,* pp. 202–3, no. 138, fig. 48.

9. Henry Mercer, *The Bible in Iron,* revised, corrected, and enlarged by Horace H. Mann (1914; 3d. ed. reprinted, Doylestown, Pa.: Bucks County Historical Society, 1961), pls. 5, 242–44, 248. Mercer referred to the "17 BATSTO 70" plate as the "Squirrel Hunt."

Deborah Dependahl Waters

Is It Phyfe?

▼ TO HAVE AN *American house, furnished in the American manner with furniture of American design and manufacture — that is the ambition of many a good American housewife. And when it is achieved she has a home of great simplicity and charm, of comfort and good taste.*

Perhaps the most distinctive type of American furniture is that which came to us originally from the workshop of Duncan Phyfe, a New York City cabinetmaker. Although a Scotchman by birth, Phyfe may rightly be called America's foremost furniture designer and maker.

Mrs. Charles Bradley Sanders,
How to Know Good Furniture
(New York, 1924)

Is it Phyfe? is a question contemporary consumers often ask furniture showroom staff, interior designers, and antique dealers while shopping for furnishings. "Phyfe" is more than the surname of the best-known nineteenth-century New York City furniture craftsman, Duncan Phyfe (1768–1854). Through the efforts of generations of dealers, collectors, curators, and furniture manufacturers, "Phyfe" has become a generic term used to identify American-made furniture in the "antique" or neoclassical style, inspired by the forms and ornament used in classical Greece and Rome. Manufacture of furniture in the neoclassical taste continued well into the mid-nineteenth century. Renewed interest in Phyfe's furniture, and in neoclassical furniture generally, began with the colonial revival movement in the latter half of the nineteenth century, from the old-time kitchens at various Sanitary Fairs during the Civil War era to the celebration of the nation's centennial in 1876 and the subsequent centennials of the ratification of the Constitution and the inauguration of Washington. Even today, neoclassicism continues as a focus of decorating trends. This article explores the continuing challenge of separating the products of the shops of Phyfe and his early nineteenth-century New York contemporaries from later copies and adaptations.[1]

Duncan Phyfe arrived in New York City from Albany not later than 1792, when he became a member of the General Society of Mechanics and Tradesmen of the City of New York, a charitable and educational organization that gave the newcomer a network of contacts and prospective customers. *The New York Directory and Register, for 1793* listed him as "Duncan Fife," joiner, at 2 Broad Street, not far from Federal Hall where George Washington's first inauguration had been held four years earlier. There he shared quarters with turner and rush-bottom chairmaker Vincent Tillou. By 1795, Phyfe had moved his shop to Partition (now Fulton) Street, where he conducted business until his retirement in 1847 and continued to live until his death seven years later. Over the course of his fifty-five-year career, Phyfe employed family members as well as journeymen and apprentices, whose numbers and names have largely escaped the historical record.[2]

In the absence of any surviving daybooks or ledgers, a group of approximately forty bills from Phyfe identifies some of the shop's clientele and suggests the diversity of woods available, as well as the variety of furniture forms produced. Although only a few labeled examples of his furniture are known, Phyfe achieved considerable celebrity in his lifetime. Attesting to the high reputation of his products was an advertisement for the sale of used household furnishings that appeared in the February 20, 1817, issue of the *New York Evening Post*. The advertiser noted that the sale "consists of almost every article necessary for a small and genteel family, and is but three years old; was made by Phyfe and other respectable persons." In 1840, Phyfe was among the cabinetmakers and furniture manufacturers who endorsed products of varnish manufacturer P. B. Smith & Co., 139 Maiden Lane, New York, in an advertisement published in the *Alexandria Gazette and Virginia Advertiser*. The fifth edition of *Wealth and Biography of the Wealthy Citizens of New York City* (1845), compiled by Moses Yale Beach, noted that Phyfe "Commenced in Fulton street, where he now is, a poor cabinetmaker, and has now the largest and most fashionable establishment in the county."[3] His reputation today as an innovator in design and as a producer of furniture of the highest quality is largely due, however, to the promotional efforts of New York cabinetmaker Ernest F. Hagen (1830–1913).

Hagen, described in an obituary published in the *New York Times* on June 8, 1913, as an "expert appraiser and collector of art objects," was a native of Hamburg, Germany. He and his family arrived in New York in June 1844. The following year, his father apprenticed him (at the age of fifteen) to a firm of German cabinetmakers, Krieg and Dohrmann, at 106 Norfolk Street, where he remained until 1853. Hagen was too young to have been a journeyman in Phyfe's shop, which closed in 1847. After leaving his masters, he worked in several shops along Broadway below Bleecker before securing employment with the two hundred-man manufactory of Charles A. Baudouine at 335 Broadway (fig. 1).[4]

When Baudouine closed his business in 1855–1856, Hagen traveled west, working in Milwaukee, St. Louis, and New Orleans. He returned to New York in 1858 and formed a partnership with his old friend and shopmate, J. Matthew Meier, under the name of Meier and Hagen. In 1867, they moved to 213 East 26th Street, where they built a dwelling that included living quarters for Hagen and his family and a shop. The Meier family lived next door. Meier and Hagen specialized in the manufacture of extension dining tables for the wholesale trade during the first years of the partnership, when they worked at the bench with two or three hands and earned little more than their expenses. By 1870, the firm employed ten men, on average, and had no mechanized equipment. The partnership continued until 1888, producing a

Figure 1 Two pages from a scrapbook compiled by Ernest F. Hagen, New York City, 1892–1906. Included are clippings of newspaper articles quoting Hagen and labels of New York cabinetmakers, removed from furniture that Hagen apparently restored and/or sold. (Courtesy, Museum of the City of New York, gift of Bernard & S. Dean Levy, Inc., and Mr. and Mrs. Benjamin Ginsburg; photo, Helga Studio.)

wide range of furniture including "Eastlake" and "Clarence Cook" bookcases and designs by Louis Comfort Tiffany, for whom they produced a variation on the ladder-back chair as recorded in the order books on May 7, 1885—"10 Maple Colonial Dining Chairs with webbing seats in leather and leather backs to Special Design," plus two armchairs.[5]

Meier and Hagen also copied pieces from such fashionable New York furniture and decorating firms as Herter Brothers, Leon Marcotte, and Sypher and Co. For other clients, Hagen's shop altered genuine eighteenth-century antiques, like a slant-front desk that received "2 new webb feet" and a carved shell on the fallboard. The desk cost Hagen $10.00, and the alterations totaled $38.75; he charged his client $95.00. Meier and Hagen refurbished and sold old furniture described in the firm's order books as "Chippendale," "Sheraton," and "Phyfe's Antique," as well as reproductions in "Phyfe's pattern." On June 15, 1886, Meier and Hagen billed a client for "1 Phyfe's Arm Chair (antique) in XVI Century old blue plush & fancy bronze nails 35.00, 1 small chair to match (reproduction) 22.00."[6]

The Meier and Hagen shop probably used old wood to fabricate the swivel-top card table illustrated in figure 2, which has a partially legible paper label. The lower edge of the skirt has an empty channel, where a string of brass was probably once inlaid. Hagen noted in a 1905 newspaper interview that "the ruins of irreparable damaged old pieces furnish the modern cabinetmaker with the very best seasoned mahogany."[7] Although the guilloche and waterleaf carving on the legs and supports (fig. 3) are related to motifs used on early nineteenth-century neoclassical furniture, the combi-

Figure 2   Card table with a partially legible paper label of Meier and Hagen (active 1858–1888), New York City, 1885–1888. Mahogany and mahogany veneer. H. 30", W. 39¹/₄", D. 19¹/₄". (Courtesy, New York State Museum, gift of the Wunsch Foundation; photo, Gavin Ashworth.)

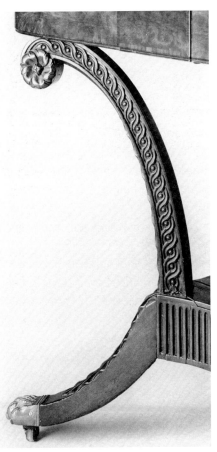

Figure 3   Detail of the support on the card table illustrated in fig. 2. (Photo, Gavin Ashworth.)

nation is not traditional. When viewed under ultraviolet light, the top and base of the table fluoresce differently, indicating the presence of a shellac on the upper portion and a resin varnish on the base.

After Meier's withdrawal from the firm, Hagen continued the business as "Ernest F. Hagen, cabinetmaker," until about 1905, when his eldest sons Frederick E. and Henry A. took over. One antique that passed through the firm after Meier's withdrawal is a dressing glass (figs. 4–6), which Hagen noted was "at one time the property of General Van Horne [1746–1801]/ bought at the 'Floyd' sale/on west 12 Street New York City/March 1890." Hagen purchased the dressing glass at the sale of "colonial relics" belonging to the late Benjamin Floyd, 124 West 12th Street, Manhattan, held on March 27, 1890. According to the *New York Times's* coverage of the sale, "Mr. Floyd was the grandson of Gen. David Van Horne of Revolutionary fame and had many mementos of that distinguished gentleman." Hagen apparently got a bargain, for "low prices prevailed all through the sale."[8]

Hagen is perhaps best known today for his "Personal Reminiscences of an Old New York Cabinetmaker," excerpts of which were published in *Antiques* in December 1943 and November 1963. He illustrated his memoirs with sketches of furniture forms, including one that documented the infringement of his former employer, Charles A. Baudouine, on John Henry Belter's patent for manufacturing laminated chair backs. As Hagen's interest in Duncan Phyfe grew, he sought out Phyfe family descendants and relevant documents. Following an interview with Phyfe's nephew, Duncan Phyfe of Jersey City, New Jersey, Hagen noted that the younger Phyfe recalled that his uncle was "always working . . . and after retiring from business kept . . . at the bench making small things for his folks which they still

Figure 4 Dressing glass, American or English, 1790–1810; labeled by Meier and Hagen, with "Meier" crossed out in ink, ca. 1890; Mahogany, mahogany veneer, and lightwood stringing with pine. H. 20½", W. 21¾", D. 18½". (Courtesy, Newark Museum, gift of John Babcock Morris; photo, Gavin Ashworth.)

Figure 5 Detail of the inscription on the drawer of the dressing glass illustrated in fig. 4. (Photo, Gavin Ashworth.)

Figure 6 Detail of the label on the dressing glass illustrated in fig. 4. (Photo, Gavin Ashworth.)

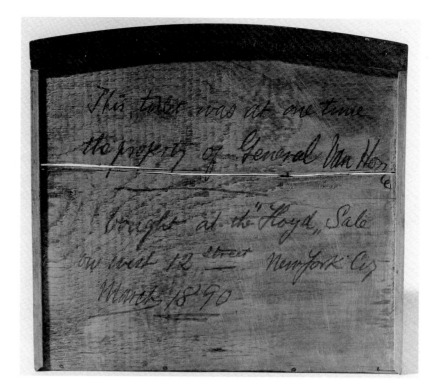

preserve." A dressing glass that descended in the family of Eliza Phyfe Vail is one such item (fig. 7). By 1894, Hagen's observations were being quoted in newspaper articles on old New York furniture, such as one published in the August 12 issue of the *New York Sun* (fig. 8). He recorded his findings in notes transcribed as "Personal Experiences of an Old New York Cabinet Maker" and "Duncan Phyfe Notes." These documents and later versions of them (all in the Winterthur Museum Library) provided the basis for most twentieth-century knowledge about Duncan Phyfe.[9]

The popularity of the Hudson-Fulton Exhibition, held at the Metropolitan Museum of Art in 1909, and the first major exhibition to display American decorative arts along with American paintings and sculpture, encouraged the collection of what had been considered "used furniture." Included was a collection of furniture attributed to the Phyfe workshop,

Figure 7 Dressing glass attributed to Duncan Phyfe, New York City, after 1847. Mahogany and mahogany veneer. H. 19⁹/₁₆", W. 12¹/₄", D. 9⁷/₈". (Private collection, on loan to the Museum of the City of New York; photo, Helga Studio.)

Figure 8 "Old New York Furniture," *New York Sun*, August 12, 1894; from a scrapbook compiled by Ernest F. Hagen, 1892–1906. (Courtesy, Museum of the City of New York, gift of Bernard & S. Dean Levy, Inc., and Mr. and Mrs. Benjamin Ginsburg; photo, Helga Studio.)

assembled by R. T. Haines Halsey (1865–1942) with the assistance of Ernest F. Hagen. Through Halsey, Henry Watson Kent (secretary of the board of trustees of the museum and organizer of the American section of the show) obtained Hagen's biographical notes on Phyfe and used them in his catalogue essay on American furniture. Kent also requested Hagen's help in identifying the furniture assembled by the exhibition committee.[10]

Collector Francis P. Garvan acquired much of the Halsey collection in 1929 and presented it to Yale University the following year. A second Metropolitan Museum of Art exhibition, "Furniture Masterpieces of Duncan Phyfe," which was organized by Halsey and Charles Over Cornelius in 1922, was the first museum exhibition devoted to the work of a single American cabinetmaker. Among the lenders were Mrs. Giles Whiting and Mrs. Harry Horton Benkard, both collectors. The exhibition and its companion publication, with measured, detailed drawings by Stanley J. Rowland, stimulated additional interest in Phyfe and his furniture.[11]

Included in the 1922 exhibition was one of a pair of New York five-leg card tables with double elliptic tops owned by Mrs. Harry Horton Benkard (fig. 9). It was illustrated in the accompanying publication as plate 20, but affixed to the underside of the top is a Hagen shop label (fig. 10). Are this

1894

THE SUN, SUNDAY, AUGUST 12

PHYFE WINDOW SEAT.

PHYFE SOFA.

OLD NEW YORK FURNITURE

EARLY CABINETMAKERS WHOSE WORK IS PRIZED HIGHLY.

Duncan Phyfe's Beautiful Productions—Allison's Chippendale Sideboards — The Meeks Brothers' Haircloth and Mahogany Chairs—Jersey Makers Famous.

There dwells some blocks northwest of the German quarter a German cabinetmaker who is in love not only with his trade, but also with its traditions. He has gathered a small but precious library bearing upon his trade, and has acquired a knowledge of antique furniture that enables him to recognize, in addition to various styles, the work of the earlier American masters of his craft. His library includes many old New York directories, and he gloats over the names of the

town region that was once the cabinetmaking quarter was Michael Allison of Vesey street. Allison often marked his work. He made beautiful Chippendale sideboards of a more durable quality than much of the Chippendale furniture, for, notwithstanding the fame of Chippendale, much of the furniture bearing his name is far from first rate. Allison did some work in rosewood, as did Phyfe, but he was chary of this wood in large articles, because of its liability to crack. Indeed, the old cabinetmakers were most fastidious as to materials. They used the best Santo Domingan and Cuban mahogany, and a famous importer of mahogany used to call his best wood Duncan Phyfe's logs.

John and Joseph Meeks were famous cabinetmakers during the first half of the century, and much of their work remains, ugly, but durable. Heavy mahogany chairs, of no particular style and hideous with black hair-cloth seats, are now and then recognized as the handiwork of the Meeks brothers. They made great sideboards, four-posters, and the like, and, although they produced little that would now be called beautiful, they had a great vogue about fifty years ago. The Meeks brothers are said to have

precision, while the more elaborate carving of larger pieces were marvels of the art. The renovation of Duncan Phyfe's work is expensive because of the care and time required. Phyfe was fond of introducing the figure of the lyre into his furniture. It appears in chairs, in swinging mirrors, and in various pieces, large and small. He seldom chose to mark his work, and only experts are able now to recognize it.

As Phyfe used to employ fully one hundred of the most skilful journeyman cabinetmakers in New York, and as his furniture was of the most durable sort, there is still a great deal of his work in existence. It is seldom for sale, and when any of it is sent to the auction room it is usually disposed of at private sale. A maiden lady who died a few years ago at the age of 94

fully printed card that reads thus: "Made and sold by Matthew Egerton, Jr., New Brunswick." Egerton was famous rather less than a century ago as one of the best cabinetmakers of the nearby Jersey towns. His work went to the homes of many well-known north Jersey families, and it turns up for sale in New York and elsewhere. The best of it is as good as any cabinet work of the period.

The cabinetmakers whose work belongs to the early years of this century and the last decade of the preceding one imitated English and French models rather than the work of the colonial Dutch and of New England cabinetmakers. New York had become rich by that

BITS OF ORNAMENTATION.

earlier cabinetmakers as they appear upon the time-stained pages of those volumes.

"There never was better furniture made than the best of our day," he said the other day, "but a few of the early cabinetmakers were wonderfully skilful. Duncan Phyfe was the greatest of them all," he added with enthusiasm. "He deserves greater fame than he won. He did more for taste in American furniture than Chippendale and the English cabinetmakers ever did."

Duncan Phyfe's name and trade appear in the New York directory of 1802. His place of business was at 35 Partition street (now Fulton

made their workmen take oath not to copy the firm's ugly patterns.

Charles Fredericks, who advertises in the Directory of 1816 his cabinetmaking shop at 17 Bowery, opposite Pell street, made famous Windsor chairs in his day. They survive yet, maple painted and gilded, and with rush bottoms of astonishing durability. He also produced dumpy, stiff-looking armchairs that are models of comfort for men with long backs and long legs. Thomas Ash was a contemporary and rival of Fredericks, with a shop at 33 John street. He also advertised Windsor chairs in the Directory of 1816. His furniture is still found, but cabinetmakers complain that the public of to-day will not pay enough for Windsor chairs to justify the expenditure of good work in repairs. Such chairs do not fit with the

PHYFE CHAIR.

left behind her a full set of Duncan Phyfe furniture, the gift of her father when she was a girl of 18. The set was reproduced in mahogany by the German cabinetmaker at the order of Frederick Bronson. Mr. Bronson, Egerton Winthrop, and Mrs. Horace Hunnewell of Boston now share the original set. William Phyfe, a grandnephew of the old cabinetmaker, has a work box made by him after he had retired from business.

Phyfe imitated and improved upon the work of the famous English cabinetmakers who immediately preceded him, and his furniture has decorated a few luxurious New York homes for the better part of a century. His Empire sideboards are recognized here and there in famous dining rooms.

A contemporary of Phyfe's in the down-

time, and there was a demand for something more elegant than the old oaken furniture of New England. The taste was not for the antique, but for luxury, rich wood, elaborate carving, and the ormulu decoration of the French, and it is all these things that have come down to the present generation to be cherished as antiques and to be imitated by the cabinetmakers of to-day. The smallest scraps from the craft masters of the century's infancy are preserved and combined into new furniture.

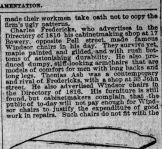

PHYFE CARD TABLE WITH FOLDING TOP.

PHYFE MUSIC TABLE.

street). He came to New York from Scotland at the age of 13, and probably learned his trade in this city. He began business about 1796, and did not give up till 1850. He made in that time a vast deal of excellent and beautiful mahogany furniture, including pieces of all sorts and sizes. Chairs were his specialty. A dozen well - authenticated Duncan Phyfe chairs sold not long ago at $22.50 each. He also made card tables with richly carved tripods, provided with an internal mechanism that caused the legs to spread or collapse as desired. The simplest carving on his small chairs was wrought with the utmost care and

luxurious appointments of modern houses, and the sale is slow.

Contemporary with the famous New York cabinetmakers of the early years of the century was a race of excellent cabinetmakers in the neighboring Jersey towns. Ichabod T. Williams, grandfather of the New York business man of that name, made excellent furniture at Perth Amboy, and the fine old houses of that quaint little city shelter many examples of his work. His sideboards were especially fine. His grandson cherishes a tall clock of his manufacture, with works made by Sayre, a famous clockmaker of Perth Amboy.

Lucky dealers in second-hand furniture sometimes come upon pieces still bearing a beauti-

CAPT. BOWER IN TIBET.

His Recent Exploration of What Is Called the Roof of the World.

Capt. Hamilton Bower, an Englishman, has recently returned from a daring trip of exploration in Tibet, the "Roof of the World." Tibet does not welcome foreign explorers, and Capt. Bower's trip was full of incident. His plan was a bold one. He made his final preparations at Leh, in Kachmirian Tibet, but he kept the object of his journey a profound secret.

Capt. Bower's Chinese passport for travelling in Chinese Turkestan was of no value in Tibet proper. Capt. Bower's plan was to push forward into Tibet without being noticed until he had gone too far to turn back. He and his companion, Dr. Thorold, represented themselves as merchants on their way to China, and succeeded in maintaining this character among the few nomads whom they met until they reached responsible officials within a few marches of Lhasa. At this point Capt. Bower and Dr. Thorold came out in their true characters and refused to be sent back by the way they came. The officials did not allow them to proceed to Lhasa itself.

The plan of these explorers involved weeks of the hardest travelling through an unknown dis-

trict lying to the north of Tibet, of which the maps give only scanty details. They lived for weeks at an elevation of from 15,000 to 18,000 feet on a plateau known as the Chang. It was thinly populated, but it abounded in game. From the north of Lhasa they came to lower elevations and more populous districts, and came out at last on the main Chinese trade road through Bethany and Lithany to the Yang-tse-Kiang.

Capt. Bower found the religion of the Tibetans a strange worship. In speaking of it he says: "In no country is religion so much en évidence. Every man has a praying-wheel in his hand, which he continually turns, even when on horseback. . . . But all this outward show means nothing but a gross superstition; in no way do the people regard their religion as being a rule of life inculcating virtue and morality; all they think is that by observing certain rules, benefit—but they know not what benefit—is obtained, and by neglecting them, calamities—but they know not what calamities—would ensue." Capt. Bower thinks that the religious question is at the bottom of the rooted objections of the Tibetans to the intrusion of Europeans in their country. The lamas objected to his entering their monasteries for fear he should see the wealth accumulated in them. Polyandry, if not a part of their religion, is sanctified by custom.

China considers all of Tibet as in some sense belonging to her, and she would undoubtedly cry "Hands off" to any other power that attempted to invade this country. As a matter of fact, the Chinese residents have little real influence, and do very much as the lamas direct.

PHYFE CHAIR.

69   IS IT PHYFE?

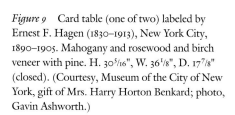

Figure 9 Card table (one of two) labeled by Ernest F. Hagen (1830–1913), New York City, 1890–1905. Mahogany and rosewood and birch veneer with pine. H. 30^{5}/$_{16}$", W. 36^{1}/$_{8}$", D. 17^{7}/$_{8}$" (closed). (Courtesy, Museum of the City of New York, gift of Mrs. Harry Horton Benkard; photo, Gavin Ashworth.)

Figure 10 Detail of the underside of the table illustrated in fig. 9. (Photo, Gavin Ashworth.)

table and its mate genuine antiques, restored by Hagen, or were they made up from old wood in the Hagen shop? The back and underside are mahoganized and varnished, treatments rarely encountered on period furniture, which suggests Hagen-shop manufacture. The method of attachment of the front legs to the skirt core also points to a late nineteenth- or early twentieth-century date of manufacture, when compared to that of a card table bearing the label of John T. Dolan's cabinet warehouse, 30 Beekman Street, 1809–1813 (fig. 11). Regional preferences employed by the Dolan shop include a veneered top over a joined core (intended to prevent warping), a treble elliptic shape for the top, and finely turned and reeded legs (fig. 12).

Perhaps exhibited, but not illustrated in the 1922 publication, was a square sofa from the Benkard collection (fig. 13). Although the basic frame dates from the early nineteenth century, the sofa has been extensively restored to repair a major break in the front seat rail. Its medial braces have been moved to accommodate pine reinforcements on the inner face of the front seat rail, and the right rear leg has been pieced at its base. Although the absence of reeding on the back of the center front legs suggests that they are original and period, the casters are not original, and the restorer shaved the front feet to make them fit. The inner face of a rear leg is inscribed "HAGEN/OCT. 1922/FEH," for Ernest F. Hagen's son and successor, Frederick E. Hagen (1868–1948). Presumably the younger Hagen undertook the work so the sofa could be included in the 1922 "Furniture Masterpieces" exhibition as a "Phyfe" piece.

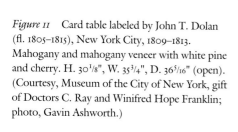

Figure 11 Card table labeled by John T. Dolan (fl. 1805–1815), New York City, 1809–1813. Mahogany and mahogany veneer with white pine and cherry. H. 30 1/8", W. 35 3/4", D. 36 5/16" (open). (Courtesy, Museum of the City of New York, gift of Doctors C. Ray and Winifred Hope Franklin; photo, Gavin Ashworth.)

Figure 12 Detail of the underside of the table illustrated in fig. 11. (Photo, Gavin Ashworth.)

With the opening of the American Wing of the Metropolitan Museum of Art in 1924, furniture manufacturers introduced reproductions of museum objects. R. T. Haines Halsey acted as an advisor for The Company of Master Craftsmen, Inc., a subsidiary of W. & J. Sloane (founded by William Sloane Coffin), active in Flushing, Queens, from 1925 to 1942. They produced "registered reproductions" for the growing middle-class market. Their advertisement for a Phyfe-style sofa, which appeared in the September 1926 issue of *Antiques*, was obviously intended to reach collectors (fig. 14). Somewhat more modest was the "Monticello—A Duncan Phyfe Adaptation" dining room suite available through the 1930 spring-summer catalogue of Sears, Roebuck and Co., with side chairs at $6.95 (fig. 15). Although the chair is relatively accurate (except for the stretchers), late nineteenth- and early twentieth-century innovations are evident in the china closet form and the novel application of broken-arch pediments to the case furniture in the suite.[12]

Museum exhibitions and publications during the 1930s continued to focus attention on Phyfe. In 1934, Joseph Downs and Ruth Ralston organized an exhibit at the Metropolitan Museum of Art titled "New York State Furniture," which included pieces labeled by and attributed to Phyfe. Then in 1939 Nancy McClelland published *Duncan Phyfe and the English Regency, 1795–1830*, which quickly became the "canon" of Phyfe scholarship and attributions.[13]

Looking for "Phyfe," that is, distinguishing period furniture from later

Figure 13 Sofa, New York City, 1810–1815;
restored by the shop of Ernest F. Hagen, 1922.
Mahogany with tulip poplar and pine. H. 37 ³/₁₆",
W. 79¹⁵/₁₆", D. 25". (Courtesy, Museum of the
City of New York, gift of Mrs. Harry Horton
Benkard; photo, Gavin Ashworth.)

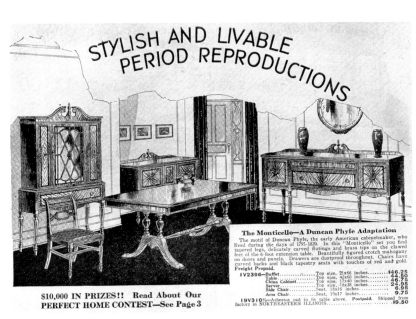

Figure 14 "The Company of Master Craftsmen,
Inc./Duncan Phyfe Furniture," W. & J. Sloane
advertisement, *Antiques* 10, no. 3 (September
1926): 156. (Courtesy, Museum of the City of
New York; photo, Helga Studio.)

Figure 15 "The Monticello-A Duncan Phyfe Adaptation," Sears, Roebuck
and Co. catalogue, Spring-Summer 1930, p. 576. Naming the dining room
suite "The Monticello" linked the "livable period reproductions" with
statesman and politician Thomas Jefferson, thereby enhancing its symbolic
value. (Courtesy, Museum of the City of New York; photo, Helga Studio.)

Figure 16 Curule side chair, New York City, 1810–1815; inscribed in ink on the inside of the front seat rail: "Thomas Cornell Pearsall made/for him by Duncan Phyfe." Mahogany. H. 32⅝", W. 17¾", D. 16¼". (Courtesy, Museum of the City of New York, gift of C. Ruxton Love; photo, Gavin Ashworth.)

reproductions and adaptations, is not particularly easy. During Phyfe's working career, New York cabinetmakers began to utilize ready-cut sheets of veneer, foot-powered mortising machines, and circular saws. In addition, later handcraft shops, like that operated by Hagen (which coexisted with both local and distant midwestern and southern furniture factories), continued to use hand-sawn and chiseled dovetails and mortise-and-tenon joints rather than machine-cut joints and dowels, and to carve decorative details by hand. To differentiate such handcrafted items from period originals, one must evaluate the artistic handling of the form and its ornament, check for evidence of use commensurate with the purported age of the object, and identify the effects of age on its condition.

The difficulties of such evaluations are illustrated by two curule-based side chairs (figs. 16, 17). Both are part of a large suite of seating furniture from the family of New York merchant Thomas Cornell Pearsall

Figure 17 Curule side chair labeled by Henry Dorr (fl. 1842/43–1862/63), New York City, 1842–1863. Mahogany. H. 32⅝", W. 17¾", D. 16¼". (Courtesy, Museum of the City of New York, gift of C. Ruxton Love; photo, Gavin Ashworth.)

Figure 18 Detail of the "H. DORR" brand on the rail of the side chair illustrated in fig. 17. (Photo, Gavin Ashworth.)

(1768–1820), who maintained a house at 43 Wall Street and another called "Belmont" at 57th Street and the East River. Based on the folding chair of the Roman magistrate, most curule or Grecian cross chairs of this type are attributed to Phyfe's shop. A sketch of a similar chair is thought to have accompanied a letter from Phyfe to his Philadelphia patron Charles N. Bancker about 1816. La Mesangere's *Meubles et Objets de Gout* (1800), however, illustrates a stool derived from the Roman curule with the cross at the front, and the 1808 *Supplement to the London Chairmakers' and Carvers Book of Prices for Workmanship*—the probable design source for the New York Grecian chair—illustrates two curule stools. New York chairmakers simply added a square back with an "ogee splat" and a single rosette.[14]

Although both chairs are constructed in similar fashion, the one branded "H. DORR" (figs. 17, 18) has slightly different proportions and carving details. Did chairmaker Dorr, who appeared in city directories from 1842/43–

Figure 19 Armchair (one of two), New York City, ca. 1815. Mahogany. H. 33", W. 20⁵/₈", D. 17¹⁵/₁₆". (Courtesy, Museum of the City of New York, gift of Captain Marion Eppley, U.S.N. Ret., in honor of John Walden Myer; photo, Gavin Ashworth.)

1862/63, make the branded chair and its mates among the Metropolitan Museum of Art group to extend the original set? Is the chair a survival, or a revival, of neoclassical design?

Ernest F. Hagen gathered materials about Duncan Phyfe and examples of furniture that he attributed to the Phyfe shop to document the man and his craft. His clients had more diverse motives for acquiring "Phyfe" furniture. To some, Phyfe, despite his post-Revolutionary working period, exemplified the self-reliant, preindustrial "colonial" artisan-craftsman. (The term "colonial" was loosely used well into the twentieth century to describe the period before the onset of modernization, about 1840.) To others, maintaining and adding to collections of family furniture reinforced their notions of superior social position in a rapidly changing society. Others simply found neoclassical designs graceful and artistic.

Two scroll-back armchairs illustrate such diverse motives. According to

Figure 20   Scroll-back armchair labeled by Ernest F. Hagen, New York City, 1905. Mahogany. H. 31", W. 19³/₄", D. 17³/₄". (Private collection; photo, Gavin Ashworth.)

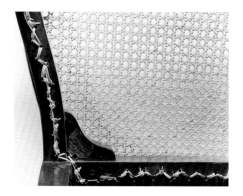

Figure 21   Detail of the underside of the seat of the armchair illustrated in fig. 20. (Photo, Gavin Ashworth.)

Figure 22   Detail of the back of the armchair illustrated in fig. 19. (Photo, Gavin Ashworth.)

Figure 23   Detail of the back of the armchair illustrated in fig. 20. (Photo, Gavin Ashworth.)

donor tradition, the chair illustrated in figure 19 and its mate belonged originally to diarist Philip Hone, who served as mayor of New York City in 1826. "Scroll sweep elbows" such as those used on these chairs cost eleven shillings (about $1.38), according to *The New-York Revised Prices for Manufacturing Cabinet and Chair Work* (1810). "Springing the front legs one way, each leg" was an additional six pence, and "preparing the front legs for lion's paws, each" cost one shilling.

Mrs. W. Sheffield Cowles, sister of President Theodore Roosevelt, probably ordered the Hagen chair with turned legs illustrated in figure 20, which is part of a set of four armchairs and two side chairs with a matching settee. Members of the Roosevelt family patronized Meier and Hagen frequently during the 1880s, often buying antiques or neoclassical-style furniture. The chair and its mates were sold during the dispersal of the Cowles estate, at Farmington, Connecticut, on May 30, 1987.[15]

To supply such a chair, Hagen bought unfinished frames from a specialist chairmaker like Jacob Dieter. Listed in the Meier and Hagen order books, Dieter charged $9.50 each for "Phyfe's Antique" mahogany chair frames. Workers in the Hagen shop carved, caned, and varnished the frame and the completed chair sold for about $25.00.

Both construction details and overall appearance mark the Hagan chair as a reproduction, although it may have been based on a period armchair he owned. Particularly significant is its lack of medial braces (fig. 21), which are dovetailed into the front and rear seat rails on period examples like Philip Hone's (fig. 19). "Sweep" or curved braces were standard on New York

Figure 24 Scroll-back side chair, New York City, 1810–1820. Mahogany. H. 32³/₄", W. 17⁷/₈", D. 16³/₄". (Courtesy, Museum of the City of New York, gift of Berry B. Tracy; photo, Gavin Ashworth.)

Figure 25 Music stool labeled by Ernest F. Hagen and inscribed in pencil "1901/Dr H (illegible)," New York City, 1901. Mahogany with oak. H. 32¼", W. 18½", D. 17". (Courtesy, Newark Museum; photo, Gavin Ashworth.)

chairs after 1802. Comparison of the crest rail carvings (figs. 22, 23), which Elizabeth Stillinger has called "seaweed," reveals subtle differences in modeling and design, with the 1905 carving lacking the crisp detailing of the earlier work.[16]

English lyre-back chairs were exported to the United States by the mid-1790s; however, the earliest evidence of their production by an American cabinetmaker is the aforementioned sketch (also depicting a curule chair) attributed to Phyfe. The lyre-back chair in the sketch has hairy shanks, lion's paw feet, and a carved crest rail. According to the fee schedule published in *The New-York Book of Prices For Manufacturing Cabinet and Chair Work* (1817), the labor charge for making a basic lyre banister was seven shillings, eight pence; stringing the lyre with brass cost an additional three pence per string (fig. 24).[17]

In 1901, the Hagen shop adapted the back scroll and lyre components to

Figure 26   Detail of the back of the music stool illustrated in fig. 25. (Photo, Gavin Ashworth.)

Figure 27   Detail of the Hagen brand on the block of the music stool illustrated in fig. 25. (Photo, Gavin Ashworth.)

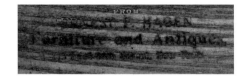

a music stool (fig. 25). Eliminating the rear legs might have weakened the joint between the side seat rail and the rear stile, so the chairmaker improvised truncated extensions. Ultraviolet fluorescence indicates that both shellac and natural resin varnish were used in different areas, and that a coloring agent was used to "antique" the carving on the crest rail (fig. 26). This finding suggests that the chairmaker used old components on an essentially new form. The stool is branded twice with Hagen's shop name and address (fig. 27). A similar base, used for a mahogany swivel-top card table, has a printed Hagen label dated 1897.[18]

As this survey has illustrated, differentiating later handcrafted furniture from that made in the workshops of Phyfe and his contemporaries can be difficult in the absence of documentation. One also must keep in mind Ernest F. Hagen's 1907 admonition that "from about 1840 to about 1865 a great deal of furniture was made there which is now sold for antique to such as don't know any better."[19]

1. Donald L. Fennimore, "Fine Points of Furniture, American Empire: Late, Later, Latest," in *Victorian Furniture: Essays from a Victorian Society Autumn Symposium*, edited by Kenneth L. Ames, published as *Nineteenth Century* 8, nos. 3–4 (1982): 46–54; Kenneth L. Ames, "Introduction," in *The Colonial Revival in America*, edited by Alan Axelrod (New York and London: W. W. Norton for the Winterthur Museum, 1985), pp. 11–12. Valley Furniture Shop, Watchung, New Jersey, advertisement for Winterthur Museum Collections/Kindel Showroom Samples featured a "Phyfe-Style Dining Table," *New York Times*, June 11, 1992, C8. This article is based upon an exhibition organized by the Museum of the City of New York, on view from March 10, 1993, to December 19, 1993. The presentation was made possible in part by a grant from William Doyle Galleries, New York. The show was subsequently installed at Boscobel Restoration, Inc., Garrison-on-Hudson, New York, where it was on view from March 2, 1994, to June 30, 1994. The scholarly assistance of Elizabeth Stillinger and Michael Kevin Brown in the exhibition's organization is gratefully acknowledged.

2. For a detailed examination of Phyfe's career, see Michael Kevin Brown, "Duncan Phyfe" (master's thesis, University of Delaware, 1978).

3. *Alexandria Gazette and Virginia Advertiser*, October 19, 1840. Moses Yale Beach, comp., *Wealth and Biography of the Wealthy Citizens of New York City comprising an alphabetical arrangement of persons estimated to be worth $100,000 and upwards, Fifth Edition* (New York: Sun Office, 1845), p. 24.

4. The most comprehensive analysis of Hagen's life and career is Elizabeth Stillinger, "Ernest Hagen—Furniture Maker," *Maine Antique Digest* (November 1988): 8D–16D; a conversation with Ms. Stillinger following the publication of that article led to the exhibition proposal that became *Is It Phyfe?*

5. Stillinger, "Ernest Hagen—Furniture Maker," p. 10D, fig. 5, reproduces the order book sketch for the Tiffany chair; two chairs and a related table are in the Art Institute of Chicago.

6. Stillinger, "Ernest Hagen—Furniture Maker," p. 12D, fig. 14, illustrates the order book sketch for the desk and the list of alterations. Three of Hagen's order books, dating from 1880 to 1886, are in the New-York Historical Society, New York. See Ruth Ralston, "Ernest Hagen's Order Books," *Antiques* 48, no. 6 (December 1945): 356–57.

7. The dated but unidentified clipping is in the Hagen scrapbook, Museum of the City of New York.

8. Stillinger, "Ernest Hagen-Furniture Maker," p. 12D; *Trow's New York City Directory*, vol. 120 (1906–1907), p. 608.

9. See Ruth Ralston, "A New York Cabinetmaker's Reminiscences," *Antiques* 48, no. 6 (December 1943): 284–85; Elizabeth A. Ingerman, "Personal experiences of an old New York cabinetmaker," *Antiques* 84, no. 5 (November 1963): 576–80. The Ernest F. Hagen Papers are in the Joseph Downs Collection of Manuscripts and Printed Ephemera, Winterthur Museum Library, Collection 32 (88 × 207); further Hagen papers are part of the R. T. Haines Halsey Papers, Collection 56 (75 × 80.36–.38).

10. Henry Watson Kent and Florence N. Levy, *The Hudson-Fulton Celebration MCMIX Catalogue of An Exhibition of American Paintings, Furniture, Silver And Other Objects of Art*, 2 vols. (New York: Metropolitan Museum of Art, 1909).

11. Charles Over Cornelius, *Furniture Masterpieces of Duncan Phyfe* (Garden City, New York: Doubleday, Page & Company, 1922).

12. *Antiques* 10, no. 3 (September 1926): 165. *Spring and Summertime, 1930 Catalogue* (Chicago: Sears Roebuck and Co., 1930), p. 576.

13. Nancy V. McClelland, *Duncan Phyfe and the English Regency, 1795–1830* (New York: W. R. Scott, Inc., 1939).

14. At Pearsall's death, the furniture went to his daughter Phoebe Pearsall, and then to her heirs. Eventually, C. Ruxton Love bought the suite at auction. He divided the group between the Metropolitan Museum of Art and the Museum of the City of New York. See Metropolitan Museum of Art, *19th-Century America: Furniture and Other Decorative Arts* (New York: New York Graphic Society, 1970), no. 17, for an armchair from the suite. Charles F. Montgomery, *American Furniture: The Federal Period* (New York: Viking Press, 1966), p. 126, no. 72a.

15. *Antiques & The Arts Weekly* (Newtown, Connecticut), June 26, 1987, p. 59.

16. The chair owned by Hagen was illustrated in Walter A. Dyer, "Chairs of Our Forefathers," *Good Furniture* 5, no. 3 (September 1915): 167.

17. The Bancker sketch is reproduced in Montgomery, *American Furniture*, p. 126, 72a. Ernest F. Hagen once owned the sketch and its companion bill and made a pencil copy of the drawing in his scrapbook (Museum of the City of New York). The sketch came to the Winterthur Library with the R. T. Haines Halsey Papers.

18. *Sotheby's Arcade Auctions, Silver, Decorations, American and English Furniture, Rugs and Carpets*, sale no. 1491, New York, January 31, 1995, lot 2615. Two other lots in that sale had Hagen labels: a period sideboard renovated by Hagen (lot 2406) and a mahogany slant-front desk partially composed of eighteenth-century elements (lot 2614).

19. Ernest F. Hagen, "Personal Experiences of an Old New York Cabinet Maker," Ernest F. Hagen Papers, Joseph Downs Collection of Manuscripts and Printed Ephemera, Collection 32 (88 × 207).

Peter Follansbee and
John D. Alexander

Seventeenth-Century Joinery from Braintree, Massachusetts: The Savell Shop Tradition

▼ O N E   O F   T H E most sophisticated joinery traditions in seventeenth-century New England flourished in Braintree, Massachusetts. Unlike most New England towns, Braintree was settled during the early seventeenth century by colonists from Boston rather than by a cohesive group of English immigrants. In 1634, the Massachusetts court ordered "that Boston shall have convenient inlargement att Mount Wooliston." This section of Suffolk County, named for a short-lived expedition by Captain Richard Wollaston in 1624, became known as Braintree.[1]

The earliest references to the woodworking trades in Braintree are deeds involving sawyers Samuel Allen and William Penn during the late 1650s. Wood was an extremely important commodity in early New England. In 1646, the town officials approved:

> A grant . . . that every man that is an inhabitant of the Towne shall have Liberty to take any timber off the Common for any use in the Towne [provided] . . . they make not sale of it out of the Towne and in case any shall make sale of it out of the Towne either in boards or bolts or any other wayes whole or sawne they shall pay for every tunne of timber five shillings a tunne to the Towne.[2]

Surviving records suggest that the most active families of woodworkers were the Belchers and Savells. Gregory Belcher (b. 1606) settled in Braintree in 1639 and remained there until his death in 1674. He and his sons, Moses (b. 1635) and Samuel (b. 1637), were carpenters, as were Samuel's son and grandson, both named Gregory. Moses Belcher's inventory listed expensive furniture, but none of his possessions indicate that he was a joiner. It is, however, quite likely that he was both a furniture maker and a carpenter.[3]

The Savells are the most plausible makers of the furniture discussed in this article. William Savell, Sr., apparently immigrated to New England from Saffron Walden, Essex, England (probably during the early to mid-1630s), and married Hannah Tidd before settling in Braintree after 1639. Her father John was a tailor in Charlestown and, later, Woburn, Massachusetts. Savell remarried twice and had six children altogether. The names of his earliest apprentices are not known, but he probably had several before his son John (b. 1642) began his training.[4]

Savell never held any town position, and there is no record of him receiving a grant or being made a freeman; however, he owned a considerable amount of property when he died in 1669. The total value of his estate was £798.17, and his inventory listed a "house and barn & a bitt of meadow" valued at £90, "John's house shop barn & land" valued at £120, "Tables stooles chayres chests & wooden ware" valued at £8.4, and "Cart wheels plow chaynes with joiners stuff [a reference to oak] & ceder boults" valued at £19.3.6. In his will, dated February 1668, William Sr. left John "the whole House & barn & shop & tooles, stuffe as Timber pertaining to his trade" and instructed that his "sonn William . . . live as an Apprentice with . . . John Savel . . . until hee bee 21." An article of agreement attached to the will also specified that his wife, Sarah (Mullins Gannett), receive the "whole estate . . . she brought to [her husband] for her own use & to dispose of forever with a chest with drawers & a Cubbert."[5]

John Savell was made a freeman in Woburn, Massachusetts, in 1684, but he apparently remained in Braintree all his life. Town records refer to the death of "John Savil Joyner" on November 19, 1687. Few references to trades occur in these records, suggesting that John was well regarded in his profession.[6]

William, Jr., was born in 1652 and apprenticed with his brother, John. The only reference to his work is a 7s payment by the town for "dimblebees cofin" in December 1694. William died on February 1, 1699/1700, possessed of "a green carpitt & covers for chairs" valued at £1.8, "a douzen painted chair & a sealskin trunk" valued at £1.18, "a wainscott chest and a box" val-

Figure 1 Chest attributed to the Savell shop, Braintree, Massachusetts, 1660–1680. Oak and chestnut with pine and white cedar. H. 34¹/₄", W. 52³/₁₆", D. 21¹/₈". (Private collection; photo, Gavin Ashworth.) This chest may be by John Savell. It appears to be one generation later than the cupboard illustrated in fig. 2 and the chest illustrated in fig. 9.

ued at £1.1, "a square table a wainscott chest and a bedstead" valued at £2.12, tools valued at £2.10, and "timber and weare begun" valued at £3.[7]

Another joiner who was part of the Savell shop tradition is Joseph Allen (1672–1727). He probably trained with William, Jr., before marrying his master's niece, Abigail, in 1701. Allen's estate included "3 chists and one box," two axes, a hand saw, and "joyner tools."[8]

The furniture attributed to the Savell shop consists of ten joined chests, a fragment of a joined cupboard, three boxes, and a stool (see figs. 1–4, 9, 20, 21). All are distinguished by their fastidious stock preparation and meticulous joinery. The case pieces also have beautifully executed relief carving that features arches, palmettes, lunettes, and guilloches. The carving is extremely precise, and the designs vary little from piece to piece. The chests and cupboard are further ornamented with crease moldings, and at least three of the pieces have remnants of original paint.[9]

Furniture historian Henry Wood Erving attributed these pieces to Windham County, Connecticut; however; the provenance of two of the chests strongly suggests that they originated in Braintree. One (fig. 1) originally belonged to John (1630–1716) and Ruth (Alden) (1634–1674) Bass, who married in Braintree on February 3, 1657. John was born in Saffron Walden and immigrated with his parents, Samuel and Anne Bass, about 1633. Ruth Alden was the daughter of John Alden and Priscilla Mullins of Plymouth and Duxbury. Like the other chests in the group, this example is constructed of riven (split) and hewn stock. The frame and panels are oak, the original four-board lid is chestnut, and the floorboards are cedar—a wood listed in the inventory of William Savell, Sr.[10]

A similar chest (fig. 21) has an early recovery history in Braintree. Tradition maintains that Charles Hibbard French (1877–1919) received it as a wedding present from an uncle who found the chest in a barn there. The French family was in Braintree by 1640, when John French received a land grant near the Monatiquot River.[11]

The Art of Joinery
A basic knowledge of conventional seventeenth-century stock preparation and joinery techniques is essential for understanding the more distinctive practices utilized by the makers of this group. The most important technique for constructing joined furniture was the drawbored mortise-and-tenon. A fragment of a wall cupboard attributed to the Savell shop (fig. 2) has clear evidence of drawboring. The joiner drove the pegs through holes that were offset intentionally (the hole in the tenon is closer to the shoulder than is the hole in the mortise), which made the joints draw together tightly (fig. 5). The amount of offset required for drawboring was minimal. Joseph Moxon's *Mechanick Exercises* (1678) recommended a difference of "about the thickness of a shilling." This process also caused the pegs to kink like the ones illustrated in figure 6.[12]

All seventeenth-century New England joiners utilized drawboring, but few were as meticulous as the tradesmen in this shop. Most joiners undercut the front shoulders of their tenons very slightly and cut the rear shoul-

Figure 2   Fragment of a cupboard attributed to the Savell shop, Braintree, Massachusetts, 1640-1670. Oak. (Courtesy, Winterthur Museum; photo, Gavin Ashworth.) This cupboard and the chest illustrated in fig. 9 probably represent the work of William Savell, Sr.

Figure 3   Desk box (front and side views) attributed to the Savell shop, Braintree, Massachusetts, 1670–1700. Oak with pine. H. 10³/₄", W. 22³/₄", D. 15 3/4". (Courtesy, Aetna Inc.; photo, Gavin Ashworth.)

Figure 4   Stool attributed to the Savell shop, Braintree, Massachusetts, 1640–1680. Oak. H. 23½", W. 18", D. 11". (Courtesy, Metropolitan Museum of Art.)

Figure 5   Detail of the door frame of the cupboard illustrated in fig. 2, showing the offset of the drawbored holes. (Photo, Gavin Ashworth.)

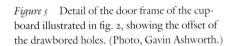

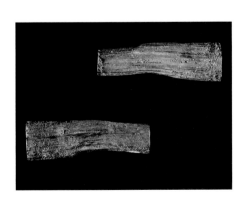

Figure 6   Detail of two pegs from the door frame of the cupboard illustrated in fig. 2. (Photo, Gavin Ashworth.)

Figure 7 Diagram of (*a*) typical seventeenth-century New England mortise-and-tenon joint, (*b*) barefaced mortise-and-tenon joint, (*c*) Savell shop mortise-and-tenon joint. (Drawing, Peter Follansbee; art work, Wynne Patterson.)

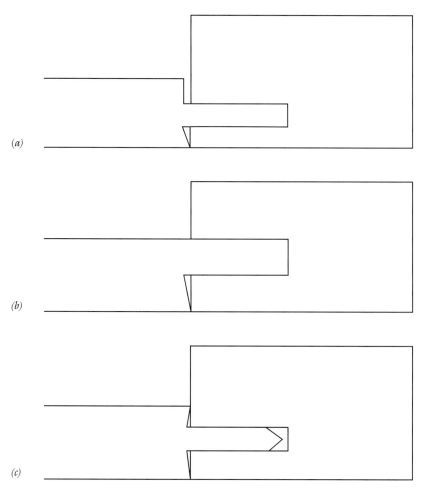

(*a*)

(*b*)

(*c*)

ders on or just inside the scribed layout line (fig. *7a*). As a result, their joints fit tightly on the front of the piece of furniture, but the rear shoulders of their tenons fail to make contact with the mortised edge of the frame. Some New England joiners constructed their furniture with "barefaced" tenons, which have no rear shoulder at all (fig. *7b*); however, the survival of numerous seventeenth-century case pieces built with joints that appear substandard to modern observers is testimony to the strength of drawboring. These joints were based on the use of green wood. Although the stiles distorted as they dried, the rear shoulders of the tenons were out of the way, or omitted altogether, so that the stiles could not press against the inside shoulder and shove the tenon out of the joint. By contrast, the Savell joiners took the time and trouble to square their stock, plane it clean and even, and cut two-shouldered tenons that fit tightly against the entire mortised surface (figs. *7c*, 8). This standard of precise workmanship was instilled during their training, which must have been rigid given the consistent stock preparation, joinery, and carving of the furniture in this group.[13]

Most stock for seventeenth-century New England furniture was riven from green or unseasoned logs. Riving was an extremely fast, labor-efficient method of extracting wood from a log. One man could reduce a log into rough stock quite easily, whereas two were needed for sawing. This factor was important in seventeenth-century New England where labor was in short supply. In addition, riving allowed the artisan to see each piece as it came from the log, giving him more control over the selection of the wood.

All of the pieces attributed to the Savell shop combine riven and sawn stock. The joined chests typically have a sawn pine panel in the rear, and several examples have sawn floorboards and drawer bottoms. The board chest with joined front illustrated in figure 9 is extremely unusual because its end

Figure 8 Detail of a mortise-and-tenon joint on the chest illustrated in fig. 1. (Photo, Gavin Ashworth.)

Figure 9 Chest attributed to the Savell shop, Braintree, Massachusetts, 1640–1670. Oak with pine. H. 20³/₈", W. 47¹/₈", D. 18¹/₂". (Courtesy, Smithsonian Institution, Greenwood Collection; photo, Gavin Ashworth.) This chest and the cupboard illustrated in fig. 2 probably represent the work of William Savell, Sr.

Figure 10 Detail of the hatchet marks on the inner face of the front rail of the cupboard illustrated in fig. 2.

boards are mill-sawn oak. A 1661 deed between George Ruggles and his son, John, referred to "Woodland . . . within a mile or thereabouts of the Saw mill of or in the said Town of Braintree." The occurrence of mill-sawn oak in seventeenth-century New England furniture is very rare.[14]

For optimum results, the joiner rived his stock shortly after felling a tree. Not only did green wood split more easily than dry wood, but reducing the log into more manageable sections made transporting it to the shop a simpler task. To make his initial splits, the joiner used a "beetle" (a large wooden mallet reinforced with iron rings to prevent the head from splitting) to drive in large iron wedges. As the sections of the log became more manageable, he used a froe (a tool with a flat blade and wooden handle) and a maul (a heavy wooden club) to rive out his stock quickly. After positioning the froe along the middle of the stock, he struck the back of the blade, burying the tool into the wood. At this point, he set the maul aside and pulled the handle to and fro. This levering action lengthened the split in the wood. The joiner could partially control the direction of the split by exerting pressure on the lower half of the breach while levering the froe. Therefore, a piece could sometimes be saved, even though the split began going astray.[15]

The joiner positioned his splits so that the radial surface of the log would become the working face of each piece. The working face was the reference for all stock dimensioning and layout, so it had to be flat and true. Because of its greater dimensional stability, the radial plane was less susceptible to distortion from moisture loss than the tangential (or growth ring) plane. The radial surface also planed and carved more easily than did the tangential surface.[16]

Most seventeenth-century woodworkers rived their stock slightly oversized, then dressed it with a joiner's hatchet (a small version of a broadaxe). Using short, controlled strokes, a skilled tradesman could produce accurate, clean surfaces; however, the main function of the tool was gross removal of waste. The joiner used the hatchet and froe to bring the work piece to near-

Figure 11 Approximate 1/2-scale drawing of (*a*) Plymoth Colony pentagonal stile and the billet it is riven from; (*b*) Savell shop rectangular stile and the larger billet required to produce it. (Drawing, Peter Follansbee; art work, Wynne Patterson.)

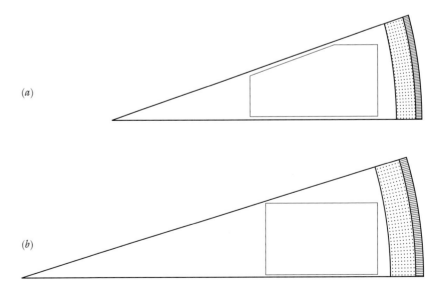

(*a*)

(*b*)

Figure 12   Detail of the layout lines of a mortise-and-tenon joint on the chest illustrated in fig. 1. (Photo, Gavin Ashworth.) The height of the mortise is indicated by the upper scribe line.

Figure 13   Detail of a door frame mortise and tenon on the cupboard illustrated in fig. 2. (Photo, Gavin Ashworth.) The scribe lines from the mortise gauge are visible on the mortise member.

finished dimensions as quickly as possible, thereby reducing the amount of planing. The inner face of the front rail of the cupboard (fig. 10) has hatchet marks left from the hewing process. Here, the joiner neglected to plane the marks away because this surface is hidden from view.[17]

Like the splitting process, planing involved a progression from coarser to finer tools. The joiner used a "fore" plane (a plane with a convex blade and a wide throat for taking a heavy shaving) to remove any natural deviations in the stock, then he removed the resulting furrows with a smooth plane. If the riven stock was clear enough, he could omit the first step and go straight to the smooth plane. Unlike many New England joiners, the tradesmen in the Savell shop planed the front stiles of their case pieces to a rectangular cross-section rather than to a polygonal one (figs. 8, 11). The former process involved more time and labor.[18]

After preparing the stock, the joiner laid out his work with a square and an awl. He used a mortise gauge to scribe the thickness of the mortise-and-tenon joints. The incised lines left from these tools often extend beyond the edges of the mortises and tenons, enabling us to measure the joints accurately (figs. 12, 13). This information is helpful in linking related pieces together and in making distinctions between the individual members of one shop tradition. The furniture attributed to the Savell shop also has alignment marks—triangles and arrows—on the inside faces of the stock.[19]

Conventional shouldered tenons could be cut very quickly. The saw cut that defined the shoulder was the most critical (see figs. 7 *a–c*). If the stock was straight-grained, the joiner simply split the cheeks off the tenon using a wide chisel or a small cleaver. Alternately, he sawed them down to the shoulder. If the tenon was too thick, the joiner pared the cheeks with a wide chisel. Although some seventeenth-century tenons are flat-ended, those of the cupboard door frame are pointed to allow them to seat in the torn fibers in the bottom of the mortise (fig. 13).[20]

To chop the mortises, the joiner used a mallet and a mortise chisel—a deep-bladed chisel made to withstand heavy blows and to function as a lever for prying out the waste. Often the ends of the mortises were crushed by the levering action. The joiner could work aggressively because green wood cut more easily than did drier timber.

Although it was advantageous to fabricate certain parts of the chest from green wood, during assembly some components needed to be drier than others. Pegs had to be bone dry. If they shrank from moisture loss after assembly, the joints could fail. The tenons needed to be dry enough to resist the pegs being driven into them; otherwise, the peg would deform the tenon instead of drawing it into the mortise. Chest panels and floorboards also needed drying. If a joiner installed the panels wet, subsequent shrinkage would cause them to slip from side to side. Likewise, excessive shrinkage across the width of floorboards would cause gaps. By contrast, the moisture content of the stiles had no effect on the joint.

Generally, the sizes of the parts of a joined object conform to their priority in the drying scheme. Pegs, which need to be the driest, were the smallest in cross-section and, therefore, dried very quickly. Tenons, which were typically about $5/16$" in thickness, also dried quickly owing to their dimensions and the fact that wood loses moisture more rapidly through the end grain.[21]

Savell Shop Joinery

Two of the pieces attributed to the Savell shop have structural features that are rare in New England. The cupboard and chest illustrated in figures 2 and

Figure 14　Detail of the board-and-frame construction of the chest illustrated in fig. 9. (Photo, Gavin Ashworth.)

Figure 15　Detail of the hole cut by a piercer on the cupboard illustrated in fig. 2. (Photo, Gavin Ashworth.)

Figure 16 Detail of the carving on the door panel of the cupboard illustrated in fig. 2. (Photo, Gavin Ashworth.) Although a number of hands were involved in the carving of Savell shop pieces, there was virtually no attempt to try anything new.

9 have joined fronts whose stiles are rabbeted to the board sides and attached with three, 3/8"-square wooden pegs at each side (see fig. 14). Seventeenth-century New England furniture with joined fronts and board cases is extremely rare. The joiner used a piercer (a fluted reaming bit with a lancet point) to bore the holes for the pegs. The counterclockwise direction of the boring is indicated by the pattern of the torn fibers in the hole. Piercers do not cut end grain as well as long grain. As the bit made the transition from the long grain to the end grain, it dug in and left cusps at diagonally opposite "corners" of the hole (fig. 15). All of the smaller peg holes on the Savell shop pieces were bored clockwise. The best explanation for the counterclockwise boring of the larger peg holes is that the 3/8" piercer had one defective lip, and was simply used the other way. The compression of the fibers around the holes reveals that the wood had a high moisture content when the joiner drove in the square pegs. Drier wood is less compressible and would have split long before deforming to this degree.[22]

The joined fronts and board cases of the cupboard and chest provide another link to William Savell, Sr. Chests from Saffron Walden, his probable birthplace, feature this type of construction but have different decoration. A more detailed study of the construction of Saffron Walden chests would be necessary, however, to establish a definitive connection to the Braintree group.[23]

The cupboard and chest share other features that suggest they are by the same hand. Their carving (figs. 16, 17) is more assured, more modeled, and more elaborate than that of the fully joined chests in the group (see figs. 1,

Figure 17 Detail of a carved panel on the chest illustrated in fig. 9. (Photo, Gavin Ashworth.)

Figure 18 Detail of a carved panel on the chest illustrated in fig. 1. (Photo, Gavin Ashworth.)

Figure 19 Detail of a carved panel on the chest illustrated in fig. 20. The carving is less competent than that of figs. 16–18.

20). Although the latter have essentially the same design elements (figs. 18, 19), the execution of the carving is somewhat "mechanical." Presumably, the better carving is that of the shop master, who probably trained in England. The narrow panels flanking the door on the cupboard and the front panels on the chest are concave (figs. 2, 17). The carver probably hollowed them to heighten the illusion of depth in his relief work. This feature may have been an option, since some of the chests in the group have flat panels (figs. 1, 18–20).

Although the chests attributed to the Savell shop can be divided into two distinct groups based primarily on the execution of their carving, their layout and joinery are remarkably consistent (see chart, p. 104). All have mortise-and-tenon joints cut so that the inside shoulders of the tenons make contact with the mortised members and all have alignment marks to orient components and prevent them from getting inverted during assembly. Seven chests vary less than 3/4" in width across the front. Although this degree of precision and attention to detail is unusual for seventeenth-century New England joinery, the methods used to achieve it provide insight into the work habits of the joiners in the Savell shop.

The joiner's goal was to produce a chest 52" wide, but to do so he had to adjust the dimensions of individual components. In the riving process, the most difficult pieces of wood to extract were the wide panels. The joiner split them from radial bolts, which were usually an eighth or a sixteenth of

Figure 20   Chest attributed to the Savell shop, Braintree, Massachusetts, 1660–1690. Oak and chestnut with pine. H. 32⁵/₁₆", W. 51³/₄", D. 21¹/₄". (Courtesy, Museum of Fine Arts, Boston, gift of Charles Hitchock Tyler.)

the whole log. The amount of straight, clear wood found between the twisted, knotty juvenile wood at the center of the tree and the sapwood just under the bark varied depending on a number of factors. Though the joiner might have had a panel width in mind when he rived his stock, he often had to settle for whatever size panels the tree would yield. In seventeenth-century joinery, close enough was good enough. On these chests, the widths of the visible panels (not including the feathered edges that fit into the grooves in the frame) vary from 8" to 8⅞", so the joiners adjusted the width of the muntins to maintain an approximate overall width of 52" (see chart, p. 104).[24]

Three of the surviving chests fall short of the "standard" size. Two have narrow panels about 8" wide (figs. 9, 21). To produce a 52" chest the joiner would have had to make the muntins over 4" wide, which would be architecturally disproportionate. The third chest, which is illustrated in Luke Vincent Lockwood's *Colonial Furniture in America* (1901), probably represents the work of a joiner somewhat removed from the main shop tradition. This tradesman could have made a standard 52" chest with only a half-inch alteration to the muntin width, but instead he chose to produce a chest 50¼" wide. Other aspects of his dimensioning depart from the shop norm; the drawers of his chest are only 5" high, and the panels are only 12" tall. Both of these deviations could be attributed to this chest being a two-drawer example, were it not for another two-drawer chest with standard dimensioning (see chart, p. 104). In addition, some of the facade moldings and the layout and execution of the carving differ from the rest of the group.[25]

On all of the Braintree chests, the framing of the floors and configuration of the rear rails is distinctive. The neatly planed, pentagonal floor rails (front and side) are grooved to receive the feathered edges of the floorboards, which are nailed down onto the lower rear rail (fig. 23a). Floorboards supported by the rear rail are unusual in New England joined furniture. Typically, they are nailed up to a higher rail. On some of the chests attrib-

Figure 21   Chest attributed to the Savell shop, Braintree, Massachusetts, 1660–1680. Oak with pine and cedar. H. 22⅜" (without lid), W. 49⅜" (case), D. 20⅛". (Courtesy, Winterthur Museum Decorative Arts Photographic Collection.) This chest may be by John Savell.

Figure 22   Chest attributed to the Savell shop, Braintree, Massachusetts, 1660–1680. Oak with pine. H. 24⁹/₁₆", W. 51½", D. 20½". (Private collection; photo, Dan Gair.)

uted to the Savell shop, the floorboards are joined with a modified tongue and groove. Many tongue-and-groove joints were cut with matching planes, but the joiners in the Savell shop cut the groove with a plow plane and formed the tongue by running a rabbet on the top edge of the adjoining board and bevelling its underside (fig. 24).[26]

The construction of the rear frame also distinguishes the Savell chests from other New England work (fig. 25). The most distinctive feature is the lack of muntins. All of the chests have one large, horizontal pine back panel with feathered edges at the sides and top. The edges fit into grooves in the rear stiles and top rail, both of which have their flat faces inside the chest. The lower rail (or rails when drawers are used) is positioned under the floor and in front of the panel, and the panel is nailed to the rear rail (figs. 23*b*, 25). Another New England case piece with this unusual structure is a cupboard attributed to the John Taylor shop of Cambridge, Massachusetts. Taylor (d. 1683) was described as the "College Joyner" in 1638. The existence of only one Taylor cupboard with rear framing like the Braintree group suggests that William Savell, Sr., may have worked in Taylor's shop.[27]

Both shops also employed dovetail drawer construction. The Savell join-

Figure 23 Detail showing the floor framing of
(*a*) the chest illustrated in fig. 1 (interior) and (*b*)
the chest illustrated in fig. 22 (exterior). (Photos,
Gavin Ashworth and Dan Gair.)

Figure 24 Detail of the modified tongue-and-
groove joint used on the floorboards and the bottom of the drawer of the chest illustrated in fig. 1.
The bevel on the underside is slightly concave.

Figure 25 Detail of the construction of the rear frame of the chest
illustrated in fig. 1. (Photo, Gavin
Ashworth.) The joiner slid the
panel into the frame from below.
See also fig. 23*b*.

Figure 26 Detail of the drawer construction of the chest illustrated in fig. 1. All of the Savell shop drawers are "side hung" and have one large dovetail nailed through the side. (Photo, Gavin Ashworth.)

ers used a half-blind dovetail to join the drawer sides to the front (fig. 26), rabbeted the drawer back to receive the sides, and secured both joints with nails. They also rabbeted the front to receive the bottom boards and nailed them to the lower edges of the drawer sides and back. Most seventeenth-century New England drawers are simply rabbeted and nailed. Dovetail construction is generally thought to indicate London or continental influence.[28]

In a 1641 petition, William Savell, Sr., stated that he was a "Cambridge joyner" and that he had worked for Nathaniel Eaton, the first professor at Harvard. Eaton had been instructed to oversee the construction of "such edifices as were . . . necessary for a college & for his own lodgings." Unfortunately, there is no record of the work Savell did for him. Eaton was dismissed from his position in September 1639, and when Henry Dunster took over as president of the college in 1641, the interiors were unfinished. Savell probably left Cambridge shortly after filing his petition, for his first son, John, was born in Braintree in 1642.[29]

Although the rear framing of the Braintree chests and the Taylor cupboard is unusual in Anglo-American furniture, it is relatively common on kasten from the Netherlands and areas of Dutch cultural influence. Two early New York examples (Winterthur Museum acc. 52.49 and 57.87.1) have rived clapboard backboards, feathered into grooves in the stiles and nailed to interior rails that are tenoned into the rear stiles. The joinery of these kasten is also more precise than that of most contemporary English work. These connections suggest that Savell or his master trained with or were influenced by northern European joiners in England.[30]

The objects attributed to the Savell shop are among the most carefully made examples of seventeenth-century New England furniture. Others are more elaborate, but none demonstrate comparable stock preparation and joinery. Minor variations in the execution of the carving indicate different hands; however, the framing of comparable forms is virtually identical. This consistency in construction reflects the restrictive nature of apprenticeship in the Savell shop. Given William Savell's probable training in Saffron Walden, the furniture attributed to his shop may represent one of the "purest" English vernacular traditions that flourished in the colonies.

ACKNOWLEDGMENTS   For their assistance with this article, the authors thank Joyce Alexander, Luke Beckerdite, Tara Cedarholm, Edward S. Cooke, Jr., Ted Curtin, Mary Follansbee, the late Benno M. Forman, Debra Hamilton, H. Hobart Holly, William Hosley, Charles Hummel, Rodris Roth, Robert Tarule, and Malcolm Walker. Special thanks are due Robert Trent for his unflagging support and critical review.

1. H. Hobart Holly, *Braintree, Massachusetts, Its History* (Braintree, Mass.: Braintree Historical Society, 1985), pp. 29–30. Nathaniel B. Shurtleff, ed., *Records of the Governor and Company of the Massachusetts Bay in New England* (Boston: Press of William White, 1853), vol. 1, 1628–1641, p. 119. Seventeenth-century Braintree included the present-day city of Quincy (except North Quincy) and the towns of Braintree, Holbrook, and Randolph.

2. For Samuel Allen, see Suffolk Deeds, bk.1, p. 90. For William Penn, see Suffolk Deeds, bk. 1, p. 299. Extracts from the town records are in Samuel A. Bates, ed., *Records of the Town of Braintree, 1640–1793* (Randolph, Mass.: Daniel H. Huxford Printer, 1886), p. 4.

3. Waldo C. Sprague, *Genealogies of the Families of Braintree, Massachusetts, 1640–1850*. This microfilm collection of index cards is published by the New England Historic Genealogical Society in cooperation with the Quincy Historical Society. Bates, ed., *Records of Braintree*, p. 640.

4. For Savell's origin, see Roger Thompson, *Mobility and Migration: East Anglian Founders of New England* (Amherst: University of Massachusetts Press, 1994), p. 40. William Savell's sister, Anne, was baptised in Saffron Walden (Extracts from the Register of Baptisms, Saffron Walden Church, copy on file at Quincy Historical Society, Quincy, Mass.). For information on Savell, his wives, and children, see *New England Historical and Genealogical Register* 3:247; and Bates, ed., *Records of Braintree*, pp. 633, 635, 637, 716. For John Tidd, see Thomas B. Wyman, *The Genealogies and Estates of Charlestown in the County of Middlesex and Commonwealth of Massachusetts, 1629–1818*, 2 vols. (Boston: David Clapp & Son, 1879), 1:78. Tidd's will, dated February 9, 1656, reads: "to my beloved wife Alice the house . . . all the land and orchard . . . then to come and remain to my 3 Grand children, Benjamin Savell Hannah Savell and my son Samuels daughter equal between them . . . I give to my two Grand Children Jno & Samuel Savel twenty shillings" (Middlesex County Probate Records, vol. 1, no. 2258, p. 78). Although the Savells are the most plausible makers of the furniture discussed in this article, our principal focus is on the objects and their construction.

5. Suffolk County Registry of Probate, no. 501, Massachusetts State Archives, Boston (hereinafter cited as SCRP).

6. James Savage, *A Genealogical Dictionary of the First Settlers of New England*, 4 vols. (1860–1862; reprint ed., Baltimore, Md.: Genealogical Publishing Company, 1965), 4:27, 28. The Woburn reference may have to do with the will of John Savell's grandfather, John Tidd. Tidd left John 20*s* (Middlesex County Probate Records, vol. 1, no. 2258, p. 78). Bates, ed., *Records of Braintree*, p. 664.

7. Sprague, *Genealogies of the Families of Braintree*. Bates, ed., *Records of Braintree*, p. 30. SCRP, no. 2560.

8. Joseph Allen was the brother of Samuel and Benjamin Allen, both of whom were wheelwrights. See appendix for entries concerning them. For more on the Allen family, see Sprague, *Genealogies of the Families of Braintree*. For Joseph Allen's inventory, see SCRP, no. 5452. An administration bond filed with the inventory refers to him as a "Joyner."

9. The stool has thorough planing, precisely cut joints, and the same crease molding as the group A and group B chests (see chart, p. 104). The authors thank Rob Tarule for calling this stool to their attention. The only other Braintree piece known to the authors is a square-post

chair illustrated in Irving Phillips Lyon, "Square-Post Slat-Back Chairs," in *Pilgrim Century Furniture,* edited by Robert F. Trent (New York: Main Street/Universe Books, 1976), p. 40, fig. 2.

10. Henry Wood Erving, *Random Notes on Colonial Furniture* (Hartford, Conn., 1931), pp. 22–23. John Bass's baptism is listed in Extracts from the Register of Baptisms, Saffron Walden. For more on John and Ruth Bass and their families, see Robert Charles Anderson, *The Great Migration Begins: Immigrants to New England, 1620–1633,* 3 vols. (Boston: New England Historic Genealogical Society, 1995), pp. 122–27; Charissa Taylor Bass and Emma Lee Walden, *Descendants of Deacon Samuel & Ann Bass* (Freeport, Ill.: Wagner Printing Co., 1940), p. 9; and Bates, ed., *Records of Braintree,* pp. 716, 640. The chest illustrated in fig. 20, and another in the Isabella Stewart Gardner Museum have original lids that are also chestnut. The lids are made of three and two boards, respectively. Richard H. Randall, *American Furniture in the Museum of Fine Arts, Boston* (Boston: by the Museum, 1965), pp. 6–7, no. 6, states that the lid of the Museum of Fine Art's chest (fig. 20) is ash.

11. Conversation between the authors and the current owner. John French is in Sprague, *Genealogies of the Families of Braintree.*

12. Joseph Moxon, *Mechanick Exercises; or the Doctrine of Handyworks,* 3d ed. (London, 1703; reprint ed., Mendham, N.J.: Astragal Press, 1994), p. 88.

13. A chest attributed to Ipswich, Massachusetts, joiner Thomas Dennis (Winterthur Museum, acc. 82.276) has barefaced tenons on the lower side rails. Barefaced tenons are common in joined chair frames. For a slightly different version of a barefaced tenon, see Robert Blair St. George, *The Wrought Covenant: Source Material for the Study of Craftsmen and Community in Southeastern New England 1620–1700* (Brockton, Mass.: Brockton Art Center, 1979), p. 38.

14. George Ruggles to John Ruggles, March 13, 1661, Suffolk Deeds, 14 vols., Boston, 1880–1906, 13:183–84. For more on mill sawing, see Benno M. Forman, "Mill Sawing in Seventeenth Century Massachusetts," *Old Time New England* 60, no. 220 (spring 1970): 110–30.

15. For more on riving and the construction of furniture with green wood, see John D. Alexander, *Make a Chair from a Tree* (Newton, Conn.: Taunton Press, 1978); Benno M. Forman, *American Seating Furniture* (New York: W. W. Norton, 1988); Robert F. Trent, "What Can a Chair and a Box Do for You?" *Maine Antique Digest* 15, no. 4 (April 1987); 10C–13C; Drew Langsner, *Green Woodworking* (1987; reprint ed., Asheville, N.C.: Lark Books), pp. 76–89, 157–59; and Mike Abbott, *Green Woodwork: Working Wood the Natural Way* (East Sussex, Eng.: Guild of Master Craftsmen Publications, 1992). Beetles and wedges are commonly listed in seventeenth-century probate inventories. Often just the beetle rings are mentioned, presumably because the wooden component was deemed to be of no value. Henry Mercer, *Ancient Carpenters Tools* (1929; reprint ed., Doylestown, Pa.: Bucks County Historical Society, 1975), pp. 11–14, describes the froe as a "thick-backed, rigid, dull-bladed steel knife, about fifteen inches long and three and a half inches wide, hafted at right angles to its blade." The joiner often placed his stock in a brake—a form of workhorse. Brakes were made in an endless variety of configurations. J. G. Jenkins, *Traditional Country Craftsmen* (1965; revised ed., London, Boston, and Henley, Mass.: Routledge & Kegan Paul, 1978), p. 33, fig. 6, illustrates several forms. In his discussion on hoopmaking, Jenkins stated that "the whole purpose of the cleaving brake was to hold the hazel in place at every conceivable angle while it was split" (ibid., p. 32). See also Scott Landis, *The Workbench Book* (Newtown, Conn.: Taunton Press, 1987), pp. 169, 170; and H. L. Edlin, *Woodland Crafts in Britain* (London: B. T. Batsford, 1949), chapter 15.

16. Shrinkage on the radial plane is roughly half of that on the tangential plane (R. Bruce Hoadley, *Understanding Wood* [Newton, Conn.: Taunton Press, 1980], chapter 4).

17. The joiner's hatchet is held in one hand; it is also called a broad, or side, or hewing hatchet. The joiner typically placed the wood on a stump of convenient height. Holding the piece at a slight angle, the joiner chopped a series of scoring cuts to the desired depth. He then oriented the stock to a nearly vertical position and swung down along these scoring cuts, chopping away at the wood (the flat back of the hatchet faced the face of the stock). See Alexander, *Make a Chair from a Tree,* p. 38.

18. For more on the use of the various planes, see Moxon, *Mechanick Exercises,* pp. 64–74; Charles F. Hummel, *With Hammer in Hand* (1968, reprint ed., Charlottesville: University Press of Virginia, 1982), pp. 105–24; and W. L. Goodman, *The History of Woodworking Tools*

(London: G. Bell and Sons, 1964), pp. 56–84. The whole issue of how a seventeenth-century joiner held his stock for planing is one for further study. Moxon recommended: "To plane this Square, lay one of its broad Sides upon the Bench, with one of its ends shov'd pretty hard into the Teeth of the Bench-hook, that it may lie the steddier" (Moxon, *Mechanick Exercises*, p. 81). With its irregularly tapered cross-section, riven stock often required shimming to steady it. For an excellent illustration of a late sixteenth- or early seventeenth-century English woodworking shop, see Forman, *American Seating Furniture*, p. 45, fig. 13.

19. See Mercer, *Ancient Carpenters Tools*, pp. 60, 63, fig. 60. Generally speaking, the marking gauge has one pin and scribes a single line. The mortise gauge has two pins and scribes a pair of parallel lines. We have broken the Savell shop pieces into three distinct groups; one of several determining factors is the thickness of the mortise chisel used. See chart, p. 104.

20. We have found no evidence of sawn tenon cheeks in New England furniture; however, the practice probably existed in England owing to the poor quality of the wood there.

21 . These conclusions regarding the moisture content of the various parts of joined furniture are based on independent shop work by the authors and by Rob Tarule and Ted Curtin.

22. Two chests from Portsmouth, New Hampshire, have joined fronts and board cases (Jonathan Fairbanks and Robert F. Trent, eds., *New England Begins:The Seventeenth Century*, 3 vols. [Boston: Museum of Fine Arts, Boston, 1982], 3:536, no. 492; Brock Jobe, ed., *Portsmouth Furniture: Masterworks from the New Hampshire Seacoast* [Boston: Society for the Preservation of New England Antiquities, 1993] pp. 89–91).

23. See Penny Rumble, "Some East Anglian Chests," *Regional Furniture* 5 (1991): 42–50, figs. 6, 9. This hybrid structure also occurs on a mid-sixteenth-century chest illustrated in Victor Chinnery, *Oak Furniture: The British Tradition* (Suffolk, Eng.: Antique Collector's Club, 1979), p. 421, fig. 4: 20.

24. For more on the importance of measuring construction dimensions, see Alexander, *Make a Chair from a Tree*, p. 18. For studies that analyze layout, see Robert Blair St. George, "Style and Structure in the Joinery of Dedham and Medfield, Massachusetts, 1635–1685," in *American Furniture and Its Makers,* edited by Ian M. G. Quimby (Chicago: University of Chicago Press for the Winterthur Museum, 1979), pp. 1–47; and Robert Tarule, "The Joined Furniture of William Searle and Thomas Dennis: A Shop Based Inquiry into the Woodworking Technology of the Seventeenth Century," (Ph.D. dissertation, Graduate School of the Union Institute, 1992). Studies of seventeenth-century shop traditions would benefit tremendously from a uniform and extensive approach to measuring. St. George's article and Tarule's dissertation come close to providing this type of detail.

25. Erving, *Random Notes on Colonial Furniture*, pp. 22, 23. This chest is also illustrated in Luke Vincent Lockwood, *Colonial Furniture in America* (New York: Charles Scribner's Sons, 1901), p. 24, fig. 9. Two chests attributed to the Savell shop do not have drawers (figs. 21, 22). The latter reportedly belonged to Jonathan Fiske (1774–1864) of Medfield, Massachusetts, and his wife Sally Flagg (1772–1865). In 1798, Fiske bought a house, land, and tannery from Oliver Adams (1777–1848) of Medfield. Oliver's grandmother was Jemmima Morse (1709–1785). Her father, Joshua, married Elizabeth Penniman (1675–1705) of Braintree. Joshua's second wife and Jemmima's mother was Mary Paine, who was also from Braintree. It is possible that the chest entered the Adams family through one of these marriages and that it was included in the sale from Oliver Adams to Jonathan Fiske (George M. Fiske, *The Migration of Jonathan Fiske and Sally Flagg* [Auburndale, Mass.: privately printed, 1923], n.p.; Irving P. Lyon to Cornelia B. Fiske, March 15, 1938, private collection; Andrew Adams, *A Genealogical History of Henry Adams of Braintree, Massachusetts and His Descendants, 1632–1897* [Rutland, Vt.: Tuttle Company Printers, 1898], p. 21). William S. Tilden, *History of the Town of Medfield, Massachusetts, 1650–1886* (Boston: George H. Ellis, 1887), pp. 392, 441.

26. The most notable exception is a group of chests from Plymouth colony (see St. George, *Wrought Covenant*, p. 28, fig. 1a, p. 38, fig. 20a).

27. For more on the John Taylor shop, see Robert F. Trent, "Joiners and Joinery of Middlesex County, Massachusetts, 1630–1730," in *Arts of the Anglo-American Community in the Seventeenth Century,* edited by Ian M. G. Quimby (Charlottesville: University Press of Virginia, 1975), pp. 123–48. Other Taylor cupboards have a feathered pine panel nailed onto the outside of the rear frame (conversation between the authors and Robert F. Trent).

28. For more on London and continental influences, see Benno M. Forman, "The Chest of Drawers in America, 1635–1670: The Origins of the Joined Chest of Drawers," *Winterthur Portfolio* 20, no. 1 (spring 1985): 1–30; and Robert F. Trent, "The Chest of Drawers in America:

A Postscript," *Winterthur Portfolio* 20, no. 1 (spring 1985): 31–48.

29. Edward Everett Hale, ed., *Note Book kept by Thomas Lechford, Esq. Lawyer, in Boston, Massachusetts Bay, from June 27, 1638 to July 29, 1641* (Camden, Me.: Picton Press, 1988), pp. 410–11. Savell's petition is undated but seems to fall about 1641. Josiah Quincy, *The History of Harvard University*, 2 vols. (Cambridge, Mass.: John Owen, 1840), 1:452. This material is also discussed in *Harvard College Records, Publications of the Colonial Society of Massachusetts*, vol. 15 (Boston: by the Society, 1925), pp. xvii–xxii. Although no new lodgings were built for Eaton, repairs were possibly made to his house, which was formerly William Peyntree's. In a ca. 1650 letter, Dunster described conditions when he took over as president:

> They had finished ye Hall yet wthout skreen table form or bench. . . . No floar besides in & above ye hall layd, no inside sepating [separating?] wall; made nor any one study erected throughout the hous. Thus the work fell upon mee 3d 8ber 1641 wch by ye Lords assistance was so far furthered yt ye students dispersed in ye town & miserably distracted in their times of discourse came into commons into one house 7ber 1642. (*Harvard College Records*, p. 7)

Records of several towns returned to Boston, *New England Historic Genealogical Register*, vol. 3, p. 247.

30. See Peter Kenny, Frances Gruber Safford, and Gilbert T. Vincent, *American Kasten: The Dutch Style Cupboards of New York and New Jersey, 1650–1800* (New York: Metropolitan Museum of Art, 1991), p. 43, fig. 33, for a kast with rear framing similar to the pieces attributed to the Savell shop (see pages 10–15 for details on the construction of Dutch kasten). For information on continental woodworkers in England, see Benno M. Forman, "Continental Furniture Craftsmen in London: 1511–1625," *Furniture History* 5 (1971): 94–120; S. W. Wolsley and R. W. P. Luff, *Furniture in England: The Age of the Joiner* (New York and London: Praeger Publishers, 1969), pp. 12, 13. Wolsley and Luff note that immigrant artisans can be linked to many architectural carvings, including those at Audley End, in Saffron Walden.

Appendix

Woodworking Craftsmen in Braintree

Samuel Allen (d. 1699)   Allen arrived in Braintree by 1639 and was referred to as a "sawier" in a 1658 deed. He died in Braintree in 1669. His widow and son Joseph sold his son Samuel of Bridgewater "twelve Acres of Land . . . within the township of Brantry . . . neere the sawmill." His grandsons, Joseph, Samuel, and Benjamin Allen, were all woodworkers. (*Sources: Suffolk Deeds*, bk. 1, p. 90, bk. 8, p. 23; Waldo C. Sprague, *Genealogies of the Families of Braintree, Massachusetts, 1640–1850* [microfilm collection of index cards published by the New England Historic Genealogical Society in cooperation with the Quincy Historical Society].)

Samuel Allen (1674–1725)   Samuel was a shipwright and a wheelwright. His inventory listed four lots of cedar swamp, several pieces of furniture, and a variety of tools and materials associated with his trades:

one chest with drawers	03-00-00
large square table a little table with draw	01-10-00
two little tables	00-14-00
seven chests	03-10-00
six chairs	00-18-00
half a dozen chairs in the kitchen	00-12-00
3 spinning wheels	01-00-00
one hatchet	00-15-00
ten dozen of spokes for cart wheels	01-00-00
two saws	02-12-00
one broad axe	00-12-00
two adzes and other carpenters tools	03-00-00

two narrow axes and two hammers	00-06-00
one grindstone	00-12-00
ship timber	03-00-00

Samuel's brother Benjamin was also a wheelwright, and his brother Joseph was a joiner. (*Sources*: Sprague, *Genealogies of the Families of Braintree*; Suffolk County Registry of Probate [hereinafter cited as SCRP], no. 5139.)

Joseph Allen (1672–1727)   See text.

Joseph Bass (1665–1733/34)   Joseph was the son of John Bass and Ruth Alden and the husband of Mary (Belcher). He may have apprenticed with his father-in-law, Moses Belcher, a Braintree carpenter. Joseph Bass was also related to the Savells. His grandmother, Anne, was the sister of William Savell, Sr. Joseph moved to Boston about 1705 and became a "wharfinger." Assuming that he completed his training about 1686, Joseph could have worked in Braintree for approximately twenty years before moving. (*Sources:* Sprague, *Genealogies of the Families of Braintree*; Suffolk County Registry of Deeds, no. 90, p. 256.)

Samuel Bass (d. 1726)   Samuel was the son of Samuel Bass and Mary Howard and the grandson of Deacon Samuel Bass and Ann Savell. Town records referred to him as "Samuel Bass-carpenter" to differentiate him from his cousin Samuel Bass (1660–1751), son of John Bass and Ruth Alden. (*Sources:* Charissa Taylor Bass and Emma Lee Walton, *Descendants of Deacon Samuel & Ann Bass* [Freeport, Ill.: Wagner Printing Co., 1940], pp. 13–15; Samuel A. Bates, ed., *Records of the Town of Braintree, 1640–1793* [Randolph, Mass.: Daniel H. Huxford Printer, 1886], pp. 28, 29, 31, 37–39.)

Deacon Gregory Belcher (1664–1727)   The son of Samuel Belcher, Gregory was referred to as a wheelwright, carpenter, shipwright, and ship carpenter in Braintree records. He died on July 4, 1727, "in the 63 year of his age being killed with a plough." His estate included barrels, tubs, wooden ware, five "low chairs," six "black chairs," a "great chair," three chests, a "case of drawers," a "square table," "sundry tools," and a "glew pot and kettle." The Selectmen's Records document work done by Gregory Belcher, but it is unclear whether they refer to Deacon Gregory or his son, Gregory:

1713/14	Gregory Belcher mending the school house	00-14-00
1714/15	Gregory Belcher for a table for the school house and	00-06-00
1715/16	Gregory Belcher mending the school house	00-10-00
1724	Gregory Belcher for G. Welly coffin	00-10-00

Gregory Belcher (1691–1727/28), who was described as a ship carpenter in an administration bond, died shortly after his father, on January 20, 1727/28. (*Sources:* Sprague, *Genealogies of the Families of Braintree*; SCRP, no. 5475; Selectmen's Records for the Town of Braintree, 1688–1757, microfilm, Genealogical Society, Salt Lake City, Utah [hereinafter cited as Selectmen's Records].)

Gregory Belcher (1606–1674)   Gregory Belcher was a carpenter. He was born in County Warwick in 1606 and received a land grant in Braintree in 1639. His inventory listed a few tools, furniture—"3 chests, 2 boxes, 2 hanging cupboards, 3 tables 6 stools six chairs 6 cushions"—and a "servant" Henry, who was probably an apprentice. Belcher's earlier servant was "Andrew Rounsimon, . . . a Scotish man dyed 8th 31 1657." Belcher's widow Katherine died in 1680. Presumably, much of the furniture listed in her inventory was her husband's: "the cupboard with the lock and some small things 5s," "6 cushions 10s another cupboard 4s," "a great press 20s, 2 chests 2 boxes 20s," and "a press and chairs 4s 6 tables 2 stooles." (*Sources:* Bates, ed., *Records of Braintree*, p. 636; SCRP, no. 720; SCRP Misc. Docket; Sprague, *Genealogies of the Families of Braintree.*)

Moses Belcher (1635–1691) Moses Belcher was the son of immigrant Gregory Belcher. Braintree records refer to Moses as a carpenter, and the quantity and values of furniture in his inventory suggest that he was relatively successful.

seven chests	01-00-00
five boxes one trunk	01-00-00
two chests in parlour	02-00-00
one cupboard	03-00-00
four tables three joint stools	02-05-00
13 chairs	00-16-00
2 dozen cushings	02-00-00
for Richard Russel's time	08-00-00
one cradle two cupboards	00-14-00
axes saws beetle and wedges	00-10-00
saws augers old iron other lumber	03-00-00

The cupboard valued at £3 is one of the most expensive listed in Braintree inventories. Richard Russel was probably an apprentice. (*Sources:* Sprague, *Genealogies of the Families of Braintree*; SCRP, no. 1875.)

Samuel Belcher (1637–1679) Samuel was a younger son of Gregory Belcher. Although his inventory does not list any tools, both Samuel and his son, Deacon Gregory Belcher, were carpenters. Perhaps Samuel's tools went to Gregory, who had yet to finish his training at the time of his father's death. (*Sources:* Sprague, *Genealogies of the Families of Braintree.*)

Samuel Hayden (ca. 1630–1676) Samuel was born in Dorchester and moved to Braintree with his father, John, by 1640. When Samuel died in 1676, his inventory included planes and "toules" worth £1.16. Although Samuel's trade is unknown, two of his brothers may have been carpenters. A 1676 deed mentions a "wharfe to bee set down . . . by Jonathan Hayden & Nehemiah Hayden of Brantrey." No inventories survive for Jonathan (1640–1718) or Nehemiah (1647/48–1717), although the Selectmen's Records list some payments made in 1716/17 to Nehemiah Hayden, Sr., for "nails and work done" and to Benjamin Hayden for "boards for schoolhouse." Another brother, John (1635–1718), received £4 in 1688 "for plastering the meeting house and whiting of it." (*Sources:* Suffolk Deeds, bk. 10, p. 121; Selectmen's Records; Sprague, *Genealogies of the Families of Braintree*; SCRP, no. 829.)

John Mills (1674–1749)   John was a carpenter who received £3 for "repaireing the meeting house" in Braintree in 1701. (*Sources:* Bates, ed., *Records of Braintree*, p. 50.)

Stephen Paine (1652–1690)   Stephen was the son of Stephen Paine and Hannah Bass. His death is mentioned in the town records: "Steven Paine a devout Christian a cunning artificer, and ingenious to admiration died in the flower of his age of the small pox May 14, 1690." Unfortunately, his trade is not indicated in any surviving documents. His inventory included:

a great chest and box	01-00-00
fower chests	00-12-00
a great table and two little ones and 4 joynt stooles	02-00-00
fower great chayrs and ten little ones	01-12-00
log chaine	00-12-00
draught chaine and a payre of horse chaines	00-10-00
two axes	00-06-06
drawing knife and fork tines	00-03-00
hewd timber and slitt work for a frame	03-00-00

His wife was Ellen Veasey, daughter of William Veasey. They had a son, Stephen Paine (1682–1720?), who may have been a joiner in Boston. (*Sources:* Bates, ed., *Records of Braintree*, p. 658; SCRP, no. 1952.)

William Penn (d. 1688)   Penn was a "sawyer" who owned property in Braintree by 1647. A 1684 deed refers to the sale of his "upper landing place where the Saw pitts are." The deed also gave the purchaser the right to set up a mill, suggesting that Penn had not done so. Penn died in Boston about 1688. (*Sources:* Suffolk Deeds, bk. 1, p. 299, bk. 10, p. 29.)

Martin Saunders (1631–1706)   A 1675 deed refers to Saunders as a "howse carpenter." (*Sources:* Suffolk Deeds, bk. 9, p. 240.)

John Savell (1642–1687)   See text.

William Savell, Sr. (d. 1669)   See text.

William Savell, Jr. (1652–1699/1700)   See text.

John Shepard (d. 1650)   Shepard's inventory lists "carpenter tooles" worth £4.8.3 and a grindstone. (*Sources:* SCRP, Misc. Docket.)

Robert Taft (d. 1724/25)   "Robert Tafft of Braintree" is first mentioned in an August 20, 1679, building contract with John Bateman of Boston. Bateman agreed to pay "for the transportation of the sd frame of the sd Cellar and house from Brantrey the place where it is to bee framed to Boston." Taft died in Mendon in 1724/25. Mendon records refer to him as both a joiner and a housewright. (*Sources:* Abbott Lowell Cumings, "Massachusetts and Its First Period Houses: A Statistical Survey," in Colonial Society of Massachusetts, *Architecture in Colonial Massachusetts* [Boston: by the Society, 1979], pp. 196–99.)

Robert Twells (Twelves, Tweld) (ca. 1620–1696/97)   Twells first appears in Braintree records in 1645. He was part of a committee that met in 1674 "about the rebuilding of the corne mill being demolished by fier." Twells's inventory included woodworking tools, and his death notice in the town records stated that: "Robert Tweld who erected the South Church at Boston died March 9th 1696/97 aged 77 or thereabout." (*Sources*: Bates, ed., *Records of Braintree*, pp. 17, 693; SCRP, no. 2369.)

Peter Webb (ca. 1650–1717/18)   Webb was a joiner and a miller (his father, Christopher, and brothers John and Samuel, were also millers). Peter's wife was Ruth Bass (1662–1700), whose brother, Joseph was a Braintree joiner. Probate records for Webb refer to him as a "joyner," and his inventory included "2,030 foot of boards." (*Sources*: Bass and Walton, eds., *Descendants of Deacon Samuel & Ann Bass*, p. 15; SCRP, no. 3998.)

William Veasey (1616–1681)   Born in Gumley, England, Veasey arrived in Braintree by 1643. His inventory listed "a thousand of board" valued at £1.15 and £15.8 "due from several persons upon the sawmill account." (*Sources*: Sprague, *Genealogies of the Families of Braintree*; SCRP, no. 1182.)

Chart

Figure no. or object location	Stiles	Panels	Muntins	Width	Mortise chisel	Molding	Floor boards	Carving
Figure 9	$2^{15}/_{16}$"–$3^{1}/_{16}$"	8"–$8^{1}/_{8}$"	3"	$47^{1}/_{8}$"+	$^1/_{16}$" ?	round with quirks	does not apply	Group A
Figure 1	$3^{3}/_{8}$"	$8^{13}/_{16}$"–$8^{7}/_{8}$"	$3^{3}/_{8}$"	$52^{3}/_{16}$"	$^1/_{4}$"	round with quirks	riven, tongue and groove	Group B
Aetna Inc.	$3^{1}/_{4}$"	$8^{3}/_{4}$"	$3^{1}/_{2}$"	$52^{1}/_{4}$"	$^1/_{4}$"	round with quirks	riven, tongue and groove	Group B
Figure 22	3"	$8^{1}/_{2}$"–$8^{5}/_{8}$"	$3^{3}/_{4}$"	$51^{1}/_{2}$"	$^5/_{16}$"	round with quirks	riven, tongue and groove	Group B
Figure 21	$3^{1}/_{4}$"	$8^{1}/_{16}$"–$8^{1}/_{8}$"	$3^{1}/_{2}$"	$49^{3}/_{8}$"	$^5/_{16}$"	round with quirks	riven, tongue and groove	Group B
Figure 20	$3^{5}/_{16}$"	$8^{7}/_{16}$"–$8^{1}/_{2}$"	$3^{11}/_{16}$"–$3^{3}/_{4}$"	$51^{3}/_{4}$"	$^3/_{8}$"	plow with ogees	butted	Group C
Gardner Museum	$3^{5}/_{16}$"	$8^{5}/_{16}$"	$3^{7}/_{8}$"–$3^{15}/_{16}$"	$51^{9}/_{16}$"	$^3/_{8}$"	plow with ogees	tongue and groove	Group C
Wadsworth Atheneum	$3^{5}/_{16}$"–$3^{3}/_{8}$"	$8^{3}/_{4}$"	$3^{3}/_{8}$"	$51^{13}/_{16}$"	not measured	plow with ogees	butted	Group C
Private collection	$3^{5}/_{16}$"–$3^{3}/_{8}$"	$8^{5}/_{16}$"–$8^{7}/_{16}$"	$3^{13}/_{16}$"–$3^{7}/_{8}$"	$51^{5}/_{8}$"	not measured	plow with ogees	oak, tongue and groove replaced	Group C
Private collection	$3^{3}/_{16}$"–$3^{1}/_{4}$"	$8^{1}/_{2}$"–$8^{9}/_{16}$"	$3^{3}/_{16}$"–$3^{1}/_{4}$"	$50^{1}/_{4}$"	not measured	round with quirks	oak, butted	Group D

Jonathan Prown and
Richard Miller

The Rococo,
the Grotto, and
the Philadelphia
High Chest

▼ W H O   W I L L *not agree with Hawthorne's observation, that "After all,
the moderns have invented nothing better in chamber furniture than those chests
which stand on four slender legs, and send an absolute tower of mahogany to the
ceiling, the whole terminating in a fantastically carved ornament"?*

William Macpherson Horner, Jr.
Blue Book of Philadelphia Furniture

The pedimented and carved Philadelphia high chest of drawers (fig. 1) has
been long celebrated as an outstanding "rococo" furniture form. Although
this stylistic categorization is correct, the logic used to support it reveals a
fundamental misunderstanding of key rococo principles. First, the overall
form and visual weight of the Philadelphia high chest epitomize an earlier
baroque aesthetic (fig. 2). Furthermore, the classically inspired architectonic
facade is wholly antithetical to the more exuberant continental taste (fig. 3),
and the relative decorative restraint and symmetry of the carved ornamentation is only marginally rococo. The same stylistic anachronisms characterize other Philadelphia "rococo" forms. A slab table (fig. 4), recently
described as "one of the most imposing examples of Philadelphia rococo
furniture," displays a rhythmically undulating shape that unmistakably
reflects a baroque rather than a rococo tradition. Whereas the ornate carving on the legs is "raffled" in the rococo manner, it nevertheless is symmetrical and baroque in inspiration. In short, analyses of Philadelphia rococo
furniture overlook the original European rococo style, or *genre pittoresque,*
with its frenzied decoration and themes of surprise, subversion, deception,
and female sexuality. Guided instead by a connoisseurship that emphasizes
aesthetics and an adherence to Palladian ideals, conventional analyses inter-
pret Philadelphia rococo furniture and, in particular, the high chest in terms
of the *British* rococo—a highly politicized artistic style that replaced the
boisterous, feminized, and erotic character of the original French model
with a more sedate and masculine baroque or classical facade. As a result,
understanding of the Philadelphia high chest has been incomplete.[1]

To be sure, the architectonic character of the Philadelphia high chest
echoes the conspicuous classicism of the British rococo, which reflected
England's desire to emulate the model of Republican Rome. Many
Philadelphia high chests were produced by immigrant British cabinetmakers and carvers. These British parallels, however, represent only one part of
the Philadelphia high chest story. An analysis that moves outside of existing

Figure 1 High chest of drawers, Philadelphia, 1765–1775. Mahogany with yellow pine, tulip poplar, and white cedar. H. 99", W. 43½", D. 25". (Courtesy, Metropolitan Museum of Art, John Stewart Kennedy Fund, 1918.)

Figure 2 High chest of drawers, Philadelphia, 1740–1750. Walnut with cedar and gum. H. 96¼", W. 43", D. 23⅛". (Courtesy, Winterthur Museum.)

Figure 3 Bureau with cabinet, Germany, probably Dresden, ca. 1750. Kingwood; mother-of-pearl, ivory, brass, ormolu mounts. H. 107½", W. 50", D. 29⅛". (Courtesy, Victoria and Albert Museum.)

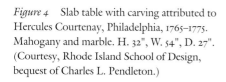

Figure 4 Slab table with carving attributed to Hercules Courtenay, Philadelphia, 1765–1775. Mahogany and marble. H. 32", W. 54", D. 27". (Courtesy, Rhode Island School of Design, bequest of Charles L. Pendleton.)

decorative arts standards reveals a hidden facet of the Philadelphia high chest that directly links it with the continental rococo.

This essay will consider the high chest's role as an active player in the remarkable cross-cultural drama called the continental or full rococo—a drama typically referred to as an eighteenth-century innovation, but which in fact, represents an amalgamation of many concepts rooted in antiquity, among them wild naturalism, overt sexuality, classical expression, and, most importantly, the richly symbolic grotto. By offering a new way of looking at the Philadelphia high chest, this paper reexamines and reinterprets the form's visual vocabulary, which exists not only to adorn but also to inform. Such an approach necessarily suspends the Apollonian ideal that is the foundation of the traditional decorative arts view and instead emphasizes the need to *think* rococo and to recognize the style's fantastic exploration of things Dionysian and mythological. It also emphasizes the power of metaphorical thought, a way of seeing and perceiving favored by classically educated rococo patrons but less familiar to modern observers, whose interest in the lessons of ancient mythology has given way to what Joseph Campbell calls the "news of the day" and "problems of the hour." In sum, this new reading of the Philadelphia high chest entails moving our critical gaze away from the abstract ideal of spiritual order and toward the earth itself, where we must conceptually enter the primordial ooze in search of the grotto, the very soul of the rococo.[2]

Just what is the rococo? Typically described as an innovative style in the arts, the rococo is firmly rooted in the Enlightenment. In *The Idea of Rococo,* William Park asserts that even though the rococo style did not blossom in all parts of eighteenth-century Europe, the beliefs that governed and nurtured the style were everywhere:

> However one regards history, the eighteenth century appears as the time of crisis, a time of extraordinary transformations, probably the most extraordinary that have ever taken place—feudal to bourgeois, classic to romantic, aristocratic to democratic, hierarchic to egalitarian, agricultural to industrial, religious to secular, from God the creator to man the creator.

The rococo was fueled by the cultural fission of the Enlightenment, an era characterized not only by its promotion of rational thought but also by the development of sociopolitical liberalism and the public articulation of unorthodox, hedonistic, and erotic forms of expression. For instance, the free thinking spirit of the Enlightenment promoted the progressive notion that nature is inherently good, which in turn inspired the rococo and its enthusiastic exploration of sexuality, desire, and pleasure. Rococo design is a spatial analogue of this "enlightened" way of thinking, and the style's fundamental spirit of inquiry, eroticism, and defiance is plainly expressed through its adoption of the S-scroll or serpentine line as a primary motif. The feminine and fluid S-scroll, sensually depicted in Jean-Honoré Fragonard's *Mme. Guimard* (fig. 5), is more than just a graceful gesture of asymmetry, more than just Hogarth's "line of beauty." The S-scroll opens the closed baroque C-scroll and effectively undermines the actual and implied architectonic strength of the earlier fashion. It is a brazen gesture that embodies

Figure 5 Jean-Honoré Fragonard, *Mme. Guimard*, Paris, 1769. Oil on canvas. (Courtesy, Louvre Museum, Cliché des Musées Nationaux, Paris; photo, Giraudon/Art Resource, New York.)

Figure 6 Francois Boucher, *Hercules and Omphale*, Paris, ca. 1731–1734. Oil on canvas. (Courtesy, Pushkin Fine Art Museum, Moscow; photo, Scala/Art Resource, New York.)

the fundamental rococo spirit so long neglected in traditional analyses and invariably hidden beneath a veil of aesthetic jargon.[3]

A diverse range of continental expressions embody the full rococo style. For instance, rococo mythological paintings overturn preceding baroque mythological traditions. Gone are the heroic, masculine gods who symbolized the glories of Louis XIV and the French monarchy, and in their place appear gods, goddesses, and fabled figures who better express essential rococo themes. Typical of this new mythology is Francois Boucher's *Hercules and Omphale* (fig. 6), which depicts a scene of great carnal intensity. In a disheveled bedchamber, the powerful Hercules passionately embraces Omphale, to whom he has been indentured for a year. Their uninhibited sexual activity, of a sort never so frankly expressed in classical texts, is all the more accentuated by the collapsing bed curtains and toppling gilt rococo table. Boucher's overt celebration of erotic love and sexuality epitomizes the way in which rococo interpretations of mythology subvert the orthodox didacticism of the baroque style.[4]

Perhaps even more expressive of key rococo themes are continental genre paintings. Fragonard's *The Swing* (fig. 7) depicts a young woman at the apex

Figure 7 Jean-Honoré Fragonard, *The Swing*, Paris, 1767. Oil on canvas. (Courtesy, Wallace Collection, London; photo, Art Resource, New York.)

of her arc, a position brought about by the efforts of a naive cleric who pulls the swing rope. The young male courtier, who lies on the ground below the swing, gazes upon the woman's unusually long, exposed legs. More provocatively, he also can see directly into the dark recesses of her pink, flowerlike dress, which serves as a direct allusion to her sexual anatomy. As Dore Ashton notes, the woman and her frilly dress in this rococo image represent a colorful and sexually suggestive opening reminiscent of Mallarmé's sensual reference to the "flower that is absent from all bouquets." Even the rake that lies in the foreground is sexually charged, referring to the French verb *ratisser*, "to rake," a common eighteenth-century euphemism for coitus and illicit behavior.[5]

The rococo's obvious allusions to female sexuality are revealed in other ways as well. Regarded as an interior decorative style, the rococo is associated with the increasing power of women as arbiters of taste. In eighteenth-century France—the ideological center of the rococo style—the self-aggrandizing vision of Louis XIV and his court yielded to the more delicate, provocative, and democratic artistic sensibilities of leading female tastemak-

Figure 8 Salon de la Princesse, Hotel de Soubise, Germain Boffrand, Paris, 1735. (Giraudon/Art Resource, New York.)

Figure 9 Castello, villa near Florence, Italy, grotto before 1550. (Courtesy, Dr. Naomi Miller.)

ers, most notably Madame de Pompadour and the Comtesse Du Barry, mistresses of Louis XV. The feminized nature of the full rococo also is revealed through the application of gendered terms such as "the shepherdess" to describe seating furniture forms, terms that are grammatically presented in the feminine voice. In fact, most of the words used by eighteenth-century and modern observers alike to describe the rococo style mirror those traditionally used to describe women. Examples include tender, delicate, soft, intimate, diminutive, erotic, playful, lighthearted, curvaceous, and pleasant, in addition to more obviously pejorative words such as frivolous, superficial, disordered, and dissolving. Even the basic formal motifs of the rococo refer to female sexuality and fertility. In the western cultural tradition, rocks, shells, and small woodland animals are invariably connected with "Mother Nature." Feminine associations also emerge in the frequent rococo references to water and the fecund seasons of spring and summer. All of these deliberately covert and carefully coded symbols were readily understood by literate eighteenth-century patrons. As Mary Sheriff suggests, "part of the pleasure taken in the [rococo] erotic symbol was the pleasure of deception; the beholders who decoded these images were pleased and amused because they could clearly perceive the sexual discourse hidden from innocent eyes."[6]

The feminized character of the rococo is perhaps most evident in its unwavering ideological allegiance to the grotto—indeed, the rococo style is the grotto style. The relationship between the grotto and the rococo is clearly seen in the fully developed rococo interior (fig. 8), which strives to emulate the wildly naturalistic interiors of garden grottoes (fig. 9). Rococo furniture, wallpaper, carpets, and other furnishings visually merge to create a unified, grotto vision. The rococo's ideological affiliation with the grotto is further evidenced by the very word "rococo," a pejorative term coined around the turn of the nineteenth century, well after the demise of the continental style. The word reflects the joining of two French nouns associated with the grotto: "rocaille," the rockwork found in caves and grottoes, and "coquillage," the shellwork used to adorn grotto walls, ceilings, and floors. As a primary source for rococo concepts and motifs, the grotto is essential to understanding the eighteenth-century continental style.[7]

More than just a cave or a hole in the ground, the grotto encompasses a wide range of emotional and intellectual experiences. Naomi Miller describes the grotto as the realm of endless contradictions, a place that, like the rococo style itself, is defined by an inherent lack of definition. The grotto provides shelter and protection, yet evokes mystery and fear. It is a site of contemplation and poetic inspiration, but also the arena of intellectual chaos; a sacred underground temple, but also the location of Bacchic orgies. Miller suggests that ultimately the grotto is best understood as "a metaphor of the cosmos," something that can be experienced but never fully understood. The grotto and, by extension, the rococo represent places where Apollonian ideas about morality confront primal Dionysian desires and where the rational, classical mind comes unraveled.[8]

Eighteenth-century allusions to the grotto are directly linked to the

Renaissance traditions of the grotesque. Inspired by the fifteenth-century unearthing of Nero's Golden Palace in Rome and a revived interest in the ancient caves along the Adriatic coast, artists and writers alike began to combine familiar Christian messages with the newly rediscovered and often controversial ancient motifs, including the grotto. During the fifteenth and sixteenth centuries, the grotto emerged as a popular literary theme, most notably in pastoral poetry. About the same time, classically-inspired humanist gardens were built with full-scale grottoes that ranged from wildly sensual places (fig. 10), resplendent with coquillage and evocative sculpture, to more architecturally classical spaces that nevertheless retained the same chaotic grotto themes. By the seventeenth century, nature was surpassed by both art and science in these man-made grottoes, with the addition of fantastic waterworks and fountains that played music. The essential concept of the grotto, however, transcends any single time, place, or artistic style. As a "metaphor of the cosmos," the grotto universally represents birth, sexuality, and death—themes intimately connected to the highly feminized rococo and, as we will suggest, to the Philadelphia high chest itself.[9]

The gendered character of the grotto derives from its basic form. Literally, the cave or grotto is shaped like a vagina. Both the grotto and female genitalia are traditionally depicted as sacred or secret places and sensually equated with darkness and dampness. European writers and artists, most of them men, have long alluded to the feminine and erotic aspects of the grotto. The lecherous Bacchus typically appears in a mythological grotto surrounded by a chaotic, orgiastic scene. In like manner, Ovid's erotic and poetical landscapes are filled with suggestive references to dripping grottoes; St. Augustine's submission to sexual temptation takes place in a grotto. Canto Four in Alexander Pope's widely read poem *Rape of the Lock* (1714), a classically inspired text that nevertheless reveals many characteristic rococo attributes, describes the libidinous Cave of Spleen. Evocative grotto themes were also apparent to the amorously minded Thomas Jefferson, who in the months leading up to his marriage was inspired to design a hillside grotto at Monticello. John Keats's romantic poem *La Belle Dame Sans Merci*, written in 1819, explicitly details the human sex act through metaphorical descriptions of male and female genitalia: the former described as a "pacing steed," and the latter as an "elfin grot." Procreative implications of the grotto include its depiction as the orifice of Mother Earth, and the act of entering the grotto is commonly equated with entering a womb. The Bible not only refers to the Grotto of the Nativity but also to other grottoes from which the earth, firmament, plants, and animals were spawned. As Miller explains, the grotto frequently is characterized as "a generative organ, the archetype of the maternal and the site of a mystery."[10]

At the same time, the grotto and the female genitalia it metaphorically represents are associated with death or consumption. For example, the mythological Grotto of Ephesus tests the chastity of young women. If the woman who enters the grotto is not chaste, discordant sounds are heard, and she disappears, consumed by the grotto. But if musical sounds emerge, the young woman is a true virgin and escapes unharmed; in a sense, she is

Figure 10   La Bastie d'Urfé, Forez, Italy, grotto 1551. (Courtesy, Dr. Naomi Miller.)

Figure 11   Sacra Bosco, Bormazo, Italy, ca. 1550–1570. (Courtesy, G. Putnam and Co., New York.)

Figure 12   Jean Mondon, *Le Galand Chasseur*, Paris, 1736. Engraving on paper. (Courtesy, Metropolitan Museum of Art, Harry Brisbane Dick Fund, 1930.)

born again. Such characterizations of the grotto as a place of both creation and destruction reflect the ancient concept of the *vagina dentata* or "toothed vagina." Rooted in the Greek idea of *lamiae*—lustful she-demons whose name meant both mouth and vagina—the *vagina dentata* embodies an ancient notion that the soul resides in both the mouth and the genitals. Several Renaissance grottoes literally depict the *vagina dentata*. The gaping, ogre-like figure (fig. 11) that guards the Sacra Bosco in Italy is a visual archetype of the *vagina dentata*; the Sacra Bosco also was called the Gate of Hell or Mouth of Hell, widely understood allegories for female genitalia. The sexual, procreative, and consumptive character of the grotto reveal it to be a highly gendered concept that is explicitly linked to the rococo.[11]

The connection between the grotto and the rococo is clearly revealed in Jean Mondon's 1736 engraving *Le Galand Chasseur,* or *The Gallant Hunter* (fig. 12). A young woman sits next to a kneeling young hunter; her right hand suggestively grasps the barrel of the hunter's rifle. At her feet lie the rewards of the hunt. The dog symbolizes the young man's loyalty and amorous desire and may also refer to Circe, the sorceress in Homer's *Odyssey* who had the power to tame men by turning them into subservient beasts.

Figure 14   Center ornament from
a high chest of drawers,
Philadelphia, 1760–1768.
Mahogany. H. 11³/8". (Courtesy,
Philadelphia Museum of Art.)

Figure 13   Gottlieb Leberecht Crusius, *Capriccio*,
Germany, 1762. (Courtesy, Staatliche Museen
Preussischer Kulturbesitz, Kunstbibliothek,
Berlin; photo, Marburg/Art Resource, New
York.)

The hunter has one arm around the woman's back, while the other points
provocatively toward her lap, where in typical rococo fashion the light is
most highly focused. Rather than dismiss his advances, the smiling woman
also points to her lap. The overt sexual character of the image is further pro-
claimed by the grotto entrance above, which literally and figuratively alludes
to the young woman. Bordered with excitedly raffled edges and emitting a
torrent of water, this motif is unmistakably vaginal in character. A manifestation of midwife Jane Sharp's 1671 description of female genitalia as "the
wellspring," this grotto entrance doubly functions as a sexual metaphor for
the hunter's impending conquest of the young woman and her ability to
render the man subordinate. The overt eroticism, surprise, and female sexuality of Mondon's illustration make it a visual manifesto of the rococo
style. Its vibrancy and sensuality is all the more pronounced when con-
trasted with the depictions of dying nature and sexual impotency that
emerged on the continent in the 1760s and 1770s, signaling the end of the
rococo style. A notable example is Gottlieb Crusius's engraving of a vacant,
womblike, weed-covered grotto entrance, fronted with a flaccid phallus
(fig. 13).[12]

The grotto entrance in Mondon's engraving unmistakably reveals the
original rococo meaning of the asymmetrical cartouche, perhaps the most
widely recognized rococo motif and one that appears with great frequency
on Philadelphia high chests (fig. 14). Stylistically, the rococo cartouche
echoes seventeenth-century auricular cartouches, many of which are either
graphically anatomical (fig. 15) or directly related to the *vagina dentata* (fig.
16). For example, a Dutch *tazza* or cup (fig. 17) in the auricular style is distinguished not only by its sexually suggestive, cartouche-shaped bowl but
also by the actively disrobing lovers who sit on the rim. The word cartouche

itself is rooted in the Italian word *cartello* or "little card," which in turn implies that a cartouche literally sends a message. The message that emanates from the cartouche atop a Philadelphia high chest has nothing to do with peanuts, kidney beans, cabochons, or any of the other conventional decorative arts descriptions of the motif; rather, the rococo cartouche is a stylized grotto entrance, which serves as a metaphorical portal leading to an entirely new understanding of the style. Like the biblical serpent who tempted Adam, this seductive opening beckons the viewer to partake of the mysterious pleasures and wonders within (fig. 18). As Miller explains, "to enter [the grotto] is the significant act; for to enter is to acknowledge the distance between outside and inside, between reality and illusion, between nature and art." The high chest cartouche attracts the viewer toward a place where conventional notions about order and morality give way to a series of chaotic dualisms that are intimately linked to the rococo: good (God)

Figure 15 Jacobus Lutma, *Festivities* (from a twelve-part series), Holland, 1654. Illustrated in Rudolph Berliner and Gerhart Egger, *Ornamentale Vorlagebläter* (Munich: Klinkhardt & Biermann, 1981), fig. 1006.

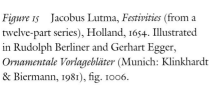

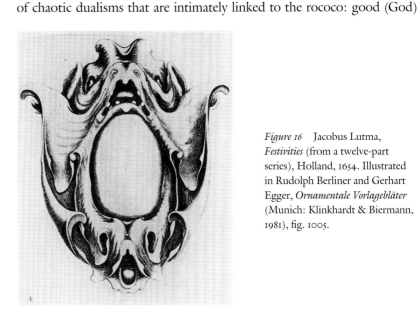

Figure 16 Jacobus Lutma, *Festivities* (from a twelve-part series), Holland, 1654. Illustrated in Rudolph Berliner and Gerhart Egger, *Ornamentale Vorlagebläter* (Munich: Klinkhardt & Biermann, 1981), fig. 1005.

Figure 17 Adam van Vianen, tazza, Utrecht, 1618. Silver. (Courtesy, Rijksmuseum, Amsterdam.)

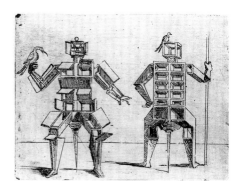

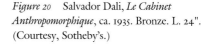

versus evil (Devil), sacred versus profane, order versus chaos, classical versus aclassical, symmetry versus asymmetry, beauty versus the sublime, Apollonian versus Dionysian, contemplation versus disorientation, comfort versus fear, and ultimately, male versus female. These dualisms—which arouse both fear and curiosity and create perceptual as well as emotional chaos—embody the fundamental appeal of the rococo style. E. H. Gombrich suggests that human delight is found on the edge of confusion, where certain truths are revealed that otherwise may not be reached by conscious effort. The radical asymmetry and grotto themes of the rococo create the same delightful confusion, and so, too, does the Philadelphia high chest of drawers.[13]

The complex, grotto-inspired character of the Philadelphia rococo high chest emerges most clearly when the form is analyzed in anthropomorphic terms. Although this strategy may appear unusual, the words used to describe the high chest suggest otherwise. The furniture term "chest" itself implies a connection to the human chest because both can be read as receptacles of essential human belongings: the human chest holds vital organs, whereas the high chest holds vital material possessions such as clothes, jewelry, and private papers. One eighteenth-century Virginia inventory meticulously details the use of the family high chest for the storage of children's clothing. In this context, the high chest acts as a sort of nurturer or surro-

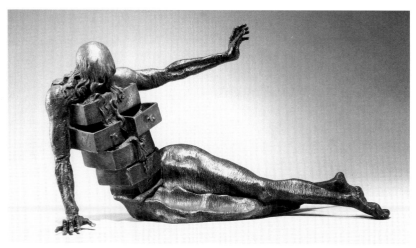

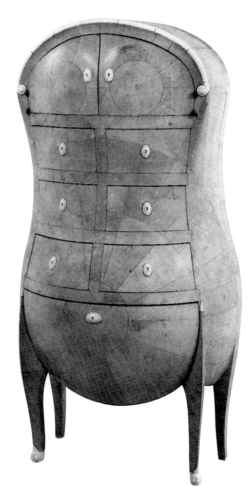

Figure 21 André Groult, high chest of drawers, Paris, ca. 1935. H. 59", W. 27⁷/₁₆", D. 12⁷/₁₆". (Courtesy, Claude Boisgirard Auctioneer.)

gate mother who provides essential family needs, a role also described by Gaston Bachelard. He noted that chests, with their diverse and ordered storage compartments, are "veritable organs of the secret psychological life" and that without them "our intimate life would lack a model of intimacy." Other literal associations between the human form and tall chests of drawers include the innovative, early seventeenth-century drawings of Braccelli (fig. 19), as well as recent designs such as Salvador Dali's *Le Cabinet anthropomorphique* (fig. 20) and a conspicuously feminized, early twentieth-century French high chest (fig. 21). Furthermore, eighteenth-century references to Philadelphia high chests, including the 1786 price list of cabinetmaker Benjamin Lehman, regularly employ anthropomorphic terms, among them "head," "knees," and "feet." Modern analysts have added "toes," "waist," and "back," as well as human-related terms like "skirt," "apron," and "bonnet." In short, basic terminology and related figurative associations directly link the high chest to the human body.[14]

To be sure, this anthropomorphic reading of the rococo high chest radically diverges from traditional analyses and, as suggested at the start of this essay, demands a renewed appreciation for the power of metaphorical thought—the very key to understanding the rococo. The ability to think and see metaphorically characterizes most preindustrial cultures but is largely suppressed in modern society. Even highly rational and enlightened

Figure 22 High chest of drawers, Philadelphia, 1765–1775. Mahogany and mahogany veneer with yellow pine, tulip poplar, and white cedar. H. 97³/₄", W. 42¹/₄", D. 25¹/₂". (Courtesy, Metropolitan Museum of Art, John Stewart Kennedy Fund.)

Figure 23 Berea Masonic Lodge No. 114, A.F. & A.M., Gloucester, Virginia, ca. 1950.

eighteenth-century culture, with all of its scientific and intellectual advancements, resounded with metaphorical thought. Birthing and mourning traditions, shared activities like dining and dancing, and private activities like bathing and sex all mirrored ancient ritualistic customs. The children of affluent eighteenth-century Europeans and Americans, for example, wore coral necklaces, not only for decorative purposes but also to keep alive an older way of warding off evil and "fascination." The Philadelphia high chest similarly reflects an older way of seeing and perceiving. Some of its visual metaphors are easily read, whereas others are more elusive. Jules Prown suggests that the most obvious design elements on objects generally represent ideas so widely understood by makers and patrons that they are never fully explained. Less conspicuous design elements, however, often represent ideas that are not fully understood and that have been consciously or subconsciously repressed. An anthropomorphic reading of the high chest and a consideration of its subtle decorative motifs reveal an equally complex conceptual framework and further indicate the form's fundamental rococo character. [15]

Consider a typical Philadelphia high chest (fig. 22) viewed from a distance of fifteen or twenty feet. From this perspective, the distinctive carved ornamentation starts to become secondary to the overall form; the high chest seems to lose much of its rococo character. In traditional terms, what remains is a baroque case. Something else appears as well, however. From the front, the appearance and stance of the high chest is quite human. Like us, the high chest can be seen as a bilaterally symmetrical biped with attenuated legs. The upper section of the form is reminiscent of a torso, which is demarcated from the lower section by a clearly defined waist. At the top are elements that suggest a head, with the scrolled pediment resembling rounded shoulders or flowing hair. Admittedly, these are visual parallels of the simplest sort, and similar human attributes appear on other artifacts, such as a mid-twentieth-century Virginia building (fig. 23) with a facelike facade; however, the highly symbolic and rococo character of the high chest is revealed in many other ways as well.

Figure 24 Detail of the carving on a high chest of drawers, Philadelphia, 1765–1775. (Chipstone Foundation; photo, Gavin Ashworth.)

Figure 25 Detail of the carving on a high chest of drawers, Philadelphia, 1763–1768. (Courtesy, Yale University Art Gallery, Mabel Brady Garvan Collection.)

Figure 26 Detail of the carving on a dressing table, Philadelphia, 1750–1760. (Courtesy, Art Institute of Chicago, gift of the Antiquarian Society through the Jessie Spalding Landon Fund.)

Echoing the ancient concept that the soul resides in the mouth and genitals, the carved decoration on the Philadelphia high chest is concentrated at the top and bottom, or in the head and groin. This carefully placed carving consists of flowers, shells, and foliage, all of which are common visual metaphors for sex, sexuality, and fecundity. Although some high chests have clearly delineated flowers and shells (fig. 24), many others have carved

Figure 27 Georgia O'Keeffe, *Jack-in-the-Pulpit, No. IV*, 1930. Oil on canvas. (Courtesy, National Gallery of Art, Washington, Alfred Stieglitz Collection, bequest of Georgia O'Keffe.)

shells that are so raffled they are virtually indistinguishable from a flower (fig. 25). Like the enticing pink dress in Fragonard's *The Swing,* high chest carving expresses visually and thematically the overt sexuality of the rococo style. The carved foliage on one Philadelphia dressing table (fig. 26), a form sold en suite with a matching high chest, is unmistakably vaginal in character—reminiscent not only of seventeenth-century auricular cartouches and Mondon's dripping grotto entrance but also of more recent interpretations, like Georgia O'Keeffe's sensual paintings of flowers (fig. 27). Both in placement and concept, the central floral motif on Philadelphia high chests emphatically announces the key rococo themes of eroticism and female sexuality.[16]

Just as symbolically charged are the carefully placed shells, which in true rococo fashion are often depicted from both the front and rear (fig. 28). This reversal simultaneously invites and excludes, reveals and conceals, and perfectly mirrors Boucher's evocative front and rear juxtaposition of the two figures in his 1759 study, *Two Nudes* (fig. 29). Procreative and sexual allusions

Figure 28 High chest by Henry Clifton and Thomas Carteret (cabinetmakers), Philadelphia, 1753. Mahogany with yellow pine, tulip poplar, and white cedar. H. 96", W. 45", D. 22½". (Courtesy, Colonial Williamsburg Foundation.)

for the shell begin with the fact that many sea creatures gestate and live in shells. In western cultural traditions, the shell is associated with birth and fecundity, and its womblike quality is characterized in Bachelard's observation that "an empty shell, like an empty nest, invites daydreams of refuge." Furthermore, the mythological goddess Venus first emerged from a large shell, and her dolphin-driven chariot is in the form of a shell. As both the Goddess of Love and the Goddess of Lust, Venus epitomizes the essential rococo/grotto dualism between the Apollonian and Dionysian; she repre-

Figure 29 Francois Boucher, *Two Nudes*, Paris, ca. 1759. Black chalk drawing on paper. (Private collection; photo, courtesy Colin Bailey.)

Figure 30 Jean-Honoré Fragonard, *Storming the Citadel*, Paris, ca. 1771–1773. (Courtesy, Frick Collection, New York.)

sents higher and more heavenly forms of love, but also baser and more earth-bound forms of sexuality. Long connected both with grottoes and erotic themes, the sexually assured Venus (fig. 30) is a primary rococo persona. Eighteenth-century terms like "delights of Venus," "feast of Venus," and "dance of Venus" were widely understood euphemisms for sex and sexuality. The highly influential early eighteenth-century Swedish taxonomist Carolus Linnaeus, in addition to cataloging flowers and plants in terms of human anatomy and sexual behavior, described clams—one of which he named the *Venus Diane*—in terms of female anatomy, from the internal "labia" and "vulva" to the adjacent "buttocks" and "anus." A similar approach was taken by the French scientist Robinet, who graphically described the conch of Venus in terms of a woman's vulva. Such evidence suggests that the owners of a carved, Philadelphia high chest not only confronted an anthropomorphic furniture form covered with a wide array of sensual visual metaphors but also perhaps engaged either consciously or subconsciously in an erotic tryst with Venus herself.[17]

The rococo character of the Philadelphia high chest is further revealed through its mixed sexual messages. Though most of the motifs on the high chest relate to the female body or to feminized themes, the massive size and imposing stance reflect classical and masculine attributes, which more often are associated with the forceful scale of baroque architecture and are invariably linked to British and American rococo furniture. Yet this contrast is perfectly in keeping with the playful spirit of the rococo. Even the rococo S-scroll alludes to both masculine and feminine ideals. The mid-eighteenth-century English artist and satirist William Hogarth illustrates women's corsets and the Medici *Venus* to suggest the perfect S-scroll, but he also depicts the male calf muscle and the Farnese *Hercules* for the same purpose (fig. 31). Equally complex are rococo dances that begin with the men pursuing the women, only to reverse these roles. These dances are decidedly rococo with their wildly asymmetrical Z-shaped or S-shaped step patterns. Gender ambiguity even characterizes the letters that Philadelphia merchants wrote to one another during the late colonial period. In describing their business losses and vulnerability to risk in a credit economy, these merchants conspicuously adopted a feminine persona and spoke in feminized language. The dual sexual personae of the high chest, like eighteenth-century dances or the discourse between colonial merchants, is surprising, deceptive, subversive, and, in the end, quintessentially rococo.[18]

Figure 31   William Hogarth, *Analysis of Beauty, Plate I*, London, 1753; reissued, ca. 1835 by James Heath. (Courtesy, Colonial Williamsburg Foundation.)

Admittedly, no concrete evidence has surfaced to prove that educated rococo patrons looked at the carved flowers, shells, and foliage on high chests and directly associated them with the wild themes of the rococo. On the other hand, patrons in Philadelphia or any other western cultural center did not encounter rococo objects and ideas in a void. Europeans and Americans alike participated in a *rococo culture,* and essential rococo themes resounded not only in the arts but also in Enlightenment literature, science, and philosophy. Texts from Pope's *Rape of the Lock* (1714) to John Cleland's *Fanny Hill: Memoirs of a Woman of Pleasure* (1748) and Henry Fielding's *Tom Jones* (1769) were openly erotic and explored the rococo concepts of reversal and transformation. The same is true of Samuel Richardson's *Pamela* (1741) and *Clarissa* (1748), the former being the first novel published in America, printed in Philadelphia by Benjamin Franklin. The novel, a new and distinctively rococo literary form, provocatively explored libidinous themes within a domestic framework and frequently criticized the aristocracy and traditions of the royal court. In Great Britian, where the anti-monarchical Whigs were the most ardent supporters of the rococo, the novel, with its thematic focus on reversal and transformation, was played out in repeated thrusts for liberty—not only sexual liberty but also social and political liberty. In fact, the political rather than the sensual character of the rococo appears to have been the style's primary appeal in Great Britain. Ironically, the political character of the rococo might also have been paramount in America, a liberty-seeking colony that was acutely aware of the increasing political and psychic distance between it and British governmental policy.[19]

Eighteenth-century patrons also were steadily reminded of key rococo concepts through their knowledge of classical mythology. Ovid's *Metamorphoses* and works by Horace, Juvenal, and Lucretius revealed fundamental thematic linkages to the rococo; so, too, did the widely popular and overtly sexual poems attributed to the fourth-century Gaelic warrior Ossian. During the eighteenth century, a familiarity with mythology was more than just an integral part of daily intellectual life. As Jean Starobinski argues, it was "a condition of cultural literacy, essential if one wanted to enter in those conversations in which every educated man would sooner or later be invited to participate." Certainly this condition was true in eighteenth-century Philadelphia, where Benjamin Franklin and other influential social leaders extolled the virtues of classical mythology and where surviving inventories of personal libraries and retail book vendors document the local interest in classical learning. A small number of Philadelphians— mostly orthodox Quakers—denounced the classics, whose questionable characters and themes were "shocking to every system of Morality." Even so, supporters and opponents alike recognized the ideological parallels between classical mythology and the grotto-inspired rococo.[20]

One of the most widely recognized examples of Philadelphia furniture with a carved mythological panel is the "Madame Pompadour" high chest (fig. 32), so named because of the carved female bust that surmounts the pediment. From an anthropomorphic standpoint alone the presence of a

Figure 32 High chest of drawers, Philadelphia, 1765–1775. Mahogany and mahogany veneer with yellow pine, tulip poplar, and white cedar. H. 91³/₄″, W. 44⁵/₈″, D. 24⁵/₈″. (Courtesy, Metropolitan Museum of Art, John Stewart Kennedy Fund, 1918.)

woman's head at the top of a high chest is highly meaningful and thoroughly in keeping with the rococo spirit of the form. Equally significant is the suggestively placed hole on the center of the skirt, a gesture that brings to mind the sexual character of the grotto entrance, the asymmetrical car-

Figure 33 Detail of the carving on the lower drawer of the high chest illustrated in fig. 32.

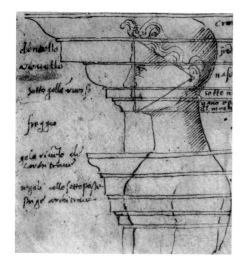

Figure 34 Francesco di Giorgio Martini, *Trattati di archittetura ingegneria e arte militare,* Italy, sixteenth century. (Courtesy, Beineke Rare Book and Manuscript Library, Yale University.)

touche, and other female-associated rococo motifs. The carved image of two swans on the bottom drawer (fig. 33), inspired by a chimneypiece design in Thomas Johnson's *A New Book of Ornaments* (London, 1762), may relate to the mythological love story of Leda and Jupiter, or more likely to the common depiction of paired swans as an allegory of love. Here again, the traditions of classical mythology are linked to essential rococo themes.[21]

Classically educated Philadelphians also had a heightened understanding of the high chest's architectural features, which reveal additional rococo themes. Although commonly associated with rationality, order, logic, and mathematical precision, classical architecture is rooted in traditions that are decidedly non-rational and imperfect. In *The Lost Meaning of Classical Architecture,* George Hersey describes the forgotten origins of classical architecture and, while doing so, uncovers much about the lost rococo character of the Philadelphia high chest. Hersey fundamentally questions why modern western cultures continue to use classical designs and concepts:

> Why do architects erect columns and temple fronts derived ultimately from ancient Greek temples, when ancient Greek religion has been dead for centuries, when the temples themselves were not even buildings in the sense that they housed human activities, and when the way of life they expressed is extinct?

One answer is that classical architecture survives because its basic precepts remain intact. Knowingly or unknowingly, allusions to classical architecture keep alive ancient ways of seeing and perceiving. A latter-day interpretation of these ancient motifs, the Philadelphia high chest is specifically based upon the classical column. Both the high chest and the classical column are vertically oriented, tripartite compositions. The column has a base, shaft, and capital; the high chest has legs, a main case, and a pediment. The typical dimensions of a Philadelphia high chest reveal a strong understanding of classical systems of proportion. Most importantly, both the high chest and the classical column are literally connected to the human form (fig. 34) and metaphorically tied to basic rococo themes.[22]

Hersey unveils the lost rococo meaning of the classically inspired high chest through his consideration of original Greek architectural terms, many of which must be understood as tropes, or words used in a figurative sense.

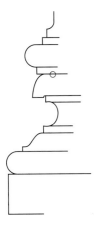

Figure 35 Drawing based on a sketch for a pilaster base in the Medici Chapel by Michelangelo, Florence, Italy, 1519–1534. Original sketch at Casa Buonarroti, Florence.

Figure 36 Hughes Sambin, female term from *Oeuvre de la Diversité des Termes,* 1572. (Courtesy, Beineke Rare Book and Manuscript Library, Yale Univeristy.)

An example is the Greek word for *foliage*, which alludes not only to leafage but also to hair, specifically to the coils of hair used in sacrificial offerings. Revealingly, the foliage on the body of the Philadelphia high chest is most highly concentrated in what can be seen as the head and groin (see figs. 24–26). Other descriptive terms for specific parts on classical columns reveal additional human connections. The Greek word for the column *base* means both foot and footwork, the latter a reference to the dances performed at sacrificial rituals; *cavetto* and *torus* moldings on the bases of columns allude to the ropes that bound the feet of sacrificial victims; *flutes* signify both the bunched shafts traditionally gathered by the victorious warrior and the folds in a Grecian sacrificial gown; *capital* represents the Greek word for head, whereas *volutes* allude to both hair and sacrificial horns; *dentils* come from the word for teeth and recall the ornaments on sacrificial trees. The deep, shadow moldings on the bases of columns are called *scotia*—the Greek goddess of darkness and the underworld—and symbolize the ancient concept of darkness or shadow as not just the absence of light but as "a vapor that was dark because it was dense with the tiny mote-like souls of the dead" (fig. 35). Finally, the swelling of the classical column shaft is called *entasis*, a Greek word that means tension or straining and alludes to the essential human and sacrificial themes of the column (fig. 36). The highly symbolic meanings of these ancient motifs survived into the eighteenth century through the study of Greek and Latin, through the reading of classical mythology, and through the strong influence of architectural treatises by Vitruvius and others who recounted the origins of the classical orders. Because rococo patrons thought in metaphorical and mythological terms, they necessarily regarded the column as more than just a type of building support. Instead, the symbolic nature of the classical column and, by extension, the classically inspired Philadelphia high chest paralleled perceptions about the grotto and the rococo.[23]

In sum, a wide range of literal and metaphorical evidence strongly suggests that the Philadelphia high chest is more than just a stylish, eighteenth-century case furniture form. Instead, the high chest can be seen as an active rococo player whose essential rococo character is revealed through its overt sexuality, its blurred gender signals, its evocative classical allusions, and its expressed liberty from baroque, Apollonian, masculine ideals. Even the larger-than-life scale of the otherwise feminized Philadelphia high chest is perfectly in keeping with rococo ideology. Early critics of the rococo regularly denounced the style's perversion of realistic proportions. They were offended, for example, that an ornate rococo tureen might have an accurately sized insect next to a lobster or rabbit of identical size. As with the nonhuman scale of the high chest, however, this type of variation epitomizes the subversive and contradictory spirit of the rococo. An identical strategy appears in Jonathan Swift's novel *Gulliver's Travels* (1726), a fully developed rococo text that manipulates the existing world order by contrasting the giant with the minuscule. As with Swift's Brobdingnagian giants, the otherwise human-looking Philadelphia high chest similarly distorts reality and expresses the form's inherent rococo nature. Like the Renaissance

grotesque style from which it emerged, this rococo expression suspends conventional western patterns of belief and order and instead exists as a visual and emotional experience unburdened by dogma.[24]

Whether this alternative reading of the Philadelphia high chest expands our understanding of other American furniture forms remains to be seen. Do the provocatively placed open hearts on Delaware Valley high chests (fig. 37), for instance, suggest a parallel type of gendered object? Or do the diverse skirt designs on New England high chests indicate both male (fig. 38) and female (fig. 39) attributes? The broader understanding of rococo ideology presented in this essay additionally points toward alternative ways of reading other kinds of eighteenth-century artifacts, including some not currently thought of as rococo. Among these is Charles Willson Peale's painting of Nancy Hallam, which depicts the actress performing a

Figure 38 High chest of drawers, New England, ca. 1750. (Courtesy, Israel Sack, Inc., New York.)

scene from Shakespeare's *Cymbeline* (fig. 40). Hallam is situated in front of a grotto entrance, dressed like a man to fool an unwanted courtier. Peale's direct grotto allusion as well as his thematic focus on deception, surprise, and maybe even eroticism suggest a conscious attempt to paint in a rococo style, a designation rarely applied to eighteenth-century American painters but perhaps appropriate for Peale, William Williams, John Singleton Copley, and others. These and many other avenues of research remain open, but

Figure 39 High chest of drawers, Preston area of Connecticut, 1770–1790. Cherry, birch, and maple with yellow poplar, chestnut, white pine, and oak. H. 82³/₄", W. 39", D. 19⁷/₈". (Courtesy, Yale University Art Gallery, Mabel Brady Garvan Collection.)

the anthropomorphic characteristics of the Philadelphia high chest *explicitly* reflect mythological, metaphorical, and cultural conditions.[25]

This essay has followed an unconventional path. Ultimately, it agrees with the traditional rococo categorization of the Philadelphia high chest, but for very different reasons. The primary difference lies in a reading of the rococo as an amalgamation of deeply rooted human concepts and as a formal and thematic expression intimately linked to earlier ways of seeing and

Figure 40 Charles Willson Peale, *Nancy Hallam in Cave Scene from Cymbaline*, Annapolis, Maryland, 1771. Oil on canvas. 50" × 40¹/₄". (Courtesy, Colonial Williamsburg Foundation.)

perceiving. More than a frivolous style centered around lighthearted eroticism, and more than an ephemeral stylistic whim, the rococo represents an important manifestation of enlightened eighteenth-century thought. The rococo themes that resonate from the Philadelphia high chest may shock our post-Victorian sensibilities and our carefully crafted understanding of colonial life, which remain the ideological foundation of traditional analyses of American rococo furniture; but these themes are readily comprehensible when considered in an eighteenth-century cultural context. There, the Philadelphia high chest emerges as a mythic rococo figure—one directly connected to the ancient idea of the grotto and to the traditions of classical mythology. Much as rococo paintings communicate the innate character rather than the literal appearance of a given subject, the high chest clearly expresses its own rococo character.[26]

In the end, the symbolic importance of the high chest remains as vital today as it was two centuries ago. Joseph Campbell reminds us that modern culture retains virtually all of the essential myths and concepts of the past, and that ancient ways continue to "line the walls of our interior system of belief like shards of broken pottery in an archaeological site." The

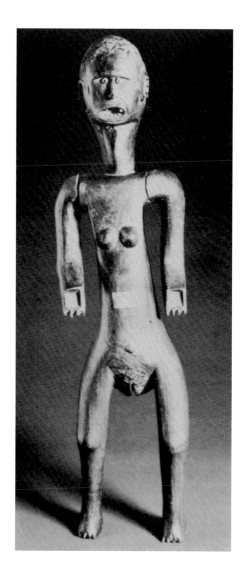

Figure 41 Female figure, central Tanzania, ca. 1900. (Courtesy, Sotheby's).

Philadelphia high chest is one such "shard" that connects past to present and that suggests surprising parallels to other, seemingly unrelated cultural expressions (fig. 41). Certainly, the high chest has yet to reveal all of her innate mysteries.[27]

ACKNOWLEDGMENTS The authors are indebted to Susan Shames and the staff at the Colonial Williamsburg Foundation Library, to the staff at the Bryn Mawr University Library, and to Jim Green of the Library Company of Philadelphia for their generous research assistance. Similar research help was provided by Martha Halpern and Jack Lindsey of the Philadelphia Museum of Art, and by Luke Beckerdite of the Chipstone Foundation. Thanks also to the curatorial staff at the Colonial Williamsburg Foundation for their suggestions and to Albert Sack, Colin Bailey, and Naomi Miller for providing photographs. This essay was read by William Park of Sarah Lawrence College, George Hersey of Yale University, Barbara Carson of the College of William & Mary, Robert Blair St. George of the University of Pennsylvania, Graham S. Hood of Colonial Williamsburg, and Jules D. Prown of Yale University. Their thoughtful suggestions are deeply appreciated. Finally, our deepest gratitude goes to Katherine Hemple Prown of the College of William & Mary, whose technical and intellectual contributions to this work are immeasurable.

1. Though often thought of as a creation of the Victorian period, the term highboy, along with tall boy, can be documented in an eighteenth-century British context, most often in reference to a tall chest of drawers. The term's use in America, and in particular in Philadelphia, is not recorded. For insight into the possible cultural and phrenological significance of the terms "highboy" and "lowboy," see Lawrence W. Levine, *Highbrow/Lowbrow: The Emergence of Cultural Hierarchy in America* (Cambridge: Harvard University Press, 1988). The foliated carving that adorns the tympana and drawers on many Philadelphia high chests is often associated with a rococo sense of delicacy and flow; however, this type of ornamentation is usually symmetrical and mirrors sixteenth- and seventeenth-century published designs. For examples, see Rudolf Berliner and Gerhart Egger, *Ornamentale Vorlageblätter: Des 15. Bis. 19 Jahrhunderts* (Leipzig: Klinkardt & Bierman, 1926). Morrison Heckscher and Leslie Greene Bowman, *American Rococo: Elegance in Ornament, 1750–1775* (New York: Harry N. Abrams, 1992), pp. 191–93, fig. 129. Another well-known Philadelphia slab table (Metropolitan Museum of Art) is more in line with conventional continental rococo expression. Its rococo character is also revealed in the central carved figure on the skirt, a figure recently described by Heckscher and Bowman as a "plump-cheeked girl, indefinably oriental in character" (Heckscher and Bowman, *American Rococo,* p. 192). Though the unacknowledged prototype for the girl holding a bird, found on a pier glass design in the 1st edition of Thomas Chippendale's *The Furniture and Cabinet Maker's Director* (pl. 146), does appear to be Oriental, the Philadelphia interpretation clearly depicts a Caucasian. Moreover, she is dressed in common mid-eighteenth-century theatrical garb, which this essay will argue is more in keeping with the prominent rococo use of costume as a means of attaining role reversal, deception, and surprise. Although some British objects directly reflect the continental rococo style, the vast majority reflect the tempered British taste.

2. John Dixon Hunt, *Garden and Grove, The Italian Renaissance Garden in the English Imagination: 1600–1750* (Princeton, N.J.: Princeton University Press, 1986), pp. 182–83. For example, Thomas Chippendale's *The Gentleman and Cabinetmaker's Director* (London, 1754), long considered a "rococo" design book, is centered around a knowledge of the ideals of classical architecture. Chippendale largely ignored the meaning of the continental rococo style. After about 1730 the high chest was out of fashion in London. Joseph Campbell with Bill Moyers, *The Power of Myth* (New York: Doubleday, 1988), pp. 3–5.

3. William Park, *The Idea of Rococo* (Newark: University of Delaware Press, 1992), pp. 11–13, 19. Paul-Gabriel Boucé, *Sexuality in Eighteenth-Century England* (Manchester, Eng.: Manchester University Press, 1982), p. 6.

4. Park, *Idea of Rococo,* p. 19. Colin Bailey, *Loves of the Gods: Mythic Painting From Watteau to David* (New York: Rizzoli, 1992), pp. 372–76.

5. For a full analysis of the metaphorical themes of *The Swing,* see Donald Posner, "The Swinging Women of Watteau and Fragonard," *Art Bulletin* (March 1982): 75–88. Dore Ashton, *Fragonard in the Universe of Painting* (Washington and London: Smithsonian Institution Press, 1988), p. 15. Mary D. Sheriff, *Fragonard: Art and Eroticism* (Chicago: University Press of Chicago, 1990), p. 109. This suggests alternative meanings for the English word "rake," for example as used by William Hogarth in his widely distributed series of engravings titled *The Rake's Progress.*

6. Witold Rybczynski, *Home: A Short History of an Idea* (New York: Penguin Books, 1987), pp. 94–95. There are few rococo buildings, and those that exist are in Europe; see Park, *Idea of Rococo,* pp. 32, 52–55. Witold Rybczynski suggests that a crucial difference exists between French and British rococo interior style, namely that the latter was aimed at "gentlemen." British cabinetmakers took it for granted that women would have no interest in furniture and furnishings, and the increasing role of women as arbiters of taste and decoration in Great Britain only began to emerge toward the end of the rococo period; see Rybczynski, *Home,* pp. 116–17. Sheriff, *Fragonard,* pp. 27–29, 107. Sheriff notes a symposium on this topic, "Social Implications of the Rococo Style: Images of Women," held at the University of Missouri, October 1987.

7. Rybczynski, *Home,* pp. 92-95. C. T. Carr, "Two Words in Art History: II. *Rococo,*" *Forum for Modern Language Studies* 1, (1965): 267. Michael Snodin, ed., *Rococo: Art and Design in Hogarth's England* (London: Trefoil Books, 1984), p. 27. Heckscher and Bowman, *American Rococo,* p. 1.

8. For the purposes of this article, the term grotto will be used exclusively, although throughout western literature the word "cave" has been used interchangeably. Naomi Miller,

Heavenly Caves: Reflections on the Garden Grotto (New York: George Braziller, 1982), p. 7.

9. Geoffrey Galt Harpham, *On the Grotesque: Strategies of Contradiction in Art and Literature* (Princeton: Princeton University Press, 1982), pp. 23–30. Miller, *Caves,* pp. 7, 59. Barbara Walker, *The Woman's Encyclopedia of Myths and Secrets* (San Francisco: Harper and Row, 1983), pp. 355–57.

10. Miller, *Caves,* pp. 15, 20, 33, 119. Park, *Idea of Rococo,* pp. 89–91. Pope first published the poem with two cantos in 1712; in 1714 it was enlarged to include five cantos. Rhys Issac, "The First Monticello," in *Jeffersonian Legacies,* edited by Peter S. Onuf (Charlottesville: University Press of Virginia, 1993). At the time of his marriage Jefferson had not yet started the project, and he seemingly lost interest in the idea thereafter.

11. Walker, *Encyclopedia,* pp. 1035–37. Many gods and goddesses, like the Hindu goddess Kali, are both creators and destroyers.

12. Metropolitan Museum of Art, New York. On its own, the theme of hunting or pursuing represents a common sexual metaphor. For example, Fragonard's painting *The Pursuit,* from the four canvases titled *The Progress of Love,* depicts a young man aggressively tracking a young woman. Thanks to William Park for this reading of Mondon. For more on the use of dogs as erotic symbols in rococo art, see Donald Posner, *Watteau: A Lady at Her Toilet* (London: Penguin Books, 1973), pp. 76–83. Jane Sharp, *The Midwive's Book* (London, 1671), cited in Antonia Fraser, *The Weaker Vessel* (New York: Alfred A. Knopf, 1984), p. 51. Many of these images of impotency emerged in Bavaria, where Elector Max III Joseph declared in 1770 the official end of the rococo style.

13. Some auricular cartouches merge the genital features with interpenetrating monsters, grotesques, and animals. Others have shell-like parts that nevertheless are decidedly skeletal and specifically pelvic in shape. E. H. Gombrich, *The Sense of Order: A Study in the Psychology of Decorative Art* (New York: Cornell University Press, 1984), pp. 241–42. Both the peanut and kidney bean are thematically associated with the rococo and are common sexual metaphors. For example, "fava," the Italian word for bean, also is a slang term for female genitalia; for rococo connection, see this essay. Miller, *Caves,* p. 123. Gombrich, *Sense of Order,* pp. 6–9, 279.

14. Dawson Papers, Library of Congress, Microfilm Manuscripts Collection, Washington, D.C. Gaston Bachelard, *The Poetics of Space* (New York: Orion Press, 1964), p. 78. Bachelard sees similar attributes in desks and wardrobes. William Macpherson Horner, *Blue Book of Philadelphia Furniture: William Penn to George Washington,* (1935; reprint ed., Alexandria: Highland House Publishers, 1988), pp. 110–11.

15. Jules D. Prown, "The Truth of Material Culture: History or Fiction," in *History From Things,* edited by Steven Lubar and W. David Kingery (Washington: Smithsonian Institution Press, 1993), p. 3.

16. Such anthropomorphic parallels suggest the possibility for a new reading of other rococo forms, notably looking glasses and tall case clocks. A matching high chest for the dressing table has not yet been identified. For more on gender and furniture, see Laurel Thatcher Ulrich, "Furniture as Social History: Gender, Property, and Memory in the Decorative Arts," in *American Furniture,* edited by Luke Beckerdite and William Hosley, (Hanover, N.H.: University Press of New England for the Chipstone Foundation, 1995), pp. 39–69.

17. Bailey, *Loves of the Gods,* pp. 422–27, pl. 50 and fig. 5. Male costumes during the Renaissance often included a codpiece in the form of a shell. Bachelard, *Poetics,* p. 107. Miller, *Caves,* p. 20. Sheriff, *Fragonard,* p. 190. Boucé, *Sexuality,* p. 9. Roy Porter, "The Secrets of Generation Display'd: *Aristotle's Masterpiece* in Eighteenth-Century England," in *Unauthorized Sexuality in Eighteenth-Century England,* edited by Robert P. McCubin, a special issue of *Eighteenth-Century Life* 9 (May 1985): 7. Stephen Jay Gould, "The Anatomy Lesson," *Natural History* 104, no. 12 (December 1995): 10–15. The authors thank Michelle Erickson for calling this reference to their attention. Robinet saw this as but one of the many examples of how nature "has multiplied models of the generative organs, in view of the importance of these organs" (J. B. Robinet, *Philosophical Views on the Natural Gradation of Forms of Existence, or the Attempts Made By Nature While Learning to Create Humanity* [Amsterdam, 1768], cited in Bachelard, *Poetics,* p. 114).

18. For more on gender attributes of rococo versus baroque, see Miller, *Caves,* p. 113. Candace Clements, "Unexpected Consequences: The Councours de Peinture of 1727 and History Painting in Early Eighteenth-Century Paris" (Ph.D. dissertation, Yale University, Department of Art History, 1992), UMI 93-08969. Toby Ditz, "Shipwrecked: Imperilled Masculinity and

the Culture of Risk among Philadelphia's Eighteenth-Century Merchants," paper presented to the Department of History, Johns Hopkins University, January 1993. Thanks to Anne Verplank and Robert Blair St. George for providing this reference.

19. Park, *Idea of Rococo,* pp. 23–34, 46, 96–106. Linda Colley, "The English Rococo: Historical Background," in *Rococo: Art and Design in Hogarth's England,* (London: Victoria and Albert Museum, 1984), pp. 10–17.

20. During the 1760s, a large selection of "newly discovered" writings by Ossian were published by James Macpherson, writings that were fraudulently produced by Macpherson himself. Jean Starobinski, "Le Mythe au XVIIIe siècle" in *Critique,* (November 1977): 977. For examples of this classical learning trend in Philadelphia, see Edwin Wolf, *The Book Culture of a Colonial American City: Philadelphia Books, Bookmen, and Booksellers* (Oxford: Clarendon Press, 1988), pp. 171–72. Although beyond the scope of this study, it would be useful to trace documented high chests to see if more conservative or orthodox owners consciously avoided the ornate, rococo forms. This concept was examined by Deborah Federen in a lecture delivered at the Williamsburg Antiques Forum in 1992. Federen noted parallels between the ownership of Philadelphia rococo furniture and participation in the Revolutionary cause. In contrast, the ownership of more restrained architectonic forms was apparently linked to neutral or Loyalist owners. This theory cannot be statistically validated, however, because for every owner whose allegiance is documented there are many others whose political preferences are not known.

21. Other mythological panels on high chests display scenes from Aesop's *Fables,* highly moralistic tales that are a part of classical mythology. There is no compelling evidence that identifies this figure as Madame de Pompadour. For another Philadelphia case piece with a female bust, see J. Michael Flanigan, *American Furniture from the Kaufman Collection* (Washington: National Gallery of Art, 1986), pp. 90–93. Equally suggestive of the gender of certain objects is the fact that Philadelphia desk-and-bookcases, a form commonly associated with male activities, most often have carved busts of male figures. No high chests with original carved busts of men are known, rather, high chests typically have baskets of flowers, birds, or cartouches—all motifs with strong feminine associations. For illustrations of some of these ornaments, see Bowman and Heckscher, *American Rococo,* pp. 207–8, figs. 144–46. The "Pompadour" high chest is illustrated in Heckscher and Bowman, *American Rococo,* pp. 202–3, fig. 48 and pl. 138.

22. Hersey, *The Lost Meaning of Classical Architecture: Speculation on Ornament from Vetruvis to Venturi* (Cambridge, Mass.: MIT Press, 1988), p. 1. David Bayne, "Proportions of Philadelphia Rococo Casepieces," unpublished paper presented to the Furniture Conservation Program, Smithsonian Institution, 1990. Hersey, *Lost Meaning,* p. 4.

23. Hersey, *Lost Meaning,* pp. 4, 20–45.

24. Park, *Idea of Rococo,* p. 84. Harpham, *Grotesque,* pp. 38–39.

25. Thanks to Jules D. Prown for suggesting the William Williams connection.

26. Sheriff, *Fragonard,* pp. 26–29.

27. Campbell, *Power of Myth,* p. xiv.

*Maurie D. McInnis
and Robert A. Leath*

Beautiful Specimens,
Elegant Patterns:
New York Furniture
for the Charleston
Market, 1810–1840

▼ I N 1 7 7 4 , Charleston, South Carolina, was the fourth largest urban center in British North America and the largest seaport in the South. The free people living there had a per capita wealth more than ten times greater than colonists in New England and more than nine times greater than colonists in the Middle Colonies. Bostonian Josiah Quincy remarked that Charleston, "in grandeur, splendour of building, decorations, equipages, numbers, commerce, shipping and indeed in almost everything . . . far surpasses all I ever saw, or ever expected to see, in America!" Despite a relative decline in the city's economy during the early nineteenth century, Charleston still had a per free capita wealth more than three times that of Massachusetts and New York in 1860. With its superior wealth, Charleston constituted a sophisticated and perhaps unique place within the American furniture market.[1]

Before the American Revolution many of Charleston's wealthiest citizens procured their furniture and other luxury items from Europe, but during the early nineteenth century, as direct trade with Europe declined, they increasingly turned to northern cities for fashionable goods. New York eventually became the primary exporter of Charleston's agricultural staples and the principal source for goods imported from abroad. New York cabinetmakers moved quickly to assume control of the furniture market vacated by European imports. Cabinetmakers, such as Duncan Phyfe, Charles Honoré Lannuier, and others, offered richly gilded and boldly carved classical furniture for the elite market. Simple mass-produced items, often shipped as venture cargo or warehoused by local merchants and cabinetmakers, flooded Charleston's middle class market. At the same time, one New York cabinet firm, Deming and Bulkley, offered Charlestonians "beautiful specimens" of their furniture in "elegant patterns . . . which will not suffer in comparison with the best specimens ever imported from Europe" (fig. 1). Most of the New York furniture that descended in Charleston families has bold figural carving and elaborate gilded decoration based on European classical designs. These pieces represent a unique body of New York classical furniture made especially for the southern market.[2]

Imported Furniture and European Taste
At the beginning of the nineteenth century, Charleston had a long-established tradition of importing expensive European art and furniture. Perhaps more than any other Americans, Charlestonians patronized European artists such as Thomas Gainsborough, Allan Ramsay, George Romney,

Figure 1 Card table attributed to Deming and Bulkley, New York City, ca. 1825. Rosewood and satinwood veneer with white pine. H. 30", W. 37⅛", D. 18½". (Private collection; photo, Gavin Ashworth.)

Figure 2 Thomas Middleton, *Friends and Amateurs in Musick*, Charleston, 1827. Wash drawing with touches of white on paper. (Courtesy, Gibbes Museum of Art/Carolina Art Association, gift of Henry Cheves.) This 1827 drawing of Arthur Middleton's house depicts an elite Charleston interior with its large painting collection and inherited furniture from earlier periods. The rush-seated fancy chairs and sideboard are typical of northern furniture shipped to Charleston from 1810 to 1840.

Joshua Reynolds, Johann Zoffany, Benjamin West, and John Singleton Copley. Throughout the nineteenth century, Carolinians were inveterate grand tourists. The typical painting collection of a Charleston aristocrat would have included paintings thought to be by Guido Reni, Raphael, Angelica Kauffmann, Salvator Rosa, and others (fig. 2). In 1802, South Carolina planter and governor John Drayton described Charlestonians as "too much prejudiced in favour of British manners, customs, and knowledge." Drayton concluded:

> Among the richer part of the community of this state, the modes of living are similar to those of the same rank in European nations. Like them, they enter into the change of fashions; perhaps directed by many of their whims, and influenced by many of their follies. Their equipages are costly and numerous, their servants many; and hospitality throughout the state is known to be a national virtue.

Charlestonians' wealth, extravagance, and predilection for European customs inevitably influenced their taste in furnishings and interior decoration.[3]

Charlestonians were among the first Americans to demonstrate a taste for the archaeologically based, classical styles published by furniture designers such as Thomas Sheraton, Thomas Hope, George Smith, and Rudolph Ackermann. After browsing through the shops of several Parisian cabinetmakers in 1797, Charlestonian Mary Stead Pinckney (d. 1812) wrote a letter to her cousin, Margaret Izard Manigault (1768–1824), describing new-styled mahogany secretaries, console tables, and "a plain mahogany commode with bronze feet *a l'antique*." Pinckney had discovered the new taste for *vert antique* decoration and explained "the *bronze* is only as an appearance & is wood painted in imitation of bronze." Pinckney was most enthused by the furniture in the shop of Georges Jacob (1739–1814), the French cabinetmaker who employed the classical innovators Charles Percier (1764–1838) and Pierre Fontaine (1762–1853) as designers. She exclaimed, "the furniture at Jacob's. I had no idea that Paris boasted of any so beautiful. The new chairs are bewitching . . . I want to give you an idea of the new shape." Pinckney described the fashion for scroll-back chairs and the new klismos style: "The back & also the seat is all of one width, carried up very high with a gentle curve till it turns & curls back. When they are not in imitation of bronze the backs are covered like the seat, yellow striped velvet, for example, trimmed with deep fringe orange & black, &c., and the end of the curve on the back of the chairs also trimmed." A Parisian friend of Pinckney's cousin envisioned Margaret Manigault reclining on a sofa in the "Greek manner." She wrote, "If by a magic wand I could evoke in your bedroom a mahogany sofa trimmed with a handsome green material embroidered in brown and a draped Etruscan fringe in the most Greek manner it seems that I would see you resting there with greater ease."[4]

Despite such tantalizing documentary evidence, surviving furniture suggests that Charlestonians imported the great majority of their classical furniture from England rather than from France during the early nineteenth century. One of the most important examples of English classical furniture

Figure 3 Painted armchair, English, ca. 1815. Woods unrecorded. H. 34½", W. 18", D. 20". (Private collection; photo, Gavin Ashworth.)

Figure 4 Detail of the gilded diapering and chinoiserie decoration on the armchair illustrated in fig. 3. (Photo, Gavin Ashworth.)

with a Charleston history is the set of black and gold japanned seating furniture owned by General Thomas Pinckney (1750–1828). The surviving set includes eight armchairs (fig. 3) and one side chair in the klismos form, and a recamier sofa. Each piece is decorated in imitation of Chinese lacquer, with gilded decoration on a black ground and polychrome-painted chinoiserie scenes on the backs of the chairs and on the sweeping scroll arms of the recamier sofa; each scene is surrounded by gilded cell-pattern diapering (fig. 4). A nearly identical set (except for the tablets that depict English pastoral landscapes) belonged to Pinckney's brother and his wife, General Charles Cotesworth and Mary (Stead) Pinckney. Their furniture typifies the Charleston taste for brightly gilded and painted furniture and represents the highest end of English Regency design. These suites are the precursors of future New York imports, for although the source for imported goods changed, Charlestonians' taste for carved and gilded classical furniture remained constant. Margaret Manigault noted this predilection when describing her brother's house:

> [It] is in excellent order, & very handsomely furnished. The Drawing Room with rich Chintz curtains lined with yellow, a beautiful rich carpet, chairs & sofas of cane of the most fashionable make, handsomely painted & gilt. They are black & gold with thick yellow cushions.[5]

The 1807 Embargo and the War of 1812

Charleston's reliance on Europe for fashionable furniture was disrupted by a nine-year series of events that included the British and French blockades of 1806, Thomas Jefferson's embargo in 1807, the non-intercourse acts of 1809, and the War of 1812. Economic historians generally consider this period the principal turning point in Charleston's antebellum commercial history. Previously, Charleston had enjoyed great prosperity as a center for trans-Atlantic trade with Europe and the West Indies, especially following the American Revolution when the city's merchants capitalized on America's neutral position in the English and French conflict, serving as the leading depot for shipping between Europe and the West Indies. The economic depression created by the blockade, the embargo, the non-intercourse acts, and the War of 1812 decimated Charleston's mercantile community to the extent that it never fully recovered. Artist Charles Fraser recalled how the embargo's results were "extensively and so ruinously experienced." In his 1854 *Reminiscences*, Fraser explained that during this period, "Capital declined, vessels disappeared, prices fell, produce accumulated . . . non-intercourse, embargo, war, paralyzed commercial enterprize; and so great, at length, became their [Charleston merchants'] depression, that scarcely a ship was owned in Charleston . . . grass was growing upon our wharves."[6]

The impact of the embargo and the war on consumerism is documented in letters from Margaret Izard Manigault to her mother, Alice Delancey Izard. In February 1809, Manigault remarked, "The effects of the Embargo are so severely felt here that there have been few parties this winter. Those families which used to give them are constrained to remain quietly in the country & live upon their poultry." One month later, Manigault lamented over how the embargo prevented her and her husband from celebrating the marriage of their nephew, Arthur Middleton (1785–1837), to Alicia Hopton Russell (1789–1840), the daughter of Nathaniel Russell (1738–1820), Charleston's leading post-Revolutionary merchant. "I cannot help wishing," she wrote, "that we too could welcome the bride into her new family. But we are not provided & the China, & glass, & even Candlesticks, & spoons, & various we thought of . . . which the circumstances of the Times will not allow us to procure." The collapse of direct trade with Great Britain forced Charlestonians to find new sources for many of their luxury goods. In 1811, Margaret Manigault informed her mother that she had just received from New York a set of white and gold painted fancy chairs with Grecian decoration in "a modern handsome shape." She concluded with satisfaction, "When I want chairs again, I shall certainly send to New York for them!"[7]

The English furniture industry struggled to maintain its position in

Charleston after the resolution of the War of 1812. In 1817, for example, Charles Cotesworth Pinckney imported an extensive set of English-made, rosewood seating furniture stamped by Gillows. Writing from London, Isaac Coffin assured the Pinckneys that their new furniture was "all the fashion in the Houses of the first Nobility and Gentry in England . . . made by Mr. Gillow at Lancaster . . . the first Upholsterer in the Kingdom." Similarly, upholsterers Barelli, Torre & Co. advertised in 1819:

> ELEGANT WINDOW CURTAINS, Of rich Crimson Damask, lined with yellow silk and ornamented with fine colored Brocade Lace, with gilt cornices and an Eagle in the centre, finished after the fashion and style of those used in the best rooms in England, having been just imported from London by order of a gentleman in Carolina, who declined taking them, being too rich a Furniture for his Country Seat.

From 1818 until 1821, Charleston merchant John Woddrop regularly imported and advertised as venture cargo an assortment of "London made furniture," consisting of "fashionable Sideboards, sets of Dining Tables, Secretaries and Book Cases, Chests of Drawers, Looking Glasses, and a variety of cane seat Chairs." By 1821, however, imported English furniture was less affordable, and Woddrop's last advertisements suggest that he had retired from the furniture trade: "The Articles remaining on hand are offered at prices considerably under cost and charges." The 1824 tariff act placed a 30 percent ad valorem tax on foreign furniture, sounding the final death knell for Charleston's tradition of importing English furniture. Merchant J. N. Cardozo recalled that, by this time, "the class of merchants who grew out of the direct foreign trade of Charleston with the ports of Europe . . . had withdrawn from business or were dead. . . . The Russells, Crafts, Winthrops, Tunnos, Hasletts, Hazlehursts, were replaced by those who were connected with the indirect trade through Northern ports—with the shipment of produce through New York."[8]

New York Furniture for the Charleston Market

In the early decades of the nineteenth century, shipments of northern-made furniture and other domestic goods began arriving in Charleston as makers and merchants sought to expand their markets by capturing a portion of the potentially lucrative southern trade. There were several different channels through which local patrons could purchase northern goods. The four primary sources were speculative cargo shipped to Charleston, cabinet warehousing by local merchants, supplementary warehousing by local cabinet-makers, and custom commissions requested by a local patron. In the late 1810s the market was crowded with furniture from London, New York, Philadelphia, Boston, Salem, and Providence, Rhode Island. As the market settled in the 1820s, Philadelphia chairmakers managed to establish control over a significant portion of the fancy and Windsor chair market, whereas New York makers established their control over the remainder of the furniture market. By the 1830s, even the competition from Philadelphia had faded away, and New York reigned supreme as furniture supplier to the Charleston market.

Venture Cargo

One of the ways that northern furniture first reached the Charleston market was through speculative or venture cargo. Numerous advertisements featured assorted furniture being sold on or near the wharves, sometimes directly from the ship itself—as in 1815 when three-dozen fancy chairs and six-dozen Windsor chairs arrived on board the sloop *Schoharie*. Most often this furniture was from New York or Philadelphia, but cabinetmakers from elsewhere also tested the waters. The most common channel of distribution was for a chairmaker or furniture maker to consign his goods to either a general retail merchant or a furniture retailer in Charleston. It was also quite common for the shipmaster himself to buy goods in his home port and bring them to Charleston. At that point he either sold them himself, consigned them to a local auction house, or sold them to a local merchant.[9]

During the earliest years of this speculative trade, most of the venture cargo was aimed at the middle and lower ends of the market. Shipments were usually small, consisting of only a few dozen chairs or fewer than a dozen case pieces. Most of the local distributors were merchants who maintained shops near the wharves rather than furniture retailers. In January 1816, Edward Gamage and Co. offered their most extensive assortment to date, which included a few sets of bamboo chairs and gilded chairs, three-dozen Windsor chairs, three-dozen slat-back chairs, two-dozen bent chairs, and one set of tortoise chairs. That same month the mercantile firm of S. Davenport & Co. offered two secretary-and-bookcases, two bureaus, two ladies' work tables, one sideboard, and two dressing tables. Despite the occasional offering of case pieces, chairs remained the most frequently offered speculative cargo. In 1818, for example, merchant J. D. Stagg advertised New York fancy chairs of the "latest fashion," including eight-dozen slat-back chairs, one-dozen scroll-fret chairs, one-dozen burr-back chairs, and one-dozen ball-back chairs, all in elaborately ornamented, gilded curled maple.[10]

Auction firms sold much of the speculative cargo shipped to Charleston. In 1816, Morton A. Waring offered "a quantity of excellent . . . furniture" that included card, dining, and chamber tables, a wardrobe, a set of drawers, a bed, and japanned chairs. When William A. Caldwell & Co. offered a quantity of New York furniture in 1820, they suggested that local cabinetmakers attend, for all the furniture was to be sold cheap for cash in order to "close a consignment and to meet advances made thereon." Obviously, some of the speculative cargo ventures were more successful with Charlestonian patrons than others.[11]

Although the makers of venture cargo furniture generally remained anonymous, some individuals tried to capitalize on the cachet of "name-brand" goods. In 1819, the Charleston Auction Establishment advertised furniture of "superior quality and workmanship" by J. L. Everitt of New York. The description of Everitt's furniture implies that it was intended for the upper end of the Charleston market. Included in the sale were gilded pier tables with marble tops, Grecian plain and dolphin sofas, and an assortment of tables, bureaus, and presses. During the same year, New York cabinetmaker John Budd advertised French bedsteads, portable desks, and a variety of table forms. Neither Budd nor Everitt advertised in Charleston subsequently, which suggests that their trips were not as successful as they had hoped. Although advertisements for venture cargo were common during the late 1810s, they diminished as more secure channels of distribution were established during the 1820s and 1830s.[12]

Warehousing

The success of northern-made speculative cargo in Charleston encouraged some merchants in the late 1810s to focus exclusively on retailing furniture. Typically these merchants stocked large quantities of New York and Philadelphia goods. In their advertisements they tried to attract potential customers by offering a wider range of goods at lower prices than did local cabinetmakers.

Although New York ultimately dominated the Charleston market in the second quarter of the nineteenth century, Providence and Philadelphia cabinet- and chairmakers also found substantial patronage, especially in the late 1810s and the early 1820s. Providence cabinetmaker William Rawson managed his family's wareroom in Charleston from 1816 to 1820. The Rawsons did not, however, find sufficient patronage to justify staying, especially after a fire in 1820 destroyed much of their stock. Shipping records reveal that Philadelphia's early trade with Charleston was substantially more lucrative. From 1820 to 1840, Philadelphia ships carried more furniture to Charleston than to any other American city—nearly 6,000 pieces. The vast majority was seating furniture; only a few Philadelphia case pieces were exported.[13]

Several northern warehousing businesses advertised in Charleston between 1783 and 1805, but none seem to have met with any success. The earliest successful ventures, which began in 1811, may have profited from the disruption of trade precipitated by the 1807 embargo and the non-intercourse acts. In the March 2, 1811, issue of the *Charleston Courier*, local cabinetmaker Jacob Sass and his son, Edward, reported that they had a sizable quantity of Philadelphia chairs and settees. Perhaps encouraged by the success of these early shipments, Edward left his father's business and began his own "Northern Warehouse," advertising Philadelphia Windsor and fancy chairs. Although Philadelphia chairs dominated the Charleston market initially, their popularity declined during the 1820s and 1830s. In 1821, over 1,400 Philadelphia chairs arrived in Charleston, but by 1826 that number had dropped by nearly 40 percent, and in 1836 no chairs were listed in cargoes of Philadelphia ships entering Charleston harbor.[14]

As the popularity of Philadelphia furniture declined, the demand for New York furniture grew. The earliest Charleston retailer specializing exclusively in New York furniture was Richard Otis. In 1817, Otis advertised furniture "just landing" from New York, including looking glasses, mantle piece glasses, dressing glasses, cornices, fancy and Windsor chairs, a cellaret and a bureau. Early success encouraged Otis to expand his offerings and to import more expensive pieces. The following year he advertised four sideboards, a secretary-and-bookcase, a selection of wardrobes, and tea, card, and work tables. As new shipments arrived, Otis frequently placed short announcements in the paper. One indicated that he had thirty-dozen fancy and Windsor chairs and that he was receiving twelve-dozen more. The new Windsor chairs were priced from $18 to $35 per dozen and the fancy chairs from $38 to $100. Although it is unclear that Otis was an artisan, his advertisements always emphasized that carving and gilding could be executed with dispatch. In 1818, a carver and gilder named Van Nostrand (probably Samuel or Jacob) announced that he had just returned from New York and was resuming work at Otis's shop. The following year, Otis referred to Van Nostrand and another New York artisan whose last name was Christie in an advertisement listing bed and window cornices, frames for looking glasses, portraits and prints, brackets, and curtain ornaments—all objects suitable for carving. Otis also noted that these tradesmen could regild any old work or carve and bronze sofa feet and other furniture components. Advertisements by Richard Otis do not appear in the Charleston papers after 1820. Many furniture merchants established stores in Charleston, but most only remained in business for a few years.[15]

Supplementary Warehousing

Although retail merchants came and went, the popularity of northern furniture clearly affected the local cabinetmaking trade. In the 1820s and 1830s, Charleston's cabinetmaking industry declined, both in the number of artisans and in the lucrativeness of their businesses. To remain competitive, many local cabinetmakers supplemented their own products with northern imports. During the same period, the furniture industry in Philadelphia and New York grew rapidly. In the northern cities, large shops employed numerous apprentices, journeymen, and specialized labor to keep production costs down. By contrast, most of the cabinetmaking shops in Charleston remained relatively small, employing only a few journeymen and apprentices. Local shops were unable to match the volume and prices of their northern competitors, and they lacked the highly specialized workforce required to produce the ornately carved, gilded, and painted furniture that appealed to wealthy Charlestonians.[16]

English-trained cabinetmaker Richard Gouldsmith began working in Charleston in 1816. In 1820, he advertised only Charleston-made goods, but by 1824 he was supplementing his own work with a variety of "splendid" articles of "first rate" quality from New York: "sofas, music chairs, elegant pillar and claw breakfast tables, very handsome, rich carved four-poster Mahogany bedsteads . . . [and] a variety of elegant Dressing Bureaus." Charleston upholsterer and cabinetmaker John J. Sheridan was also an English immigrant who began working in Charleston in the early 1820s. He made carved mahogany bedsteads and sofas and sold them along with a full range of imported fancy and Windsor chairs. In 1827, he hired "a New York Ornamental Painter, who paints and ornaments old chairs and settees, in the New York and Philadelphia style" and urged his customers to apply quickly, "as the young man is about to return to the North shortly." The following year, Sheridan recommended that his customers have their old chairs "painted and ornamented in either the Philadelphia or New York style." Whereas modern furniture historians may deliberate over whether a chair was made in New York or Philadelphia, nineteenth-century Charlestonians obviously knew the difference.[17]

Few of Sheridan's advertisements in the 1820s emphasized "Charleston made," but by 1830, he, Gouldsmith, and other local cabinetmakers placed that designation at the head of their advertisements or emphasized it in bold capital letters. The timing of this new self-awareness was not coincidental. From 1828 to 1834, the city was obsessed with the political divisions wrought by the Nullification Crisis. At the heart of the debate were conflicts between northern and southern interests. Some extended the argument, encouraging Charlestonians to support local artisans rather than northern concerns. After such issues were raised in the Charleston press, many Charleston cabinetmakers emphasized the fact that their goods were locally made. There is little evidence, however, that the appeal of local production had any substantial impact on patronage. Although Charlestonians were passionate about their politics, they did not let it stand in the way of personal gratification when it came to luxury goods.[18]

Custom Commissions

Another way in which Charlestonians obtained furniture was through directly commissioning New York cabinetmakers. Some northern tradesmen made a special effort to position themselves in the southern market. In newspapers across the South, New York cabinetmaker Charles Christian reported that he had "principally adapted his business for Southern demand," was offering his work at 5 percent below New York prices, and was urging the public to contact him by letter.[19]

It is unknown whether any Charlestonians attempted to contact Christian, but they certainly patronized other New York cabinetmakers. Some placed their orders during visits to New York, whereas others had friends or family members in the city act as their agents. In a July 31, 1834, letter, Alicia Hopton Russell Middleton scolded her sister-in-law in New York for recommending the most elaborate examples of sofas and tables, "bound with brass or inlaid," for their plantation. While heavily carved, gilded, brass-bound, and inlaid furniture was appropriate for a Charleston townhouse, Middleton deemed it too expensive and too lavish for her country seat.[20]

A series of letters among another circle of Charleston's prominent women describe the process of securing a commission for custom-made New York furniture. In March of 1812, Sarah Elliott Huger of Charleston, then living in New York, sent sketches of furniture by Duncan Phyfe to her friend and cousin, Harriott Pinckney Horry, and wrote:

> Enclosed are two drawings of furniture, rather uncouthly executed, but yet I think some idea of the originals is conveyed. Our next neighbor Mr. Gelston has two communicating rooms furnished by Mr. Phyfe (from whom I got the sketches) with considerable taste; but if mahogany is too expensive, I can find you painted chairs and settees with either rush or cane bottoms, & whatever colour you feel a predilection for, transmit it, painted on paper or wood; a dozen chairs with two settees of the latest fashion will cost $144, made of cane, if rush, $120, the shape is quite plain and nothing like the mahogany; in fact

Figure 5 Gilbert Stuart, *Sarah I'on Lowndes,* Washington, D. C., ca. 1803. Oil on canvas. (Courtesy, Gibbes Museum of Art/Carolina Art Association, bequest of Mrs. Royal Phelps Carroll.)

there is a great difference in the appearance as there is in price; two Sofas and twelve chairs of Mahogany of the best taste will be $500.[21]

Apparently Phyfe's sketches did not suit Horry's taste, for six months later she had still not forwarded instructions, prompting Huger to write, "I was quite mortified not to have heard from you about the furniture; I fear the drawings I enclosed were not as Tasty as you wished." As for the style of the furniture, Huger assured her friend, "we have had nothing newer." Huger was more concerned over the shipment of the suite. She recommended, "in these disastrous Times," that Horry not "think of incurring the risk of the seas" and promised "to procure a sketch of something more fashionable" after the war.[22]

Huger's warning about the "risk of the seas" apparently persuaded her friend to wait for the war to end. At that time, Horry, acting as an intermediary for her friend Sarah I'on Lowndes (fig. 5), once again contacted Huger to coordinate the procurement of an extensive suite of furniture. Intended as a wedding present for Lowndes's daughter, the suite was to consist of card and pier tables, "drawing room chairs . . . at least 18 in number to have cain seats and cushions covered with chintz not of a very large pattern, and not to require washing very often, Sophas of your taste and Curtains with fringe to the draperies."[23]

Huger gave Lowndes's sketches for the seating furniture to New York chairmakers Jesse Ellis and Stephen Wheaton (in partnership, 1815–1817), who specialized in painted maple fancy furniture. On October 21, 1815, Huger wrote Horry:

> The sofas or lounges will cost more than you supposed, $60 is the price of the common shape, but the fashionable ones according with the design enclosed to Mr. Wheaton will cost $75 each. The chairs $9, but they will be extremely plain without gilt or ornament of any kind. This I confess is as much in concordance with *my* taste as *your* directions; but whether Mrs. Lowndes will agree with us in this simplicity of choice I am doubtful of as some floating remembrance of her toilette decorations induce me to suppose that she by no means estimates ornament as superfluous.[24]

For card and pier tables, the ladies commissioned Duncan Phyfe (1768–1854), New York's preeminent cabinetmaker of the period; however, delays in procuring the furniture forced Huger to complain:

> What shall I say to you about Mrs. Lowndes' Furniture? In truth I feel mortified in confessing that it is impossible for me to prophesy when the good lady will receive the card and pier tables. Mr. Phyfe is so much the United States rage, that it is with difficulty now, that one can procure an audience even of a few moments; not a week since I waited in company with a dozen others at least an hour in his cold shop and after all, was obliged to return home, without seeing The *great man;* however a few days since . . . I had the great good fortune to arrive at his house just at the moment he was entering and consequently extorted from him another promise that the furniture should certainly be finished in three weeks . . . The Tables from $325 to $350; Phyfe says he cannot tell precisely what will be the price.

Finally, in March the Lowndes' furniture was safely packed aboard the schooner *South Carolina* and directed to the care of Lowndes's Charleston

Figure 6 Side chair attributed to Duncan Phyfe, New York City, ca. 1815. Mahogany; secondary woods and dimensions unrecorded. (Private collection; photo, Israel Sack, Inc., New York.)

Figure 7 Detail of the carved lyre back of the side chair illustrated in fig. 6.

factor, Kershaw, Lewis and Company. Huger assured that final bills from Phyfe and Ellis & Wheaton would be sent promptly, "on one of the many vessels sailing constantly for Charleston." From September 1815 to March 1816, the Lowndes' commission for custom-made New York furniture had taken a total of nearly seven months to fulfill.[25]

Sarah Elliott Huger's letters detail the process of acquiring custom furniture from New York: the exchange of sketches between cabinetmaker and patron; communication between the tradesman and client regarding design, materials, and price; submission and approval of samples (paint); and arrangements for payment and shipping. More importantly, her letters show one means by which styles for furniture, ornaments, and interior decoration were transmitted from one American city to another. On March 5, 1816, Huger wrote Horry, "I think you will admire [the pier table] as a remarkably chaste and tasteful ornament, but I must confess that the Card Tables neither accorded with my *Fancy* or *Directions*. . . . Articles by the way that are now become obsolete in drawing rooms, which should only exhibit marble Tables in every pier, and a round centre one, corresponding in marble and finish with the side ornaments." In her final critique of the Lowndes' seating furniture, Huger commented, "Tell Mrs. Lowndes . . . that her Furniture is by no means as handsome as I wished it, or as the nature of the wood could admit of. The chairs for example should certainly have been scrolled backed, to Correspond with their attendant Lounges, and I think an insertion of gilt moulding in place of the black line would prove more appropriate to Drawing Room display."[26]

Benjamin Huger's method of securing furniture was somewhat different. He simply sent his factors a list of specifications with terms for payment and delivery:

> Eighteen Chairs of maple with Cushions, neat and fashionable, but without guilding
> Two Sophas Do. to answer the above
> A pier table Do.
> A pair of Card tables Do.
> A Carpet and hearth Rug Do.
> As soon as the cost of the above can be ascertained & the amount communicated, it shall be remitted to New York or a bill may be drawn on me and presented to my Factors in Charleston, Messrs. Keating, Simons & Sons. The articles may also be shipped to the same Gentlemen if no Vessel offers for Georgetown.

Huger also attached a sketch of the pier table that included dimensions—"3 feet, 8 inches across the front and 3 feet, 1 inch high"—based on those of the room for which it was intended.[27]

Although none of the furnishings ordered by Lowndes and Huger are known, several pieces of furniture documented and attributed to Duncan Phyfe have nineteenth-century histories of ownership in Charleston. A set of cane-seated, lyre-back chairs (fig. 6) that descended in the family of Arthur Middleton probably represent a custom commission. Representing the very best of Phyfe's work, they have delicately carved lyres with acanthus leaves and brass strings (fig. 7), acanthus carving on the front legs, and

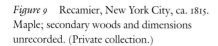

Figure 8 Side chair, New York City, ca. 1815. Mahogany with ash. H. 33", W. 16³/₄", D. 22". (Private collection; photo, Gavin Ashworth.)

gilded hairy paw feet. A similar set (see fig. 8) descended in the Alston-Pringle family during their residence in the Miles Brewton house. These chairs also have lyre backs with brass strings, but their crest rails are turned, their legs are plain, and their paw feet are not gilded. Chairs with these features have traditionally been attributed to Phyfe's workshop, but it is likely that at least a half-dozen New York cabinetmakers made comparable examples. More closely allied to the Sarah Elliott Huger letters, however, is a cane-seated tiger maple recamier with gilded and *vert antique* winged paw feet (fig. 9), originally from the family of two Charlestonians, Benjamin Huger Read and his wife Mary Julia (Middleton).[28]

Several pieces of furniture in the style associated with French-born New York cabinetmaker Charles Honoré Lannuier (1779–1819) also have Charles-

Figure 9 Recamier, New York City, ca. 1815. Maple; secondary woods and dimensions unrecorded. (Private collection.)

ton histories. This group includes a pair of card tables that descended in the Ravenel-Frost family (fig. 10). Both tables have caryatid supports, paw feet, gilded and *vert antique* decoration, and classical ormolu mounts and brass

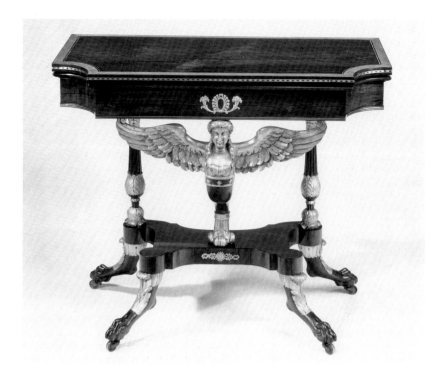

Figure 10 Card table attributed to Charles Honoré Lannuier, New York City, ca. 1815. Mahogany; secondary woods and dimensions unrecorded. (Private collection.)

inlay. Nearly identical pairs belonged to John Wickham of Richmond, Virginia, and James Bosley of Baltimore, Maryland. All of these objects reflect the high level of quality expected by wealthy southerners.[29]

Deming and Bulkley

The letters between Huger and Horry document the difficulties of long-distance commissions and help explain the popularity of warehoused and venture cargo furniture. There was one firm, however, that offered extremely sophisticated furniture without the hassles associated with long-distance commissions — Deming and Bulkley. Like other northern cabinet firms, the partnership between Brazilia Deming (1781–1854) and Erastus Bulkley (1798–1872) engaged in the venture cargo trade with Charleston; however, their furniture was intended for the upper end of the market. Deming and Bulkley's early successes encouraged return trips, and after a few years they established a retail storefront on King Street where, for more than twenty years, they set the standard for furniture retailing in Charleston.

Their longevity was due to a number of factors. Instead of retailing a random selection of imported goods, they focused on their own furniture, which they continued to manufacture in New York. By having Bulkley reside in Charleston, they also became acquainted with local patrons and their tastes. At their "Cabinet Furniture, Piano Forte, and Carpet Ware-Rooms," Charlestonians could take advantage of New York prices and still receive the personal attention that custom work demanded. Additionally, Deming and Bulkley carried a wide variety of domestic goods ranging from the most elaborate and costly drawing room furniture to simple Windsor chairs; from fabulous silk draperies and cornices to Venetian blinds; from expensive Brussels carpets to the most basic matting.[30]

The firm's association with Charleston began in 1818 when Erastus Bulkley arrived with a shipment of furniture from New York. Working with a local merchant, he advertised several times, offering such items as pillar and claw card and tea tables, extension dining tables, pier tables, Grecian sofas, and sundry other items. In the summer, he announced that he was about to return to New York and was receiving orders for furniture. He promised his firm would "obligate themselves to furnish their friends and customers with such articles as may be wanting, of the latest fashion, and of the best workmanship." When Bulkley returned in the fall, he endeavored to make his store the premier source for furniture in Charleston. On December 18, 1818, he advertised daily arrivals of "elegant . . . Cabinet Furniture, from their Manufactory in New York," and boasted, "this Furniture, for Elegance of Style and excellence of Workmanship, is equal, if not superior to any ever imported to this City." His latest shipment included pier, card, tea, and work tables; secretaries; bureaus; mahogany and maple bedsteads; Grecian couches with embossed morocco leather; "lovers Grecian" and other sofas; and French presses. In the fall of 1819, Bulkley thanked his patrons for their liberal support and announced that he had once again returned from New York with an elegant assortment of furniture. He also advertised that any article in the furniture line could be ordered from "their" manufactory in New York.[31]

The second party alluded to in Bulkley's earliest advertisements remains anonymous; however, Bulkley was in partnership with Deming by 1820. Deming first appears in the New York City directory in 1805, in partnership with William Turner. Brazilia was born in Wethersfield, Connecticut, and his brother, Simeon, was a cabinetmaker. Erastus Bulkley was also born in Wethersfield and was Deming's first cousin, once removed. When Erastus first ventured to Charleston in 1818, he was only twenty years old. Given the fact that most trade apprenticeships terminated at the age of twenty-one, it is likely that Bulkley went to Charleston on behalf of a New York manufacturer or merchant, discovered a lucrative market, and convinced his cousin to join him and to produce furniture for his southern clientele.[32]

Although Deming and Bulkley advertised "the latest New York fashions," much of their furniture made for the Charleston market manifests regional, and perhaps class, variations in taste. Deming and Bulkley recognized this distinctive taste during their first years of retailing in Charleston. In 1821, Bulkley advertised "elegant furniture after any pattern they may choose *or* [emphasis added] the latest New York fashions." He emphasized his firm's "taste, faithful workmanship, and punctuality" and added that "unquestionable references" were available from other Charleston patrons.[33]

Unlike William Rawson, who advertised furniture "sold low for cash," and John J. Sheridan who maintained a "Cheap Furniture Warehouse," Deming and Bulkley constantly referred to the ornamented, refined, and elegant nature of their goods—not their low prices. They appealed to wealthy Charlestonians by boasting that their furniture could not "be surpassed by any in the world, for elegance and neatness, strength and durability." Deming and Bulkley were probably aware of the Charlestonian penchant for English goods, and their marketing strategy capitalized on that taste.[34]

As a way of introducing their work to a wider Charleston audience, Deming and Bulkley raffled a set of drawing room furniture in 1820:

> *An Elegant Sett of Rose Wood Furniture*
> *To be Raffled*
> A most superb and complete set of Rose Wood Drawing Room FURNITURE, consisting of:
> One pair elegant Rose Wood Card Tables
> One dozen do. do. Chairs
> One   do. do. Grecian Sofa
> One   do. do. Pier Table, with an Italian Marble Top, and Glass in the back, 36 by 22 inches.
>   The whole sett is made of real Rose Wood, with a Border, in imitation of a Grape Vine, around every piece of it. This Furniture was manufactured in one of the first Warehouses in NY, of the latest-fashion, and warranted workmanship, and is, without exception, the richest and most elegant sett in the city.
>
> ALSO
> A Mahogany Grecian SOFA.
> The whole is valued at 1000 Dollars. There will be Fifty Chances, at 20 Dollars a chance.

The description of the furniture emphasized its elaborate gilded decoration and the lavish use of exotic rosewood—both of which were considered the height of fashion and certainly accorded with the European-derived tastes of the city's elite. Charlestonians were well acquainted with the latest English designs through their travels and through English design books, such as Rudolph Ackermann's *The Repository of Arts, Literature, Commerce, Manufactures, Fashions and Politics* (1809–1828). Ackermann, for example, specifically recommended rosewood for drawing room furniture and gilding for important decorative details. For a sofa of a "higher class . . . the frame-work would be entirely gilt in burnished and matt gold," whereas one of "less splendour" would be "carved work partially gilt." The enthusiasm for Deming and Bulkley's "justly admired" suite was sufficient to warrant their production of another set of rosewood furniture consisting of a dozen chairs, a sideboard, a pier table, a dressing table, and a pair of card tables, each supported by a spread eagle. Deming and Bulkley claimed that these latter articles could not be surpassed by any in the world and they urged the public to examine them and judge for themselves.[35]

The significance of Deming and Bulkley's strategy and the uniqueness of the Charleston market are clearly illustrated when one compares their New York and Charleston advertisements. In Charleston they offered "the richest and most elegant" furniture available, but in New York they stressed price. A typical New York advertisement referred to mahogany furniture of "the best workmanship, and good seasoned wood . . . as reasonable as any made in the same style" and rosewood furniture at "reasonable" prices.[36]

Deming and Bulkley's Charleston wareroom was so successful that they rarely advertised after 1825, though they occasionally announced the arrival of unusual items such as piano fortes. Surviving furniture and receipts indicate that they established themselves as the premier suppliers of elaborate furniture for wealthy patrons as well as of mass-produced furniture for the middle class. Families who had earlier patronized cabinetmakers in England and New York increasingly relied on Deming and Bulkley. Their list of clients included Governor William Aiken, son-in-law of the Mrs. Lowndes so frustrated with Duncan Phyfe; Daniel Elliott Huger, whose sister Sarah coordinated Mrs. Lowndes's purchases from Ellis & Wheaton and Duncan Phyfe; and Colonel Thomas Pinckney, whose father owned the English Regency black and gilded chairs discussed earlier. In the 1820s and 1830s, these men turned to Deming and Bulkley.

Deming and Bulkley's business grew until they eventually became interior decorators. When the young but extremely wealthy Hugh Swinton Ball built his new home in the Charleston suburbs, he commissioned their firm to supply the furniture, specially ordered, for his entire home. When Ball died shortly thereafter, in the wreck of the steamship *Pulaski*, his house and furniture were auctioned:

> Elegant Private Residence . . . together with all the FURNITURE, which is of the latest fashion, made to order by Bulkley, of New-York, particularly adapted to the arrangement of the Building. The House has been very recently built, is of the best materials, and finished in the modern style, with folding doors. To each chamber is attached a commodious Dressing Room.

The auctioneer obviously thought that Bulkley's name would encourage more persons to attend the sale. Ball's inventory provides an indication of both his wealth and his elaborate and extensively decorated home; his estate was valued at nearly $100,000, including more than 150 slaves on two plantations. The furniture inventories list several pier tables with marble tops, a set of dining tables, a marble slab table, a center table, a dozen mahogany hair-cushioned chairs, a rocking chair covered in red velvet, a divan, eight mahogany cushioned chairs with spring seats, and two benches to "suit the above." The house also contained Brussels carpets, bronzed chandeliers, expensive looking glasses, and a fairly extensive art collection, including Washington Allston's *Spalatro and the Bloody Hand*, other works by contemporary American artists, and Old Master paintings from Europe.[37]

Deming and Bulkley Furniture
Considering the enormous amount of furniture sold by Deming and Bulkley, it is surprising how few labeled or documented pieces survive; yet, by using the stylistic and structural details of these objects as a benchmark, we can attribute a larger body of furniture to their firm. For the most part, these pieces belonged to very wealthy patrons. Furniture made for the middle class is less discernable; however, a few labeled examples suggest the full extent of Deming and Bulkley's production.

An elaborate marble-top center table (fig. 11) made for South Carolina governor Stephen D. Miller (1787–1838) is closely based on English Regency prototypes. A letter from Deming and Bulkley to Miller details the packing of this table in Charleston for delivery to Miller's home near Camden, South Carolina:

Figure 11   Center table by Deming and Bulkley, New York City, 1828. Rosewood veneer with white pine and ash. H. 30½", Diam. 36". (Private collection; photo, Gavin Ashworth.)

Figure 12 Design for a round monopodium or table illustrated on pl. 39 in Thomas Hope, *Household Furniture and Interior Decoration* (1807). (Courtesy, Winterthur Museum.)

Figure 13 Detail of the freehand gilded decoration on the pedestal of the center table illustrated in fig. 11. (Photo, Gavin Ashworth.)

Figure 14 Design for a center table illustrated in Rudolph Ackermann's *Repository of Arts, Literature, Commerce, Manufactures, Fashions and Politics*, May 1825, pp. 305–6. (Courtesy, Winterthur Museum.)

We went on board ourselves and assisted in stowing it for we were desirous to do all in our power to get it to you in as fine order as possible, if proper care is taken of it after it reaches Camden you will receive it safe. There is two of the boxes in particular that must be handled with all possible care, and not receive any jarring. To wit: the box containing the two mirrors. . . . The other box alluded to is that which contains the top to the centre table. It is of the very finest Egyptian marble and the finest piece by far that we have ever met with. It must be carried with the edge of the box up which we have directed. The contents of the box is marked on the outside to your residence.

In form, the center table is remarkably similar to one published in Thomas Hope's *Household Furniture and Interior Decoration* (1807). Hope's "round monopodium or table" (fig. 12) features a three-sided concave support, decorated with inlay and supported by a carved base terminating in lion paw feet. Deming and Bulkley's table is also supported by a three-sided concave support over a base with lion paw feet (fig. 11). The decorative motifs on the center table resemble those depicted in European design books. For example, the gilded dolphins on the concave support are reminiscent of those forming the base of a table illustrated in the *Repository* (fig. 14), and the design in the center of the support (fig. 13) is virtually identical to the inlaid ornament shown on Hope's "round monopodium."[38]

The designs (three repeats) on the skirt of the center table feature swans drinking from a fountain with double-sided human masks (fig. 15) and floral reserves. Like the form of the table, the swans have close parallels in Hope's *Household Furniture,* and a nearly identical swan appears in an early nineteenth-century Birmingham trade catalogue for ormolu mounts. All of these designs have clear classical antecedents.[39]

On the center table, the ornamental painters in Deming and Bulkley's shop used three types of freehand gilding to imitate the decorative effects of carving, ormolu mounts, and die-cut metal inlay. The faces of the dolphins on the support (fig. 13) have incised lines and black ink penwork, which gives them a three-dimensional effect. Conversely, the absence of shading on the overlapping circles of the plinth makes the gilding look like die-cut brass or gold.

The swan and fountain motif is repeated on a pair of card tables attributed to Deming and Bulkley (fig. 16). The skirts of the card tables have elab-

Figure 15 Detail of the gilded swan decoration on the skirt of the center table illustrated in fig. 11. (Photo, Gavin Ashworth.)

orate cell-pattern diapering, similar to that on the Pinckney family chairs, and "gilding to imitate inlaid brass" on the bottom edge (figs. 4, 17). This illusionistic device, which also occurs on the skirt of the Miller table (fig. 15), was recommended by several English designers. The pedestals of the Pinckney tables are grained in imitation of rosewood, like the support of the center table, and further ornamented with freehand gilding in the form of a classical lyre—another motif common in English design books. Their tops are veneered with rosewood and ornamented with a freehand gilded basket of flowers surrounded by a grapevine border, and when open, the original stamped red velvet playing surface is visible. The tables rest on concave, four-sided plinths with canted corners supported by four ebonized paw feet with gilded acanthus leaf carving. Even in its unconserved state, the gilded decoration presents a dazzling contrast with the dark rosewood ground.[40]

The card tables belonged to General Thomas Pinckney (1750–1828) or one of his sons, Colonel Thomas Pinckney (1780–1842) or Charles Cotesworth

Figure 16 Card table attributed to Deming and Bulkley, New York City, ca. 1825. Rosewood veneer and mahogany with white pine. H. 29½", W. 36", D. 18". (Courtesy, Charleston Museum; photo, Gavin Ashworth.)

Figure 17 Detail of the gilded swan decoration and cell-pattern diapering on the skirt of the card table illustrated in fig. 16. (Photo, Gavin Ashworth.)

Figure 18 Edward Greene Malbone, *Colonel Thomas Pinckney*, Charleston, ca. 1804. Watercolor on ivory. (Courtesy, Gibbes Museum of Art/Carolina Art Association.)

Pinckney (1789–1865) (fig. 18). In 1828, when Colonel Thomas Pinckney's new residence in Charleston was nearing completion, he ordered $1,330.50 of goods from Deming and Bulkley. Although the bill of sale does not survive, an inventory of Pinckney's house does. Since no other furniture purchases were recorded in his account book, it is likely that most of the furnishings in Pinckney's Broad Street residence came from Deming and Bulkley. The furniture in the drawing room was the most expensive, and it included two rosewood sofas, an ottoman, two armchairs, two taborets, eighteen chairs, four light rosewood chairs, seven satin damask window curtains, one marble-top center table, two marble-top pier tables, two card tables, four pictures, one flower stand, two firescreens, two Wilton carpets and rugs, and two chandeliers.

The contents of the room were valued at $1,500. The appraisers were not just being generous either. Their evaluation clearly reflected a hierarchy in the quality of the furniture in that room as compared with the other rooms in that house and in Pinckney's plantation homes. In Pinckney's Charleston house, the next most expensive room was the parlor. Its eighteen mahogany chairs, two mahogany settees, one mahogany footstool, one mahogany sideboard, miscellaneous tables, and five moreen window curtains and shades were valued at only $286.50. Apparently, the appraisers of the Pinckney estate believed the furniture in the drawing room was of truly exceptional quality and style. One can only speculate whether or not the Pinckney card tables were the ones mentioned in his inventory. Clearly, however, when Pinckney wished to create a grand room he turned to Deming and Bulkley for his decorating needs.[41]

With their elaborate gilded decoration, the Miller center table and the Pinckney card tables may seem gaudy to modern eyes, but during the early nineteenth century they were the height of fashion. Several English authors published instructional manuals with gilding designs and information on materials and techniques. The ornamental gilders in Deming and Bulkley's shop produced exceptional work, and Charlestonians recognized it. On February 3, 1824, the *Charleston Courier* published a letter written under the pseudonym "Franklin":

> The writer of this, however, cannot pass unnoticed, the elegant patterns of Cabinet Work, executed by Messrs. DEMING & BULKLEY, of this city. There are two pieces of this work, which will not suffer in comparison with the best specimens ever imported from Europe, either in point of taste or workmanship. Those who are desirous of examining the works of American ingenuity, may be gratified by calling at their Ware-House, in King-street. We will not be so unjust as to suppose that so much talent and industry will go unrewarded by the liberal citizens of Charleston.

Although praising Deming and Bulkley for their "American ingenuity," the writer nevertheless compared their work to the best imported furniture from Europe. "Franklin's" statement reveals that his frame of reference and that of his audience was European furniture. Deming and Bulkley's understanding of this attitude unquestionably contributed to their success.[42]

Closely related to the Pinckney and the Miller tables are ten card tables

Figure 19 Card table attributed to Deming and Bulkley, New York City, ca. 1825. Rosewood veneer with white pine, tulip poplar, and oak. H. 29¼", W. 37¼", D. 18¾". (Courtesy, Charleston Museum; photo, Gavin Ashworth.)

and a pier table with Charleston histories and six tables associated with families in Georgia and other areas of South Carolina. When viewed as a group, there are certain details that recur in varying combinations, almost as if there was a menu of decorative options from which to choose. These include canted-corner or D-shaped tops; rosewood veneer or rosewood graining; a stamped red velvet playing surface; gilded grapevine borders; a gilded basket of flowers on the top; gilded motifs in imitation of ormolu; a gilded stenciled or inlaid brass border on the skirt; a concave, four-sided plinth with canted corners; carved or painted dolphin feet; and carved or painted eagle designs.

Two of the finest card tables attributed to Deming and Bulkley's shop (see fig. 19) were acquired in the early twentieth century by the Roebling family of Charleston. Both have rosewood veneers and freehand gilded decoration, but instead of a painted pedestal they have extraordinary, carved eagle supports. The tops are decorated with a gilded basket of flowers and a grapevine border (fig. 20) virtually identical to those on the Pinckney tables. The eagle support and the grapevine border are especially important because Deming and Bulkley mentioned both details in their advertisements. The rosewood suite raffled in 1820 featured "a Border in imitation of a Grape Vine, around every piece of it." The same year, they advertised another set of rosewood furniture that included "a pair of Card Tables, supported by a Spread Eagle." Deming and Bulkley described the second suite as "much superior" to any offered previously and claimed that several pieces were equivalent to any in the world. Three pairs of spread eagle, rosewood card tables attributed to Deming and Bulkley survive, suggesting that their "superior" furniture appealed to Charleston tastes. One pair virtually identical to the Roebling tables descended in the Wragg family of Charleston. Family tradition maintains that Dr. William Wragg purchased them in France while studying medicine there in the early nineteenth century. Evidently, Deming and Bulkley were so successful in producing furniture equated with European examples that their legacy fell victim to their marketing strategy.[43]

Several other New York cabinet shops made tables with spread eagle supports, but few are as robust or as anatomically accurate as those of the Roebling tables, which have the most sculptural carving attributed to Deming and Bulkley's shop. Carved from white pine blocks, laminated for thickness, the eagle support of the table illustrated in figure 19 has a gilded and painted head that protrudes beyond the skirt and powerful claws that grasp a *vert antique* rock that rests on the plinth below. The skirt is decorated with freehand gilding like those of several other tables in the group. These designs are derived from classical ornaments, and they imitate, in both style and placement, the ormolu mounts of French Empire furniture. The shape of the plinth is virtually identical to those on the Pinckney card tables, but it has a different gilded border and four dolphin feet rather than lion's paws. Although slightly faded, the top also has its original stamped red velvet playing surface (fig. 21).[44]

A card table (figs. 1, 22) with dolphin supports descended in the Alston-

Figure 20 Detail of the grapevine border and flower basket on the top of the card table illustrated in fig. 19. (Photo, Gavin Ashworth.)

Figure 21 Detail of the velvet playing surface on the card table illustrated in fig. 19. (Photo, Gavin Ashworth.)

Figure 22 Card table illustrated in fig. 1 opened to the original velvet playing surface. (Photo, Gavin Ashworth.)

Figure 23 Detail of the grapevine border and satinwood edging on the top of the card table illustrated in fig. 22. (Photo, Gavin Ashworth.)

Pringle family. Although it lacks the gilded basket of flowers found on several other tables in the group, it has a rosewood top with a grapevine border and satinwood edging (fig. 23). The classical motif on the skirt is based on English designs, and the gilding is enlivened by delicate penwork that simulates the more modeled and expressive surface of ormolu. Recent conservation confirmed the presence of *vert antique* and gilded decoration.[45]

Ten card tables with either dolphin supports or dolphin feet have nineteenth-century Charleston provenances. The Huger family example, illustrated in figure 24, was considerably less expensive than the Roebling and Alston-Pringle tables. It has mahogany veneers instead of rosewood, simple carved dolphins, and no freehand gilded decoration. The only ornament on the skirt is a narrow strip of die-cut brass banding. The rope-twist balusters and dolphins had gilded and *vert antique* decoration; however, the acanthus leaves that enlivened the design of the Roebling feet are absent on the Huger example.

English and French design books and furniture attest to the popularity of the dolphin motif, which was commonly associated with the goddess Venus in antiquity. Although dolphins occur on nineteenth-century furniture from New York and Philadelphia, the tables and seating forms attributed to Deming and Bulkley suggest that this motif achieved a special status in

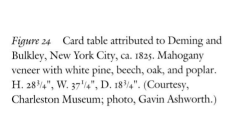

Figure 24 Card table attributed to Deming and Bulkley, New York City, ca. 1825. Mahogany veneer with white pine, beech, oak, and poplar. H. 28³/₄", W. 37¹/₄", D. 18³/₄". (Courtesy, Charleston Museum; photo, Gavin Ashworth.)

Figure 25 Card table, English, ca. 1813. Rosewood veneer with brass inlay; secondary woods and dimensions unrecorded. (Courtesy, Royal Pavilion, Brighton, England.)

Charleston. English sources for dolphins include Thomas Sheraton's *Cabinet Dictionary* (1803), which has four plates with dolphin motifs, and Ackermann's *Repository* (fig. 14). In Britain, dolphin designs were especially popular after Lord Nelson's victory at Trafalgar. A suite of dolphin-carved furniture (fig. 25) was commissioned in memory of Lord Viscount Nelson and presented to Greenwich Hospital in 1813 and 1815. It was placed in the Governor's House, only to be viewed by visitors "of distinction." Like the tables attributed to Deming and Bulkley, English examples typically have four carved dolphins supporting the base. The one illustrated in figure 25 also has a cross-banded top, brass inlay, and a painted and gilded pedestal. Whether the dolphin motif appealed to Charlestonians because of its association with antiquity, because of its use on English and French furniture, or for purely stylistic reasons is unknown; however, the substantial number of surviving tables indicates that it was popular with wealthy consumers as well as with those of lesser means.[46]

Stylistically related to this large group of dolphin card tables is a dolphin-foot recamier (fig. 26) that belonged to Colonel William Washington (1785–1830). The back of the recamier has a carved eagle battling a serpent (fig. 27), whose tail curls down to the seat in a scrolling volute. The carving appears to be by the same hand that carved the eagle support of the Roebling table (fig. 19). The front rail and arms are veneered with rosewood and inlaid with brass anthemia and rosettes (fig. 28), and the entire form is supported by four carved dolphin feet with gilded and *vert antique* decoration. The feet are double-tenoned into the frame like those of the card tables.[47]

A related sofa that descended in the Ravenel family (fig. 29) also has a

Figure 26 Recamier attributed to Deming and Bulkley, New York City, ca. 1830. Rosewood veneer and mahogany with oak, ash, and poplar. H. 38½", W. 90½", D. 25". (Courtesy, Charleston Museum; photo, Gavin Ashworth.)

Figure 27 Detail of the crest rail on the recamier illustrated in fig. 26. (Photo, Gavin Ashworth.)

Figure 28 Detail of an arm, foot, and brass inlay on the recamier illustrated in fig. 26. (Photo, Gavin Ashworth.)

carved eagle and serpent crest and dolphin feet; however, the eagle and serpent are not as sculptural and appear to be by a different hand. By contrast, the dolphin feet on the sofa and the recamier are virtually identical. Such variations are to be expected in the products of large shops that employed several specialists. Furthermore, the brass inlays on the sofa are negatives of those on the Washington recamier, much like *premier parti* and *contra parti* in European boulle decoration.

Deming and Bulkley's advertisements indicate that they sold a large number of chairs, from the finest rosewood examples to the most basic Windsors. Only one documented chair is known, a lyre-back armchair with hairy paw feet (fig. 30) that shares several details with the tables attributed to Deming and Bulkley's shop. It is grained in imitation of rosewood and decorated with freehand gilding. Like the Roebling, Pinckney, and Alston-Pringle tables, the armchair features a grapevine border on the front of the lyre and on both the inside and outside surfaces of the scrolled arms (figs. 31, 32). The lyre terminates in miniature eagle heads (fig. 31) similar to those on the Roebling card table (fig. 19) and the Washington recamier (fig. 27). Additionally, the gilded decoration on the front seat rail is closely related to that on the skirt of the Alston-Pringle and Roebling card tables (figs. 1, 19, 30). In 1821, Erastus Bulkley presented this "elegant chair" to St. John's Lutheran Church "to be placed at the Altar for the use of the minister." Documentation for similar chairs includes the 1823 inventory of Joseph Yates, which listed "12 Small & 2 Elbow imitation Rose Wood Chairs & 2 Grecian Couches" valued at $160.[48]

A pair of cane-seated fancy chairs that descended in the Porcher family have similar rosewood graining and gilded decoration (fig. 33). The turned crest rails are decorated with gilded eagles (fig. 34), and the scrolled splats and front seat rails have classical ornaments. The seat rail designs resemble the trompe l'oeil ormolu decoration on the St. John's armchair and on many of the card tables attributed to Deming and Bulkley.

In contrast to the aforementioned furniture, a few pieces documented to Deming and Bulkley suggest the character of the furniture they made for the middle class. In 1825 and 1828, planter William Lucas placed several orders with Deming and Bulkley, the first for a pair of card tables, a sofa,

Figure 30 Armchair by Deming and Bulkley, New York City, 1821. Maple. H. 33", W. 20½", D. 17½". (Courtesy, St. John's Lutheran Church; photo, Gavin Ashworth.)

Figure 31 Detail of the grapevine border and carved eagle heads on the lyre back of the armchair illustrated in fig 30. (Photo, Gavin Ashworth.)

Figure 32 Detail of the grapevine border on the arms of the armchair illustrated in fig. 30. (Photo, Gavin Ashworth.)

Figure 33 Painted side chair attributed to Deming and Bulkley, New York City, ca. 1825. Maple. H. 33³/₄", W. 16³/₄", D. 21¹/₂". (Private collection; photo, Gavin Ashworth.)

Figure 34 Detail of the freehand gilded eagle on the crest rail of the side chair illustrated in fig. 33. (Photo, Gavin Ashworth.)

Figure 35 Sideboard by Deming and Bulkley, New York City, 1825. Mahogany veneer with tulip poplar and white pine. H. 52¹/₂", W. 66³/₁₆", D. 24⁵/₈". (Private collection; photo, Museum of Early Southern Decorative Arts.)

and a sideboard. The sideboard, which descended in the Lucas family with its bill of sale (fig. 35), is typical of the plainer furnishings that Charlestonians preferred for their plantation houses. Lucas was apparently satisfied with his purchase, for in 1828 he ordered a work table, an end dining table, carpeting, and candle shades. The two surviving bills do not list any fancy chairs, but a bamboo side chair also in the Lucas family is marked in chalk, "D & B," and may have been purchased from them.[49]

A pier table with feet similar to those on the Lucas sideboard and a marble-top center table (fig. 36) have labels from Deming and Bulkley's Charleston wareroom. The one on the center table states:

DEMING & BULKLEY,
Manufacturers,
No. 56 Beekman-Street, New-York.
Sold at their
CABINET FURNITURE, PIANO FORTE,
AND CARPET WARE-ROOMS,
No. 205 King-Street,
Charleston, So. Ca.

Such labels are relatively common on mass-produced furniture made for export and stock-in-trade. The center table has an "Egyptian" marble top; however, it may have been a stock item as well.[50]

Figure 36 Center table with partial label by Deming and Bulkley, New York City, ca. 1835. Mahogany veneer with ash and white pine. H. 29½", Diam. 35¾". (Private collection; photo, Museum of Early Southern Decorative Arts.)

Figure 37 Secretary-and-bookcase with partial label by Deming and Bulkley, New York City, ca. 1835. Mahogany veneer with cedrela, white pine, and tulip poplar. H. 87½", W. 73½", D. 48½". (Private collection; photo, Gavin Ashworth.)

Figure 38 Detail of the Deming and Bulkley label on the secretary-and-bookcase illustrated in fig. 37. (Photo, Gavin Ashworth.)

Figure 39   Aiken-Rhett house, Charleston, 1817; with 1833 and 1858 additions. (Courtesy, Historic Charleston Foundation.)

Figure 40   Interior of the Aiken-Rhett house with original furnishings, photographed in 1918. The whereabouts of the dolphin card table in the lower lefthand corner is unknown. (Courtesy, Historic Charleston Foundation.)

The only labeled piece for which the original owner is known is a secretary-and-bookcase (figs. 37, 38) from a pair originally owned by Governor William Aiken (son-in-law of Sarah Lowndes). Aiken was one of Charleston's wealthiest citizens, owning more than seven hundred slaves in 1844. Like the labeled pier table and center table, Aiken's secretary-and-bookcase demonstrates that Deming and Bulkley's work had shifted toward the new "Grecian plain style" by the 1830s. Advocated by European designers such as Thomas King, this new style emphasized "chaste contour and simplicity of parts." New York's ability to produce furniture in this style was no doubt enhanced by the increasing arrival of German-trained cabinetmakers familiar with the Biedermeier style then popular in central Europe.[51]

Aiken substantially remodeled his Charleston house during the late 1830s (figs. 39, 40) and apparently refurnished it with New York furniture. The surviving Aiken furniture includes the two secretary-and-bookcases, a dining table, two bedsteads, two demi-lune ottomans, a tabouret, a wardrobe, a marble-top dressing table, and two sideboards with their companion cellarets (fig. 41). The secretary-and-bookcase (fig. 37) is the only labeled piece, but evidence suggests that many of the other items came from Deming and Bulkley as well. The sideboards and cellarets (fig. 41) were designed to fit into Aiken's new dining room. In 1839, Francis Kinloch Middleton described a ball held there:

> last night I was at the handsomest ball I have ever seen—given by Mrs. Aiken—Miss Lowndes that was—they live near Boundary street (now Calhoun) in a house he has added to & furnished very handsomely—2 floors were entirely thrown open—the orchestra from the theatre played for the dancers—and the supper table was covered with a rich service of silver—lights in profusion, & a crowded handsomely dressed assembly.

These sideboards and the other furnishings Aiken purchased for his home were important components of an elaborate physical space he created to

showcase his wealth and his taste. Made of the most expensive materials—"Egyptian" marble, white marble, highly figured mahogany veneer—they were intended solely for the display of his silver and ceramics.[52]

It is not known exactly when or why Deming and Bulkley went out of business in Charleston. They were listed in the 1840 city directory at 205 King Street, when Erastus Bulkley was additionally listed as a marble agent at 49 Broad Street, but not in the following one published in 1849. Their success in the Charleston market is suggested by New York City records. While Bulkley lived and worked in Charleston, Deming's wealth increased steadily. From 1810 to 1840, the value of Deming's real estate grew from $1,400 to $13,500 and his personal property from $200 to $10,000. Deming and Bulkley continued to appear in New York City directories until 1850, just four years before Brazilia's death. In 1852, Bulkley found a new partner in German emigré cabinetmaker Gustave Herter (1830–1892). Their firm also produced ornate furniture for an elite clientele, primarily by custom order. A financial notice described Herter as a "practical mechanic" and Bulkley as a "close, careful businessman" worth over $80,000 and "formerly of Deming and Bulkley, a successful firm producing high quality furniture with a branch in Charleston." Documentation pertaining to Deming and Bulkley's New York and Charleston ventures remains scarce, but the extraordinary carved and gilded furniture attributed to their shop attests to their success in producing high-quality, European-styled objects for the upper-class Charleston market. These objects represent an important new body of American furniture in the classical style.[53]

ACKNOWLEDGMENTS The authors thank Mr. Gavin Ashworth, Mr. William N. Banks, Mr. Luke Beckerdite, Mr. David Beevers, Ms. Wendy A. Cooper, Mrs. Ashby Farrow, Mr. and Mrs. George E. Grimball, Mr. and Mrs. Samuel L. Howell IV, Mrs. Richard Hutson, Mr. Peter M. Kenny, Mr. Chris Loeblein, Mr. and Mrs. Peter Manigault, Mr. Charles Moffatt, Dr. Edward F. Parker, Mr. and Mrs. Robert Prioleau, Mrs. Karen Rabe, Mr. and Mrs. Daniel Ravenel, Mr. J. Thomas Savage, St. John's Lutheran Church, Mr. and Mrs. Joseph Torras, and Mrs. Deborah Dependahl Waters for their generous assistance with this article.

1. The calculation of per free capita wealth is skewed in Charleston's favor, for it omits slaves who made up approximately 50 percent of the population; however, when calculated as a per capita amount, Charleston's wealth was still twice as great as New England and the Middle Colonies. For more on the economic history of South Carolina, see Peter A. Coclanis, *The Shadow of a Dream: Economic Life and Death in the South Carolina Low Country, 1670–1920* (New York: Oxford University Press, 1989); the statistics cited here are taken from pp. 116, 125. See also, Alice Hanson Jones, *The Wealth of a Nation To Be: The American Colonies on the Eve of the Revolution* (New York: Columbia University Press, 1980), pp. 54, 58, 380. Josiah Quincy, *Memoir of the Life of Josiah Quincy Jun. of Massachusetts* (Boston, 1825), p. 73. In 1860, the per capita wealth in Charleston was $800, in Massachusetts, $600, and in New York, $625. Coclanis, *Shadow of a Dream*, p. 128.

2. *Charleston Courier*, February 3, 1824.

3. For more on British furniture imported in Charleston, see Milby Burton, *Charleston Furniture 1700–1825* (Columbia: University of South Carolina Press, 1970), pp. 7–8, 13–16; M. Allison Carll, "An Assessment of English Furniture Imports into Charleston, South Carolina, 1760–1800," *Journal of Early Southern Decorative Arts* 11, no. 2 (November 1985): 1–18; J. Thomas Savage, "The Miles Brewton House, Charleston, South Carolina: The Interior and Furnishings," *Antiques* 143, no. 2 (February 1993): 300–7. For general information on British trade with Charleston after the American Revolution, see the chapter "The Return of the British Merchants," in George C. Rogers, Jr., *Evolution of a Federalist, William Loughton Smith of Charleston (1758–1812)* (Columbia: University of South Carolina Press, 1962), pp. 97–111. For more on the Charlestonian experience with the grand tour, see Maurie D. McInnis, "The Politics of Taste: Classicism in Charleston, 1815–1840" (Ph.D. dissertation, Yale University, 1996). John Drayton, *A View of South-Carolina* (Charleston, S.C.: W. P. Young, 1802), pp. 217, 221.

4. Mary Stead Pinckney to Margaret Izard Manigault, October 5, 1797, Manigault Papers, South Caroliniana Library, University of South Carolina, Columbia. Josephine du Pont to Margaret Izard Manigault, September 10, 1800, as quoted in Betty-Bright P. Low, "Of Muslins and Merveilleuses: Excerpts from the Correspondence of Josephine du Pont and Margaret Manigault," *Winterthur Portfolio* 9 (Charlottesville: University Press of Virginia for the Winterthur Museum, 1974), p. 66.

5. Margaret Izard Manigault to Alice Delancey Izard, November 25, 1808, Izard Papers, Library of Congress (hereinafter cited as IP, LC). Surviving furniture and probate inventories document Charleston's enthusiasm for gilding, carving, and rosewood furniture. For example, Dr. Alexander Baron's drawing room had "2 London made cane bottom sophas $50; 12 [London-made, cane-bottom] . . . chairs $120; 1 pr. Sattin wood card tables $20; 1 [pr. satin-wood] . . . tea tables $10 . . . [and] 5 Window Curtains & Cornices London made, $250." Although Charleston County inventories are not very descriptive, occasional notations indicate the prevalence of gilded seating furniture. Ed Power had "12 Green & gilt chairs $36" in his drawing room; Col. Charles W. Bulow had "12 gilt chairs" in his back parlor; William Lowndes had "12 Gilt chairs with cane bottoms, $18" in an unspecified room; and William Brisbane's drawing room had "a rich guilt Grecian Sopha with damask Cushions $120; a dozen Chairs with damask Cushions $175" (Inventory of Dr. Alexander Baron, May 6, 1819, Charleston County Probate Court, Bk. F, 1819–1824, pp. 53–56; Inventory of Ed Power, May 24, 1819, Bk. F, 1819-1824, pp. 70-1; Inventory of Col. Charles W. Bulow, July 1823, Bk. F, 1819–1824, pp. 562–64; Inventory of William Lowndes, October 23, 1823, Bk. F, 1819–1824, pp. 582–83; Inventory of William Brisbane, 1822, Bk. F, 1819–1824, pp. 414–17, 495–98). Examples of painted and gilded English neoclassical furniture with Charleston histories include a set of nine armchairs (ca. 1800) with an Allston family history and a pair of armchairs (ca. 1805) with a Bacot family history, all in the collection of the Historic Charleston Foundation.

6. Charles Fraser, *Reminiscences of Charleston* (1854; reprint ed., Charleston, S.C.: Garnier & Company, 1969), p. 14.

7. Margaret Izard Manigault to Alice Delancey Izard, February 5, 1809, March 12, 1809, December 22, 1811, IP, LC.

8. Isaac Coffin to the Misses Pinckney, July 12, 1817, Charles Cotesworth Pinckney Papers, LC; this set of Gillows chairs is in a private collection. The Barelli, Torre & Co. advertisement is in the *Charleston Courier*, March 20, 1819. For Woddrop's advertisements, see the *Charleston Courier,* January 6, 1818; January 19, 1819; January 1, 1820; January 8, 1820; February 19, 1821. For more on the 1824 tariff, see William W. Freehling, *Prelude to Civil War: The Nullification Controversy in South Carolina, 1816–1836* (New York: Harper & Row, 1966), pp. 106–8; and Rogers, *Evolution of a Federalist*, pp. 374–76. J. N. Cardazo, *Reminiscences of Charleston* (Charleston, S.C.: Joseph Walker, 1866), pp. 11–13.

9. *Charleston Courier*, October 23, 1815. Information concerning the marketing of furniture in Charleston was derived from the city's newspaper advertisements and U.S. Bureau of Customs, Outward Coastwise Manifests, District of Philadelphia (hereinafter cited as USBC, OCM, DP). Unfortunately similar records do not survive for New York, but one assumes that the early channels of distribution were similar. For more on the extent of Philadelphia's coastwise and foreign trade, see U.S. Bureau of Customs, Outward Coastwise Manifests, District of Philadelphia, Record Group 36–1059, National Archives, Washington, D.C.; and Kathleen M. Catalano, "Cabinetmaking in Philadelphia 1820–1840: Transition from Craft to Industry," in *American Furniture and Its Makers, Winterthur Portfolio* 13, edited by Ian M. G. Quimby (Charlottesville: University Press of Virginia, 1979), pp. 81–91.

10. *Charleston Courier*, January 3, 1816 (Gamage); January 23, 1816 (Davenport); January 6, 1818 (Stagg).

11. *Charleston Courier*, February 8, 1816. *City Gazette and Commercial Daily Advertiser*, June 16, 1820.

12. *City Gazette and Commercial Daily Advertiser*, January 1, 1819 (Everitt). *Charleston Courier*, January 1, 1819 (Budd). The New York directories list John L. Everitt as a cabinetmaker from 1808 to 1837 and John Budd from 1819 until 1844. The authors thank Peter M. Kenny and Deborah Dependahl Waters for this information.

13. The fire in Rawson's wareroom was reported in the *Charleston Courier*, February 21, 1820. Advertisements indicate that Rawson stocked a full range of furniture including bureaus, sideboards, bedsteads, chairs, and breakfast, tea, and card tables. His advertisements usually mentioned that the furniture was from the north, but they did not specify Providence. Rawson's Charleston label is on a sideboard (Museum of Early Southern Decorative Arts [hereinafter cited as MESDA] research file S-14321) and a set of drawers with a dressing glass published in Paul H. Borroughs, *Southern Antiques* (New York: Bonanza Books, 1931), pp. 147, 158. For more on William Rawson's association with Charleston, see Forsyth M. Alexander, "Cabinet Warehousing in the Southern Atlantic Ports, 1783–1820," *Journal of Early Southern Decorative Arts* 15, no. 2 (November 1989): 28. For a comparison of the amount of furniture shipped from Philadelphia to various U.S. cities, see Catalano, "Cabinetmaking in Philadelphia," p. 83.

14. For more on warehousing in the South, see Alexander, "Cabinet Warehousing," pp. 1–42. Information about Philadelphia furniture imports was compiled from USBC, OCM, DP, for 1821, 1826, 1831, and 1836.

15. *Charleston Courier*, January 2, 1817; *Charleston Courier*, January 3, 1818; *Charleston Courier*, February 17, 1818. For other advertisements by Otis, see *Charleston Courier*, January 8, 1818, January 31, 1818, and March 31, 1818. For Van Nostrand, see *Charleston Courier*, March 13, 1819. "Van Nostrand" may have been either Samuel Van Nostrand who is listed in the New York directories in 1819, 1821, 1823, and 1824, or Jacob Van Nostrand who is listed in the New York directories from 1812 to 1817 and from 1819 to 1825. No information on the carver named "Christie" is known. The authors thank Peter M. Kenny for this information.

16. The evolution of the furniture industry in Philadelphia is discussed in Catalano, "Cabinetmaking in Philadelphia," pp. 87–91. For more on the decline of the Charleston cabinetmaking trade, see McInnis, "The Politics of Taste," chapter six.

17. For information on Gouldsmith and Sheridan, see Burton, *Charleston Furniture*, pp. 93, 94, 120. For Sheridan's advertisements, see *Charleston Courier*, March 14, 1827, and *Charleston Courier*, March 3, 1828.

18. *Charleston Courier*, February 20, 1820; *Charleston Courier*, April 3, 1824. In a public address, artist Charles Fraser lamented the fashion for visiting the north and buying northern goods:

Not to speak of the fascinations which annually draw into their vortex so many of our fellow citizens, and so much of our money—not to speak of the preference given to Northern workmen by the votaries of fashion—not to mention that reliance upon their labour for almost every article of use, which paralyzes industry at home.

See Charles Fraser, *An Address delivered before the Citizens of Charleston, and the Grand Lodge of South-Carolina, at the Laying of the Corner Stone of a new College Edifice, with Masonic Ceremonies, on the 12th January, 1828* (Charleston: J. S. Burges, 1828), p. 17. For more on the Nullification crisis and its effect on the artisan community, see William H. and Jane H. Pease, *The Web of Progress: Private Values and Public Styles in Boston and Charleston, 1828–1843* (Athens, Ga.: University of Georgia Press, 1991); Freehling, *Prelude to Civil War*; and McInnis, "The Politics of Taste," chapter six.

19. *Charleston Courier*, February 15, 1817.

20. Alicia Hopton Russell Middleton to Euretta Barnewall Middleton, July 31, 1834, Cheves-Middleton Papers, South Carolina Historical Society, Charleston (hereinafter cited as SCHS).

21. Sarah Elliott Huger to Harriott Pinckney Horry, March 17, 1812, Mrs. St. Julien Ravenel Family Papers (hereinafter cited as SJRFP), SCHS.

22. Sarah Elliott Huger to Harriott Pinckney Horry, October 15, 1812, Anna Wells Rutledge Papers, SCHS.

23. Mary I'on Lowndes married Frederick Rutledge Kinloch, March 16, 1816. Harriott Pinckney Horry Rutledge to Harriott Pinckney Horry, September 20, 1815, SJRFP.

24. The Paris firm, J. Boris, Antiquités Longchamp, 83 Rue de Longchamp, offered a set of labeled Ellis & Wheaton fancy chairs of curled maple in 1991. The label reads:

ELLIS & WHEATON, Fancy Chair Manufacturers, No. 15 Bowery-Lane, Keep constantly on hand a large and elegant assortment of Japan Furniture, Settees, Couches, Rocking, Sewing and Fancy Chairs. Orders thankfully received, and carefully executed. N.B. Old Chairs repaired, painted, and gilt, in the newest fashion and on the lowest terms.

The label is dated "Oct. 26 1816" and signed by Stephen Wheaton, with the following hand-written invoice: "Mr. Westfield/ Ten Curl mapel [sic] fancy Chairs at $5.50 each/ Eight Ball Do. at $5/ to painting 8 winsor [sic] Chairs/ to painting fancy Do./ $104.50" (J. Boris to Deborah Dependahl Waters, Curator of Decorative Arts, Museum of the City of New York, December 13, 1991). For more on Wheaton, see Charles Montgomery, *American Furniture, The Federal Period* (New York: Viking Press, 1966), p. 457. Sarah Elliott Huger to Harriott Pinckney Horry, October 21, 1815, SJRFP.

25. Sarah Huger had previously commissioned tables from Duncan Phyfe for her brother-in-law John Wells, who wrote to her on July 25, 1815: "select a carpet for our two lower rooms with proper tables for the front room and a tea-table for the back room. Chairs will also be wanting.... The tables you will get better at Phyfe's than elsewhere" (as quoted in Nancy McClelland, *Duncan Phyfe and the English Regency 1795–1830* [New York: William R. Scott, Inc., 1939], pp. 304–7). Sarah Elliott Huger to Harriott Pinckney Horry, January 4, 1816, and March 5, 1816, SJRFP.

26. Despite this advice, surviving furniture and probate inventories indicate that the card table remained an extremely popular item of furniture throughout the period covered in this article. Sarah Elliott Huger to Harriott Pinckney Horry, March 5, 1816, SJRFP.

27. Benjamin Huger Papers, n.d., South Caroliniana Library, University of South Carolina. For another example of New York furniture ordered for a South Carolinian, see Elizabeth D. English, "House Furnishings of the 1830's As Described in the Letters of Martha Keziah Peay," *South Carolina Historical and Genealogical Magazine* 43, no. 2 (April 1942): 69–87. Martha Keziah Peay wrote on September 2, 1830, enclosing a list for furniture that included:

2 Pier Tables & 1 Centre Table/ 1 Tea Table - 2 Foot Stools/ 2 Grecian Sofas (with elastic bottoms)/ 1 set Dining Tables/ 1 Side Board (with marble top)/ 1 Secretary and Bookcase/ 2 Candle Stands/ 1 Large handsomely carved Bed Stead/ 2 Perfectly Plain Bed Steads/ 2 Wash Stands - One suitable for the carved Bedstead, & the other plain/ 1 Dressing Table - 1 Easy Chair for chamber/ 1 Wardrobe (with a recess on one side for hanging up dresses)/ 1 Set Cane bottom Chairs for Drawing Room.

Eventually, part of the furniture order was diverted to Philadelphia through the help of Mrs. William Chaloner. On December 8, 1830, Peay's furniture was shipped from New York to the care of John Robinson, her father's Charleston factor, with bills of lading and invoices from

New York cabinetmaker Alexander P. W. Kinnan for the pier tables, a center table, two sofas, a work table, a tea table, and a pair of benches, totaling $426.00; and from the looking glass maker Charles Del Vecchio for two pier glasses and a chimney glass, totaling $82.00. The goods were shipped by steamboat from Charleston to Columbia, South Carolina, on January 13, 1831.

28. Albert Sack, *Fine Points of Furniture: Early American* (New York: Crown Publishers, Inc., 1950), p. 61, illustrates one of the Middleton family chairs and identifies it as made for Arthur Middleton (1742–1787), a signer of the Declaration of Independence; however, the set was probably made for his nephew, Arthur Middleton (1785–1837) and Alicia Hopton Russell Middleton (1789–1840) of Bolton Plantation. "Middleton of South Carolina," *South Carolina Historical and Genealogical Magazine* 1, no. 3 (July 1900): 242–45, 253–55. For more on these chairs, see Katherine Gross Farnham, "Living with Antiques: The Gordon-Banks House in the Georgia Piedmont," *Antiques* 102, no. 3 (September 1972): 432–50. The Read family recamier is illustrated and discussed in Farnham, "Living with Antiques," pp. 432–50. "Middleton of South Carolina," p. 248.

29. For more on the Wickham and Bosley tables, see Wendy A. Cooper, *Classical Taste in America, 1800–1840* (New York: Abbeville Press, 1993) pp. 170–71; and Newark Museum, *Classical America 1815–1845* (Newark, N.J.: Baker Printing Co., 1963), pp. 36–37, 74.

30. The quotation is taken from a labeled card table, MESDA research file S-8866. Evidence from directory listings and other sources suggests that Bulkley resided in Charleston and Deming remained in New York.

31. Deming and Bulkley's first advertisement is in the *City Gazette and Commercial Daily Advertiser*, January 5, 1818. Other advertisements appeared in the *Gazette* on March 10, 1818, and in the *Charleston Courier* on June 3, 1818. Bulkley sold his first shipment at the store of Henry Loomis, identified as a "hardware merchant" in *The Directory and Stranger's Guide for the City of Charleston* (Charleston: Schenckand Turner, 1819), p. 62; *Charleston Courier*, December 28, 1818. *City Gazette and Commercial Daily Advertiser*, November 22, 1819. Charleston was marked by seasonal rhythms. In the winter, especially from January to March, planters lived in town, and the city was crowded and active. In the summer, many residents left for cooler climes. Although escaping the heat of Charleston's near tropical climate was part of the reason, the strongest motivation was the various fevers (yellow fever, "stanger's fever," etc.) that tended to plague the city during the summer months. Bulkley's yearly excursions to New York were consistent with this movement.

32. The authors thank Peter M. Kenny for the New York directory references to Deming and Bulkley. From 1805 to 1809, Deming was in business with William Turner. From 1810 to 1820 he is listed alone at various addresses, and from 1820 to 1826 (the last year of Kenny's research) Deming is listed with Bulkley. The family genealogy is outlined in Donal Lines Jacobus, *The Bulkeley Genealogy* (New Haven, Ct.: privately published, 1933), pp. 658, 661, 663. Simeon Deming is best known for a sideboard he made for Governor Oliver Wolcott (1726–1797) of Connecticut (J. Michael Flanigan, *American Furniture from the Kaufman Collection* [Washington: National Gallery of Art, 1986], pp. 208–11).

33. *City Gazette and Commercial Advertiser*, June 28, 1821. *Charleston Courier*, June 24, 1822.

34. *Charleston Courier*, March 7, 1820 (Rawson); *Charleston Courier*, January 1, 1826 (Sheridan). *City Gazette and Commercial Daily Advertiser*, November 20, 1820 (Deming and Bulkley).

35. *Charleston Courier*, April 12, 1820. *City Gazette and Commercial Daily Advertiser*, November 20, 1820. Pauline Agius, *Ackermann's Regency Furniture and Interiors* (Ramsbury, England: Crowood Press, 1984), pp. 18, 27. The issues of Rudolph Ackermann, *The Repository of Arts, Literature, Commerce, Manufactures, Fashions and Politics* from which the above quotations are drawn are vol. 1, no. 2, pl. 38 (December 1809): 411; vol. 1, no. 5, pl. 16 (March 1811): 222; vol. 2, no. 1, pl. 20 (April 1816): 244; vol. 2, no. 11, pl. 9 (February 1821): 128.

36. The authors thank Peter M. Kenny for information on the New York advertisements. *New York Evening Post*, October 7, 1819, and July 22, 1820.

37. Huger's purchases are documented by receipts dated May 29, 1821, and May 14, 1832, Bacot-Huger Papers, SCHS. *Charleston Courier*, January 24, 1838. The success of Deming and Bulkley is also supported by the rather substantial number of surviving receipts, greater than for any other cabinetmaker, retailer, or warehouser of furniture in Charleston from 1815–1840. Of the forty-one surviving receipts for furniture purchased in Charleston from 1815–1840, twelve (30 percent) are for the firm of Deming and Bulkley. Five receipts (12 percent) survive for Cowperthwait, four (9 percent) for Richard Gouldsmith, and four (9 percent) for William Enston. The remainder are scattered between ten other cabinetmakers and retailers. Out of

fourteen entries in account books for cabinetmakers and retailers, Deming and Bulkley are listed in four separate entries (30 percent). For Hugh Swinton Ball's inventory, see Charleston County Probate Inventories, Bk. H, 1834–1844, pp. 326–30, 359–65, August 29, 1838. Washington Allston's *Spalatro and the Bloody Hand* is discussed in William H. Gerdts and Theodore E. Stebbins, Jr., *"A Man of Genius," The Art of Washington Allston* (Charlottesville: University of Virginia Press, 1979), p. 151.

38. The authors thank Wendy A. Cooper for bringing this table and letter to their attention. Deming and Bulkley to S[tephen] D. Miller, April 26, 1829, Charleston, Chestnut Family Papers (microfilm edition, 1979), State Historical Society of Wisconsin. Thomas Hope, *Household Furniture and Interior Decoration,* with introduction by David Watkin (1807, reprint ed., New York: Dover, 1971). For more on gilding techniques, see Donald L. Fennimore, "Gilding Practices and Processes in Nineteenth-Century American Furniture," and Cynthia Moyer, "Conservation Treatments for Border and Freehand Gilding and Bronze-Powder Stenciling and Freehand Bronze," in American Institute of Conservators, *Gilded Wood: Conservation and History* (Madison, Ct.: Sound View Press, 1991), pp. 139–51, 332–34.

39. The bodies of the swans on the skirt of the Deming and Bulkley table are similar to those on a stand in plate 21 of Hope's *Household Furniture*, but the fountain from which they are drinking is more like that on a dressing glass in plate 14. The trade catalogue is in the Victoria & Albert Museum, press no. M61e. A pier table labeled by Joseph Barry (Metropolitan Museum of Art) has a nearly identical ormolu mount (Jillian Ehninger, "With the Richest Ornaments Just Imported from France: Ornamental Hardware on Boston, New York, and Philadelphia Furniture, 1800-1840" [master's thesis, University of Delaware, 1992]).The decoration trailing the swans is similar to that behind a pair of winged lions drinking from a fountain in plate 15 of Hope's *Household Furniture*.

40. The quotation appears in Nathaniel Whittock, *The Decorative Painters' and Glaziers' Guide* (London, 1827), p. 20, and is taken from John Morley, *Regency Design, 1790–1840* (New York: Harry N. Abrams, 1993), p. 409. For more on the technique used to produce such borders, see Moyer, "Conservation Treatments for Border and Freehand Gilding," p. 332. Lyres abound in the design books of the period and are especially prevalent in Thomas Hope's *Household Furniture*.

41. Although it is possible that General Pinckney acquired these tables late in life (his second wife was considerably younger than he), they were probably purchased by his son. Colonel Pinckney purchased furniture from Deming and Bulkley in 1828. Colonel Pinckney's house on Broad Street was one of the most elaborate residences built in Charleston in the 1820s. The drawing room was on the second floor—an arrangement common in Charleston. That room extended across the front of the house and had extremely bold and deeply carved woodwork. The ceiling was sixteen feet high. The payment to Deming and Bulkley is recorded in Colonel Thomas Pinckney's account book with his factors, North, Webb & Osborne (Colonel Thomas Pinckney Estate Account Book, Charleston Library Society.) The furniture in Pinckney's Broad Street house was valued at $2,965.50, whereas that at his rice plantation, Fairfield, was valued at only $170. This difference provides a clear indication of the contrast between the utilitarian nature of the furnishings at his plantation home and the elaborate nature of the furnishings at his Charleston home, where Pinckney is known to have entertained lavishly during Charleston's social season. If these tables were purchased by General Thomas Pinckney and used at his plantation, El Dorado, as oral tradition maintains, then they may have been the "1 pair Square Card Tables" listed in his wife's inventory taken in 1843 (Charleston County Probate, Bk. A, 1839–1844, pp. 425–31).

42. A center table illustrated in Cooper, *Classical Taste in America*, p. 128, is decorated with elaborate freehand gilding, cut-brass inlay, and carving. Although not as elaborate as the Deming and Bulkley examples, it is described as "indicative of the most expensive New York workmanship." *Charleston Courier*, February 3, 1824. See George Smith, *Ornamental Designs after the Antique* (London, 1812); Rudolph Ackermann, *Selection of Ornaments* (London, 1817–1819); Thomas King, *Designs for Carving and Gilding* (London, ca. 1830); and Nathaniel Whittock, *The Decorative Painters' and Glaziers' Guide* (London, 1827). There are close parallels between Deming and Bulkley's work and several plates reproduced from design books in Frances Collard, *Regency Furniture* (Woodbridge, Eng.: Antique Collectors' Club, 1985).

43. For more on this related group of dolphin tables, see J. L. Sibley Jennings, *Dolphin Tales: The Discovery of Related Southern Furniture of Exceptional Quality and Northern Mis-Attribution, or, Move Over Lannuier* (Washington, D.C.: by the author, 1990). Although the authors dis-

agree with Jennings's conclusions regarding the origin of this group, his research was vital in grouping these pieces and determining their provenances. *City Gazette and Commercial Daily Advertiser*, April 11, 1820 and November 20, 1820. For more information on the Wragg card table, see Jennings, *Dolphin Tales*, p. 15.

44. For a French piece with ormolu mounts and an American history, see Cooper, *Classical Taste in America*, fig. 44. Ormolu mounts were often imitated by English cabinetmakers. Thomas Hope recommended the use of inlay instead of ormolu because inlay would not attract as much dirt and dust. Frances Collard, *Regency Furniture*, p. 93. Ormolu mounts were occasionally used but were more frequently imitated on American furniture. For other New York spread eagle card tables, see David L. Barquist, *American Tables and Looking Glasses in the Mabel Brady Garvan and Other Collections at Yale University* (New Haven, Ct.: Yale University Art Gallery, 1992), pp. 225–30.

45. For more on penwork, see Fennimore, "Gilding Practices," p. 147.

46. For more on the popularity of dolphins in nineteenth-century classical American furniture, see Cooper, *Classical Taste in America*, p. 150. The authors would like to thank David Beevers, Keeper of Preston Manor, Brighton, England, for information about the furniture made for Greenwich Hospital, now part of the collection of the Royal Pavilion, Brighton.

47. The recamier descended in the family of Colonel William Washington of Charleston. Notes made by Anna Wells Rutledge indicate that its mate was exactly the same, only reversed (Anna Wells Rutledge Papers, SCHS).

48. Vestry minutes, November 10, 1821, St. John's Lutheran Church. Inventory of Joseph Yates, 1823, Charleston County Probate Court, Bk. F, 1819–1824, pp. 495–98.

49. Deming and Bulkley's relatively liberal credit policy is documented by these two surviving bills. The 1825 bill records the purchase of the sideboard ($90) and the card tables ($75) in August and the sofa ($95) in November. Lucas paid for all of the items in late November. The 1828 bill for $186.30, which also spanned several months, was partially paid for by barrels of rice instead of cash. Photographs of the bills are in MESDA research files S-8624 and S-8624a. It is likely that Deming and Bulkley did not manufacture their own fancy chairs but instead purchased them from other makers. Beginning in 1826, they received shipments of chairs from Philadelphia chairmaker David Lindal. For specific shipments see USBC, OCM, DP, November 4, 1826; March 9, 1827; June 2, 1827; July 23, 1827; November 21, 1827; January 8, 1828; July 11, 1828; and June 4, 1831. The chairs were probably decorated by Deming and Bulkley's workmen.

50. MESDA research files S-8866, S-13560.

51. *Neo-Classical Furniture Designs, a reprint of Thomas King's "Modern Style of Cabinet Work Exemplified,"* introduction by Thomas Gordon Smith (New York: Dover, 1995).

52. William Aiken was the son of a Scots-Irish immigrant. He served as a state legislator, senator, and governor and was a member of the U.S. House of Representatives. A visitor to his plantation estimated that Aiken owned between 700 and 800 slaves (*Charleston Courier*, July 19, 1844). For more on the Aiken-Rhett house, see William Nathaniel Banks, "The Aiken-Rhett House, Charleston, South Carolina," *Antiques* 139, no. 1 (January 1991): 234–45. Francis Kinloch Middleton to Francis Kinloch, February 24, 1839, Charleston, Cheves-Middleton Papers, SCHS.

53. *Charleston Directory and Stranger's Guide* (Charleston, S.C.: T. C. Fay, 1840) p. 12. The authors are grateful to Deborah Dependahl Waters and Peter M. Kenny for sharing information on Deming and Bulkley in New York City directories and tax assessment books in the New York City Municipal Archives. Katherine S. Howe, Alice Cooney Frelinghuysen, Catherine Hoover Voorsanger, et al., *Herter Brothers: Furniture and Interiors for a Gilded Age* (New York: Harry N. Abrams, 1994), pp. 39–40, 63, 225–26.

*Roger Gonzales and
Daniel Putnam
Brown, Jr.*

Boston and New York
Leather Chairs:
A Reappraisal

▼ D U R I N G   T H E   L A S T few years of his life, Winterthur Museum curator Benno M. Forman developed an intriguing theory that three early eighteenth-century leather chairs in that institution's collection (see fig. 1) originated in New York rather than in New England as had previously been thought. Two are very similar to another leather chair (fig. 4) that Museum of Fine Arts, Boston, curator Richard H. Randall, Jr., had earlier dubbed a "Piscataqua," or Portsmouth area, version of the Boston leather chair. Forman's catalogue, *American Seating Furniture: 1630–1730*, identified nine characteristics that distinguished New York chairs from what he called "standardized" Boston chairs. In an article titled "Hidden in Plain Sight: Disappearance and Material Life in Colonial New York," historian Neil Kamil took Forman's argument one step further. Kamil maintained that many of the chairs he and Forman attributed to New York were the products of Huguenot artisans who immigrated to that city after the revocation of the Edict of Nantes in 1685.[1]

This article presents two arguments that dispute Forman's and Kamil's attributions. The first is that the leather chairs in Winterthur's collection are Boston chairs made during the first decade of the eighteenth century. They were the first seating forms to have evolved from the low-back "Cromwellian" chairs (or stools) made there from about 1640 to 1700 (figs. 2, 3). These "first-generation" leather chairs differ from Forman's "standardized" Boston chairs, not because they were made in a different region but because they were made at an earlier date. The second argument is that New York leather chairs have consistent turning patterns and construction details that differ from contemporary Boston examples.

The Forman Attributions
Forman outlined the following nine characteristics as distinguishing New York chairs:

1. "New York chairs have complex, turned stiles with a short column, and either balls or short balusters atop long balusters. Flat bottom-caps (half round turnings) above the balusters are common."

2. "On chairs that have barrel-like turnings on the stile between the seat rail and the lower back rail, the barrels have fat rings at their tops and bottoms."

3. "The rear feet go straight down to the floor on the back side and are chamfered on the forward side."

4. "Some chairs have double side stretchers, often of oak, and these are thicker than those on the Boston examples."

Figure 1   Side chair, Boston, 1700–1710. Maple and oak. H. 43⅝", W. 17⅝", D. 14¾". (Courtesy, Winterthur Museum.)

5. "When the side and rear stretchers are rectangular in section rather than turned, the rear stretcher enters the rear legs at the same point that the side stretchers do."

6. "When the front stretcher of a New York chair is turned, its ends terminate in blocks, which are joined to blocks on the front legs by mortise and tenon joints."

7. "In order to get a sufficiently bold turning on such stretchers, a piece of wood thicker than the legs is used. Upon final assembly the front stretcher is fitted flush with the front of the legs and thus overhangs in the back, often more than ¼"."

8. "On this chair [a carved-top leather chair that Forman attributed to New York] it [the top line of the upholstery on the back] is straight, with the characteristic slit through which the upholstery is pulled and tacked; on the usual Boston chairs, it is a rounded arch . . . that echoes the arch on the bottom edge of the front stretcher."

9. A "hollow crest rail is common to New York chairs."[2]

Although Forman was correct in asserting that leather chairs were made in New York and Kamil has documented the extensive involvement of Huguenot tradesmen in that city's chairmaking industry, seven of the nine features cited by both authors as characteristics of New York chairs are actually features of first-generation Boston chairs. The two other characteristics are typical of both first- and second-generation Boston seating.

With its double side stretchers and complex post turnings, the side chair illustrated in figure 4 is an excellent example of a first-generation Boston chair with all of Forman's "New York" characteristics. It features a leather seat and back panel, which were the most important visual components of baroque leather chairs regardless of their place of manufacture. The upholsterer used iron tacks to fasten the leather to the back of the crest and brass nails to secure it to the front faces of the stiles and rails. He also used brass nails to fasten the leather strips that cover the rough edges of the seat upholstery. The back of the chair is unupholstered, leaving the linen foundation for the marsh grass stuffing visible.[3]

Second-generation Boston leather chairs, most of which date after 1710, are the only ones Forman attributed to that city (see fig. 5). They typically have long columnar turnings flanking the back panel, scored cylindrical turnings above the seat, rear feet that rake backward, single side stretchers, and a rear stretcher positioned above the side stretchers. In addition, their back panels are often double nailed and unstuffed.[4]

The "Boston" Stretcher and the Evolution of Baroque Leather Chairs

The strongest evidence for attributing the first-generation leather chairs to Boston rather than to New York is their stretcher turnings. All have blocks at both ends and double opposed balusters (the inner one smaller than the outer one) flanking a central ring (see figs. 1, 4, 6*b*). Identical stretchers occur on seventeenth-century Boston low-back chairs (see figs. 3, 6*a*) and second-generation Boston leather chairs (see figs. 5, 6*c*), whose New England origins have never been disputed. The front stretchers on first- and second-generation side chairs are consistently 14½" wide, the same dimension as many of the ball-turned stretchers on earlier Boston low-back chairs (see fig. 2). Elongated versions of this pattern (fig. 6a–c) occur on the front stretchers of Boston armchairs (fig. 7), which typically have wider seats, and on the medial and rear stretchers of Boston easy chairs made during the first two decades of the eighteenth century.[5]

Three other characteristics cited by Forman—straight rear legs with chamfered faces, double side stretchers, and rear stretchers set level with the bottom side stretchers—are also features of Boston low-back chairs (figs. 2, 3). The side chair illustrated in figure 3 is the only example with a "Boston" stretcher and with baluster turnings above the seat; nevertheless, it represents a transition between low-back chairs with square seats and ball turnings (see fig. 2) and first-generation chairs with high backs and trapezoidal seats (see figs. 1, 4).[6]

Figure 2   Side chair, Boston, 1650–1700. Maple and oak. H. 36", W. 18", D. 15¼". (Courtesy, Winterthur Museum.)

Forman also believed that New York leather chairs had rear posts with more complex turnings than their Boston counterparts. During the late seventeenth and early eighteenth centuries, however, large numbers of English cane, turkeywork, and leather chairs (fig. 8) with similarly complex turnings were exported to the colonies, where they undoubtedly influenced regional turning patterns such as those on first-generation leather chairs (see figs. 1, 4). As the first-generation chairs passed out of fashion about 1710, the short baluster or barrel and ring elements above the rear seat rails became simple scored cylinders, and the columns on the back posts became elongated as the number of turned elements was reduced. At the same time, Boston chairmakers eliminated the upper side stretchers and raised the rear stretcher. Figures 2–5 illustrate the structural and stylistic changes that occurred as low-back chairs evolved into first-generation chairs and as they, in turn, evolved into second-generation chairs. From the high-back second-genera-

Figure 3 Side chair, Boston, 1685–1700. Maple and oak. H. 35½", W. 18½", D. 18½". (Private collection; photo, Gavin Ashworth.)

Figure 4 Side chair, Boston, 1700–1710. Maple and oak. H. 44½", W. 18⅜", D. 16". (Courtesy, Saint Louis Art Museum, gift of Mr. and Mrs. E. J. Nusrala.)

Figure 5 Side chair, Boston, 1710–1720. Maple and oak. H. 47½", W. 18", D. 14½". (Private collection; photo, Gavin Ashworth.)

Figure 6 Composite detail showing (from top to bottom) the front stretchers of the (*a*) late seventeenth-century, Boston low-back chair illustrated in fig. 3; (*b*) first-generation Boston leather chair illustrated in fig. 1; (*c*) second-generation Boston leather chair illustrated in fig. 5. (Photo, Gavin Ashworth.) The armchair illustrated in fig. 25 has an identical rear stretcher of the same dimensions as those illustrated here.

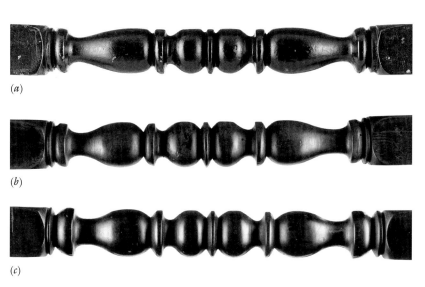

(*a*)

(*b*)

(*c*)

tion chairs (fig. 5), it was only a short leap to the Boston "crook'd back" chairs that were in vogue after 1720.[7]

Another feature that characterizes many first-generation, Boston "plain top'd" leather chairs is a slight hollowing of the back rails (fig. 9). Almost imperceptible on an upholstered and stuffed back, the concavity is readily apparent when the upholstery is removed and the chair is viewed from above. Late seventeenth-century English chairs occasionally had such backs, and many were imported into the colonies. No second-generation Boston chairs have this detail, however, nor do any first-generation "carv'd top" chairs, presumably because the hollowing would have made carving more difficult.

Several of the modifications exhibited by second-generation Boston chairs stemmed from efforts to simplify and expedite their construction. The elimination of details, such as turned elements, upper side stretchers, and hollow backs, reduced the costs of making the chairs, giving Boston chairmakers a competitive edge in the marketplace. Indeed, the prevalence of the "Boston" stretcher, with its consistent 14½" length, suggests that artisans mass-produced individual components to achieve a higher level of efficiency. During the seventeenth century, Boston turners produced stretchers, table legs, pillars, and spindles for joiners, so it is logical to assume that this practice also occurred later.[8]

Not all of the attributes of second-generation Boston chairs resulted from efforts to simplify construction. The addition of a backward rake to the rear legs was a response to the increased height of the chair backs. The backs of most first-generation chairs are about 27¾" high (seat to finial), whereas those of some second-generation examples are as high as 31½". Although the backs became taller, their pitch remained constant, making the later examples prone to tip over. The raked rear legs were more labor intensive, but they were necessary for stability (fig. 5).

On first- and second-generation chairs, customers could choose design features that affected both appearance and price, for example "carv'd top" or "plain top'd." The carved-top, first-generation chair illustrated in figure 10 has a carved front stretcher and a conforming crest rail with a slit for the leather upholstery—a characteristic that Forman attributed to New York. This chair, however, also has turned rear posts that are virtually identical to a "plain top'd" side chair with a "Boston" front stretcher, dual side stretchers, straight rear legs with a chamfered heel, and other attributes of first-generation Boston workmanship (fig. 11). Considering the widespread importation of English leather and turkeywork chairs into the colonies, some of which undoubtedly had carved crests with slits (see fig. 8), it is surprising that Forman chose to "regionalize" this detail. New Yorkers apparently pre-

Figure 7 Armchair, Boston, 1700–1710. Maple and oak; original leather upholstery. H. 47¼", W. 23½", D. 22⅜". (Courtesy, Museum of Fine Arts, Boston, Arthur Tracy Cabot Fund.)

Figure 8 Side chair, probably London, 1685–1700. Woods and dimensions unrecorded. (Photo, Symonds Collection, Decorative Arts Photographic Collection, Winterthur Museum.)

Figure 9 Detail of the hollow back of the side chair illustrated in fig. 29. (Courtesy, Milwaukee Art Museum, Layton Art Collection.)

Figure 10 Side chair, Boston, 1700–1710. Maple and oak. H. 47 5/8", W. 17 3/4", D. 14 1/2". (Private collection; photo, Gavin Ashworth.) The carving on this chair is closely related to that on the New York side chair and New York armchair illustrated in figs. 23 and 24 and the Boston armchair illustrated in fig. 25.

Figure 11 Side chair, Boston, 1700–1710. Maple and oak. H. 46", W. 17 3/4", D. 15". (Private collection; photo, Gavin Ashworth.) The rear legs have been improperly restored to incorporate the backward rake.

ferred the less expensive "plain top'd" chairs. In a 1709 letter to his New York agent Benjamin Faneuil (b. La Rochelle, France, 1658, d. New York 1719), Boston merchant Thomas Fitch (1668/9–1736) wrote, "I wonder the chairs did not sell; I have sold a pretty of that sort to Yorkers since, and tho some are carv'd yet I make six plain to one carv'd; and can't make the plain so fast as they are bespoke, so you may assure . . . customers that they are not out of fashion here."[9]

Figures 5 and 12 show two second-generation Boston side chairs with virtually identical back posts. The only vestige of first-generation workmanship on either chair is the distinctive "Boston" stretcher on the "plain top'd" example (fig. 5); both chairs have single side stretchers, raised rear stretchers, scored cylinders above the seats, and elongated columnar turnings on the back posts. A side chair with related post turnings (fig. 13) has an arched crest similar to that of the chair illustrated in figure 12. Although the carving designs are similar (figs. 14, 15), they are clearly by different hands. The carver of the crest rail illustrated in figure 15 was considerably more adept with his parting tool (a V-shaped tool used for making deep shading cuts). During the second decade of the eighteenth century, chairs with banister backs, flag seats, and "Prince of Wales" crests were less expensive alternatives to these second-generation, "carv'd top" leather chairs. Some of these examples also have "Boston" front stretchers.[10]

In addition to the ubiquitous "Boston" stretcher, construction details shared by first- and second-generation chairs suggest a common origin.

Figure 12 Side chair, Boston, 1710–1715. Maple and oak. H. 47³/₈", W. 18", D. 14³/₄". (Private collection; photo, Gavin Ashworth.)

Figure 13 Side chair, Boston, 1710–1715. Maple and oak. H. 48", W. 18", D. 14³/₄". (Private collection; photo, Gavin Ashworth.) This chair retains the first-generation feature of a slit crest rail.

Forman argued that the end blocks of the front stretchers overhung the backs of front legs because New York chairmakers used thicker stock for the front stretchers in order to achieve bolder turnings. On all of the chairs examined for this article, however, the stock for the legs and front stretchers is the same thickness. The overhang resulted from Boston chairmakers planing the back sides of the front leg blocks (fig. 16), which allowed them to join the side stretchers to the legs at right angles (fig. 17). Another distinctive Boston construction detail is the chamfering of the back legs (fig. 18). Aside from this slight chamfer, the back legs are square, and, unlike the

Figure 14 Detail of the carved crest rail of the chair illustrated in fig. 12. (Photo, Gavin Ashworth.)

Figure 15 Detail of the carved crest rail of the chair illustrated in fig. 13. (Photo, Gavin Ashworth.)

Figure 16 Detail of the construction of the side chair illustrated in fig. 11, showing the planed surfaces of the front leg squares and overhang of the front stretcher. (Photo, Gavin Ashworth.)

front legs, they are not planed away on the sides to continue the visual lines of the side stretchers along the surfaces of the legs, as they would be on New York chairs.[11]

All of the Boston side chairs Forman attributed to New York have dual side stretchers, and all of the armchairs have single side stretchers; however, the number of side stretchers is not an indicator of a chair's place of origin. Seventeenth-century, Boston low-back side chairs invariably had double side stretchers (fig. 2), and contemporary armchairs, following English fashion, invariably had one.[12] This rule also applies to first-generation Boston armchairs with rectangular or turned stretchers such as the ones illustrated in figures 7 and 25. Although Forman recognized that all leather side chairs had rectangular side stretchers, he asserted that those on New York chairs were thicker than those on Boston chairs; however, stretcher thicknesses varied in both cities. Some of the first-generation chairs that Forman attributed to New York have thin stretchers with "barefaced tenons" (a tenon with one shoulder). These tenons, which were easier to cut and required less stock than conventional two-shouldered tenons, are often found on Boston Cromwellian chairs. When Boston chairmakers eliminated the upper

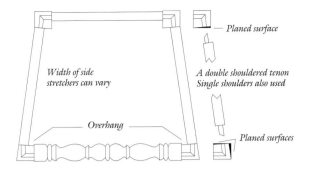

Figure 17 Diagram showing how the seat rails and stretchers join the front and rear legs on first- and second-generation Boston chairs.

Width of side stretchers can vary

— Planed surface

A double shouldered tenon
Single shoulders also used

Overhang

Planed surfaces

Figure 19 Side chair, New York, 1700–1710. Maple and oak. H. 44³/₈", W. 17³/₄", D. 14¹/₂". (Private collection; photo, Gavin Ashworth.) This chair was found in Newburgh, New York.

Figure 18 Detail of the side chair illustrated in fig. 11, showing the characteristic chamfering on the rear legs of first- and second-generation Boston chairs. (Photo, Gavin Ashworth.)

stretchers on second-generation chairs, the remaining side stretchers needed the additional bearing surface of a second shoulder—requiring thicker stock—to prevent the frame from wracking.[13]

New York Chairs: Some Distinguishing Features

Documentary and material evidence indicates that New York artisans made leather chairs in imitation of Boston and English seating, at least for a while. From 1700 to 1710, New York merchants such as Benjamin Faneuil and Abraham Wendell imported and sold large numbers of Boston leather chairs. Such chairs would have provided ready design sources for local artisans. Huguenot chairmaker Richard Lott purchased at least one set of carved-top leather chairs from Thomas Fitch. Lott probably intended to sell the chairs, but he may also have used them as models. When New York chairmakers copied imported examples, they did so within the context of their own craft traditions. Their turning patterns and construction methods thus differ significantly from those utilized by their Boston counterparts (figs. 19, 20).

On New York chairs, the turned baluster just above the seat is shallow (figs. 19, 20), whereas on Boston chairs this turning is more robust (fig. 1). The upper turnings of the back posts also differ depending on the chair's origin. Boston chairs have columns ending in reels, whereas New York chairs have more classically correct, quarter-round capitals; furthermore, none of the chairs that the authors attribute to New York incorporate the standard "Boston" stretcher. Instead, most "plain top'd" New York chairs have a block and turned front or medial stretcher with an extra ball just inside the block (fig. 21).[14]

Figure 20 Side chair, New York, 1700–1710. Maple and ash. H. 44¼", W. 17⅝", D. 14½". (Private collection; photo, Gavin Ashworth.)

Figure 21 Detail of the front stretcher of the side chair illustrated in fig. 19. (Photo, Gavin Ashworth.) The characteristic elements are the extra balls on the outer ends. See also figs. 20, 24, and 28.

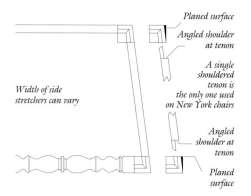

Width of side stretchers can vary

Planed surface

Angled shoulder at tenon

A single shouldered tenon is the only one used on New York chairs

Angled shoulder at tenon

Planed surface

Figure 22 Diagram showing how the seat rails and stretchers join the front and rear legs on New York chairs.

Another critical distinction between Boston and New York chairs can be seen in the joinery of the frame. When New York chairmakers constructed trapezoidal seats, they left the leg blocks square and planed away only the outside edge in order to align it with the side stretchers (fig. 22). As a result, the side stretchers connect to the rear legs and front legs at oblique angles, and the front stretcher blocks do not overhang on the back sides, as they do on Boston chairs. The rear legs of New York chairs are also square and unchamfered rather than being shaped like those of figure 18. All of these features are present on the side chairs illustrated in figures 19, 20, and 23.

The turning details and construction methods are also different on armchairs from the two regions. The armchair shown in figure 24 is constructed in the New York manner, whereas the one in figure 25 is constructed in the Boston manner. The latter armchair has a 14½" "Boston" rear stretcher identical to the front stretchers illustrated in figure 6. That the same stretchers could be used on both side chairs and armchairs is another example of the efficiencies achieved by Boston artisans. The two armchairs also have different rear posts, medial stretchers, and arm supports. The urn and baluster supports of the New York armchair (fig. 24) are related to the turnings on contemporary gateleg tables from that city (fig. 26).[15]

One intriguing parallel between these armchairs (figs. 24, 25) and the side chairs illustrated in figures 10 and 23 is that the carving on their crests and their front stretchers is remarkably similar. Assuming that the chairs shown in figures 10 and 25 are Boston made and the other two chairs (figs. 23, 24) are New York made, one explanation for this similarity is that a Boston carver exported piecework to New York; however, no documentary evidence of this practice has been located. Another possibility is that a carver moved from one city to the other. A New York armchair that descended in

Figure 23 Side chair fragment, New York City, 1700–1710. Maple and oak. H. 38", W. 17 3/4", D. 14 1/2". (Private collection; photo, Gavin Ashworth.) This chair was found in Greenwich, Connecticut.

Figure 24 Armchair, New York City, 1700–1710. Maple with oak. H. 52", W. 24 3/4", D. 17 1/2". (Courtesy, Chipstone Foundation; photo, Gavin Ashworth.)

the Van Cortlandt family (fig. 27) has related carving, but it appears to be by a different hand. The carving on the Van Cortlandt chair, which is somewhat less accomplished, probably represents the work of a local tradesman. The turnings and stance of the Van Cortlandt armchair differ from the other New York seating included in this study; however, it has square legs rather than chamfered ones like contemporary Boston chairs.

The predecessors of these New York leather chairs also differed from their seventeenth-century Boston counterparts. Although seventeenth-century New York chairs are exceedingly rare, an unusual turned and joined armchair shows several departures from standard Boston construction (fig. 28). The seat is trapezoidal rather than square like those of Boston low-back chairs (see fig. 2), and the side rails join the square legs at oblique angles in the New York manner. In addition, the front stretcher relates directly to the side stretchers of a late seventeenth- or early eighteenth-century New York escritoire (at the Metropolitan Museum of Art). The meticulous stock prep-

Figure 25 Armchair, Boston, 1700–1710. Maple with oak. H. 53³/₄", W. 23⁷/₈", D. 16³/₈". (Courtesy, Museum of Fine Arts, Boston, gift of Mrs. Charles L. Bybee; photo, Edward A. Bourdon, Houston, Texas.)

Figure 26 Gateleg table, New York City, 1690–1720. Mahogany with maple, yellow poplar, and oak. H. 28⁷/₈"; top: 40³/₄" × 44¹/₂" (open). (Courtesy, Museum of the City of New York, gift of the Reynal family; photo, Gavin Ashworth.)

Figure 27 Armchair, New York, 1700–1710. Maple with oak and hickory. H. 47¹/₂", W. 25¹/₂", D. 27". (Courtesy, Historic Hudson Valley.) The feet are replaced and the finials are incorrectly restored.

aration and joinery of the chair contrasts with contemporary Boston chairs, many of which were mass-produced objects made for a burgeoning local market and the export trade. Slight variations in the turnings on individual Boston chairs suggest that specialists turned the legs and stretchers while others assembled chairs from bins of parts. Often the seat and side rails (generally of red oak) bear signs of being riven and dressed hurriedly.[16]

Boston chairmakers' efforts to expedite production may explain why the widths of their side stretchers vary so much. Within fairly wide tolerances, Boston makers could use whatever stock was on hand. When thin stock was available, the stretchers could have barefaced tenons, but when a wider piece was handy a second shoulder could be added. Or, when the stretcher width was not sufficient to allow a full second shoulder, the chairmaker simply cut one shoulder narrower than the other. New York makers were much more precise and more regimented in their production methods. On the side chairs illustrated in figures 19, 20, and 23, the side stretchers are dressed to a uniform thickness of ³/₄", and they have barefaced tenons that are ³/₈" thick.

The ledgers and letterbooks of Thomas Fitch document numerous shipments of Boston leather chairs to New York between 1700 and 1720. In 1706, Fitch wrote Benjamin Faneuil, "I would have sent yo some chairs but could scarcely comply with those I had promised to go by these sloops." Given the date of this letter, it is likely that Fitch was referring to first-generation chairs. Boston merchant-upholsterers, such as Fitch, purchased chairs from several different chairmakers, who in turn commissioned piecework from turners, carvers, and other specialists. The New York chairs dis-

Figure 28 Armchair, New York, 1680–1700. Maple stained red. H. 44¼", W. 22½", D. 22¼". (Private collection; photo, Christopher Zaleski.)

Figure 29 Side chair, Boston, 1700–1710. Maple and oak. H. 45⅝", W. 18⅛", D. 15¼". (Courtesy, Milwaukee Art Museum, Layton Art Collection; photo, Richard Eells.)

cussed above suggest that tradesmen in that city mounted a brief response to Boston imports during the first decade of the eighteenth century; however, the development of faster and less expensive methods of production in Boston—manifest in the turnings and construction of second-generation chairs—and that city's expanding venture cargo trade evidently stifled the competition in New York. This would explain why there are no New York versions of fully developed, single-side-stretcher, second-generation Boston chairs.[17]

The Perils of Relying on Provenance
Considering the vast quantity of seating imported by merchants such as Faneuil and Wendell, a New York provenance is insufficient for determin-

ing a leather chair's origin; nevertheless, in attributing Winterthur's first-generation Boston chairs to New York, Forman relied heavily on the oral history of the side chair illustrated in figure 29. The chair reportedly belonged to artist Pieter Vanderlyn, who immigrated to New York City in 1718. If Vanderlyn owned the chair, he undoubtedly purchased it second-hand. Not only does the chair have a "Boston" stretcher, but its construction, double side stretchers, and complex post turnings suggest that it pre-

Figure 30 Side chair, Boston, 1700–1710. Maple and oak. H. 46³/₄", W. 18", D. 14³/₄". (Private collection; photo, Gavin Ashworth.)

Figure 31   Side chairs, possibly New Hampshire, 1700–1710. Maple and oak. H. 47½", W. 17¾", D. 15". (Private collection.)

dates Vanderlyn's arrival by about a decade. Many chairs that are clearly of Boston origin have eighteenth-century histories in New York, and some even bear the initials of successive New York owners. In light of all this, Forman's extrapolation of a New York origin for Winterthur's first-generation chairs, using the history of the Vanderlyn chair, is unpersuasive.[18]

By contrast, a Boston-area provenance for a first-generation chair is meaningful, since there is virtually no evidence of leather chairs being imported there from any other colonial port. A side chair with a "Boston" front stretcher and first-generation construction details (fig. 30) has a nineteenth-century label that reads, "This chair belonged to Rev. Thomas Potwine born in Boston Oct. 8, 1731, ordained E. Windsor May 1, 1754. Died November 15, 1802 . . . by E. Simons." Simons owned the chair and its mate (at the Yale University Art Gallery) prior to 1891, when Irving Whitehall Lyon illustrated one in *The Colonial Furniture of New England*. Although the label does not prove that the chair originated in Boston, it adds to the circumstantial evidence. Similarly, several second-generation details occur on a couch advertised in the March 1984 issue of *Antiques* and labeled: "Bed belonged to Rev. Daniel Shute, D. D. (1722–1802) of South Hingham, Mass., ordained pastor in Hingham in 1746." The couch has an arched "Prince of Wales" crest similar to those illustrated in figures 14 and 15, elongated columns, scored cylinders above the seat, and raked rear legs. The only Boston construction detail missing is the chamfering on the legs, which is unnecessary because of the long rectangular seat. All of these details point to a Boston origin, as the label suggests.[19]

Although the majority of the chairs examined by the authors fit neatly into the structural and stylistic paradigms established for Boston and New York, a few have disparate features. A pair of side chairs recently discovered in Maine (fig. 31) are similar to first-generation Boston chairs (see. fig. 1), but their turnings are less sophisticated and more indicative of rural work. As Randall suggested, Boston-trained artisans who moved to the Piscataqua region probably made such chairs for a short period of time. Eventually, however, they undoubtedly succumbed to the competition from Boston imports, just as their counterparts in New York, Philadelphia, and other regions of colonial America did.[20]

The evidence presented here clearly shows how first-generation Boston chairs relate to the seating forms that both preceded and followed them. These first-generation chairs would be completely out of context if they were constructed in New York. Changing fashions affected turning styles and basic chair forms, but most of the structural modifications that occurred in Boston seating between 1700 and 1720 reflect efforts to expedite production, reduce cost, and achieve a more elegant vertical look. The account books and letterbooks of Fitch and his apprentice Samuel Grant (fl. independently ca. 1728), colonial shipping records, and other documentary sources indicate that Boston artisans and their merchant-patrons produced vast quantities of chairs and dominated the coastal trade in seating until the mid-eighteenth century. The assertion that New York mounted a successful response to Boston imports is incompatible with this evidence and distorts the history of colonial industry and commerce.[21]

ACKNOWLEDGMENTS For assistance with this article, the authors thank Mark Anderson, Jean Blair, Allison Perkins Brown, Nannie W. T. Brown, Jonathan Fairbanks, Benjamin Faucett, Patricia E. Kane, Peter M. Kenny, John T. Kirk, Mario Martinez, Henry Merriman, Richard Stevenson, and Wayne Utley.

1. Benno M. Forman, *American Seating Furniture: 1630–1730* (New York: W. W. Norton for the Winterthur Museum, 1988), pp. 288–94, 320–26. Richard H. Randall, Jr., "Boston Chairs," *Old Time New England* (summer 1963): 13. Forman, *American Seating Furniture*, p. 311. Neil D. Kamil, "Hidden in Plain Sight: Disappearance and Material Life in Colonial New York," in *American Furniture,* edited by Luke Beckerdite and William N. Hosley (Hanover, N.H.: University Press of New England for the Chipstone Foundation, 1995), pp. 191–249.

2. Forman, *American Seating Furniture*, pp. 289–91.

3. The preferred leather was "russia" leather, tanned near St. Petersburg and exported to the colonies by London merchants. The leather was cross-hatched and dyed red. For more on russia leather, see Geoff Garbett and Ian Skelton, *The Wreck of the Meta Catharina* (Redruth, England: St. George Printing Works, Ltd., 1987), pp. 23–42; Robert F. Trent, "17th Century Upholstery in Massachusetts," in *Upholstery in America & Europe from the Seventeenth Century to World War I,* edited by Edward S. Cooke, Jr. (New York and London: W. W. Norton & Co., 1987), pp. 39–50; and Brock Jobe, "The Boston Upholstery Trade," in Cooke, ed., *Upholstery in America & Europe*, pp. 69–71. In colonial terminology, an upholstery "nail" referred to a brass-headed fastener and a "tack" to an iron fastener. For more on stuffing materials, see Trent, "17th Century Upholstery in Massachusetts," p. 39; and Jobe, "The Boston Upholstery Trade," p. 78. The grass on this example is probably *Distichlis spicata*, or spike grass.

4. Forman cited these characteristics and noted that the cylindrical turnings above the seat "are invariably scored about 3/8" (1cm) from their ends" (Forman, *American Seating Furniture*, p. 290).

5. For examples of Boston easy chairs, see Forman, *American Seating Furniture*, pp. 363, 367; advertisement by John Walton, Inc., *Antiques* 120, no. 2 (August 1981): 206. Roger Gonzales first recognized the "Boston" stretcher. He also developed the chronological framework for the Boston seating presented here and was the first to observe the distinctive stylistic and structural details of the New York chairs illustrated in figs. 19, 20, and 23.

6. For an excellent discussion of seventeenth-century, Boston low-back chairs, see Trent, "17th-Century Upholstery," p. 39. Forman discusses the connections between New York and Boston chairs in *American Seating Furniture*, pp. 292–93.

7. The Cane-Chair Makers Company noted in 1680 that "about the year 1664, cane-chairs came into use" and were esteemed "for their Durable Lightness, and Cleanness from Dust, Worms and Moths which inseparably attend Turkey-work, serge and other stuff chairs and couches, to the spoiling of them and all furniture near them" (Peter Thornton, *Seventeenth Century Interior Decoration in England, France & Holland* [New Haven and London: Yale University Press, 1978], p. 202). Gertrude Z. Thomas argues that cane chairs became fashionable shortly after the marriage of Charles II to Catherine of Braganza (Gertrude Z. Thomas, *Richer than Spices* [New York: Alfred A. Knopf, 1965] p. 58). A small number of Boston leather chairs have ball-turned posts (see Herbert Cescinsky and George Leland Hunter, *English and American Furniture* [Garden City, N.Y.: Garden City Publishing Company, 1929], p. 74). For an English leather chair with ball-turned posts, see John T. Kirk, *American Furniture and the British Tradition to 1830* (New York: Alfred A. Knopf, 1982), p. 232, fig. 737. For illustrations of "crook'd back" chairs, see Richard H. Randall, Jr., *American Furniture in the Museum of Fine Arts, Boston* (Boston: by the Museum, 1965), pp. 165–67; Dean F. Failey, *Long Island is My Nation: The Decorative Arts and Craftsmen, 1640–1830* (Setauket, N.Y.: Society for the Preservation of Long Island Antiquities, 1976), p. 25; and Forman, *American Seating Furniture,* pp. 333–52.

8. For references to this kind of specialization in the seventeenth century, see Jonathan L. Fairbanks and Robert F. Trent, eds., *New England Begins: The Seventeenth Century*, 3 vols. (Boston: Museum of Fine Arts, Boston, 1982), 2:288–89. During the 1730s, Boston turners John Underwood, Daniel McKillister, and Daniel Swan produced legs, drops, and finials for the city's cabinetmakers (Brock Jobe, "The Boston Furniture Industry, 1720–1740," in *Boston Furniture of the Eighteenth Century,* edited by Walter Muir Whitehill, Brock Jobe, and Jonathan Fairbanks [Boston: Colonial Society of Massachusetts, 1974], p. 15).

9. For an English or Dutch chair with a leather back and slit crest rail, see fig. 8. A late seventeenth-century side chair with a slit, carved crest rail, hollow back, carved stretcher, and "barley-twist" front legs, stretchers, and rear posts is illustrated in Oswaldo Rodriguez Roque, *American Furniture at Chipstone* (Madison, Wis.: University of Wisconsin Press, 1984), p. 107. This chair reportedly descended in the Pritchard family of Milford, Connecticut. As quoted in Forman, *American Seating Furniture*, p. 283.

10. A banister-back side chair with a "Prince of Wales" crest is illustrated in Forman, *American Seating Furniture*, p. 317. In place of the typical leather back panel, this chair has four turned banisters that match the back posts. All of the stretchers are fully turned and inserted into holes drilled into the legs. The turned legs also attach to the seat rails in this manner, rather than having pegged mortise-and-tenon joints. The rear legs rake backward like those of second-generation Boston leather chairs.

11. Only a few quick strokes were required to plane the legs to the desired shape. The original stock had to be square so that the front leg could be turned properly. It was quicker to plane the surface with the grain rather than rip it with a saw. The angles of the three block surfaces differ slightly, indicating that they were planed separately. The construction illustrated in fig. 17 did not last long. On later "crook'd back" Boston leather chairs, the front legs are usually chamfered, like the earlier chairs, whereas the rear legs are square.

12. For seventeenth-century, English low-back armchairs with single side stretchers, see Kirk, *American Furniture and the British Tradition*, p. 221, fig. 676; and Victor Chinnery, *Oak Furniture: The British Tradition* (Woodbridge, England: Antique Collectors' Club, Baron Publishing, 1979), p. 278. For a Boston example, see Fairbanks and Trent, eds., *New England Begins,* 3:532–33.

13. For a Boston Cromwellian chair with barefaced tenons, see Heritage Plantation of Sandwich, *A Cupperd, Four Joyne Stools & Other Smalle Things: The Material Culture of Plymouth Colony* (Sandwich, Mass.: Heritage Plantation, 1994), p. 129, no. 137.

14. Forman, *American Seating Furniture*, p. 301, fig. 169, shows a detail of two Boston chairs

with undercut blocks and reel-shaped capitals. New York chairs have more attenuated post turnings than Boston examples, but the space between the seat rail and the lower back rail is about the same. Because New York turnings occupy more of the vertical space, there is less room for the square stock of the back leg; thus, the turning shapes and size of the exposed blocks beneath them can help verify a chair's New York origin. Similar columns appear on other examples of New York furniture (see the ca. 1700 escritoire in Marshall B. Davidson and Elizabeth Stillinger, *The American Wing at The Metropolitan Museum of Art* [New York: Alfred A. Knopf, 1985], p. 108). The extra ball on New York stretchers is also found on turned elements of New York tables from that period. See Peter M. Kenny, "Flat Gates, Draw Bars, Twists, and Urns: New York's Distinctive, Early Baroque Oval Tables with Falling Leaves," in *American Furniture,* edited by Luke Beckerdite (Hanover, N.H.: University Press of New England for the Chipstone Foundation, 1994), p. 122.

15. A second-generation "plain top'd" Boston armchair (Art Institute of Chicago, acc. 1989.57) has a rear stretcher of the same design and dimensions as that of the chair shown in fig. 25. Forman attributed the latter chair to New York even though the finial and underarm turnings are in the Boston style (Forman, *American Seating Furniture*, p. 288). For a Boston chair with similar turnings and finials, see Kenny, "Flat Gates, Draw Bars, Twists and Urns," p. 124, fig. 30. Kenny also illustrates several New York tables with urn and baluster turnings on pp. 115–17, figs. 19–21; p. 123, fig. 29.

16. New York's chairmaking community was considerably more diverse than Boston's and included artisans of English, French, and Dutch descent (see Forman, *American Seating Furniture,* pp. 321–24; and Kamil, "Hidden in Plain Sight").

17. Forman, *American Seating Furniture*, pp. 292, 285. As quoted in Kamil, "Hidden in Plain Sight," p. 196. Although the New York chairs have double side stretchers like first-generation Boston chairs, the authors believe the New York examples shown in figs. 19 and 20 are contemporary with second-generation Boston ones. This would explain why the turnings on New York chairs sometimes bear more resemblance to Boston second-generation chairs.

18. Forman, *American Seating Furniture*, p. 326. The Vanderlyn chair is also attributed to New York in Robert F. Trent, "The Early Baroque in Colonial America: The William and Mary Style," in *American Furniture with Related Decorative Arts 1661–1830: The Milwaukee Art Museum and Layton Collection,* edited by Gerald W. R. Ward (New York: Hudson Hill Press, 1991), pp. 68–69. For other Boston chairs with New York histories, see Joseph T. Butler, *Sleepy Hollow Restorations: A Cross-Section of the Collection* (Tarrytown, N.Y.: Sleepy Hollow Press, 1983), p. 53; Failey, *Long Island is My Nation,* p. 26, fig. 23; and Roderic H. Blackburn, "Branded and Stamped New York Furniture," *Antiques* 119, no. 5 (May 1981): 1131.

19. The Potwine family originated in Boston and resided briefly in Hartford before settling in Coventry, Connecticut, about 1740. There is no evidence that Thomas Potwine had any ties to New York (Franklin Bowditch Dexter, *Biographical Sketches of the Graduates of Yale College with Annals of the College History: October, 1701-May, 1745* [New York: Henry Holt and Company, 1885], pp. 265–66). Irving Whitehall Lyon, *The Colonial Furniture of New England* (1891; reprint ed., Boston and New York: Houghton Mifflin, 1925), p. 171, fig. 69. The Yale chair is illustrated in Patricia Kane, *300 Years of Seating Furniture* (Boston: New York Graphic Society, 1975), pp. 60–61. The couch is illustrated in an advertisement by Bernard & S. Dean Levy, Inc., *Antiques* 125, no. 3 (March 1984): 492.

20. The chairs are discussed in the May 1994 issue of *Maine Antique Digest*, p. 14C. Auctioneer Ronald Bourgeault advertised a first-generation-type side chair with a Portsmouth history in the December 1984 issue of *Maine Antique Digest*, p. 40D. The chair has a classic "Boston" front stretcher, but the back posts and finials more closely resemble those of the chairs shown in fig. 31.

21. For more on the export of leather chairs from Boston, see Forman, *American Seating Furniture*, pp. 281–302; and Kamil, "Hidden in Plain Sight."

F. Carey Howlett

Admitted into the Mysteries: The Benjamin Bucktrout Masonic Master's Chair

▼ EVERYTHING THAT *strikes the eye more immediately engages the attention, and imprints on the memory serious and solemn truths. Hence Masons have universally adopted the method of inculcating the tenets of their order by typical figures of allegorical emblems.*

William Preston
Illustrations of Masonry, 1772

On the evening of May 28, 1774, members of the Williamsburg Lodge of the Most Ancient and Honourable Society of Free and Accepted Masons gathered for a Master's Lodge—the ritual reenactment of the murder, burial, and disinterment of Hiram Abif, legendary stonemason and builder of King Solomon's Temple. Seven aspiring master Masons prepared to assume the role of Hiram Abif. Entering the lodge one at a time, each encountered three "unworthy brethren" in search of the secrets of Masonry. Refusing to reveal the mysteries of the Craft, the candidates were ritually struck down by "assassins" wielding stonemason's tools. Wrapped in shrouds, the candidates experienced the desolation of Hiram's burial until "resurrected" by their brethren, led by John Minson Galt, a prominent physician in Williamsburg and deputy master of the lodge (fig. 1).[1]

This ritual was not unusual during the rapid growth of the Williamsburg Lodge in the years before and during the Revolutionary War. Two candi-

Figure 1   From Johann Martin Bernigeroth "Les Costumes des Francs-Macons dans leurs Assemblees," ca. 1745. (By permission of the Board of General Purposes of the United Grand Lodge of England.) This rare French print depicts the Masonic third-degree ritual: the raising of the master Mason. Although the "teardrop" symbol is associated specifically with French Masonry, other elements are characteristic of the British ritual.

dates, Edmund Randolph and Henry Tazewell, came from wealthy Virginia families. Both were twenty years old, had recently completed legal study at the College of William and Mary, and were commencing what would become distinguished careers in public service. Randolph probably was influenced by his uncle Peyton Randolph, provincial grand master of Virginia Freemasonry, speaker of the Virginia House of Burgesses, and president of the First Continental Congress. Candidate William Yates was a professor at the College of William and Mary and son of the college's president. During the 1770s, the Williamsburg Lodge attracted liberal-minded faculty, clerics, and students, who esteemed Freemasonry for its antiquity, enlightened rationalism, and Newtonian scientific idealism.

The next three candidates provide an interesting contrast in education, wealth, and social status. Michael McCarty worked as a guard at the powder magazine in 1762, John Lockley was a barkeeper at Mrs. Vobe's Tavern in 1774, and, although Walter Battwell's profession is unknown, he was not a man of means. In 1775, the lodge ordered its treasurer to "pay to Brother Battwell the Sum of Twelve Pounds for his relief . . . Brother Battwell to have a free seat in the Lodge and invited free to all feasts." Masons believed that assisting the distressed "is a duty incumbent on all men, but particularly on Masons, who are linked together by an indissoluble chain of sincere affection."[2]

The last candidate, Benjamin Bucktrout, was neither poor nor privileged, and it is unlikely that his education approached that of Randolph, Tazewell, or Yates. Bucktrout immigrated to Williamsburg from London in 1765 and subsequently became a successful cabinetmaker and merchant, serving such distinguished patrons as Robert Carter, the Blair family, and Governor Botetourt. In the mid-1770s, Bucktrout was also one of the most active members of the Williamsburg Lodge.[3]

The admission of Bucktrout and others of lower social standing into the Williamsburg Lodge underscores a significant shift in the membership of Freemasonry. During the early eighteenth century, Freemasonry was the domain of progressive members of the social and intellectual elite, who espoused a philosophy of universal brotherhood, egalitarianism, and religious toleration. By midcentury, Masons began acting upon their ideals, as the tenets of the Ancient and Honourable Society attracted men of a lower station in life. In the words of Williamsburg Reverend James Madison, "Man, created by the great Author of all Things was formed for equality. Those artificial Distinctions which Societies introduce, Masonry obliterates. Following Nature as her Guide, she extends her Arms to all, whether the humble Cottage be their Lot, or whether raised to the most exalted stations. Benevolence, Integrity, and Charity are the only Discriminations that she knows, and these are such as Nature herself have established."[4]

Although the American rebellion against British authority was still a few years away, a quiet social revolution had already begun, partly in the guise of Masonic ceremony and celebration. As fraternal ties united men of increasingly diverse backgrounds, Freemasons gathered to experience ancient rituals, to derive lessons from the symbols emblazoned on lodge furnish-

Figure 2 Masonic master's chair by Benjamin Bucktrout, Williamsburg, Virginia, 1769–1775. Mahogany with walnut; painted and gilded ornament, original leather upholstery. H. 65 1/2", W. 31 1/4", D. 29 1/2". (Courtesy, Colonial Williamsburg Foundation; photo, Hans Lorenz.)

ings, to listen to moral and philosophical discourse, and to feast, drink, and observe "that Harmony, Decorum, and friendly Intercourse, which characterize the Brotherhood, and are so agreeable to the Laws of Masonry."[5]

The Bucktrout Masonic Master's Chair

A master Mason and senior steward of the Williamsburg Lodge, Benjamin Bucktrout created the most elaborate ceremonial chair produced in the American colonies (fig. 2). This Masonic master's chair, which probably

Figure 3   Masonic master's chair, Williamsburg Lodge No. 6, Williamsburg, Virginia, 1765–1770. Mahogany. H. 52¼", W. 29½", D. 26¼". (Courtesy, Williamsburg Lodge No. 6, A.F. & A.M.; photo, Hans Lorenz.)

dates between 1769 and 1775, is the only signed example of Williamsburg furniture. As such, it clearly documents cabinetmaking practices in that city and sheds light on the aspirations of eighteenth-century Freemasonry in Virginia.

Bucktrout's Masonic master's chair was one of several made in the South prior to the Revolution (see figs. 3–6). Although speculative Freemasonry was founded in England in 1717 and established in America by the 1730s, very little lodge furniture or three-dimensional Masonic art made before 1750 survives in England or America. A few British chairs bearing Masonic

Figure 4　Masonic master's chair, Fredericksburg Lodge No. 4, Fredericksburg, Virginia, ca.
1775. Mahogany with walnut. H. 42½", W. 27½",
D. 18⅞". (Courtesy, Fredericksburg Lodge No.
4, A.F. & A.M; photo, Museum of Early
Southern Decorative Arts.) The Fredericksburg
Lodge was chartered by the Grand Lodge of
Scotland in 1758. The symbol of the sundial on
this chair associates it with Scottish Freemasonry.

emblems date from the late seventeenth century (probably made for lodges
of working, or "operative," stonemasons), but the real tradition of ceremonial lodge furniture dates from the third quarter of the eighteenth century.
In fact, the Grand Lodge of England, which chartered at least five eighteenth-century Virginia lodges, acquired its own ceremonial furniture only
after building Freemason's Hall in London in 1775.[6]

The master's chair occupied a place of special significance within the
lodge room—a carefully contrived setting symbolically representing the
interior of King Solomon's Temple. Wherever Masons met, they laid out

Figure 5 Masonic chair, Union Kilwinning Lodge No. 4, Charleston, South Carolina, ca. 1770. Mahogany; ash slip seat. H. 53 ½", W. 27½". (Collection of the Museum of Early Southern Decorative Arts.) The painted square and compass cover an original inlaid plumb rule, indicating that this chair served the senior warden of the lodge.

the lodge room according to that allegorical plan, effectively conveying a sense of mystery, solemnity, authority, and tradition. Placed on the east wall of the room, the chair associated the worshipful master with the rising sun. Just as the sun was the source of celestial light, the master was a source of knowledge and enlightenment. Traditionally, three steps led up to the chair, suggesting the progression through the three symbolic degrees of Masonry (representing three levels of self-knowledge) to the state of virtue exemplified by the worshipful master.

The identity of the lodge that first owned Bucktrout's chair is a mystery, but the chair stood for over two hundred years in Unanimity Lodge No. 7 in Edenton, North Carolina. Unanimity Lodge accepted the chair on July

Figure 6   Masonic master's chair attributed to Richard Hall, Royal White Hart Lodge No. 2, Halifax, North Carolina, ca. 1765. Walnut; yellow pine slip seat. H. 48 9/16", W. 24", D. 17" (seat). (Courtesy, Royal White Hart Lodge No. 2, A.F. & A.M.; photo, Museum of Early Southern Decorative Arts.)

6, 1778, as a gift from a ship's captain named George Russel, who, legend states, had been entrusted with the chair by a lodge in Virginia for safe-keeping during the Revolution. When the lodge in Virginia failed to reestablish, Russel presented the chair to Unanimity Lodge.[7]

Unanimity Lodge tradition maintains that Bucktrout's master's chair was one of three commissioned for lodges in Virginia by "Lord Baltimore." This unlikely patron's name is probably a corruption of Lord Botetourt, royal governor of Virginia from 1768 to 1770. A similar tradition accompanies the master's chair made for the Williamsburg Lodge (fig. 3). Bucktrout pro-vided furniture for the Governor's Palace and supervised arrangements for Botetourt's funeral. Although the governor may have commissioned the Bucktrout chair for a lodge in Norfolk, which claimed the chair in letters dated 1811 and 1815, evidence suggests that Bucktrout made it for use in the Williamsburg Lodge by Peyton Randolph, provincial grand master of Virginia.[8]

Nothing is known about Bucktrout's training, but his master's chair dem-

Figure 7 Detail of the carved dolphin leg on the chair illustrated in fig. 2. (Photo, Hans Lorenz.)

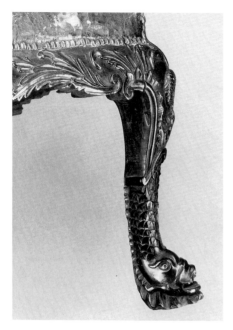

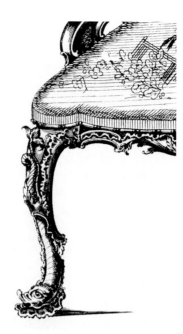

Figure 8 Detail of plate 21 in Thomas Chippendale's *The Gentleman and Cabinet-Maker's Director,* 1st ed. (London, 1754). (Courtesy, Colonial Williamsburg Foundation.)

Figure 9 Detail of the stamped signature and layout lines for the carving on the back of the Composite capital on the chair illustrated in fig. 2. (Photo, F. C. Howlett.)

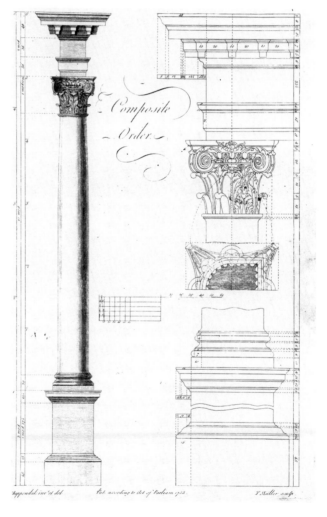

Figure 10 "Composite Order" from Thomas Chippendale's *The Gentleman and Cabinet-Maker's Director,* 1st ed. (London, 1754). (Courtsey, Colonial Williamsburg Foundation.)

Figure 11 Masonic chair illustrated on plate 25 of Thomas Chippendale's *The Gentleman and Cabinet-Maker's Director*, 3d ed. (London, 1762).

Figure 12 Preconservation view of the chair illustrated in fig. 2, showing many of the symbolic elements missing or obscured by darkened varnish and overpaint. (Photo, Hans Lorenz.)

onstrates a familiarity with urban British style. The dolphin legs are virtually identical to those of a French chair illustrated on plate 21 of the first edition of Thomas Chippendale's *The Gentleman and Cabinet-Maker's Director* (1754) (figs. 7, 8), a book that belonged to at least one other Williamsburg cabinetmaker. Similarly, Bucktrout's Corinthian and Composite capitals are based on those in plates 4 and 5; the acanthus leaves are remarkably similar and the scribe lines on the reverse of the capitals duplicate the proportional relationships presented in the *Director* (figs. 9, 10).[9]

Although Bucktrout borrowed individual details from the *Director,* he ignored Chippendale's design for a master's chair (fig. 11). The *Director* design, though more elaborate than most extant chairs, represents the approach generally utilized by makers of Masonic furniture. The symbols— a blazing sun and the stonemason's tools—serve as focal points, but they are grafted onto a conventional seating form. Bucktrout's chair represents an inventive, possibly unique, departure from the standard approach to

Masonic chair design. Whereas the legs, seat rails, and arms are a synthesis of London and Williamsburg stylistic details, the back is entirely symbolic. Impressively, this conceit applies not only to the ornament but also to the very structure and composition of the design.

The major framing elements of the back are symbols derived from classical architecture (fig. 12). Corinthian columns support the arch and keystone, and a central Composite column supports the bust of the worshipful master. The area within this framework is composed entirely of emblems of the Craft. In the center are the three great lights—the compass, square, and "Volume of the Sacred Law"—the most recognized symbols of eighteenth-century Freemasonry. The lights are overlaid with the five-pointed star, a juxtaposition unfamiliar to twentieth-century American Masons but of probable symbolic importance during Bucktrout's time. Surmounting the columns are the three lesser lights—the sun, moon, and worshipful master—which comprise the secondary symbolic triad of Freemasonry. Between the columns are the working tools of the Craft: the 24" gauge, trowel, plumb rule, level, mallet, and gavel. Each tool was important symbolically and some served as "jewels"—insignias of the lodge officers. At the base are the jewels of the secretary (crossed quills) and the treasurer (crossed keys), apparently included to complement the officers' jewels above.[10]

The Colonial Williamsburg Foundation acquired the Bucktrout chair in 1983 and began conservation in 1989. Historical research, traditional connoisseurship, and scientific analysis helped place the chair within its historical context. The conservation treatment drew upon this research and contributed to it, as new discoveries about the physical nature of the chair's symbols gave insights into their meaning.

Origins of Masonic Symbolism

The Bucktrout chair embodies the rich, obscure tradition of Masonic symbolism, a tradition rooted in medieval stonemasonry and Renaissance Neoplatonism. Most apparent is the influence of the medieval, guildlike association of working or "operative" stonemasons. The use of masons' tools as symbols, the wearing of aprons, the practice of gathering in "lodges," the Hiramic legend, and the levels or degrees within the Craft—entered apprentice, fellowcraft, and master—all derive from the medieval stonemason's trade. Fourteenth-century manuscripts indicate the practical function of the early lodges: ensuring quality workmanship, instituting wage policies, and protecting the trade's secrets. The lodges also established guidelines for the moral conduct of members, developed trade-oriented symbols to represent desirable values, and created a mythical history that stressed the secret knowledge, honor, and antiquity of the trade.

During the seventeenth century, operative stonemasonry incorporated an amalgam of esoteric ideas from outside the trade. These ideas influenced the gradual transformation of stonemasonry from an operative craft organization into a purely speculative society, combining sociability with an allegorical system of moral instruction. The symbolism of the new "speculative" Freemasonry reflected this transformation, as the organization expanded its imagery to include a rich mixture of emblems, hieroglyphics, and symbols associated with several arcane schools of late Renaissance thought. The medieval craft organization provided a structural and symbolic foundation, but the speculative Freemasonry that developed in England and spread across the world evolved into an entirely different organization.

The transformation of stonemasonry accompanied a change in lodge membership that occurred during the seventeenth century. Early in the century, operative stonemasons, already of a higher social standing than most tradesmen, began accepting members of the gentility into their lodges. Gentlemen such as Sir Robert Moray and Elias Ashmole joined Masonic lodges during the 1640s. Both men were members of the Royal Society with strong scientific, philosophical, and antiquarian interests. In 1688, Randle Holme wrote of his decision to "honor the Fellowship of the Masons because of its Antiquity." Masonry fed on the seventeenth-century passion for antiquity; the past was a source of fundamental truths, and the stonemasons' lodge, through its rituals and symbols, represented an unbroken tradition of ancient, secret wisdom.[11]

The stonemasons' association with architecture also appealed to educated gentlemen. Renaissance scholars revered Vitruvius, who believed that an architect must "be educated, skilful with the pencil, instructed in geometry, know much history, have followed the philosophers with attention, understand music, know the opinions of the jurists, and be acquainted with astronomy and the theory of the heavens." By joining a lodge, gentlemen consciously identified themselves with the great architects—masters of many disciplines and creators of edifices intended to elevate the human spirit. The classical orders of architecture gained special significance in the symbolism of the new Freemasonry. As physical manifestations of the philosophy of the ancients, they represented important universal ideals.[12]

Another attraction was stonemasonry's emphasis on secrecy and its association with occult practices. Among early stonemasons, cryptic signs, handshakes, and the "Mason's word" enabled members of the transient craft organization to recognize and to communicate covertly with one another. This secrecy gave Freemasonry the aura of an occult mystery, and the Craft became associated with a number of arcane Neoplatonic philosophies.

Neoplatonists, who fused classical philosophy with Renaissance mysticism, conceived of the universe as a unity of spirit and matter. For Christian Europe, this conception represented a new way of looking at the world: Spiritual truth was no longer dependent upon divine revelation, and man could understand the metaphysical world by studying the natural world. A branch of this philosophy, Hermeticism, focused on the writings of Egyptian alchemist and astrologer Hermes Trismegistus. Renaissance antiquarians justifiably considered stonemasons' lodges to be repositories of ancient Hermetic tradition, since stonemasons had long revered Hermes as the source of the principles of geometry.

Neoplatonists believed that the mysteries of the universe could be unraveled by combining the mathematical and scientific models of the Egyptians and the Greeks with the empirical endeavors of medieval alchemists and

Figure 13   Frontis of James Hasolle, esq., *Chymical Collections* (London, 1650). (By permission of the Board of General Purposes of the United Grand Lodge of England.) The frontis of this seventeenth-century alchemical text has symbols later incorporated into speculative Masonry.

astrologers. This approach became a simultaneous pursuit for spiritual and worldly knowledge. The alchemist's quest for the philosopher's stone, the material that could change base metals into gold, became an allegory for the human quest for spiritual perfection.[13] Whether spiritual or proto-scientific, Neoplatonic philosophy was linked with symbolism. The specific symbols of the Hermeticists reflected their desire to harness the creative powers of the universe; thus, the tools of geometry (the compass and square) and astrological symbols (sun, moon, and star) had special meaning. To the Hermetic philosopher, the linkage of an evanescent idea with a material object created something greater than the idea or the object alone. As embodiments of matter and spirit, symbols contained the truth of nature and divinity (fig. 13).

The Jewish mystical literature known as the Caballa also infused Neoplatonic philosophy, eventually influencing the symbolism of Freemasonry. Central to the Caballistic tradition is the concept of an incomprehensible, infinite being, perceptible only through the symbolic grouping of divine emanations: a hierarchy of three triads (physical, moral, and spiritual) arranged on three pillars (justice, middle, and mercy), all supported by a tenth emanation (Kingdom). Known collectively as the tree of life, these emanations symbolized both the microcosm (archetypal man) and the macrocosm (universe).[14]

Symbolism pervaded Neoplatonic philosophy, embodying its essential concepts: the unity of matter and spirit, of object and idea, and of man and the universe. Symbolism gave rise to the expression of unutterable truths, the comprehension of fathomless mysteries, and the revelation of natural principles. With symbolism as their medium, the alchemists and philosophers of the late Renaissance fashioned the last of the western "holistic systems of knowledge . . . where no art, science or technology was intelligible without its cosmological, ethical, and 'existential' presuppositions and implications."[15]

The pillars, triadic arrangements, celestial bodies, artisan's tools, classical orders, and geometric designs on the back of the Bucktrout chair represent a fusion of late Renaissance mysticism with the rituals of medieval stonemasonry (see fig. 12). By the time Bucktrout made this chair, however, these symbolic vestiges of archaic philosophies had been invested with new meaning. The western world experienced a dramatic transformation during the early eighteenth century, a transformation both reflected in and fostered by Freemasonry. Significantly, much of this change was wrought by one of the last of the great alchemists—Sir Isaac Newton. Newton established the foundations for modern science, altering perceptions of the universe and of humanity in the process. Newtonian philosophy, along with concurrent strains of the new Enlightenment thinking—the religion of nature and the perfectibility of man—resonated within the lodges of the Freemasons. The old symbols and rituals of the Craft resonated as well.

Freemasonry in the Eighteenth Century
The Ancient and Honourable Society of Freemasons traces its formal orga-

nization to 1717, when four lodges assembled at the Goose and Gridiron Tavern in London to form a Grand Lodge. Freemasonry, which became the most successful of the eighteenth-century secret societies, envisioned itself as more than just a "club." Sociability was important, but from the beginning Freemasonry established a much higher goal: the moral and spiritual development of its initiates through a universal system transcending religion, politics, and all other constructs of man. To accomplish this goal, Freemasonry adapted its long tradition of symbolism and ritual to the new philosophies of the Enlightenment.

The most influential leader in this new Freemasonry was Huguenot John Desaguliers, a member of the Royal Society and a colleague of Sir Isaac Newton. An accomplished scientist, Desaguliers was noted as the great popularizer of Newton's scientific discoveries. By demonstrating and quantifying the force of gravity, Newton had taken the mysterious and unknowable and made it comprehensible. He discovered a natural law with profound spiritual implications, an unseen force that governed the motion of the entire universe. This finding was the single most important discovery of the age, not only as a scientific principle but as the basis for a new, idealistic way of looking at man's place in the universe. The spiritual mysticism of the seventeenth century yielded to a new conviction in the powers of man. Mysteries still existed, but, by using reason and his five senses, man suddenly seemed capable of solving them. It followed that, by conducting human affairs according to the same natural principles at work in the universe, man could usher in a new era of harmony, happiness, and peace.

In 1721, Presbyterian cleric James Anderson began working with Desaguliers on the *Constitutions* of the new speculative Freemasonry. Anderson rewrote the ancient "Old Charges," the old moral and ethical code of the operative stonemasons, to reflect the philosophical bent of the new organization and to address the new Enlightenment thinking. The *Constitutions* defined antiquity in terms of Newtonian philosophy, the religion of nature, and man's Masonic progress. God, "the Almighty Architect of nature and Masonry," appears not as a judge but as a benevolent creator who gave man a "Heart thoroughly instructed in the noble Science of GEOMETRY, for his own improvement and for the Instruction of his Descendants." Anderson recast the world's history as man's creative progression towards spiritual and technological perfection (fig. 14).[16]

The new "Charges" accompanying this history advocated religious and political tolerance. The first charge simply called for belief in a supreme being and "that religion in which all men agree, leaving their particular opinions to themselves . . . whereby Masonry becomes the center of union, and the means of conciliating true friendship among persons that must have remained at a perpetual distance." Masonry saw itself as a universal institution transcending any particular religious doctrine. This approach attracted English deists, many of whom were educated members of the gentry who eschewed religious dogma, "divine revelation," and sectarian exclusivism. Deists professed a simple faith in the goodness, benevolence, and wisdom of their creator, perceived rationally in the order and harmony of nature.

Figure 14   Frontis of James Anderson's *The Constitutions of the Freemasons* (London: William Hunter and John Hooke, 1723). (By permission of the Board of General Purposes of the United Grand Lodge of England.) This was the first publication authorized by the newly formed (1717) Grand Lodge of England.

Within the established church, this Enlightenment faith became known as latitudinarianism, and it found special favor among American colonists, particularly Virginia planters. In the decade prior to the Revolution, the College of William and Mary was "the most effective academic base of American deism," and the Williamsburg Lodge, which attracted many local scholars, served as the secular "Sanctum Sanctorum" for the practice of their faith.[17]

The second charge urged political moderation but upheld the individual's essential freedom of opinion: "A Mason is to be a peaceable subject to the civil powers, wherever he resides or works . . . never to be concerned in plots and conspiracies against the peace and welfare of the nation." Although a Mason who defies the state is "not to be countenanced . . . the loyal brotherhood cannot expel him from the lodge, and his relation to it remains indefeasible." The founding members of the Craft, mostly Whigs opposed to absolute monarchy, envisioned Freemasonry as an institution transcending politics. The organization, therefore, attracted those who entertained thoughts of republicanism.[18]

Anderson's *Constitutions* are crucial to understanding the transformation of Freemasonry from an operative craft into a speculative system of moral development—a system that codified the Enlightenment faith in reason and the perfectibility of man. This same faith provided much of the impetus for the tremendous social forces later expressed in the American and French revolutions and the establishment of republicanism and self-government.

The optimism of Freemasonry was based upon ideals, but it would be naive to assume that all those who took the oaths of Freemasonry were idealists. Some members were motivated more by concerns for sociability, social status, and financial advantage. Williamsburg cleric and Freemason William Bland lamented the paucity of lodges "wherein her votaries are sincere." The visible manifestations of Masonry—processions, socializing in taverns, sumptuous feasts, self-proclaimed antiquity, tools cast as symbols, and glittering jewels—smacked of superficiality to uninitiated and "unenlightened" skeptics (fig. 15). Joseph Greene, a New England Old Light Congregationalist who opposed the optimistic deism of Freemasonry, mocked the Boston Lodge's traditional Feast Day of St. John the Evangelist in his "Entertainment for a Winter's Evening": "To house of God from house of ale, And how the parson told his tale: How they return'd, in manner odd, To house of ale from house of God."[19]

Despite such criticisms, the Craft grew throughout the eighteenth century. Freemasonry sought to be a universal institution, and in a sense it succeeded. By equating sociability with the sacred, by comparing man to the universe, by combining mystery with reason, and by fusing science with morality, the Craft encompassed nearly all of the aspirations, ideals, vanities, and contradictions of the eighteenth century.

The Symbolism of the Bucktrout Masonic Master's Chair

Bucktrout's chair appears calculated to promote lessons in eighteenth-century Masonic cosmology: the belief in a harmonious world where the prac-

Figure 15   William Hogarth, *Night,* from the *Times of Day* series, London, 1738. (Courtesy, Colonial Williamsburg Foundation.) Hogarth was a Freemason who nonetheless parodied the association of the Craft with late-night drunkenness.

tice of brotherly love and moral virtue exemplifies direct conformity to the laws of nature. With its architectural framework, purposeful juxtaposition of tools, celestial bodies, inscriptions, and bust, the chair has less in common with other master's chairs than with the traditional symbolic instructional devices of Masonry—the tracing boards and floor cloths found within the lodges and the engravings accompanying Masonic texts. In a remarkable feat of design, Bucktrout successfully translated into freestanding, three-dimensional form the eighteenth-century symbolic art of Masonry—art that, because of its celestial, hieroglyphic character, appeared most often in two-dimensional form.

Pillars and Arch

Freemasonry has always glorified architecture as a sublime expression of human creativity, and the pillars and arch are quintessential symbols of the Craft. On the Bucktrout chair, the architectural elements are academically correct and structurally clever. They also have a striking graphic quality that

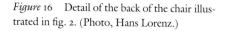

Figure 16 Detail of the back of the chair illustrated in fig. 2. (Photo, Hans Lorenz.)

amplifies their symbolic meaning. Masonic texts of the eighteenth century extolled both the aesthetic qualities and the inherent virtues of the five classical orders. By fusing these classical influences with the triad of pillars forming the Caballa's tree of life, Masonry endowed its three pillars (the "supports of a lodge") with the qualities of wisdom, strength, and beauty. The three pillars also designate the legendary grand masters—King Solomon, King Hiram, and Hiram Abif—and, by extension, the officers of a lodge.

By the early nineteenth century, the Doric, Ionic, and Corinthian orders had become formalized representations of the three pillars, but earlier artists rendered them in a variety of classical forms. For example, the master's chairs made for Williamsburg Lodge No. 6 (fig. 3) and Fredericksburg Lodge No. 4 (fig. 4) have Ionic, Corinthian, and Composite elements arranged in different sequences. The Bucktrout chair has a central Composite pilaster flanked by two Corinthian ones (fig. 16). His composition probably had dual symbolism, representing both the three pillars of Masonry and the pillars (named Jachin and Boaz) that flanked the entrance to King Solomon's Temple.[20]

According to Hiramic legend, King Solomon's Temple was a repository of secret knowledge; thus Jachin and Boaz stood at the entrance to new levels of wisdom. In the Bible, they have identical capitals of "lily-work"; consequently, English artists commonly depicted them as Corinthian columns, often surmounted by globes, celestial bodies, or the arch of heaven. In a similar fashion, Bucktrout's Corinthian pilasters act as supports for the sun, moon, and arch. The Ionic volutes of the central Composite capital, on the other hand, refer to the pillar of wisdom associated with the worshipful master, whose bust it supports.

Over time, the delicately carved capitals of the chair lost a considerable amount of detail because of their laminated construction and regular use (fig. 17). Several leaves and volutes fell off when their glue joints failed, and other losses occurred because of the carving's inherent fragility. The extreme undercutting necessary to render acanthus foliage properly produced numerous curls of weak, short-grained mahogany. To preserve the historic character of the chair, the curatorial and conservation staff chose to leave some of the old losses untouched as evidence of the chair's regular use and to repair only the most visually objectionable ones (figs. 18, 19).[21]

Bucktrout's rusticated arch of heaven is composed of two arc-sawn mahogany boards lap-joined behind the keystone. To Bucktrout and his Masonic brethren, smooth-dressed "stones" represented perfect ashlar— the ideal state of virtue and the lifelong goal of every Mason. Entered apprentices identified themselves with rough ashlar, a coarse, unformed block of stone, which was neither intrinsically moral nor innately depraved. The creation of perfect ashlar was a Lockean metaphor for human development; by progressing through the Craft degrees, "the rough external is smoothed off, and beauties, till then unknown, rise full to . . . view." The Bucktrout chair goes beyond the theme of individual perfectibility, however, to serve as a reminder that men could "bring their ideas . . . conduct

Figure 17 Preconservation detail of the right capital of the chair illustrated in fig. 2, showing numerous losses and a poor repair mimicking the form of the missing upper portion. (Photo, F. C. Howlett.)

Figure 18 Detail of the right capital of the chair illustrated in fig. 2 during treatment, which included removal of old repairs, glue, and varnish from areas of loss prior to attaching replacements. (Photo, F. C. Howlett.)

Figure 19 Post-conservation detail of the right capital of the chair illustrated in fig. 2 with replacements carved and toned to match the adjacent surfaces. (Photo, Hans Lorenz.)

. . . and institutions . . . into harmony with the universal natural order." The arch's conjoined blocks of perfect ashlar represent Masons joined in universal brotherhood—an embodiment of the Enlightenment vision of the "Heavenly City" on earth.[22]

The association of whole numbers with mystical powers is another component of Masonic symbolism. A vestige of the occult arts of the late Renaissance, Masonic number systems drew on the Pythagorean mysticism of the Hermeticists and on the secret numerical/alphabetical equations of the

Figure 20 Frontis of Thomas and Batty Langley's *The Builder's Jewel: or the Youth's Instructor, and Workman's Remembrancer* (1741; reprint ed., London: R. Ware, 1754). (Courtesy, Colonial Williamsburg Foundation.)

Caballa. In the Pythagorean system, odd integers represented male attributes, a distinction that probably accounts for their prevalence in Freemasonry.

During the eighteenth century, Masonry's mystical numerology was tempered by rationalism, but it never disappeared. The frontis of Thomas and Batty Langley's *The Builder's Jewel* (1741, 1747) has several allusions to the number three, the most perfect number in the Masonic system (fig. 20). Nearly all of the symbols occur in triadic arrangements, and each of the three pillars is labeled with one of the significant numbers of Freemasonry, III, V, and VII. Above an acacia branch marking the grave of Hiram Abif is the number 15, representing the sum of the three significant numbers as well as the fifteen days the body of the murdered master lay undiscovered.

Obvious triadic arrangements on the Bucktrout chair are the three great lights (Bible, compass, and square) and the three lesser lights (sun, moon, and worshipful master). Other numerical allusions are the nine flutes on each pillar, a possible reference to perfection, to the nine muses, to the nine worthies of Masonic legend, and to the celestial sphere (360 degrees: 3 + 6 + 0 = 9). There are twenty-seven flutes in all, a number of great significance since it is the product of three raised to the third power. The pillars taper to a width of three inches at their capitals, the same width found on the curved elements comprising the arch of heaven. The seven segments on each half of the arch suggest creation as well as the number of years required to build Solomon's Temple; and in its entirety, the fifteen blocks of perfect ashlar comprising the arch (including the keystone) recall the fifteen days of Hiram Abif's interment, the fifteen elect who founded the Society of Freemasons, and the fifteen steps of the winding staircase leading toward a life of virtue (the first three steps symbolize the three ages of man and the three degrees of Masonry, the next five represent the five senses and the five orders of architecture, and the final seven symbolize the seven arts and sciences and the seven planets).[23]

The Three Lesser Lights: The Sun, the Moon and the Worshipful Master
In a sermon delivered at Williamsburg Lodge on December 27, 1775, Reverend William Bland remarked:

> mingled with the mighty Chaos, [light] moderated its Convulsions, and gave the whole Body a Bias, to receive such Impressions as unbounded Wisdom should afterward prefer. . . . In strict Affinity to Light doth Masonry step into the Dissentions and Animosities amongst Men. . . . Need I be asked, Why we revere the Sun and Moon, seeing that the Former is the Source of Light, the Latter its Subordinate Minister.[24]

The sun, the moon, and the worshipful master were the symbolic focus for Masonry's reverence for light, yet this reverence suffused the entire institution. The Feast Days of St. John the Baptist and of St. John the Evangelist, for instance, marked the yearly progress of the sun, falling on the summer and winter solstices, respectively. Similarly, the orientation of the lodge to the east, with obeisance to the south and west, paid heed to the sun's daily travel.

Thomas Paine, who called the sun "the great emblematical ornament of Masonic lodges and Masonic dresses," observed that "Masonry . . . is the remains of the religion of the ancient Druids; who, like the magi of Persia and the Priests of Heliopolis in Egypt, were priests of the sun. They paid worship to this great luminary, as the great visible agent of a great invisible first cause." By revering the sun and the moon, Freemasons were practicing the religion of nature. This was not necessarily the pantheism of the Druids, but rather the English deism that transcended, and in many individuals supplanted, the traditions of Christianity. Deified nature was the source of light, light was the source of reason, and reason was the source of truth.[25]

Within the Freemasonic scheme of natural religion, the worshipful master was an intermediary between nature and the individual Mason. In a metaphor derived from the craft tradition, the worshipful master embodied

Figure 21   Preconservation detail of the sun on the chair illustrated in fig. 2, showing degraded bronze paint obscuring earlier layers of gold leaf. (Photo, Hans Lorenz.)

the wisdom and knowledge obtained through years of labor. He also represented cumulative human knowledge: the sum total of man's application of reason to the study of nature. By following the light of the worshipful master and by studying his teachings, the Mason could speed his progress toward virtue. The symbol of the worshipful master could call to mind King Solomon, as in the ritual of the third degree, or it could evoke the character of a more recently departed patriarch. In his Feast Day sermon on December 27, 1775, William Bland extended the language of light beyond the sun and the moon to exalt the late worshipful master of Williamsburg Lodge, Peyton Randolph, "as a bright Exemplar, to imitate and admire. . . . All North America was under his wing, but we his peculiar Care. . . . I congratulate my brethren that we once had Such a head and such a Father."[26]

Given the importance of light to eighteenth-century Freemasonry and its embodiment in the symbols of the sun, the moon, and the worshipful master, the Bucktrout chair appeared very dim when Colonial Williamsburg acquired it (fig. 21). Subsequent examination, however, revealed that the chair initially had three types of gilding: burnished water gilding, oil gilding, and shell gold (gold powders on size). These materials and their skillful application suggest that the work was done by an ornamental painter or a carver and gilder such as George Hamilton. In the July 28, 1774, issue of the *Williamsburg Gazette*, Hamilton advertised, "GEORGE HAMILTON, CARVER and GILDER, just from Britain, and now in this City, hereby informs the Publick that he intends carrying on his Business in all its Branches."[27]

Hamilton worked for cabinetmaker Edmund Dickinson, who succeeded Bucktrout as the master of the Hay shop. Like Bucktrout, Dickinson was an active member of the Williamsburg Lodge. Hamilton may also have been a Mason, for a George Hamilton appeared as a visitor at lodge meetings six times between August 1774 and February 1775. Bucktrout, who never advertised gilding, may have required Hamilton's services to complete his master's chair.[28]

Figure 22   Cross-section of a sample taken from the sun (200x), viewed with a combination of visible light and near-ultraviolet light to reveal original gilding and restoration layers. (Photo, F. C. Howlett.)

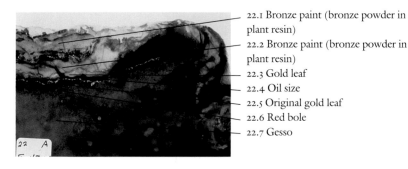

22.1 Bronze paint (bronze powder in plant resin)
22.2 Bronze paint (bronze powder in plant resin)
22.3 Gold leaf
22.4 Oil size
22.5 Original gold leaf
22.6 Red bole
22.7 Gesso

Layers of tarnished nineteenth- and twentieth-century bronze paint obscured the brilliance of the sun, and areas of long-lost gesso and gold scarred the expression on its face (fig. 21). A small finish sample taken from the sun's cheek revealed that the original surface was water gilded (three to five coats of gesso laid on the wood, followed by a thin layer of red bole topped with burnished gold leaf) and that earlier restorers had added a layer

Figure 23 Post-conservation detail of the sun on the chair illustrated in fig. 2, showing early oil gilding. (Photo, Hans Lorenz.)

Figure 24 Preconservation detail of the moon on the chair illustrated in fig. 2. (Photo, F. C. Howlett.) Two coats of dark, degraded varnish are above the mahogany.

Figure 25 Scanning electron microscope photomicrograph of a particle taken beneath the moon's lower lip (350×). (Courtesy, Conservation Analytical Laboratory, Smithsonian Institution; photo, Melanie Feather.)

of oil gilding (oil size and gold leaf) and, more recently, a layer of bronze paint (fig. 22). To preserve the historic integrity of the fragmentary water gilded surface, we removed the degraded bronze paint and left the oil gilding. Once cleaned, an acrylic coating consolidated the surface and gave the gold a luster that resembled the original water gilding (fig. 23).[29]

The moon presented a set of problems entirely different from those of the sun (fig. 24). Like the rest of the chair, this dark mahogany crescent had two later layers of opaque varnish. Common sense suggested that the moon was decorated originally, and upon close inspection we noticed a few bits of pale-colored residue lodged below the lower lip. Suspecting that these fragments were vestiges of silver-gilded decoration, we arranged for an examination of the chair at the Smithsonian Institution's Conservation Analytical Laboratory.

Examination began using an X-ray fluorescence object analyzer, an instrument used to determine the atomic elements of high atomic weight present on an object's surface. When the X-ray beam strikes the surface, each atomic element fluoresces differently. The sensor takes in the fluorescence of all the elements present, and the unit produces a printout of the combined spectra on a single graph. With computer assistance, the spectral peaks for each element present are readily distinguished.

The indistinct substance below the moon's lower lip contained calcium, iron, lead, and silver. This result tentatively confirmed our hypothesis; but the silver spectral peaks from the moon were minimal, so we decided to remove a small sample for more intensive examination (fig. 25). A scanning electron microscope incorporating energy dispersive analysis (SEM-EDX) yielded solid proof of silver gilding. The presence of calcium, lead, and iron

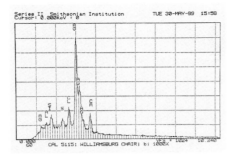

Series II Smithsonian Institution   TUE 30-MAY-89 15:58
Cursor: 0.000keV = 0

CAL 5115; WILLIAMSBURG CHAIR; b; 1000X

Figure 26   Scanning electron microscope–EDX spectrum indicating the presence of silver in the particle illustrated in fig. 25. (Courtesy, Conservation Analytical Laboratory, Smithsonian Institution.)

Figure 27   Detail of the moon on the chair illustrated in fig. 2 during treatment, showing the application of new silver leaf above an acrylic barrier coating. (Photo, F. C. Howlett.)

Figure 28   Post-conservation detail of the moon on the chair illustrated in fig. 2. (Photo, Hans Lorenz.)

also supported this conclusion, since these materials are found in gesso and bole (fig. 26).

Given this evidence, we decided to resilver the moon. To preserve the minute fragments of the original surface and the later varnish layers, we applied four coats of acrylic resin. As each layer dried, we abraded it with fine finishing paper to provide a smooth, bole-like surface for the silver leaf. A fine mist of solvent sprayed onto the acrylic surface made it slightly tacky, permitting the leaf to be laid in the traditional manner (fig. 27). After the surface dried, we distressed the leaf, toned it with watercolors, and coated it with shellac to impart color and prevent tarnishing (fig. 28).[30]

The renewed brilliance of the sun and the moon produced an unforeseen imbalance within the triad of the three lesser lights. The bust of the worshipful master, a focal point in the entire composition of the back, seemed dark in contrast to its celestial companions (fig. 29). X-radiography revealed a small area of opacity in the tassel of the master's turban, which suggested

Figure 29 Detail of the bust of the worshipful master on the chair illustrated in fig. 2. (Photo, Hans Lorenz.)

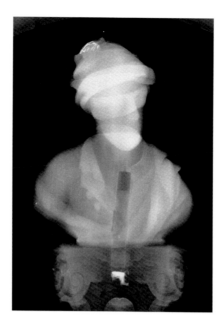

Figure 30 X-radiograph of the bust illustrated in fig. 29. (Courtesy, Robert Berry, Fabrication Division, Nondestructive Evaluation Section, NASA—Langley Research Center.)

Figure 31 Josiah Wedgwood Factory, Bust of Matthew Prior, England, ca. 1775. Basalt stoneware. H. 9", W. 5". (Courtesy, Colonial Williamsburg Foundation; photo, Hans Lorenz.)

the presence of a heavy metal pigment (fig. 30). Upon close examination of the tassel, we found remnants of early paint and, using a simple chemical test, identified it as lead white. Microscopic samples from other areas of the bust revealed no additional pigments. Although it is possible that the tassel alone was painted, it is more likely that the entire bust was originally decorated and that it subsequently received a scouring like the moon. Since analysis was inconclusive, however, the bust remains unpainted.[31]

A ceramic copy of the marble bust of poet and philosopher Matthew Prior in Westminster Abbey probably served as the model for Bucktrout's bust of the archetypal worshipful master (fig. 31). If so, Bucktrout may have attempted to simulate its stonelike surface. Lead white would have made an excellent ground coat for a marbleized surface, and the luminous quality of stone would have enhanced the visual and symbolic power of the three lesser lights; moreover, the implicit reference to the Craft of stonemasonry would have been obvious to lodge members.

Virtute et Silentio

Prior to treatment, tarnished bronze paint obscured the original surface of the small carved scroll on the keystone above the bust. During a test cleaning, the letters "VIR" began to emerge (fig. 32). By revealing the hidden inscription, we hoped to identify the lodge that owned the chair originally. Instead, we uncovered a Latin expression common on Masonic medals from the third quarter of the eighteenth century: "Virtute et Silentio"—by virtue and silence (fig. 33). In 1774, Philip Vickers Fithian of Westmoreland County, Virginia, observed his friend, Joseph Lane, "drest in black superfine Broadcloth; Gold-Laced hat; laced Ruffles; black Silk Stockings; & to his Broach on his Bosom he wore a Mason's Badge inscrib'd 'Virtute and Silentio' cut in a Golden Medal!"[32]

Virtue was a pervasive theme in eighteenth-century moral, ethical, and religious texts and in the literature and iconography of Freemasonry. In

Figure 32   Detail of the scroll on the keystone of the chair illustrated in fig. 2. (Photo, F. C. Howlett.) The letters "VIR" began to appear during removal of the degraded bronze paint.

Figure 33   Post-conservation detail of the scroll illustrated in fig. 32. (Photo, Hans Lorenz.)

1777, the new president of the College of William and Mary, Reverend James Madison, exhorted his Williamsburg brethren "to raise a lasting monument of Worth upon the Basis of Virtue supported and adorned by the grand Pillars of Charity, Benevolence and Friendship." To eighteenth-century Freemasons, the concept of virtue differed radically from that preached by dissenting Protestants. Fithian recorded the opinions of his friend, Lane, who criticized Virginia Anabaptists for "destroying pleasure in the Country; for they encourage ardent pray'r; strong and constant faith, & an entire banishment of Gaming, Dancing, and Sabbath-Day Diversions." Lane probably agreed with fellow Mason Benjamin Franklin, whose benevolent creator "delights in the Happiness of those he has created; and since without Virtue Man can have no Happiness, . . . let me resolve to be virtuous, that I may be happy, that I may please Him."[33]

Enlightenment thinkers like Franklin merged the classical model of virtue with eighteenth-century notions of sociability: The virtuous man achieved personal happiness and extended it to the lives of others by serving the public good. The Reverend Madison asked, "what objects are more worthy of the Wise and good . . . than those which lead us to promote disinterested Virtue, and to diffuse the stream of Happiness into every Heart . . . Men of such Character . . . will manifest by . . . generous and worthy actions, that they live not for themselves but for their Country the World."[34]

The juxtaposition of virtue and silence illustrates one of the greatest paradoxes of eighteenth-century Freemasonry. Although virtue was a means of uniting humanity, "Silentio" alluded to Freemasonry's legendary secrecy and exclusivity. The quality of virtue, like fraternal membership, could thus not extend to all humanity, for "the great part of mankind is not fit to be members." In 1772, William Preston wrote: "Were the privileges of Masonry to be common, or indiscriminately bestowed, the design of the institution would be subverted; for being familiar, like many other important matters, they would soon lose their value, and sink into disregard." Although the social boundaries of eighteenth-century Freemasonry gradually expanded, the organization maintained its status as a secret, exclusive orga-

Figure 34 Preconservation detail of the three great lights on the chair illustrated in fig. 2. (Photo, Hans Lorenz.)

nization. The brotherhood may have extended universal love and membership to "the distant Chinese, the wild Arab, or the American savage," but it excluded Africans, women, and those without property.[35]

The Three Great Lights and the Five-Pointed Star

The three great lights—the compass, the square, and the "Volume of the Sacred Law"—became a unified symbol about 1760. After that time, no lodge could operate unless these symbols were present in the furnishings. Their juxtaposition served to illustrate the essentially personal nature of adherence to Masonic principles. As emblems of inner spiritual guidance, they symbolized the work of the individual Mason in his progress toward wisdom and virtue (fig. 34).[36]

To eighteenth-century Freemasons, the symbolic significance of the three great lights transcended any specific moral doctrine or religious dogma. For this reason, the "Volume of the Sacred Law" represented not only the Bible of Christianity but also the universal truths contained within the scriptures of all religions. As William Preston stated in 1772, "Men of the most opposite religions, of the most distant countries and of the most contradictory opinions, are by [Masonry] united in one indissoluble bond of unfeigned affection."[37]

By eschewing dogmatism, Freemasonry sanctioned individual interpretations of the three great lights and other symbols. Christian interpretations were certainly possible. In his *Spirit of Masonry* (1775), William Hutchinson wrote:

> The SQUARE will teach us to square all our actions. . . . Our behavior will be regular and uniform, not aspiring at things above our reach, nor pretending to things above our finite capacities. . . . The COMPASSES will inform us that we should in every station learn to live within proper bounds, that we may, therefore, be enabled to contribute to the relief of the necessities and indigencies of our fellow-creatures. Hence we shall rise to notice, live with honour, and make our exit in humble hopes of compassing what ought to be the main pursuit of the most aspiring genius, a crown of glory.

For Hutchinson, these Masonic symbols embodied "divine truths" and provided direction on his Christian path toward the light.[38]

In contrast, the designer of the Bucktrout chair probably intended a more universal interpretation of the three great lights. The "Volume of the Sacred Law" on the chair is a carved and painted Bible—the sacred text one would expect to find in a colonial American lodge—but it is open to I Kings, Chapter VII, which recounts in detail the construction of King Solomon's Temple. Freemasonry traces its institutional origin to this event, and the Biblical account serves as the foundation for many of the great Masonic symbols and legends. The text, simulated on the Bucktrout chair, details the floor plan of the Temple and the orientation of its rooms—the prototype for every Masonic lodge. It also describes the ornament of the Temple, including the important pillars, Jachin and Boaz, and details events that formed the legend of the grand master, Hiram Abif.

It would be difficult for a Christian moralist to derive a lesson from I Kings, Chapter VII. The language is purely descriptive in its delineation of the form and dimensions of the Temple rooms, in its depiction of the elaborate interior ornamentation of the building, and in its discussion of the skills in woodworking, bronze casting, stonemasonry, and goldsmithing utilized by Hiram and the Temple builders. The emphasis is on human skill, industry, and ingenuity—on man as a being capable of divine creativity, building a structure dedicated to his own glory and to the glory of the "Grand Architect."

The compass and square on the Bucktrout chair also reflect this creative function. The square represents man's activities within the physical world, his moral nature, whereas the compass represents his spiritual side. Working together, they become positive tools for the moral and spiritual growth of the individual Mason. This concept is reinforced by the illustration of Euclid's forty-seventh proposition, incised on the blade of the square. To the eighteenth-century Freemason, this geometric representation of the Pythagorean theorem depicted a mathematical discovery of simple logic and beauty. As a clear example of natural law, it offered a glimpse of divine perfection.

The square and compass were essential tools for making the forty-seventh proposition comprehensible. By applying the rational science of geometry

Figure 35   Detail of the Bible during treatment, showing removal of the degraded varnish layers. (Photo, F. C. Howlett.)

Figure 36 Masonic apron presented by George Washington to General William Schuyler, ca. 1770. (Courtesy, Alexandria—Washington Lodge No. 22, A.F. & A.M.; photo, Museum of Early Southern Decorative Arts.)

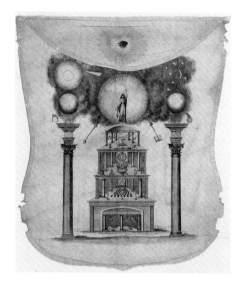

Figure 37 Floor cloth presented by Joseph Montfort to the Royal White Hart Lodge No. 2, Halifax, North Carolina, ca. 1765. (Courtesy, Royal White Hart Lodge No. 2, A.F. & A.M.; photo, Museum of Early Southern Decorative Arts.)

to his own life through the use of his square and compass—squaring all of his actions while enlarging the circle of his spiritual world—the Mason could work to achieve consonance with natural principles and, ultimately, to attain a life of divine perfection. In *Illustrations of Masonry*, William Preston wrote:

> By geometry, we may curiously trace Nature through her various windings, to her most concealed recesses. By it we may discover the power, the wisdom, and the goodness of the Grand Artificer of the Universe, and view with amazing delight the beautiful proportions which connect and grace this vast machine. By it we may discover how the various planets move in their different orbits, and mathematically demonstrate their various revolutions. . . . Numberless worlds are around us, all framed by the same Divine Artist, which roll through the vast expanse and are all conducted by the same unerring law of Nature. When such objects engage our attention, how must we improve, and with what grand ideas must such knowledge fill our minds![39]

The painted lettering and inscribed illustration of Euclid's forty-seventh proposition thus link the three great lights on the Bucktrout chair with Newtonian philosophy. Small physical clues such as these often have a marked effect on the interpretation of an object, yet after years of use and deterioration their significance may be overlooked. The preservation and stabilization of these and similar bits of evidence are, consequently, paramount in conservation treatments.

Removal of the compass and square permitted a better assessment of the Bible's fragile surface and the outline of its missing five-pointed star. In the process, it became apparent that the compass was an exact copy of a working tool, complete with movable, hinged arms. Both arms were missing their points, but they retained original oil gilding under later coats of bronze paint.

The Bible had suffered paint losses around the lettering of the chapter heading as well as in areas of the simulated text (fig. 35). Overall, the deteriorated paint had a fine craquelure and was obscured by two coats of a dark, degraded resin varnish. X-ray fluorescence and chemical tests revealed that the paint on the Bible was lead white in oil. The brown-black letters on the gesso had partially dissolved into the degraded varnish layers. As a result, removing the varnish required a combination of solvent swelling and careful mechanical removal around the perimeter of each letter. Once cleaned, two very thin coats of acrylic resin consolidated the surface, and acrylic emulsion paints and watercolors disguised the most disturbing losses.[40]

The five-pointed star originally positioned at the center of the Bible is not an important symbol in American Freemasonry; however, the star appears frequently in Masonic art from the second half of the eighteenth century. For example, a star appears below the three great lights on an apron presented by George Washington to his staff officer, General William Schuyler (fig. 36), and a blazing five-pointed star imprinted with the letter "G" predominates the imagery of a British floor cloth presented by Joseph Montfort to the Royal White Hart Lodge in Halifax, North Carolina (fig. 37).[41]

Among other things, the star was a symbol of the five points of fellowship, the points of bodily contact used to physically raise a candidate to the third or master's degree. Each of the five points is associated with a particular duty of the master Mason regarding the welfare of his brethren, so the star became a symbol of brotherly love. Illustrative of the multidimensional nature of Masonic symbols, the star also combines the symbol of archetypal man (when viewed as a stylized human figure) with that of a celestial body. The star thus speaks to the microcosm-macrocosm relationship inherent in Newtonian philosophy—the conduct of human life according to the natural laws of the universe.[42]

Two types of five-pointed stars appear in Masonic symbolism. The most common is the pentalpha, an ancient talisman of health comprised of three open, interlaced triangles formed by five interconnected lines. The pent-

Figure 38   Post-conservation detail of the three great lights and the five-pointed star on the chair illustrated in fig. 2. (Photo, Hans Lorenz.)

Figure 39 Grand master's jewel, probably Williamsburg, Virginia, 1778. Silver gilt. H. 5 ½", W. 6¼". (Courtesy, Grand Lodge of Virginia; photo, F. C. Howlett.) The jewel dates from the founding of the independent Grand Lodge of Virginia.

Figure 40 Detail of the replacement tool on the back of the chair illustrated in fig. 2. (Photo, F. C. Howlett.) The tool probably dates from the late nineteenth century.

alpha appears in Virginia iconography on the back of the master's chair belonging to Williamsburg Lodge No. 6 (fig. 3); however, the physical evidence on the Bucktrout chair is inconsistent with an openwork design. Instead, we made a solid, faceted star, a three-dimensional form in keeping with the other carved elements of the chair. Bronze paint overruns from a nineteenth- or twentieth-century touchup outlined the star's position on the Bible, suggesting that it had been gilded like other elements on the chair. The star thus received water gilding much like the original surface of the sun, artificial wear to mute the surface, toning with acrylic emulsion paints, and a coat of shellac to harmonize it with its surroundings (fig. 38).[43]

After conservation, the juxtaposition of the newly constructed gilded star with the compass and square suggested the form of an esteemed officer's jewel, much like the jewel devised in 1778 (the year Virginia lodges broke all ties with British Freemasonry) for the grand master of the newly independent Grand Lodge of Virginia—the blazing sun, compass, and quadrant (fig. 39). The five-pointed star, square, and compass, though unfamiliar to American Masons, became the jewel of English provincial grand masters in 1814 after the formation of the United Grand Lodge of England. Evidence exists that indicates earlier British use of the jewel as well, for it appears on the crest of a master's chair in the Royal White Hart Lodge in Halifax, North Carolina (fig. 6). This chair was used by Joseph Montfort, provincial grand master of North Carolina. Virginia's provincial grand master, Peyton Randolph, wore a jewel indicative of his status. Following his death, Mrs. Randolph presented his "Provincial Grand Master's Jewel, Sash, and Apron," to his Williamsburg brethren. The five-pointed star, square, and compass on the Bucktrout chair, therefore, strongly suggest that it was made for Randolph's use in the Williamsburg Lodge.[44]

The presence of two master's chairs in the Williamsburg Lodge is in keeping with its pre-Revolutionary status as the premier lodge in Virginia and with the membership of two masters. When Randolph assumed the title of provincial grand master in 1774, the Williamsburg Lodge elected John Blair to be its master. Both Randolph and Blair attended a lodge held on July 5, 1774. On that date, the Proceedings of the Williamsburg Lodge refer to Randolph as "P. G. M." and to Blair as "M." Also present at that meeting was Philadelphia artist Charles Willson Peale, who had come to paint a full-length portrait of Randolph seated in his master's chair. The painting, later given to the Library of Congress, was destroyed during the mid-nineteenth century.[45]

The Missing Tool

Although the original symbols present on the Bucktrout chair held multiple layers of meaning for eighteenth-century Freemasons, an odd replacement tool added in the late nineteenth century probably would have been unfamiliar to them (fig. 40). The long-handled object installed diagonally to the right of the Bible vaguely resembles a Mason's rake, but the rake had little symbolic importance when the chair was made. Glue lines, nail evidence, and an original mortise indicate that the orientation of the original

Figure 41 Third-degree tracing board by J. Bowring, Britain, 1819. Painted wood. (By permission of the Board of General Purposes, United Grand Lodge of England.) The English working tools of the master mason (compass, pencil, and skirret) appear in the rectangle above the arch.

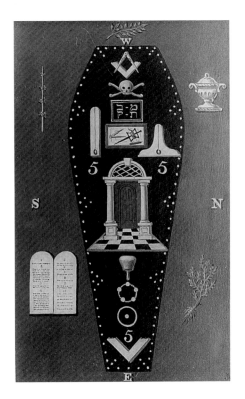

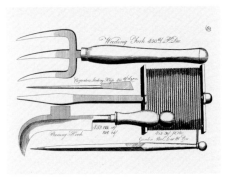

Figure 42 "Garden Reel" illustrated on pl. 62 of a Birmingham, England, tool catalogue, ca. 1798. (Courtesy, Peabody-Essex Museum.) In British Freemasonry, the tool described here as a "garden reel" is a version of the wooden "line" or "chalk line," a tool given the name "skirret" by British Freemasons.

tool echoed the position of the trowel; however, the mortise dimensions and the attachment points differ, which suggest that the missing component was a different tool.

The missing tool was probably one of the "working tools" of Freemasonry, as are all the others on the chair. In England and America, "working tools" were divided into three levels, each embodying the moral virtues ascribed to one of the three symbolic degrees of Masonry: entered apprentice, fellowcraft, and master Mason. Since the early nineteenth century, English and American Freemasons have employed nearly identical "working tools" for their entered apprentice and fellowcraft degrees, but the tools for the master Mason differ significantly. The American master Mason has a single "working tool"—the trowel. The English master has three—the compass, pencil, and skirret.[46]

Masonic historian Albert Mackey described the skirret as "an implement rotating on a center pin, whence a line is drawn, chalked, and struck to mark out the ground for the foundation of the intended structure." Early nineteenth-century English Masonic illustrations of the skirret confirm it to be a tool for laying line, consisting of a reel on a spindle above a projecting handle or spike (fig. 41). Such an implement could fit into the space for the missing tool on the Bucktrout chair. Its rectangular head would harmonize with the flanking trowel and provide a counterbalance to the mallet on the lower left. More importantly, the skirret's projecting pin would fit the attachment outline on the pilaster, and its reel would align with the mortise below the 24" gauge.[47]

Unlike the other tools on the chair, the skirret does not appear in any known eighteenth-century illustrations of Masonic symbols, nor was it an implement used by medieval stonemasons. Its origin is unknown, but given the importance of antiquity to Freemasonry, the skirret may emulate a tool discovered during eighteenth-century explorations of ancient Egyptian, Greek, or Roman archaeological sites. The earliest non-Masonic depiction of a skirret-like tool dates to about 1798 (fig. 42). A similar undated example of this tool (Colonial Williamsburg Foundation) is referred to as a "line" or "chalk line." Curiously, the term "skirret" is associated only with British Freemasons, who coined the name early in the nineteenth century.[48]

The new name probably helped distinguish the symbolism of the skirret, a tool for laying horizontal lines, from that of the "line" or "plumb," a tool used to establish verticality. Evidence of confusion concerning these "line" tools is apparent in Hutchinson's *Spirit of Masonry*: "The Line should make us pay the strictest attention to that line of duty which has been given us, or rather which was marked out to us, by our great Benefactor and Redeemer." Hutchinson's words foreshadow an early nineteenth-century reference to the symbolism of the skirret: "The Schivit Line represents the strict and undeviating line of duty marked out for our pursuit in the Volume of the Sacred Law." Both passages suggest a horizontal "line of duty" to be pursued in the physical world.[49]

Hutchinson symbolically moves the same "line" to a vertical orientation: "This line, like Jacob's ladder, connects heaven and earth together; and, by laying hold of it, we climb up to that place where we shall change this short line of time for the never-ending circle of eternity." This quote almost certainly refers to a "plumb," a simple tool consisting of a string tied to a lead weight, used to establish a vertical line. Hutchinson's extraction of "horizontal" and "vertical" moral lessons from a single implement probably reflects his genteel distance from operative stonemasonry. Such confusion could have prompted the United Grand Lodge to distinguish the horizontally employed "skirret" from its vertical counterpart.[50]

The tool missing from the Bucktrout chair may have been an early interpretation of a skirret, removed when it no longer held meaning in American Freemasonry. In addition to the physical evidence, the hierarchical arrangement of the "working tools" on the back supports this supposition. At the base are the mallet and the gavel, which have served as first-degree tools in both England and America. On the next level are two plumb rules, a level, and a square, the second-degree "working tools" in both countries. At the third level are the trowel and the compass, master Mason's tools from America and England respectively. The skirret, a third-degree tool and a "line" symbol absent on the chair, would be an appropriate substitute for the replacement tool. The entire arrangement of the chair back, then, much like illustrations found elsewhere in Freemasonry, would symbolize the progression of the individual Mason upward through the three degrees toward the light provided by the sun, moon, and worshipful master, all occurring under the arch of heaven.

An Emblem of Royalty

Despite the profusion of symbols on the Bucktrout chair, its design is incomplete. The uppermost component, an object that once rested on the cushion above the arch, is missing. The cushion has a carved and gilded, braided cord with tiny brass loops that probably held tassels (fig. 43). Tassels and cords, depicted on eighteenth-century English tracing boards (symbolic instructional devices for entered apprentices), represented, among other things, "the universal bond by which every Freemason ought to be united to his Brethren."[51]

Figure 43   Detail of the cushion above the arch on the chair illustrated in fig. 2. (Photo, F. C. Howlett.)

Cushions, however, served not as symbols but as displays for the most revered items of a lodge during processions and ceremonies. Preston's prescribed procession for the "Ceremony of Laying the Foundation Stone" included the "Bible, Square and Compass, on a crimson velvet cushion, carried by the Master of a Lodge." The cushion on Bucktrout's chair retains remnants of red paint (iron oxide) in keeping with Preston's description, but it is unlikely that this cushion bore a Bible, square, and compass, since these elements appear elsewhere on the chair.[52]

A half-circle scribed into the cushion's top surface and outlined by a few forged nail shanks almost certainly registered the base to a carved crown. A crown on the arch of the Bucktrout chair could associate the chair with Royal Arch Masonry. If so, this feature may be a clue to the original owner of the chair, since only lodges chartered by Scotland's Grand Lodge or the English "Antient" Grand Lodge typically conferred Royal Arch degrees.

Figure 44   Detail of the crown and cushion in Allan Ramsay's portrait of Queen Charlotte, ca. 1770. Oil on canvas. 96⁷/₈" × 61³/₈". (Courtesy, Colonial Williamsburg Foundation.)

It is more likely that the crown simply reflected pre-Revolutionary Masonic respect for the British monarchy. Eighteenth-century, British royal portraits often depicted monarchs posed next to their crowns, which almost invariably rest upon tasseled cushions (fig. 44). In spite of its Whiggish associations, British Freemasonry maintained favor among the nobility, who traditionally served as the grand masters of both the "Antient" and Modern branches of the Craft. In 1790, the Modern Grand Lodge elected the Prince of Wales as grand master and ordered a suite of furniture to commemorate the event. Above an arch on the grand master's chair sat a cushion bearing a crown and the Prince of Wales plumes.[53]

The colony of Virginia maintained official loyalty to the Crown until a very late date. The Williamsburg Lodge held a ceremony to lay the cornerstone of the new Capitol Landing bridge in October 1774, just after Peyton Randolph presided over the First Continental Congress. The medal laid beneath the cornerstone was inscribed, "Georgio Tertio Rege/ Comite Dunmore Profecto/ Peyton Randolph Latomorum/ proside Supremo/ Johanne Blair Proside A. L. 5774."[54]

When the break from Britain finally occurred, it happened quickly. Late in his life, Edmund Randolph recalled the fervor of the first days of the Revolution: "Not a vestige of the emblems of royalty was tolerated where the public voice could be brought to act upon it. The wall of the House of Burgesses . . . was decorated with several of them. The chair in which the speaker sat, now filled by the president of the Convention, had a frontispiece commemorative of the relation between the mother country and the colony. These had been criticized before any formal act of reprobation was taken, and all of them were at different times effaced." Ironically, the crowning piece of evidence for the missing element may be its disappearance.[55]

The Chair as a Symbol

The Masonic membership of Benjamin Bucktrout, like that of many other tradesmen, may have been a quest for improved social and financial standing. Indeed, a 1796 description of Bucktrout reveals that he had exchanged "his old greasy leather indispensibles and white cap" for a "scarlet waistcoat and . . . neat wig." At the outset of the Revolution, however, he demonstrated his "Public Spirit and Ingenuity" by building, at his own expense, a hand-mill to provide gunpowder for the Virginia militia. From 1777 to 1779, he served as purveyor of hospitals for the State of Virginia, and later in life he served as surveyor and commissioner of taxes for the city of Williamsburg. Though his activity as a Mason waned in his later years, he maintained the respect of his Masonic brethren, who invited him to their annual Feast Day of St. John in June 1812, the year before his death.[56]

Benjamin Bucktrout's personal interpretation of the symbols on his chair is unknown; nonetheless, the symbols on his master's chair connected eighteenth-century Masons such as Bucktrout with ancient traditions and an influential system of moral guidance. Through the study and conservation of this chair we are "admitted into the mysteries" of their minds and motivations. In its entirety the chair symbolizes the ideals, values, and paradoxes

Figure 45   The Benjamin Bucktrout Masonic master's chair, computer enhanced to illustrate speculations about the missing symbols. (Photography, Hans Lorenz; system work, GIST.)

of eighteenth-century Freemasonry, an organization that systematized and promulgated many of the principles of the British Enlightenment (fig. 45). This optimistic philosophy promoted ideas of tolerance, individual responsibility, and public service—ideas that must have influenced the lives of Bucktrout and his brethren, much as they contributed to the formation of the new republic.[57]

ACKNOWLEDGMENTS For assistance with this article the author thanks Marie Barnett, Robert Berry, Melanie Feather, Jay Gaynor, Wallace Gusler, John Hamill, Ronald Hurst, and Albert Skutans. I am especially grateful to Iris Heissenbuttel for her support and encouragement throughout this project.

1. William Preston, *Illustrations of Masonry* (1772; reprint ed., London: G. and T. Wilkie, 1778), p. 50. Formally incorporated into Freemasonry in the 1730s, the third-degree ritual is described in Bernard Fay, *Revolution and Freemasonry 1680–1800* (Boston: Little, Brown and Company, 1935), pp. 198–201; and Michael Baigent and Richard Leigh, *The Temple and the Lodge* (New York: Arcade Publishing, 1989), pp. 128–30. Ms. Minutes of the Williamsburg Lodge of Masons, 1773–1779 (hereinafter cited as MWLM), bound and photocopied by the Library of Congress, 1939, p. 22, Special Collections, Colonial Williamsburg Foundation Library.

2. Occupational information provided by historian Harold B. Gill, Jr. At their raising, McCarty and Lockley were "Tylers" in the lodge, a position often held by men of lesser stature, for it included duties such as keeping "the Lodge and its furnishings clean and in good order" (MWLM, p. 90). As quoted in George Kidd, *Early Freemasonry in Williamsburg, Virginia* (Richmond, Va.: Dietz Press, 1957), p. 35. In the May 18, 1776, issue of the *Virginia Gazette*, Battwell made this request: "all persons who have demands against me are desired to bring their accounts to Edmund Randolph, Esq., properly attested." Battwell remained in Williamsburg, however, and received charity from the lodge again in May 1779 (Kidd, *Freemasonry in Williamsburg*, p. 46). Preston, *Illustrations of Masonry*, p. 53.

3. Accounts with Robert Carter, 1769, 1770, 1771, Ms C2468a, Carter Family Papers, Virginia Historical Society, Richmond; Ann Blair to Mary Braxton, September 4, 1769, Blair Papers, Special Collections, Swem Library, College of William and Mary; Lord Botetourt's Account Book, November 1, 1769 (copy at the Colonial Williamsburg Foundation).

4. Sermon at the Williamsburg Lodge's Feast of St. John the Evangelist, December 28, 1778, in Ms. Proceedings of the Williamsburg Lodge of Masons, 1774–1779 (hereinafter cited as MPWLM), photocopied and bound by the Library of Congress, 1916, p. 103, copy on file in Special Collections, Colonial Williamsburg Foundation Library.

5. On December 30, 1773, the *Virginia Gazette* reported:

> Last Monday being the Feast of St. John the Evangelist, the ancient and honourable Society of Free and Accepted Masons, all habited alike, and in the proper insignia of their Order, went in Procession from their Lodge in this City to Bruton Church, where an excellent Discourse, delivered by the Reverend Mr. Andrews, a brother Mason, was preached.... After divine Service, they returned to their Lodge, and dined together; after which they gave a Ball and elegant Entertainment to a Number of Ladies, and spent the Evening with that Harmony, Decorum, and friendly Intercourse, which characterize the Brotherhood, and are so agreeable to the Laws of Masonry.

Reverend Andrews was a professor of moral philosophy, and later of mathematics, at the College of William and Mary. Other attendees included the clerk of the Governor's Council, two additional clerics, a cabinetmaker, a wigmaker, a ferry owner, a physician, the former mayor, a merchant, a musician, a tavern keeper, two silversmiths, and several members of the landed gentry. The attendees are listed in MWLM, p. 14; the biographical information came from historian Harold B. Gill and from Kidd, *Freemasonry in Williamsburg*, pp. 87–131.

6. The term "operative" is commonly used by Masonic writers and historians to distinguish working stonemasons from "speculative," or symbolic, Freemasons. Preston, *Illustrations of Masonry*, p. 303. Freemason's Hall in London was dedicated on May 23, 1776.

7. The July 6, 1778, Minutes of Unanimity Lodge No. 7 record: "Justices gave leave that the Lodge might be held in the Courthouse . . . it was accordingly moved, when Br Russel presented the Lodge with an Elegant Master's Chair for which he received thr Sincere Thanks" (as quoted in Bradford L. Rauschenberg, "Two Outstanding Virginia Chairs," *Journal of Early Southern Decorative Arts* 2, no. 2 [November 1976]: 11–20). Rauschenberg discusses variations of the story as found in the files of Unanimity Lodge, nineteenth-century North Carolina newspaper accounts, and the oral tradition of the lodge.

8. The "Lord Baltimore" legend is mentioned in Thomas C. Parramore, *Launching the Craft: The First Half Century of Freemasonry in North Carolina* (Raleigh: Litho Industries, Inc., 1975), p. 72. Norborne Berkeley, Lord Botetourt, was revered by Virginians for his commissions in

support of the College of William and Mary and the House of Burgesses. Though Lord Botetourt's Masonic connections are undocumented, his close nephew and executor of his estate, Henry Somerset, the fifth Duke of Beaufort, was grand master of the Grand Lodge of England from 1767 to 1772 (see Colonial Williamsburg DOC file for 1990-74: portrait of Henry Somerset, fifth Duke of Beaufort). The Grand Lodge of England granted charters to Williamsburg Lodge and the newly named Botetourt Lodge in Gloucester, Virginia, in November 1773 (William Moseley Brown, *Freemasonry in Virginia* [Richmond: Masonic Home Press, 1936], pp. 22, 30). Rauschenberg, "Two Outstanding Virginia Chairs," p. 11.

9. Chippendale's *Director* is listed in Edmund Dickinson's 1778 estate inventory. Dickinson was a former partner of Bucktrout and a Mason. Bucktrout was one of the appraisers of Dickinson's estate. See Wallace Gusler, *Furniture of Williamsburg and Eastern Virginia, 1710–1790* (Richmond: Virginia Museum, 1979), pp. 182–83.

10. Throughout Masonic literature, the compass is referred to in its plural form. The square is the jewel, or insignia, of the grand master; the level is the jewel of the senior warden; and the plumb rule is the jewel of the junior warden. They are traditionally worn on ribbons around the neck during lodge meetings, processions, and other events, hence the term "jewel."

11. David Stevenson, *The Origins of Freemasonry: Scotland's Century, 1590–1710* (Cambridge, Eng.: Cambridge University Press, 1988), pp. 167, 219. Randle Holme, *The Academy of Armory*, 3 vols. (1688; reprint ed., Menston, Eng.: Scolar Press, 1972), p. 393.

12. From Vitruvius, *De Architectura* (1st century, B.C.) as quoted in David Stevenson, *Origins of Freemasonry*, p. 106.

13. Hans Christian von Baeyer, *Taming the Atom: The Emergence of the Visible Microworld* (New York: Random House, 1992), p. 11; Stevenson, *Origins of Freemasonry*, pp. 79–80.

14. Albert C. Mackey, *An Encyclopedia of Freemasonry* (New York: Masonic History Co., 1921), pp. 167–68.

15. Mircea Eliade, *The Forge and the Crucible: The Origins and Structure of Alchemy*, 2d ed. (Chicago: University of Chicago Press, 1972), p. 234.

16. James Anderson, *Charges and Constitutions of Masonry* (1723; revised ed., Boston: Isaiah Thomas, 1767), p. 3.

17. Cornelius Moore, *The Ancient Charges and Regulations of Freemasonry, with Notes Critical and Explanatory* (Cincinnati, Ohio: Masonic Review Office, 1855), p. 119. Henry May, *The Enlightenment in America* (New York: Oxford University Press, 1976), p. 71.

18. Moore, *Ancient Charges*, p. 126.

19. Bland's sermon, given on December 25, 1775, is in MPWLM, pp. 38, 39. From Greene's "Entertainment for a Winter's Evening" (1750), as quoted in David S. Shields, "Clio Mocks the Masons: Joseph Greene's Anti-Masonic Satires," in *Deism, Freemasonry, and the Enlightenment*, edited by J. A. Leo Lemay (Newark: University of Delaware Press, 1987), pp. 102–26.

20. For more on these Virginia Masonic chairs, see Gusler, *Furniture of Williamsburg*, pp. 71–73, 75–79, 92–96. For a thorough discussion of Jachin and Boaz and their various permutations, see James Stevens Curl, *The Art and Architecture of Freemasonry* (London: B. T. Batsford Ltd., 1990), pp. 28–32.

21. Acetone removed the more recent layer of varnish, and an ethanol and water solution dissolved old glue residue. We adhered replacements to flat losses with hot hide glue. We attached the replacements for the jagged losses with gap-filling, carvable epoxy (Ciba-Geigy Araldite 1253) after applying a barrier of hide glue to the original surfaces (furniture conservators at Winterthur Museum pioneered this now widely accepted, reversible treatment). Once firmly attached, new leaves and volutes were carved, using gouges and chisels matching the original tool marks, then matched to adjacent original surfaces using acrylic emulsion paints, clear acrylic coatings, dry pigments, and paste wax. Where possible, new components received a stamped date of completion.

22. William Hutchinson, *The Spirit of Masonry* (1775; reprint ed., Carlisle, Eng.: F. Jollie, 1802), p. 335. The Masonic metaphor of man entering life as rough ashlar is analogous to the theories of human development put forth by John Locke. Early Masonic writers claimed Locke was a Freemason. William Preston published a letter purportedly by Locke in which the philosopher expressed his desire to join the Craft (*Illustrations of Masonry*, p. 105). Carl L. Becker, *The Heavenly City of the Eighteenth-Century Philosophers* (New Haven: Yale University Press, 1932), p. 65. The arch may also allude to Royal Arch Masonry.

23. Numerical allusions abound in Masonic texts of the eighteenth and nineteenth centuries. For a revealing parody of Masonic numerology, see Dr. Alexander Hamilton, *The History of*

the *Ancient and Honourable Tuesday Club*, 4 vols., edited by Robert Micklus (Chapel Hill: University of North Carolina Press, 1990), 2:271–72.

24. MPWLM, p. 38.

25. As quoted in Catharine L. Albanese, *Sons of the Fathers: The Civil Religion of the American Revolution* (Philadelphia: Temple University Press, 1976), p. 133.

26. MPWLM, p. 39.

27. As quoted in Gusler, *Furniture of Williamsburg*, p. 66.

28. Ibid., pp. 66, 67. Kidd, *Freemasonry in Williamsburg,* p. 135.

29. We imbedded the sample in polyester resin, ground and polished it perpendicular to the plane of the paint layers to produce a cross-section of the paint and gilding strata, and examined it with a microscope fitted with visible and UV-fluorescence light sources to achieve clear distinction of the layers. By applying three direct-reactive dyes, we were able to characterize the binders in each layer. (Magnification, 100–200×; visible light source, 50w halogen lamp; near-ultraviolet light source, 100w mercury vapor lamp with a violet cube [excitation range: 350–470nm]; direct-reactive stains Rhodamine B [reacts with lipids such as linseed oil, fluorescing red-orange], TTC [reacts with carbohydrates such as starches and gums], FITC [reacts with proteins such as casein, hide glue, and egg binders].) The size layer appeared amber in white light but fluoresced orange-red under ultraviolet light when stained with Rhodamine B. The oil-gilded surface continued around the break in the gesso, indicating that it was applied after the loss. The latest surfaces consisted of two or three coats of a resinous bronze paint. The bronze pigment particles appeared as dark flakes within the resin binder. Microscopy suggested that the oil-gilded layer remained intact across the marred face of the sun. The upper layers of bronze paint were soluble in a variety of polar solvents, but we found an acetone gel best suited to remove the bulk of the material (developed by paintings conservator Richard Wolbers: 150ml acetone, 20ml deionized water, 8ml Ethomeen C25, and 1.3g Carbopol 625). Diacetone alcohol removed the remaining residue just above the oil gilding. Last, we applied an acrylic coating to consolidate the surface and enhance the brilliance of the gold.

30. The acrylic resin is easily removable; the first two layers are 20 percent Acryloid B72 in toluene (smoothed with 600 grit wet/dry sandpaper), and the second two layers are 20 percent Acryloid B67 in a 90/10 solution of Stoddard Solvent and xylene (smoothed with 600 grit wet/dry sandpaper). A mist of Stoddard Solvent made the B67 suitably tacky for gilding.

31. To test for lead, the dispersed pigment was dissolved in nitric acid, then treated with potassium iodide, which reacted with the lead to form lead iodide.

32. Subsequent testing indicated that both the bronze overpaint and the overvarnish were soluble in acetone, but the original oil-gilded surface of the scroll was not. Unfortunately, the thinly applied lettering was partially bound up in the overvarnish, and it had a similar solubility. Since no solvent or cleaning system could successfully separate the lettering from the overvarnish, the treatment required a combination of techniques. After removing the two thick layers of bronze overpaint with an acetone gel, we applied diacetone alcohol to the darkened varnish to make it swell and soften. This method allowed us to remove most of the varnish mechanically using a micro-chisel and a stereomicroscope at 15–25× magnification. *Journal and Letters of Philip Vickers Fithian, 1773–1774*, Hunter Dickinson Farish, ed., (Charlottesville: University Press of Virginia, 1978), pp. 69–70. Although born in Virginia, Joseph Lane was a friend of Fithian's from Princeton. The motto "Virtue and Silence" appeared on the 1760 seal of England's Antients Grand Lodge (*Transactions of the Quatuor Coronati Lodge* 82, no. 2076 [1969]: 240), a rival to the premier Grand Lodge of England that chartered Williamsburg's lodge and several others in Virginia. In the third quarter of the eighteenth century, "Antient" Freemasonry, loosely tied to the Scottish and Irish Grand Lodges, introduced more elaborate symbolism and higher degrees, such as the Royal Arch degree. Although the presence of "Virtute et Silentio" on the chair suggests that it was made for a lodge practicing "Antient" Freemasonry, dissension between "Antient" and "Modern" Masons did not affect the Craft in Virginia as it did in the northern colonies. Regular intervisitation may have disseminated the symbols and mottos of both branches throughout the Virginia lodges. For a socioeconomic explanation of the rift, see Steven C. Bullock, "The Ancient and Honorable Society: Freemasonry in America, 1730–1830" (Ph.D. dissertation, Brown University, 1986).

33. As quoted in Kidd, *Freemasonry in Williamsburg*, pp. 47–49. Virtue was "the grand object in view, luminous as the meridian Sun, shines refulgent on the mind, enlivens the heart, and converts cool approbation into warm sympathy and cordial attention" (Preston, *Illustrations*

of Masonry, p. 9). Farish, ed., *Journal and Letters of Philip Vickers Fithian*, pp. 72–73. Benjamin Franklin, "Articles of Belief and Acts of Religion," in Fay, *Revolution and Freemasonry,* pp. 160–62. Franklin's simple expression exemplified the optimism of eighteenth-century Freemasonry, which tended to minimize, ignore, or reject the negative aspects of orthodox Christianity—concepts of evil, original sin, and the depravity of man. Franklin's creator was anything but judgmental: "he has created many Things, which seem purely design'd for the Delight of Man, I believe he is not offended, when he sees his Children solace themselves in any manner of pleasant exercises and Innocent Delights." The "Articles" were found in Franklin's pocket when he died.

34. As quoted in Kidd, *Freemasonry in Williamsburg*, p. 48. For a discussion of the eighteenth-century American concept of virtue, see Gordon Wood, *The Radicalism of the American Revolution* (New York: Vintage Books, 1991), p. 218.

35. From a sermon by Isaac Head, Cornwall, England, April 21, 1752, as quoted in Margaret Jacob, *Living the Enlightenment* (New York: Oxford University Press, 1991), p. 61. Preston, *Illustrations of Masonry,* pp. 21, 8. African-American Freemasonry, known as Prince Hall Masonry, dates from the American Revolution, when a group of free blacks were initiated by members of a British military lodge. It was not officially recognized by other American Masonic organizations. British and American Freemasonry remained male organizations throughout the eighteenth century. Only French Freemasons admitted women.

36. Albanese, *Sons of the Fathers,* p. 132. Albanese's date seems reasonable, based on the appearance of the three great lights on Masonic art, engravings, and furniture beginning about 1760.

37. Preston, *Illustrations of Masonry*, p. 9.

38. Hutchinson, *Spirit of Masonry*, p. 333. Hutchinson's orthodox Christian interpretation of Masonic symbols presaged more pronounced Christian influences in Freemasonry after 1800.

39. Preston, *Illustrations of Masonry*, p. 76.

40. The resin was 20 percent Acryloid B67 in Stoddard Solvent. This acrylic coating had no solvent effect on the lettering or the white paint, and it is easily removable.

41. John Bivins, Jr., *The Furniture of Coastal North Carolina, 1700–1820* (Chapel Hill: University of North Carolina Press, 1988), pp. 239–42.

42. In the old English system, which was probably used in Virginia in the eighteenth century, the points are: hand to hand, foot to foot, knee to knee, breast to breast, and hand over back. During the mid-nineteenth century, American Freemasonry substituted mouth to ear for hand to hand. Oliver Day Street, *Symbolism of the Three Degrees* (New York: George H. Doran, 1963), p. 77; and Mackey, *Encyclopedia of Freemasonry*, p. 787.

43. To gild the star, we applied a thin layer of hide glue, followed by a few coats of thin gesso (sanded until smooth), a coat of red bole, and 23K gold leaf. Straight pins attached the star to the Bible (secured in old nail holes that we filled with white pine). Spots of Acryloid B72 reinforced the pins and secured the two lower points of the star. Original nails were reused to attach the square and compass.

44. Parramore, *Launching the Craft*, p. 24. Kidd, *Freemasonry in Williamsburg*, p. 125. MPWLM, December 17, 1775, p. 37.

45. MPWLM, p. 12. Before July 5, 1774, Randolph was listed as "G. M." (grand master), which suggests that he held a special status among Virginia Masons.

46. In America, the "working tools" of the entered apprentice are the 24" gauge and the gavel. In England they are the gauge, gavel (or mallet), and chisel. In both countries, the working tools of the fellowcraft degree are the level, plumb rule, and square. For other contemporary interpretations of these tools, see W. Kirk MacNulty, *Freemasonry: A Journey Through Ritual and Symbol* (London: Thames and Hudson, 1991), pp. 20–31; and Albert Mackey, *Mackey's Revised Encyclopedia of Freemasonry*, 2 vols. (Chicago: Masonic History Co., 1946), 2:1056.

47. Mackey, *Revised Encyclopedia*, 2:947; MacNulty, *Freemasonry*, p. 49.

48. The only line-laying tools shown in Randle Holme's *Academy of Armory* (1688), Joseph Moxon's *Mechanical Exercises* (1688), and Diderot's *Encyclopedia* (1762) are simple iron pins. The *Oxford English Dictionary* lists "skirret" as a tool but ascribes both the origin of the tool and its use to nineteenth-century British Freemasonry. See the discussion of the "chalk line and reel" in R. A. Salaman, *Dictionary of Woodworking Tools* (1975; revised ed., Newtown, Conn.: Taunton Press, 1990), pp. 128–29.

49. See Mackey, *Revised Encyclopedia,* 2:784. Hutchinson, *Spirit of Masonry,* pp. 335–36. The "line" or "plumb" must also be distinguished from the vertical line tool most often referred to in Masonry—the "plumb line" or "plumb rule." According to Hutchinson, the plumb line "admonishes us to walk erect and upright . . . not to lean to a side, but to hold the scale of justice in equal poise; to observe the just medium between temperance and voluptuousness." As quoted in Graeme Love, Research Report on the "Skirret," Lodge of Research no. 218, Library Files, Shrine Temple, Washington, D.C.

50. Hutchinson, *Spirit of Masonry,* p. 336. Similarly, Hutchinson ascribed attributes of the heavy setting maul and chisel-edged gavel to his symbolic "hammer." Love's "Report on the 'Skirret'" traces the name to the early nineteenth-century Freemasons and attributes the name to the sound made as the line is pulled from the reel.

51. Mackey, *Revised Encyclopedia,* 2:1031.

52. Preston, *Illustrations of Masonry,* p. 114.

53. E. T. Joy, "Some Unrecorded Masonic Ceremonial Chairs of the Georgian Period," from *Transactions of the Quaturo Coronati Lodge,* vol. 80, reprinted in *Connoisseur* 159, no. 641 (July 1965): 163.

54. References to Royal Arch Masonry appear early in Virginia lodges. Masonic historians credit the Fredericksburg Lodge with the first Royal Arch degree ever recorded (1753). Cabin Point Royal Arch Lodge met just across the James River from Williamsburg as early as 1771. See Brown, *Freemasonry in Virginia,* pp. 22, 30. MPWLM, p. 15.

55. Edmund Randolph, *History of Virginia* (Charlottesville: University of Virginia Press, 1970), p. 262. Randolph's "History," written between 1809 and 1812, remained in manuscript form until the late nineteenth century. Virginia lodges were the first in the colonies to break ties with British Freemasonry. An independent Grand Lodge was first proposed in Williamsburg on December 3, 1776 (see transcribed MWLM in Kidd, *Freemasonry in Williamsburg,* p. 37), and formally established by 1778 (see Brown, *Freemasonry in Virginia,* pp. 49–64).

56. Mrs. Peachy Wills to Mrs. Ann Coulter, April 30–May 31, 1796, Tucker-Coleman Papers, Special Collections, Swem Library, College of William and Mary. In April 1776, John Page described Bucktrout's "elegant Machine" and the refusal of the Committee of Safety to grant Bucktrout "30 or 40 Pounds as a Reward for his Public Spirit and Ingenuity and to enable him to go on with his Plan" (John Page to Thomas Jefferson, April 26, 1776, in Julian P. Boyd, ed., *The Papers of Thomas Jefferson,* vol. 1 [Princeton, N. J.: Princeton University Press, 1950], pp. 288–89). Bucktrout probably left Williamsburg in late 1779 but returned in 1781, when his name appears on a list of suspected former members of the British army. J. Prentis to Governor Nelson, November 24, 1781, Calendar of State Papers, vol. 2, p. 260; Williamsburg Council Journals, vol. 2, p. 219; Williamsburg Land Tax Records. "At a meeting of the Lodge, June 12, 1812: Resolved that Benjamin Bucktrout be invited to dine with us on June 24 [St. John's Day]" (transcription from MWLM as quoted in Kidd, *Freemasonry in Williamsburg,* p. 62).

57. "Admitted into the mysteries" was the phrase used to signify the initiation of an entered apprentice (MPWLM, p. 98). Individuals involved in the treatment of the Bucktrout chair included Ronald Hurst, curator; Carey Howlett, project director, analysis, cleaning of gilded and painted elements, inpainting; Albert Skutans, structural treatments, fabrication of star, and re-silvering of moon; Wallace Gusler, replacement of carving losses; Leroy Graves, upholstery conservation; Jon Prown, cleaning of gilded and painted surfaces, fabrication and gilding of new rule hinge, inpainting; Julie Reilly, solvent tests, leather seat consolidation and repairs; Steve Ray, solvent tests; Martha Edwards, removal of bronze overpaint on cushion "cord"; Angela Kotakis, mechanical cleaning of brass nails. Assistance in analysis was provided by Melanie Feather of the Smithsonian Institution's Conservation Analytical Laboratory (X-radiography, X-ray fluorescence, and scanning electron microscopy); Gregory Landrey of Winterthur Museum (fluorescence microscopy); and Robert Berry of NASA-Langley (X-radiography).

Luke Beckerdite

Immigrant Carvers and the Development of the Rococo Style in New York, 1750–1770

▼ THE ROCOCO STYLE reached its peak in the American colonies between 1760 and 1775, owing to the arrival of specialized immigrant artisans, the influence of design books and furniture imports, and the economic and political situations at home and abroad. An unprecedented number of artisans immigrated during the 1760s. Most probably felt there was less competition and more opportunity for personal and social advancement in America, whereas others immigrated to escape punishment for minor criminal offenses or because of bankruptcy. In the economic decline that resulted from the Seven Years War (1756–1763), many small shops in Britain were displaced by larger firms, and patronage waned, particularly among the middle class. By contrast, America's economy flourished during and after the French and Indian War (1754–1763).

In 1756, New York merchant Philip Cuyler remarked that the war "may prove as fortunate to this place as the Last [King George's War]." Colonial merchants and entrepreneurs made fortunes privateering and provisioning the British forces and subsequently reaped the benefits of new and expanded commerce with the hinterland and the Atlantic community. James Beekman, for example, sold large quantities of dry goods in New York and in Albany, where Britain maintained a strong military presence. In his *History of the Late Province of New York* (1757), William Smith, Jr., wrote, "Never was the trade in this province in so flourishing a condition as at the latter end of the late French War." Similarly, John Watts noted that New Yorkers "have run too much into habits of luxury. . . . Changes and inconstancies of the war had allmost turned their Heads."[1]

Together with the scions of wealthy, established families, this new merchant elite was largely responsible for the spate of building that occurred in New York during the 1750s and 1760s. Between 1743 and 1760, the number of houses increased from approximately 1,140 to 2,600, and the city's population grew from 11,000 to 18,000. Artisans outside the building trades profited from the growing demand for furnishings and consumer goods and from nonimportation agreements established in response to increasing tariffs and duties imposed by the Crown. This economic and political climate encouraged domestic industries and attracted a variety of tradesmen from abroad.[2]

At least half of the carvers who advertised in New York during the third quarter of the eighteenth century were immigrants. The first to arrive was Henry Hardcastle (fl. ca. 1750–ca. 1756), who was admitted as a freeman in 1751. Little is known about his career, but the furniture and architectural work attributed to him suggests that he trained in London or another large British city during the 1740s. This training is particularly evident in his carving in Philipse Manor in Yonkers (figs. 1, 2). Although a few individual elements could be interpreted as rococo, such as the wavelike plinths of the (missing) birds in the door pediments and asymmetrical scrollwork and heron of the overmantle frieze (fig. 3), the vast majority of this work has a bold, naturalistic quality reminiscent of stone carving in British Palladian interiors of the 1720–1740 period.[3]

Figure 1 First-floor, southeast parlor, Philipse Manor, Yonkers, New York, ca. 1750. (Courtesy, Philipse Manor Hall State Historic Site, administered by the New York State Office of Parks, Recreation, and Historic Preservation; photo, Gavin Ashworth.)

Figure 2 Second-floor, southeast parlor, Philipse Manor. (Photo, Gavin Ashworth.)

Figure 3 Detail of the frieze appliqué of the chimneypiece illustrated in fig. 2.

Hardcastle's patron, Frederick Philipse III, was the third lord of Philipseburg Manor. His grandfather emigrated from Friesland to New Amsterdam during the Dutch period of rule and subsequently amassed a fortune through land speculation, slave trading, and two financially advantageous marriages. After the British conquered New Netherland in 1664, Frederick I supported the new government and was eventually rewarded with a royal patent granting manorial status to his estate. His son, Frederick II, was educated in England but returned to New York in 1716. While maintaining the family's mercantile business, he pursued a legal career culminating in his appointment to the New York Supreme Court in 1755. Frederick II enlarged and renovated Philipse Manor, but his son probably commissioned all the architectural carving in the house and installed the rococo papier-mâché ceiling in the southeast parlor on the first floor (fig. 1). The ceiling ornaments, which appear to be later than the carving, could have been provided by Roper Dawson, who advertised "a great variety of Paper Hangings and . . . Bass Relievo for Ceilings" in 1762; by carvers Nicholas Bernard or John Minshall, who advertised papier-mâché in 1769; or by an English agent or firm working directly with Philipse.[4]

Frederick III is the only individual patron associated with Hardcastle; however, furniture with carving attributed to Hardcastle's shop descended in the Van Rensselaer, Stuyvesant, and Vreeland-Gautier families. By the middle of the eighteenth century, many New Yorkers from old European families turned to England for the latest styles and fashions. Their demands helped stimulate new developments in the furniture-making trades and supported specialists like Hardcastle.[5]

Judging from his surviving work, Hardcastle maintained a relatively small shop. His only known apprentice, Stephen Dwight (DeWight, DeWhile), ran away in June 1755 and opened a shop between the Ferry Stairs and Burling Slip the following month. Hardcastle subsequently moved to Charleston, South Carolina, where he died in October 1756. Although his residence in New York was relatively short, as Dwight's master Hardcastle was the progenitor of the most enduring carving tradition in eighteenth-century New York.[6]

Stephen Dwight's career lasted from 1755 to at least 1774. Advertisements indicate that he moved his shop "into the house of Mr. Johnson Carpenter . . . near the Moravian Meeting" in 1762, that he painted portraits and taught drawing, and that he was in partnership with carver Richard Davis by 1774. Dwight and Davis may have remained in business through the Revolutionary War. Davis was the executor of Dwight's will (written in October 1785), and his name appeared in an 1805 suit involving Dwight's wife, Mary, and other beneficiaries of his estate. New York City directories listed him at various addresses from 1789 to 1798.[7]

Picture frames made for Lawrence Kilburn's portraits of New York merchant James Beekman (1732–1807) (fig. 4) and his wife Jane (Keteltas) are the only carving documented to Dwight's shop. On March 11, 1762, Beekman paid Dwight £11.10.0 for the frames and 8s for "carving four flowers for my New Roome." Presumably, the portraits, frames, and architec-

Figure 4   Picture frame by Stephen Dwight, New York, 1762. White pine, gilded. 52³/₄" × 40". (Collection of the New-York Historical Society; photo, Metropolitan Museum of Art.) The frame is on Lawrence Kilburn's portrait of James Beekman.

tural carving were for Beekman's house on Queen Street. Beekman purchased the house from his brother-in-law, Abraham Keteltas, in 1760 and almost immediately began enlarging, renovating, and refurnishing it. The "flowers" were almost certainly appliqués for the crossettes (or ears) of an architrave (see fig. 13).[8]

Dwight probably patterned his frames after the British example on Kilburn's portrait of Beekman's brother Abraham (fig. 5). All have similar scroll-and-acanthus repeats, applied flowers in the corners and reserves, and large acanthus leaves modeled in much the same manner. The most distinctive elements on Dwight's frames are the carved flowers glued in the corners. These have convex centers and concave lobed petals with small gouge cuts on the edges. The acanthus leaves have minimal detail and are roughly modeled like those on the British frame. As such, they reveal very little about Dwight's working style.

Based on stylistic and technical parallels with the work in Philipse Manor, several examples of New York furniture and architectural carving can be attributed to an artisan trained by Hardcastle. Many colonial artisans trained during the early 1750s had to adjust to new styles introduced by design books and immigrant artisans during the third quarter of the eighteenth century. New York furniture, architectural carving, and trade cards document the presence of Matthias Lock and Henry Copland's *A New Book of Ornaments* (1st ed. 1752), Thomas Chippendale's *The Gentleman and Cabinet-Maker's Director* (1st ed. 1754), and the Society of Upholsterers' *Houshold Furniture in Genteel Taste* (1st ed. 1760). Such design sources were influential; however, they never supplanted the drawing style and technical repertoire that artisans developed during their apprenticeships. Regardless of its date or stylistic derivation, the carving attributed to this anonymous artisan bears the clear imprint of Hardcastle's instruction. Dwight is the most likely candidate, since he is Hardcastle's only known apprentice and the only locally trained carver documented in New York between 1755 and 1770.[9]

Figure 5   Picture frame, British, ca. 1760. Red pine, gilded. 54 1/4" × 45 3/4". (Collection of the New-York Historical Society; photo, Metropolitan Museum of Art.) The frame is on Lawrence Kilburn's portrait of Abraham Beekman.

Figure 6   Parlor from Hampton Place, Elizabeth, New Jersey, 1760–1765. (Courtesy, Winterthur Museum.)

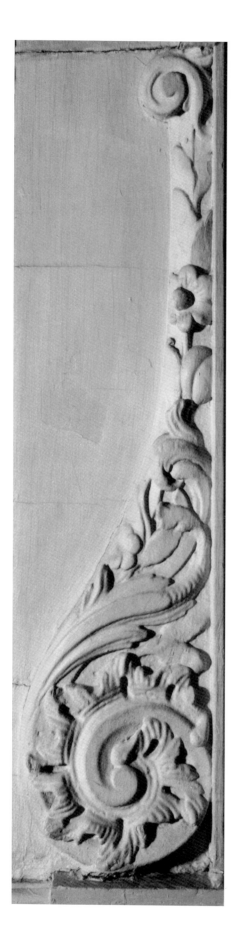

Figure 7 Detail of a truss and crossette appliqué
on the chimneypiece illustrated in fig. 6.

The earliest architectural carving in the "Hardcastle school" is on a chimneypiece from Dr. William Barnet's house in Elizabeth, New Jersey. Tradition maintains that Barnet hired local builder William Brittin to design and supervise the construction of his house, which was reportedly completed by 1763. Following Barnet's death in 1790, the house became known as "Hampton Place."[10]

The parlor (now in the Winterthur Museum) has an elaborate chimneypiece flanked by stop-fluted Doric pilasters and cupboards with molded surrounds, pulvinated friezes, and pediments matching those of the mantle (fig. 6). The upper section of the chimneypiece has a crossetted architrave with "flowers," large carved trusses, and a low, pitched pediment. Small architectural components, such as appliqués and trusses, were easily transported either by wagon or by water. In this instance they were probably shipped by boat across the West River.

Hardcastle's influence is apparent in the design and execution of the carving from Hampton Place. The large acanthus leaves curling against the edge of the architrave molding are simplified versions of those at the top of the trusses in the second-floor parlor of Philipse Manor (figs. 7, 8). All of these

Figure 8 Detail of the left truss of the chimneypiece illustrated in fig. 2. (Photo, Gavin Ashworth.)

Figure 9   Desk-and-bookcase, New York, 1750–1760. Mahogany with tulip poplar, gum, oak, and mahogany. Dimensions unrecorded. (Private collection; photo, John Walton Antiques.)

Figure 10   Detail of the relief-carved heron on the prospect door of the desk-and-bookcase illustrated in fig. 9.

Figure 11   Detail of an appliqué on the scroll-board of the desk-and-bookcase illustrated in fig. 9.

Figure 12   Chimneypiece from Mount Pleasant, New York, 1763–1765. White pine, painted. (Collection of the New-York Historical Society; photo, Metropolitan Museum of Art.)

leaves have broad, flat spines and convex surfaces articulated with multiple gouge cuts; however, the carving from Hampton Place is less accomplished. The trusses have garlands with small flowers, fruits, and simple leaf forms carved in relief on a sloping ground, whereas those attributed to Hardcastle are three-dimensional and far more realistic. The tattered foliage flowing from the large scrolls at the bottom of the trusses is the only rococo detail present in the Hampton Place carving. Hardcastle also used tattered leafage, but the similarities between these details are too generic for comparison.[11]

A desk-and-bookcase that reportedly descended in the Peter Stuyvesant family (fig. 9) is by the same artisan that carved the trusses on the chimney-piece from Hampton Place, and from the same cabinet shop as an earlier desk-and-bookcase with carving attributed to Hardcastle. Both pieces have double-ogee-shaped upper door rails, serpentine blocked interior drawers, pigeonholes with arched brackets, drawers with fully paneled bottom boards, and thin dustboards that are feathered into grooves in the drawer blades and drawer runners. The prospect door on the Stuyvesant desk-and-bookcase has a carved heron (fig. 10) that resembles the one on the frieze appliqué in Philipse Manor (fig. 3). Not only is the posture of the birds similar, but both have body feathers simulated with short, paired gouge cuts. The heron on the prospect door is, however, considerably less sculptural

Figure 14 Detail of a rosette on the chimneypiece illustrated in fig. 1. (Photo, Gavin Ashworth.)

Figure 13 Detail of a crossette appliqué on the chimneypiece illustrated in fig. 12. (Photo, Gavin Ashworth.)

Figure 15 Desk-and-bookcase, New York, 1760–1770. Mahogany with unrecorded secondary woods. H. 106″, W. 50″, D. 24¹/₂″.

than the bird on the frieze appliqué. Similarly, the flower and leaf appliqués on the scrollboard of the Stuyvesant desk-and-bookcase (fig. 11) are simplified versions of those in Philipse Manor. The execution of these naturalistic elements is more comparable to the work in Hampton Place (fig. 7).[12]

A chimneypiece from James Beekman's country house, Mount Pleasant (fig. 12), is probably two or three years later than the Stuyvesant desk-and-bookcase and the interior from Hampton Place. On January 11, 1763, Beekman noted cash "paid Abraham Anderson . . . John Anderson ["and others"] for my . . . farm ["lying and being on Turtle Bay"] . . . total cost, £738.13.6." Within a year, Beekman had spent an additional £1,967 for "utensils, and creatures . . . cost of materials, Labor, and Victuals," suggesting that work at Mount Pleasant was well underway. His account book lists payments to several tradesmen in 1764, including carpenters "Jeramiah Fowler" and "Mr. Peat," but he neglected to specify if the work was for his town or country seat. Although Dwight's name does not appear during the mid-1760s, his involvement is plausible given his previous commissions from Beekman.[13]

Like the chimneypiece in the first-floor parlor of Philipse Manor, Beekman's has a compressed broken-scroll pediment, a pulvinated frieze, and an architrave with scrolling fretwork and shallow, carved leaves. The crossette appliqués on the Beekman chimneypiece are clearly derived from the rosettes on the chimneypiece in the first-floor parlor of Philipse Manor. Both sets of flowers have broad convex petals with deeply fluted and veined depressions and flat half-petals, or sepals, in the background (figs. 13, 14). Similar rosettes also appear on a New York desk-and-bookcase said to have descended in the Cotton Mather Smith family (fig. 15).[14]

No exact source for the dog and swans (fig. 16) on the Beekman chimneypiece is known, but similar animals are depicted in eighteenth-century furniture and architectural designs, particularly those for chimneypieces, looking glasses, and pier tables. The modeling of these animals is comparable to that of the heron on the prospect door of the Stuyvesant desk-and-bookcase (fig. 10). On each the carver used short, paired gouge cuts to simulate hair or feathers.

In other respects the carving on the Beekman chimneypiece differs stylistically from that in Philipse Manor and in Hampton Place. The pediment

Figure 16 Detail of the frieze appliqué on the chimneypiece illustrated in fig. 12. (Photo, Gavin Ashworth.) The carver used short, paired gouge cuts to simulate hair and feathers. This distinctive technique appears in work attributed to Henry Hardcastle.

rosettes, trusses, pilaster "flowers," and frieze appliqué are considerably more abstract (fig. 12). The trusses and appliqué, for example, have acanthus clusters with heavy rounded lobes and tattered leaves that resemble the composite plant/shell forms common in rococo engraving (fig. 17). Although these flower and leaf elements may look different from those in Hampton Place, evidence suggests that they are from the same shop if not, in many instances, by the same hand.

In both design and execution, the carving from Hampton Place and Mount Pleasant is closely related to that in St. Paul's Chapel at Broadway and Fulton Street, built between 1764 and 1766 (fig. 18). Made of Manhattan mica-schist with brownstone coins, the chapel bears a strong resemblance to eighteenth-century churches in towns and cities throughout northern England and Scotland. Local tradition maintains that the architect was Scottish immigrant Thomas McBean; however, recent scholarship suggests that St. Paul's was designed by Peter Harrison. On June 23, 1764, the church paid £600 to "John Dies for 20th [illegible] have taken his Bond & Mortgage per order of Mr. Marston & Mr. Harrison payable [illegible] 9th June 1763."[15]

A notation on a drawing of the south elevation of the church states: "This is the plan designed for the New Church to be executed by Messrs. Gautier and Willis 17th of July 1764." Mr. Gautier, who may have been New York alderman and Windsor chair retailer Andrew Gautier, was apparently in charge of the building. Between March 25, 1762 and December 22, 1768, he received £4,689.12.4, primarily "for the use of St. Paul's Church." Most of the construction was completed by the fall of 1766. That October, the *New York Gazette* reported, "On Monday, 27th . . . the pews in St. Pauls Chapel will be let at public auction . . . and on the Tuesday following the chapel will be opened, and a sermon preached." A subsequent account of the opening described the church as "one of the most elegant edifices on the continent" and noted that "the Mayor and Corporation of the City" and Governor Henry Moore attended the service.[16]

St. Paul's is the only surviving public building in New York City with architectural carving in the rococo style. The ceiling arches spring from classical entablatures supported by large Corinthian pilasters with capitals that match the smaller one beneath the sounding board of the pulpit (figs. 18,

19). The pulpit is one of the most elaborate examples from the colonial period, featuring a carved sounding board; a stair with a carved ogee frieze, brackets, and banisters (figs. 19, 20); a variety of carved moldings; several carved appliqués; and an openwork bolection element, ornamented with strapwork shells flanked by acanthus leaves and flowers. The relief carving on the frieze and on the cartouche above the large Venetian window at the altar end are the most overt rococo details (figs. 21, 22).[17]

The cartouche has acanthus clusters with heavily rounded lobes that are modeled and articulated with chip cuts in precisely the same manner as those on the trusses and appliqué of the Beekman chimneypiece (figs. 17, 22). In addition, several of the C-scrolls framing the inscription on the cartouche have poorly defined volutes that are virtually identical to those of the chimneypiece appliqué (figs. 16, 22). Most carvers used deep vertical gouge cuts to set in their volutes, then fluted the edge of the scroll to cast them in relief, but in many instances, this artisan omitted the first step. Other elements on the cartouche are related to those in Hampton Place and Philipse Manor. The paired acanthus leaves that drop from the large scroll volutes and curl in toward the central reserve (fig. 23) have flat spines and convex

Figure 17 Detail of a truss on the chimneypiece illustrated in fig. 12. (Photo, Gavin Ashworth.)

Figure 18 Interior of St. Paul's Chapel, Broadway and Fulton Street, New York, 1764–1766. (Courtesy, St. Paul's Chapel, Parish of Trinity Church; photo, Gavin Ashworth.)

Figure 19 Pulpit in St. Paul's Chapel, New York, ca. 1765. (Photo, Gavin Ashworth.)

Figure 20 Detail of the stair leading to the pulpit illustrated in fig. 19. (Photo, Gavin Ashworth.)

Figure 21 Detail of the relief-carved frieze of the pulpit illustrated in fig. 19. (Photo, Gavin Ashworth.)

surfaces articulated with gouge cuts, like the similarly shaped leaves on the trusses of the chimneypiece from Hampton Place (fig. 7) and Philipse Manor (fig. 8). These parallels suggest that the same tradesman executed much of the carving for St. Paul's Chapel, the Beekman House, and Hampton Place, and that he trained in Hardcastle's shop.

Other carved details in St. Paul's Chapel bear a strong resemblance to work attributed to Hardcastle. The upper appliqués on the sides of the pulpit have grape leaves with complex outlines and divergent veining like those on the frieze appliqué of the chimneypiece in the second-floor parlor of Philipse Manor (figs. 3, 24). Also, although the stair brackets of the pulpit

Figure 22 Detail of the cartouche above the Venetian window in St. Paul's Chapel. (Photo, Gavin Ashworth.)

Figure 23 Detail of the acanthus leaves on the cartouche illustrated in fig. 22. (Photo, Gavin Ashworth.)

Figure 24 Detail of one of the upper appliqués on the pulpit illustrated in fig. 19. (Photo, Gavin Ashworth.)

have acanthus leaves that differ from Hardcastle's, their overall design is derived from the brackets in Philipse Manor (figs. 20, 25). These interrelationships are consistent with the notion that artisans such as Dwight developed habitual drawing and working styles during their early training.

The latest architectural carving attributed to this shop is in the entrance hall of Stephen Van Rensselaer II's (1742–1769) manor house, built in Albany between 1765 and 1768 (fig. 26). This room was one of the most important public spaces in the house, providing access to the stair hall and first-story rooms. The woodwork includes six doorways with crossetted surrounds, pulvinated friezes, and pitch pediments; four recessed, paneled windows; and an elliptical archway flanked by fluted Ionic pilasters. Shortly after the interior was completed, Stephen ordered hand-painted wallpaper depicting the four seasons. Such papers were popular in England during the third quarter of the eighteenth century. In 1754, Battersea printer Jean Baptist Jackson (ca. 1701–ca. 1780) wrote:

> By this way of printing paper, the Inventor has contrived that the Lights and Shades shall be broad and bold and give great relief to the Figures; the finest prints of all, the Antique Statues, which imitate Drawings, are introduced into Niches of chiaro obscuro in the Pannals of the Paper—these are surrounded with a Mosaic in imitation of Frames, or with Festoons and Garlands. . . . Thus

Figure 25   Detail of a stair bracket in Philipse Manor.

Figure 26   Entrance hall from Van Rensselaer Manor, Albany, New York, 1765–1768. (Courtesy, Metropolitan Museum of Art; photo, Gavin Ashworth.)

the person who cannot purchase the Statues themselves . . . may as effectively show his Taste and Admiration for the ancient Artists in this manner of fitting up and furnishing the Apartments as is the most expensive.

The wallpaper and architectural carving in Van Rensselaer's hall was part of a larger decorative scheme. Stephen originally planned to install an ornamental stucco ceiling; however, his father-in-law, Philip Livingston, advised him otherwise: "I am told You Intend to gett Stucco Work on the Ceiling of Your Hall which I would not advise You to do, a Plain Ceiling is now Esteemed the most Genteel."[18]

Although Van Rensselaer opted for a plain ceiling, he commissioned extremely elaborate architectural carving. The appliqués above the arch are almost literal copies of the spandrel design on plate 10 of Lock and Copland's *A New Book of Ornaments* (figs. 27, 28). In all probability, the carver manufactured the spandrel appliqués and other carved details for Van Rensselaer's house in New York City and then shipped them up the Hudson River. Presumably the carved details were among the last architectural components installed.[19]

In their complexity, the spandrel appliqués are matched only by the cartouche from St. Paul's Chapel. Both designs have three-dimensional scrollwork and multiple layers of acanthus leaves. Their execution required a great deal of spatial sense and sculptural ability, the latter also reflected in the birds and dog on the Beekman chimneypiece. All of the technical details associated with this carver are present on the spandrel appliqués: clusters of rounded lobes with chip cuts; poorly defined scroll volutes; and leaves with flat spines, long curled tips, and gouge cuts on their convex surfaces (fig. 29). In addition, nearly all the flower and fruit elements on the spandrel appliqués appear in the carving in St. Paul's Chapel (see fig. 24) and on the Beekman chimneypiece (fig. 12).

Many houses such as Stephen Van Rensselaer's were built or remodeled in New York during the 1760s. At least three of the five carvers who advertised during this period were British-trained immigrants. The first to arrive was John Brinner, a "Cabinet and Chair-Maker from London." In the May 31, 1762, issue of the *New-York Mercury*, he advertised:

Figure 27 Detail of a spandrel appliqué in the hall illustrated in fig. 26. (Photo, Gavin Ashworth.)

Figure 28 Design for a spandrel illustrated on plate 10 of Matthias Lock and Henry Copland's *A New Book of Ornaments* (1st ed. 1752). (Courtesy, Winterthur Museum.)

At the Sign of the Chair, opposite Flatten Barrack Hill, in the Broad-Way . . . every Article in the Cabinet, Chair-making, Carving, and Gilding Business is executed on the most reasonable Terms, with the utmost neatness and Punctuality. He carves all sorts of Architectural, Gothic, and Chinese, Chimney Pieces, Glass and Picture Frames, Slab Frames, Gerondoles, Chandaliers, and all kinds of Mouldings and Frontispieces, &c. &c. Desk and Book-Cases, Library Book-Cases, Writing and Reading Tables, Commode and Bureau Dressing Tables, Study Tables, China Shelves and Cases, Commode and Plain Chest of Drawers, Gothic and Chinese Chairs; all Sorts of plain or ornamental Chairs, Sofa Beds, Sofa Settees, Couch and easy Chair Frames, all Kinds of Field Bedsteads &c. &c.

Brinner also mentioned that he had "brought over from London six Artificers, well skill'd in the above Branches."[20]

By the fall of 1765, Brinner and his locally trained counterpart, Stephen Dwight, had another competitor—James Strachan, "Carver and Gilder, from London." Like Brinner, Strachan offered "all sorts of Picture and Glass Frames, Tables, Gerendoles, Brackets; and Candle Stands; in Oil or burnish'd Gold . . . [and] House-Carvings in Wood or Stone." Regrettably, lit-

Figure 29 Detail of the acanthus leaves on the spandrel appliqué illustrated in fig. 27. (Photo, Gavin Ashworth.)

Figure 30 Picture frame by James Strachan, New York, 1767. White pine, gilded. 43½" × 35½". (Collection of the New-York Historical Society; photo, Metropolitan Museum of Art.) The frame is on John Durand's portrait of James Beekman, Jr.

Figure 31 Chimneypiece in the first-floor parlor of Van Cortlandt House, Bronx, New York, 1760–1765. (Courtesy, National Society of Colonial Dames in the State of New York; photo, Gavin Ashworth.)

tle is known about his career. In December 1767, he received £22.4 for six carved and gilded frames for John Durand's portraits of James Beekman's children (see fig. 30). One of the most distinctive aspects of the frames is their heavy gadrooning. Gadrooned moldings are common on New York furniture from the third quarter of the eighteenth century, and it is likely that Beekman requested that the frames match other furnishings in his house. Strachan was in partnership with cabinetmaker David Davidson by October 1768 and died the following February. In the February 9, 1769, issue of the *New-York Journal or the General Advertiser*, his widow Catherine reported, "business will be carried on as usual," which suggests the involvement of Davidson or a journeyman who worked for her husband.[21]

The third carver reportedly from London was John Minshall (Minshull), who established a shop "in the Broadway, near the Old English Church" by December 7, 1769. In addition to carving a range of furniture forms and "Bed and Window Cornicing," he made "Paper Ornaments for Ceilings and Stair Cases," sold imported looking glasses, girandoles, and prints, and

Figure 32 Detail of the frieze appliqué on the chimneypiece illustrated in fig. 31. (Photo, Gavin Ashworth.)

Figure 33 Detail of the frieze appliqué on the chimneypiece illustrated in fig. 31. (Photo, Gavin Ashworth.)

Figure 34 Detail of a truss on the chimneypiece illustrated in fig. 31. (Photo, Gavin Ashworth.)

taught drawing. In 1770, Minshall urged his debtors to settle their accounts before he returned to England, but he either canceled his trip or returned to New York by October 1772 when he married Mary Stanton. Minshall subsequently moved to Hanover Square, where he advertised for an apprentice in 1775. In March of that year he offered "the greatest variety of girandoles ever imported into this city," brackets, ornaments for chimney-pieces, birds and baskets of flowers "for the top of book cases or glass frames, [and] gilt bordering by the yard," and assured his customers "that when the difference is settled between England and the colonies" his store would be "constantly supplied with the above articles." Minshall may have been a Loyalist, for a "John Michalsal" was included in a list of Loyalists in that year and a "John Minchull" subsequently fled to Shelburne, Nova Scotia, became a merchant, and built one of the largest houses in that town. "John Minchull" died in London in 1822.[22]

The architectural carving in Van Cortlandt House in the Bronx almost certainly represents the work of a London-trained carver who immigrated to New York during the early to mid-1760s (fig. 31). The house was built by Frederick Van Cortlandt in 1748 on land that his father, Jacobus, purchased from Frederick Philipse I in 1699. Not only did the Van Cortlandt and Philipse families intermarry, but Van Cortlandt family tradition maintains that Philipse Manor inspired the basic design of their house. Frederick Van Cortlandt died on February 12, 1749, leaving the house to his son Jacobus, commonly referred to as James Van Cortlandt. James probably commissioned the chimneypiece illustrated in figure 31 between 1760 and 1765.[23]

The carving on the chimneypiece is by two different artisans, one responsible for the frieze appliqué (figs. 32, 33) and urn-and-flower ornament and the other for the trusses flanking the appliqué (fig. 34). Presumably, these tradesmen were part of a large shop like John Brinner's, which employed London-trained artisans and provided "all sorts of . . . Chimney Pieces" and furniture carving. As a marketing ploy, some colonial tradesmen falsely advertised or implied London training; however, the quality of the Van Cortlandt chimneypiece suggests that its carvers may have apprenticed or worked as journeymen there.

Figure 35   Tea table, New York, 1760–1765. Mahogany. H. 29", Diam. 29". (Chipstone Foundation; photo, Gavin Ashworth.)

Given the connections between the Van Cortlandt and Philipse families and the close proximity of their houses, it is possible that the rococo bird on the Van Cortlandt chimneypiece (fig. 32) was inspired by the heron on the chimneypiece in the second-floor parlor of Philipse Manor (fig. 3). Both birds are posed in a similar manner and are framed by scrolls, leaves, and floral garlands. The execution of the work, however, is entirely different. The bird on the Van Cortlandt appliqué has overlapping feathers and over-scaled feet that rest on branches of acanthus bound by bands of ribbon. The leaves are skillfully modeled with smooth convex surfaces and long precise flutes that propel the design (fig. 33). Few examples of New York rococo carving are as workmanlike as that of the frieze appliqué. The gouge cuts used to delineate, model, and shade the leaves indicate that the carver worked efficiently and very quickly. The carver of the consoles was just as skilled, although his work differs in having tiny overlapping leaves (adjacent to the large ones curling in toward the spine) and multiple shading cuts made with a very small gouge (in relation to the size of the design).

The same two carvers were responsible for two pillar-and-claw tea tables with hairy paw feet. One (fig. 35) is by the tradesman who carved the trusses,

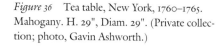

Figure 36   Tea table, New York, 1760–1765. Mahogany. H. 29", Diam. 29". (Private collection; photo, Gavin Ashworth.)

Figure 37   Detail of the edge bead and carving on the top of the tea table illustrated in fig. 36. (Photo, Gavin Ashworth.)

and the other (fig. 36) is by the artisan who carved the frieze appliqué and urn-and-flower ornament. The tables have identically shaped tops with half-round beads and simple rocaille carving (fig. 37). Although the rocaille carving varies slightly, both tops have six symmetrical, double-ogee segments separated by flats (fig. 38). This unusual shaping occurs on only one other New York table, and it appears to be from the same shop (see fig. 46). Each top has four plugged holes from having been attached to the face plate of a lathe. Face-plate turning was a fast, efficient way to relieve the ground inside the perimeter of the carved design. The legs of the tables were cut from the same template, and the birdcage balusters and pillars appear to be by the same turner. These details and the joinery of the tables indicate that they are from the same cabinet shop.

Although the design of the carving on the tables is very similar, the work is clearly by different hands. The acanthus leaves on the baluster of the table in figure 35 are more complex, with small overlapping lobes and fine shading cuts made with a very small, U-shaped gouge (fig. 39). The corresponding details on the other table are simpler, but the leaves have broader flutes (made with a larger and slightly flatter gouge) that "read" better from a distance (fig. 40). As a result of the carving, both balusters are squarish in

Figure 38 Detail of the top of the tea table illustrated in fig. 35. (Photo, Gavin Ashworth.)

Figure 39 Detail of the baluster of the tea table illustrated in fig. 35. (Photo, Gavin Ashworth.)

Figure 40 Detail of the baluster of the tea table illustrated in fig. 36. (Photo, Gavin Ashworth.)

Figure 41 Detail of the knee carving on the tea table illustrated in fig. 35. (Photo, Gavin Ashworth.)

section, and each has four design repeats separated by vertical ridges. On the table illustrated in figure 36, the ridges are aligned with the center of the legs, but on the other table these details are not aligned (fig. 35). Evidently, the carver of the latter table failed to orient his pattern with the mortises for the legs and/or the spaces between them.

The knee carving on these tables is in very high relief and features confronting C-scrolls with ruffled edges, ascending and descending acanthus sprigs, and naturalistic leaves and flowers. Again, the designs are similar, but the execution is entirely different. The leaf and flower elements illustrated in figure 41 have finer shading cuts, like the acanthus on the baluster above (fig. 39), whereas those shown in figure 42 more closely resemble the leaves and flowers on the Van Cortlandt frieze appliqué and overmantle ornament (figs. 32, 33). Of all the carved details on these tables, their feet are the most alike (figs. 43, 44). Both carvers used chip cuts and flutes to simulate swirls of hair and deep vertical gouge cuts to set in the design of the upper tufts. The sides of the feet, however, are very different. Those illustrated in figure 44 have rudimentary pad segments, whereas the feet of the other table have small tufts of hair (fig. 43), evidently intended to represent fetlocks (see also figs. 35, 36).

A paw-foot tea table with a history of ownership by Sylvanis Miller of East Hampton, Long Island (fig. 45), and a monumental claw-and-ball foot

Figure 44 Detail of a paw foot on the tea table illustrated in fig. 36. (Photo, Gavin Ashworth.)

Figure 43 Detail of a paw foot on the tea table illustrated in fig. 35. (Photo, Gavin Ashworth.)

Figure 45 Tea table, New York, 1760–1765. Mahogany. H. 29", Diam. 30". (Courtesy, Israel Sack, Inc., New York.)

table that reportedly descended in the Van Vechten family of New Jersey (fig. 46) may be from the same cabinet shop that produced the aforementioned examples, but they represent the work of two other carvers. The design of the carving on the Miller table is similar to that of the other paw-foot examples, though the work is coarse by comparison. The acanthus leaves on the baluster have numerous flips and curls that interrupt the flow of the design. With its round top and cylindrical, birdcage turnings, the Miller table was considerably less expensive than the scalloped-top versions. The carving on the Van Vechten table (fig. 47) is very different than that of the other tables; however, it has a top with symmetrical ogees separated by flats, a raised astragal bead, and simple rocaille leafage (fig. 48) like those

Figure 46 Tea table, New York, 1760–1770. Mahogany. H. 29", Diam. 45³/₈". (Courtesy, National Society of Colonial Dames in the State of New York, Van Cortlandt House; photo, Gavin Ashworth.)

shown in figures 37 and 38. The Van Vechten table and a dressing table illustrated in the January 1953 issue of *Antiques* are the only known examples of New York furniture with sheathed claw-and-ball feet. Sheathed feet occur on northern European furniture during the mid-eighteenth century, and their presence on these tables may reflect the influence of Dutch or German furniture in colonial New York.[24]

A side chair (from a set of at least twelve) that belonged to Cornelius Willett (ca. 1708–1781) of Westchester County (fig. 49) is by the same artisan that carved the Van Vechten table. Both objects have broad, flat acanthus leaves, fine shading cuts, and asymmetrical shells with rosettes separating their volutes. Although this chair likely dates from the early to mid-1760s, its double-crook stiles, splat shape, and commode seat reflect the influence of Boston chairs imported into New York from about 1735 to 1760. The rear pad feet, however, are a common Anglo–New York detail. Several simpler versions of this basic chair design survive.[25]

The shell and acanthus carving on the Van Vechten table and the Willett chairs resembles London work from the 1730s and early 1740s rather than

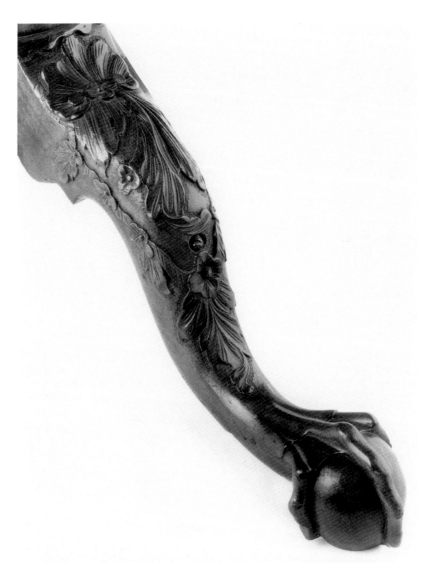

Figure 47 Detail of the knee carving on the tea table illustrated in fig. 46. (Photo, Gavin Ashworth.)

Figure 48 Detail of the edge bead and carving on the top of the tea table illustrated in fig. 46. (Photo, Gavin Ashworth.)

the more current styles expressed by the paw-foot tables and the Van Cortlandt chimneypiece. This outdated style suggests that the carver of the table and chairs trained in a town or city some distance from London. During the 1760s and 1770s, artisans immigrated to New York from Dublin, Edinburgh, Glasgow, Somerset, Bristol, Liverpool and other regional centers in the British archipelago.

One of the largest groups of New York furniture with rococo ornament appears to be the work of another carving shop with at least one artisan who probably trained outside of London. Included in this group are two china tables (one from the Halstead family of Yonkers, and the other illustrated in Luke Vincent Lockwood's *Colonial Furniture in America*); an elaborate turret-corner card table illustrated in the January 1961 issue of *Antiques*; a suite of furniture, including at least twelve side chairs, a settee, and a concertina-action card table, that descended in the Verplanck family; a set of chairs that belonged to Robert and Margaret (Beekman) Livingston; a dining table; and the side chair illustrated in figure 50. The latter chair may be the earliest example in the group. Its compass seat, double-crook stiles, and splat

Figure 49 Side chair, New York, 1760–1770. Mahogany with cherry and mahogany; oak and cherry slip seat. H. 38⅞", W. 21", D. 18½". (Courtesy, Metropolitan Museum of Art, Harris Brisbane Dick Fund, 1940.)

Figure 50 Side chair, New York, 1745–1765. Mahogany; ash slip seat. H. 38¾", W. 21½", D. 17½". (Courtesy, Bernard and S. Dean Levy, Inc., New York; photo, Helga Studio.)

pattern are based on Boston chairs, and its shell and husk knee carving has precedents in both Boston and New York furniture from the second quarter of the eighteenth century.[26]

The crest of the Boston-inspired chair has stylized acanthus carving like that on the knees of the two china tables (figs. 50–52). The leaves have exaggerated, hook-shaped curls, distinctive veining, and amorphous folds (figs. 50, 53, 54). Both china tables have serpentine rails with central tablets and conforming tops that were probably fitted with galleries. The Halstead family table has mahogany rails that are laminated for thickness (at the outer faces of the serpentine), mitered at the corners, and attached to a ¾"-thick

Figure 51 China table, New York, 1750–1765. Mahogany with gum. H. 27", W. 34³/₈", D. 21¹/₂". (Courtesy, Winterthur Museum.)

gum frame (fig. 51), whereas the other china table has solid mahogany rails that are tenoned to the leg stiles (fig. 52). On all of the tables in this group the gadrooning is cut from boards that are mitered at the corners and attached to the lower edges of the rails.[27]

The card table from the Verplanck suite has the most sophisticated joinery of any piece from the group (fig. 55). Although many eighteenth-century, British concertina-action tables survive, American ones are extremely rare. The Verplanck example has a concealed drawer (the rail between the turrets pulls out after a wooden spring lock is disengaged), hinged side rails, and sliding wooden bars that keep the rails rigid when extended. Wide mitered battens prevent the top from warping, and the playing surface is relieved to accommodate a broadcloth liner. The Verplanck table and the one illustrated in *Antiques* also have vertically laminated turrets veneered to match the grain of their front drawer (Verplanck) or rail.[28]

The side chairs (fig. 56) and settee (at the Metropolitan Museum of Art) from the Verplanck suite have shield-carved knees and feet that are virtually identical to those of the concertina-action table. The side chairs have inter-

laced strapwork splats reminiscent of several designs in the Society of Upholsterers', *Houshold Furniture in Genteel Taste* and Robert Manwaring's *The Cabinet and Chair-Maker's Real Friend and Companion* (1765); however, the New York pattern was more likely inspired by imported British seating

Figure 54 Detail of the knee carving on the china table illustrated in fig. 52.

Figure 55 Card table, New York, 1750–1765. H. 28 7/8", W. 37 1/2", D. 19" (closed). Mahogany and mahogany veneer with birch, tulip, white pine, and white cedar. (Courtesy, Metropolitan Museum of Art, gift of James De Lancey Verplanck and John Bayard Rodgers Verplanck, 1939.)

or introduced by British-trained chairmakers. The suite may have belonged New York merchant and banker Gulian Verplanck (1698–1751) and his wife, Mary (Crommelin) or, more likely, their son Samuel (1739–1820). While studying banking in Holland, Samuel married his cousin Judith Crommelin. In 1763, the couple returned to New York and moved into a house on Wall Street. Guilian's will gave Samuel the option of taking his father's "Lott of ground with the houses and buildings thereon in Wall Street near the City Hall" in exchange for £1,500 from his share of the estate.[29]

The Livingston family chairs are the most ambitious seating forms with carving attributed to this shop (fig. 57). Like all the objects in this group, these chairs have dramatic serpentine legs with slender ankles and claw-and-ball feet with small rear talons and almost no webbing. Their strapwork cyphers probably refer to Robert Livingston and Margaret Beekman, who married in 1742, rather than to their son, Robert, and daughter-in-law Mary (Stevens) who married in 1770. Most English cypher-back chairs date from the 1750s, but the Livingston examples could be as late as 1760.[30]

Figure 56 Side chair, New York, 1750–1765. H. 38¹/₂", W. 23", D. 18¹/₄". Mahogany with white pine; white oak slip seat. (Courtesy, Metropolitan Museum of Art, gift of James De Lancey Verplanck and John Bayard Rodgers Verplanck, 1939.)

Figure 57 Side chair, New York, 1750–1760. H. 41³/₈", W. 22¹/₂", D. 22". Mahogany. (Courtesy, Museum of Fine Arts, Houston; Bayou Bend Collection, gift of Miss Ima Hogg.)

Trained as an attorney, the elder Livingston's fortune increased substantially when he married Margaret Beekman, the only surviving child of Henry Beekman. The couple subsequently inherited Beekman's fortune, including his estates, Clermont and Rhinebeck. In 1765, Livingston's political opponent, Lieutenant-governor Cadwalader Cohen, wrote, "[Livingston] is heir to one of the greatest Landed estates in several parts of the Province, and involved in disputes with the poor industrious farmers, who have settled and improved the adjoining lands."[31]

The Livingstons, Beekmans, Verplancks, Van Rensselaers, and Van Cortlandts were members of a powerful aristocracy rooted in the Anglo-Dutch manorial system established during the seventeenth century. Most were landed gentlemen, merchants, professionals, and political leaders with intercolonial and transatlantic family and commercial connections. By the middle of the eighteenth century, this elite looked to England for the latest styles and customs, thus providing a ready market for immigrant tradesmen attracted by New York's rapidly expanding economy. The furniture and architectural carving presented here reflects the training of these artisans, the tastes and aspirations of their patrons, and the unique cultural and economic climate in which they flourished.

ACKNOWLEDGMENTS For assistance with this article, the author thanks Gavin Ashworth, Michael K. Brown, Laura Carpenter-Correa, Mr. and Mrs. Dudley Godfrey, Jr., Morrison Heckscher, Bernard Levy, Dean Levy, Frank Levy, Robert Lionetti, Mike Podmaniczky, Albert Sack, Peggy Scholley, Margaret Tamulonis, Joseph Tanenbaum, and the Parish of Trinity Church. I am especially grateful for the outstanding research provided by Joan Barzilay Freund and Cynthia Siebels.

1. Philip Cuyler to Dirk Vander Heyden, July 17, 1756, Cuyler Letterbook, as quoted in Virginia Harrington, *The New York Merchant on the Eve of the Revolution* (1935; reprint ed., Gloucester, Mass.: Peter Smith, 1964), p. 291. New York merchants benefited from new trade routes developed during and after King George's War. Cuyler, for example, imported tea (illegally) from Holland and sold it for a handsome profit in New York and New England (Carl Bridenbaugh, *Cities in Revolt: Urban Life in America, 1743–1776* [1955; reprint ed., New York: Oxford University Press, 1971], pp. 52–53). Philip L. White, *The Beekmans of New York* (New York: New-York Historical Society, 1956), p. 539. See also, *Beekman Mercantile Papers*, 3 vols., edited by Philip L. White (New York: New-York Historical Society, 1956). William Smith, Jr., *The History of the Late Province of New York*, edited by Michael Kammen (1757; reprint ed., Cambridge, Mass.: Belknap Press of Harvard University Press, 1972), p. 284. Letterbook of John Watts as quoted in Harrington, *The New York Merchant*, p. 233.

2. For more on New York's growth and the economic effects of war, see Bridenbaugh, *Cities in Revolt*, pp. 5, 16, passim. New York's economy suffered after the British forces departed for the Caribbean in 1761. In a letter to Moses Franks, John Watts complained, "The Reservoir of all Streams of Business and the Spring to which feeds many of them is dried up" (Letterbook of John Watts as quoted in Harrington, *The New York Merchant*, p. 280).

3. For more on Hardcastle, see Luke Beckerdite, "Origins of the Rococo Style in New York Furniture and Interior Architecture," in *American Furniture*, edited by Luke Beckerdite (Hanover, N. H.: University Press of New England for the Chipstone Foundation, 1993), pp. 15–39.

4. Ibid., p. 15. *New-York Gazette or the Weekly Post-Boy*, June 3, 1762, as quoted in *The Arts and Crafts in New York, 1726–1776: Advertisements and News Items from New York City Newspapers, Collections of the New-York Historical Society*, compiled by Rita S. Gottesman (1938; reprint ed., New York: Da Capo Press, 1970), p. 123. For advertisements by Bernard and Minshall, see ibid., pp. 126–28.

5. Beckerdite, "Origins of the Rococo Style," pp. 22–24, 27, 30, figs. 18, 33, 35.

6. *New-York Mercury*, June 30 and July 21, 1755, as quoted in Gottesman, comp., *Arts and Crafts*, p. 127: On July 21, 1755, the *New-York Mercury* reported, "STEPHEN DWIGHT, late an apprentice to Henry Hardcastle has set up his business . . . where he carves all sorts of ship and house work; also tables, chairs, picture and looking glass frames and all kinds of work for cabinetmakers, in the best manner and all at reasonable terms." The fact that Dwight established his business one month after Hardcastle's advertisement suggests that his indenture had expired or that Hardcastle had left for Charleston. Hardcastle was buried in Charleston on October 20, 1756 (D. E. Huger Smith and A. S. Salley, Jr., *Register of St. Phillip's Parish, Charles Town, or Charleston, S.C., 1754–1810* [Columbia: University of South Carolina Press, 1971], p. 282). His inventory listed two silver watches, a pair of silver buckles, a gold ring, a crosscut saw, a musket, clothing, a lot of books, and "1 Gross & half of Carving Tools" (Transcript of Charleston County, S.C. Wills, et cetera, 1756–1758, 84: 54, microfilm at Museum of Early Southern Decorative Arts, Winston-Salem, N.C.).

7. *New York Gazette,* April 12, 1762, as quoted in Gottesman, comp., *Arts and Crafts,* p. 126. See also the *New-York Mercury,* May 2, 1763 (ibid., p. 3). Davis's name appears in a 1775 list of inhabitants of New York City and a 1775 militia roll. In that year he resided at 621 William Street (see Dorothy C. Barck, "A List of Five Hundred Inhabitants of New York City in 1775 with their Occupations and Addresses," in *New-York Historical Society Quarterly Bulletin* 3 [1939]: 31; and list of New York Militia taken April 25, 1775, and reprinted in *New-York Historical Society Collections* 2 [1915]: 503). Isaac Alling vs. Mary Dwight & Ors., August 10, 1805, Chancery Court, file B. M. 307A.

8. For more on Dwight's frames, see Morrison H. Heckscher, "The Beekman Family Portraits and Their Eighteenth-Century New York Frames," *Furniture History* 26 (1990):114–20; and Morrison H. Heckscher and Leslie Greene Bowman, *American Rococo: Elegance in Ornament* (New York: Harry N. Abrams for the Metropolitan Museum of Art and Los Angeles County Museum of Art, 1992), pp. 156–57.

9. For more on New York carvers, see Gottesman, comp., *Arts and Crafts,* pp. 3, 16, 110, 124, 126–29, 132–33; and Heckscher and Bowman, *American Rococo,* pp. 153–56. Morrison H. Heckscher, "English Furniture Pattern Books in Eighteenth-Century America," in *American Furniture,* edited by Luke Beckerdite (Hanover, N.H.: University Press of New England for the Chipstone Foundation, 1994), pp. 185, 189 (6.1), 192–93, 195–97 (16.2–16.4).

10. Warren R. Dix and Lebbeus B. Miller, "Itinerary of Historical Excursions," in *Historic Elizabeth, 1664–1914: A Two Hundred and Fiftieth Anniversary of the City,* compiled by Frank Kelly (Elizabeth, N.J.: Historic Elizabeth Committee, 1914), p. 19. Theodore Thayer, *As We Were: The Story of Old Elizabethtown* (Elizabeth, N.J.: Grassman Publishing Co., 1964), pp. 113, 252. Dr. Barnet was a highly regarded surgeon during the Revolutionary War. On February 10, 1780, the *New Jersey Gazette* published Dr. Barnet's account of the British forces plundering his house: "They emptied my feather beds in the streets, broke in windows, smashed my mirrors, and left our pantry and storeroom bare. I could forgive them all but that the rascals stole from my kitchen wall the finest string of red peppers in all Elizabethtown" (as quoted in Reverend Edwin F. Hatfield, *History of Elizabeth New Jersey Including the Early History of Union County* [New York: Carlton & Lanahan, 1868], p. 484).

11. The trusses removed from the chimneypiece in the first-floor, southeast parlor of Philipse Manor may have resembled those from Hampton Court. The former are shown in an engraving in *Frank Leslie's Illustrated Newspaper* (1882) (Beckerdite, "Origins of the Rococo Style," p. 17).

12. The desk-and-bookcase with carving attributed to Hardcastle is illustrated in ibid., pp. 21–23, figs. 13–17. The author originally attributed the desk-and-bookcase illustrated in fig. 9 to Hardcastle; however, subsequent research suggests that it was carved by an apprentice, either working in Hardcastle's shop before 1755 or working independently shortly thereafter. Advertisement by John Walton, *Antiques* 85, no. 4 (April 1964): 356.

13. For the purchase of the farm, see Beekman Manuscripts, box 43, folder titled "Revolutionary Generation," as quoted in Edward A. Griggs, "Beekman Hill" (master's thesis, New York University, 1959), p. 3. Beekman's expenditures for utensils, labor, and food are discussed in White, *The Beekmans of New York* , p. 404. James Beekman Account Book Personal Affairs, 1759–1786, New-York Historical Society.

14. Advertisement by French & Co., Inc., *Antiques* 52, no. 2 (February 1950): 105. The author has not examined this desk-and-bookcase.

15. The building of St. Paul's is discussed in Parish of Trinity Church, "St. Paul's Chapel of the Parish of Trinity Church Broadway and Fulton Street," brochure, n.p.; Morgan Dir, *Historical Records of St. Paul's Chapel, New York* (New York: F. J. Huntington & Co., 1867), pp. 26–29; and Morgan Dir, *A History of the Parish of Trinity Church in the City of New York* (New York: P. G. Putnam's Sons, 1896), pp. 302–5. For more on McBean, see Gulian Verplank's letter to the editor, "Notes and Queries," *The Crayon* (New York), June 1857. Verplank and subsequent writers have speculated that McBean trained with British architect James Gibbs. John F. Millar of Williamsburg, Virginia, attributed St. Paul's Chapel to Peter Harrison (John F. Millar, "Peter Harrison, 1716–1775," brochure, n.p., copy in the archives of Trinity Parish, New York.) Trinity Parish Account Book, 1756–1769, RG2: SG1,2,3: Box 3 [2]; transcribed information provided by the Parish of Trinity Church.

16. For Gautier, see ibid.; Dir, *History of the Parish of Trinity Church,* pp. 302–5; and Gottesman, comp., *Arts and Crafts,* pp. 97, 112–13, 118, 281, 395. As quoted in Dir, *Records of St. Paul's Chapel,* p. 27.

17. According to Dir's *History of the Parish of Trinity Church,* pp. 315–16, the "sacristies were

at the eastern end, near the chancel. . . . The interior has been changed; the sacristies are now at the west end; the beautiful chandeliers have vanished; the canopied pews have disappeared; but the chancel and altar, the memorial tablets with their emblazoned arms, and the old pulpit with the Prince of Wales's feathers atop, still greet the eye." See Heckscher and Bowman, *American Rococo*, p. 25, for a ca. 1900 photograph of the interior showing the pulpit at the west end, but with the stair on the right side.

18. For more on the Van Rensselaer house and family, see Katherine Schuyler Baxter, *A Godchild of Washington: A Picture of the Past* (New York: F. Tennyson Neely, 1897), pp. 414–19; and *Some Colonial Mansions and Those Who Lived in Them,* 2 vols., edited by Thomas Allen Glenn (Philadelphia: Henry T. Coates & Co., 1898), pp. 156–68. These early publications allude to other architectural carving that may have been part of the original fabric of the house as well as to subsequent alterations made by architect Richard Upjohn. For Upjohn's alterations, see Edgar Mayhew and Minor Myers, *A Documentary History of American Interiors from the Colonial Era to 1915* (New York: Charles Scribner's Sons, 1980), p. 55. For more on the entrance hall, see Heckscher and Bowman, *American Rococo*, pp. 23–25. Jackson also wrote, "Saloons in Imitation of Stucco may be done in this manner, and Staircases in every Taste as may be agreeable. These papers being done in oil, the Colour will never fly off—no water or damp can have the least effect on it" (John Baptist Jackson, "An Essay on the Invention of Engraving and Printing in Chiaro obscuro, as practised by Albert Durer, Hugo di Carpi, etc. and the Application of it to the making of Paper Hangings of Taste Duration and Elegance," as quoted in Nancy McClelland, *Historic Wall-Papers* [Philadelphia: J. B. Lippincott, Co., 1924], pp. 144–49).

19. Heckscher and Bowman, *American Rococo*, p. 24.

20. Stephen Dwight apprenticed in New York, and nothing is known of Richard Davis's training. As quoted in Gottesman, comp., *Arts and Crafts*, p. 110. On January 3, 1763, Brinner advertised "all kinds of bedsteads, with carved or plain cornishes . . . N. B. A neat mahogany desk and bookcase in the Chinese taste to be sold" (as quoted in ibid., p. 124).

21. The *New-York Gazette or the Weekly Post-Boy*, October 24, 1765, as quoted in Gottesman, comp., *Arts and Crafts*, pp. 128–29. Strachan is one of the few American carvers who advertised stonework (ibid., pp. 128, 132). For more on the Strachan frames, see Heckscher, "The Beekman Family Portraits," pp. 116–17, 120; and Heckscher and Bowman, *American Rococo*, pp. 156–58. Strachan evidently tripped on a rope while walking along the dock near Burling's slip, fell into the river, and drowned (*Extract of Genealogical Data from the New-York Weekly Post Boy, 1743–1773*, compiled by Kenneth Scott [Washington, D.C.: National Genealogical Society, 1970], p. 125; *Genealogical Data from Colonial New York Newspapers*, compiled by Kenneth Scott [Baltimore, Md.: Genealogical Publishing Co., 1977], p. 134). Catherine married painter James Barrow on August 7, 1769 (*New York Marriage Bonds, 1753–1783,* compiled by Kenneth Scott [Middletown, N.Y.: Trumbell Publishing for the Saint Nicholas Society of the City of New York, 1972], n.p.), and died by the following February (Scott, comp., *Data from Colonial New York Newspapers*, p. 145). A February 9, 1770, notice in the *New York Gazette and Weekly Mercury* requested her debtors to make payment to Jonathan Blake, Thomas Barrow, or James Barrow (Gottesman, comp., *Arts and Crafts*, p. 129). On April 16, 1770, the *New York Gazette and Weekly Mercury* reported that the partnership between "Strachan, Widow dec'd," and John Fulkner was dissolved (Scott, comp., *Data from Colonial New York Newspapers*, p. 145).

22. Gottesman, comp., *Arts and Crafts*, pp. 16, 128, 132–33. Scott, comp., *New York Marriage Bonds*, n.p. "John Michalsal" appears in William Kelby, *Orderly Book of the Three Battalions of Loyalists Commanded by Brigadier-General Oliver De Lancey, 1776–1778* (New York: New-York Historical Society, 1917), p. 125. For "John Minchull," see Lorenzo Sabine, *Biographical Sketches of Loyalists of the American Revolution*, 2 vols. (Baltimore, Md.: Genealogical Publishing Co., 1979), 2:84. William Kelby listed a John Minshull, "Capt.," in his handwritten notebook titled "The New York Loyalists or Adherents to the British Crown in that City During the War of the Revolution," New-York Historical Society, ca. 1901, n.p.

23. For more on the Van Cortlandt family and house, see Catherine Van Cortlandt Matthews, *Historical Sketch of the Van Cortlandt House Prepared for the Society of the Colonial Dames of the State of New York* (New York: Colonial Dames, 1903), p. ix; and Baxter, *A Godchild of Washington*, pp. 297–98.

24. For more on the Miller table, see Dean F. Failey, *Long Island is My Nation: The Decorative Arts and Craftsmen, 1640–1830* (Seatucket, N.Y.: Society for the Preservation of Long Island Antiquities, 1976), p. 95, no. 113. Related feet are on a New York chest-on-chest with a history of ownership by New York and New Jersey merchant John Stevens (*Treasures of State: Fine and*

Decorative Arts in the Diplomatic Reception Rooms of the U.S. Department of State, edited by Alexandra W. Rollins [New York: Harry N. Abrams, 1991], pp. 96–98). A post card for the New York antique firm John S. Walton, Inc. illustrates another New York tea table with hairy paw feet (Winterthur Museum Decorative Arts Photographic Collection, 71.396). This table is branded "P" on the birdcage, reportedly for the Pruyn family of New York. Its knee carving features ascending and descending acanthus leaves separated by a small C-scroll. This common New York carving design also appears on a firescreen illustrated in Oswaldo Rodriguez Roque, *American Furniture at Chipstone* (Madison: University of Wisconsin Press, 1984), pp. 414–15, no. 194; and a tea table branded "PVR," presumably for Philip Van Rennsselaer (Morrison H. Heckscher, *American Furniture in The Metropolitan Museum of Art II, Late Colonial Period: The Queen Anne and Chippendale Styles* [New York: Random House, 1985], pp. 65–66, no. 23). Two exceptional pieces of New York furniture with related carving are the slab table advertised by C. W. Lyon in *Antiques* 45, no. 4 (April 1944): 161 (now at Stratford Hall in Virginia), and a card table in the collection of Bernard and S. Dean Levy; both objects have large carved reserves on the front rail. For the dressing table with sheathed claw-and-ball feet, see advertisement by Ginsburg and Levy, *Antiques* 63, no. 1(January 1953): 13; and Museum of Early Southern Decorative Arts Research File, S-4164. The author thanks John Bivins for the information on Dutch prototypes for sheathed feet.

25. Heckscher, *American Furniture in The Metropolitan Museum*, pp. 65–66, no. 23. For more on Boston's influence, see Leigh Keno, Joan Barzilay Freund, and Alan Miller, "In the Pink of the Mode: Boston Georgian Chairs, Their Export and Their Influence," in this volume. The acanthus and flower carving on the Van Vechten table and Willett chairs may have inspired that found on several New York card tables (see Morrison H. Heckscher, "The New York Serpentine Card Table," *Antiques* 103, no. 5 [May 1973]: 974–83) and chairs (see David B. Warren, *American Furniture, Paintings, and Silver from the Bayou Bend Collection* [New York: New York Graphics Society for the Museum of Fine Arts, Houston, 1975], p. 49, no. 86).

26. For more on the Halstead table, see Joseph Downs, *American Furniture: Queen Anne and Chippendale Periods* (New York: MacMillan Company, 1952), no. 374. Luke Vincent Lockwood, *Colonial Furniture in America* (New York: Charles Scribner's Sons, 1901), pp. 234–35, fig. 206. The turret-corner table advertised by Ginsburg and Levy, *Antiques* 79, no. 1 (January 1961): 39, has gadrooning and knee carving similar to that on the china tables, particularly the one from the Halstead family. For more on the Verplanck suite, see Heckscher, *American Furniture in The Metropolitan Museum*, pp. 66–67, 139–40, 174–75, nos. 24, 82, 105. The Livingston chairs are discussed in Bernard Levy and S. Dean Levy, *"Opulence and Splendor:" The New York Chair, 1690–1830* (New York: Bernard & S. Dean Levy, Inc., 1984), p. 7. The author thanks Frank Levy for the information on the dining table (Bernard and S. Dean Levy, photo no. 128). Related shell and husk designs appear on the knees of a ca. 1740 New York card table (Failey, *Long Island is My Nation*, p. 120, no. 139) and the prospect door of a ca. 1750 desk-and-bookcase with carving attributed to Henry Hardcastle (Beckerdite, "Origins of the Rococo Style," p. 21, fig. 13).

27. The author thanks Michael Podmaniczky for the information on the construction and materials of the Halstead table.

28. For more on the construction of the Verplanck table, see Heckscher, *American Furniture in The Metropolitan Museum*, pp. 174–75, no. 105.

29. The first edition titled *Houshold Furniture in Genteel Taste for the Year 1760* (London: Robert Sayer, 1760) included 180 designs on 60 plates; the second and third editions had 100 plates with about 300 designs; and the fourth edition had 120 plates with about 350 designs (Heckscher, "English Pattern Books," p. 195). For more on the Verplanck family, see Heckscher, *American Furniture in The Metropolitan Museum*, pp. 66–67; William Verplank, *The History of Abraham Isaacse Verplanck and His Male Descendants in America* (Fishkill, N.Y.: John W. Spaight, 1892), pp. 102–4; and John Caldwell and Oswaldo Rodriguez Roque, *American Paintings in The Metropolitan Museum of Art I: A Catalogue of Works by Artists Born by 1815* (New York: Metropolitan Museum of Art, 1994), pp. 94–96.

30. Warren, *American Furniture, Paintings, and Silver from the Bayou Bend Collection*, p. 25, no. 42. The author thanks Michael K. Brown for information on the Livingston chair at Bayou Bend and related English examples.

31. E. B. Livingston, *The Livingstons of Livingston Manor* (New York: Knickerbocker Press, 1910), pp. 148–51.

Figure 1 Side chair with carving attributed to John Welch, Boston, ca. 1735. Walnut and walnut veneer with maple and white pine; maple slip seat. H. 38⅝", W. 20¾", D. 18½". (Courtesy, Metropolitan Museum of Art, gift of Mr. and Mrs. Benjamin Ginsburg, 1984; photo, Gavin Ashworth.)

*Leigh Keno, Joan
Barzilay Freund, and
Alan Miller*

The Very Pink of the
Mode: Boston
Georgian Chairs,
Their Export, and
Their Influence

▼ D U R I N G   T H E first half of the eighteenth century, Boston func-
tioned as "the Metropolis of New England."[1] Within the vast market economy that linked Boston merchants to London and to the manufactures of
England, intercoastal trade offered an ideal venue for those eager to capitalize upon innovation and material growth on the domestic front. Mercantile entrepreneurship charged both the city's economy and its social structure as many sought to capitalize on the town's allure in other colonial
centers. Boston was the principal port of entry for British goods in the
colonies, and fashions from the homeland found a receptive audience in its
Anglocentric merchant class. In attempting to satisfy their own social and
cultural aspirations, Boston's elite set new standards for Anglo-aestheticism
and material culture at other colonial ports.

The relationship between fashion and commerce is most apparent in
Boston seating furniture from the second quarter of the eighteenth century.
For decades, scholars have incorrectly attributed Boston Georgian chairs to
New York or Newport, two cities with strong social and commercial ties to
Boston and two of the most important destinations for Boston venture
cargo. Confusion arose from the flawed assumption that an object's prove-
nance established its place of manufacture and that family and recovery his-
tories were a viable touchstone for defining regional characteristics.
Although provenance is an important consideration for furniture historians, it is often an indicator of retail history rather than origin.[2]

Style as a Commodity
Historians John J. McCusker and Russell R. Menard have concluded that
the quality and character of each region's exports "shaped the process of
colonial development." New Englanders were at a disadvantage because
their natural resources—products such as wheat, cattle, and fish—were of
little demand in Britain. Lacking a staple crop or rare commodity of the kind
that flourished in the plantation colonies (tobacco, rice, indigo), Boston
merchants turned to manufactures to help correct the balance of trade.
Boston-made furniture—and in particular, seating furniture—was one such
commodity. The export of such goods to other colonies challenged Britain's
role as the primary supplier of manufactured goods in British America. In a
1732 letter to Parliament, Lieutenant Governor William Gooch of Virginia
complained that:

> the People of New England are obliged to apply themselves to manufactures
> more than other of the Plantations, who have the benefit of a better soil and
> warmer climate, there has been of late much Improvements made there in all

sorts of mechanick arts. . . . Escritors, chairs and other wooden manufactures
. . . are now carried from thence to the ot[he]r Plantations, and if not prevented
will do great Damage to the Trade & Manufactures of our Mother Country.[3]

English parliamentarian Edmund Burke described Boston as the "first city of New England, and of all North America" and noted that "New England[ers] . . . are in a manner the carriers for all the colonies of North America and the West Indies, and even for some parts of Europe." He estimated that between December 1747 and December 1748, 340 vessels entered the port and 540 left for "foreign trade." In addition to transporting local manufactures, Boston vessels carried staples and other products from the middle Atlantic and southern colonies to the West Indies, Britain, and Europe. In all, Boston ships accounted for nearly 40 percent of the carrying capacity in the colonies. Boston's maritime dominance ensured that during the first half of the eighteenth century much of New York's transatlantic trade went through Boston.[4]

Boston's commercial success was rooted in the city's shipbuilding industry. In 1693, Sir Josiah Child (1630–1699), president of the British East India Company, wrote that "New England is the most prejudicial plantation to this Kingdom. . . . his Majesty has none so apt for the building of shipping." As early as 1660, Boston shipbuilders exported large ships to England, and in the early eighteenth century, Boston's shipyards boomed as Britain ordered ships during Queen Anne's War. By the end of the colonial period, nearly one-third of all British-owned ships were made in Boston. In addition, by the second quarter of the eighteenth century, approximately one-third of the city's adult male population held shares in or part ownership of a seafaring vessel. In 1749, Dr. William Douglass (1691–1752) observed that shipbuilding was "one of the greatest Articles of our Trade and Manufacture," employing and maintaining "above 30 Denominations of Tradesmen and Artificers." Many of these craftsmen were also involved in the furniture-making trades.[5]

By comparison, shipbuilding did not play as pivotal a role in the economic structure of colonial New York and Rhode Island. In 1736, George Clarke, president of the Council of New York, informed the General Assembly that the neighboring provinces were reaping handsome profits from shipbuilding, but that the trade was "neglected and little used in this Province: and yet Nature has been as bountiful to us as to them, in giving us many materials for that use." Historian Carl Bridenbaugh concluded that shipping, mercantilism, and stylistic evolution were so interdependent that New York's "failure to develop shipbuilding on a large scale" explained "in large measure the backwardness of [its] . . . arts and crafts." Rhode Islanders recognized the success of their Massachusetts neighbors, but they also lagged behind in shipbuilding and shipping. In 1721, the colony had only sixty bottoms with a 3,500 ton total burden. Twenty years later, Governor Richard Ward reported to the Board of Trade: "We have now one hundred and twenty sail of vessels belonging to the inhabitants of this colony, all constantly employed in trade."[6]

Fueled by the port's expanding economy, Boston's population and artisan community grew during the second quarter of the eighteenth century. Between 1730 and 1743, the number of inhabitants rose from 13,000 to 16,382. By comparison, New York's population grew from 8,622 to 11,000, Philadelphia's increased from 11,500 to 13,000, and Newport's rose from 4,640 to 6,200. At least 143 furniture-making tradesmen—sixty-two joiners, twenty-six cabinetmakers, twenty-two chairmakers, fourteen upholsterers, six carvers, five turners, six japanners, one glazier, and one chair caner—worked in Boston between 1730 and 1750. This number far exceeded that of any other colonial city. During the same time frame, New York had approximately thirty-five furniture-making tradesmen, including ten cabinetmakers, one chairmaker, four upholsterers, one carver, seventeen turners, and two japanners. Several of these turners may have been chairmakers, but most turners did not have the training to manufacture joined cabriole leg forms. Similarly, no chairmakers were recorded in Newport between 1730 and 1750.[7]

A thriving urban setting was essential for specialized tradesmen such as Samuel Grant (1705–1784), a Boston upholsterer who established himself in 1728 "at the Crown and Cushion in Union Street near the Town Dock." Grant's ledgers, which intermittently span the years 1728 to 1771, document the extensive activities of his shop and reveal that he was both a successful upholsterer and a merchant. Within the hierarchy of furniture-making tradesmen, the upholsterer's profession ranked among the most prestigious and the most lucrative. In *The London Tradesman* (1747), Robert Campbell wrote that an upholsterer must have "not only judgment of material but taste in Fashions . . . skill in workmanship . . . and set up as a connoisseur in every article in the house." Many upholsterers came from well-to-do families, an important background for craftsmen who needed to establish credit at the start of their careers to purchase expensive upholstery fabrics. Ultimately, some of these tradesmen capitalized upon their professional connections and became merchants.[8]

By its very nature, the upholstery business was closely tied to several other trades, the most obvious being chairmaking. Grant, for example, purchased frames from local chairmakers Thomas Dillaway, James Johnson, Samuel Ridgway, Clement Vincent, Henry Perkins, and Edmund Perkins, Sr., as well as unspecified work from joiners Daniel Ballard, John Leech (Leach), and William Pain (Payne) and from carvers Benjamin Luckie and John Welch. Artisans of Grant's stature often patronized several craftsmen to maintain a stock-in-trade for both the local market and for export.[9]

Grant also relied upon local merchants such as Charles Apthorp to act as middlemen. As former paymaster and commissary of the British forces in the colonies, Apthorp had the resources and connections to import English textiles in bulk. Among Grant's larger purchases from Apthorp were ribbon for £1767.14.7 in December 1740 and "Sundry Tabbys" for £1725.19.1 in May 1749. In lieu of cash, Apthorp often accepted upholstered furniture and services such as "work at house" or "Makeing Curtains for 4 Window headed." On October 25, 1736, Grant credited Apthorp's account with "2. doz: chairs" valued at £36, "2. Elbow ditto" valued at £10.16, a "Couch

Frame & Squab" valued at £7.7.9, and "canvas & packing" valued at £1.5. The inclusion of packing in the order suggests that these items were being prepared for shipment out of Boston. Subsequent credits to Apthorp's account were even larger. On May 13, 1741, he received "54 Leather Chairs" and "5 Elbow ditto" valued at £104, and on May 18, 1748, he received "6 Walnut compass chairs & packing" valued at £61.10. Between March of 1738 and 1748, Apthorp received at least three hundred chairs from Grant. Many of these transfers included charges for packing materials or directives to specific ships and ship captains, indicating that the chairs had been prepared for export.[10]

Several of these shipments can be tracked through clearance records for the port of Boston. For example, on April 17, 1744, Grant noted: "Charles Apthorp's Sent on Board Capt. Treco^ck 6 doz Leather Chairs" valued at £117.6. Just four days later, the *Snow Friendship,* captained by "M. Trecothick" and owned by "C. Apthorp," cleared Boston for Philadelphia with "8 doz. and 2 Leather Chairs" in its hold. At least seventy-two of those chairs were from Grant's shop.[11]

Grant had similar commercial arrangements with several other Boston merchants. On March 6, 1743/44, he charged Boston merchant Jonathan Jones £30.18 for "12 Maple Chairs @ 50/ 4 yds oxamb. & packing," and designated them for shipment "on Board his Vessell Capt. Power." The following month, the sloop *Hopewell,* captained by "Joseph Powers" and owned by "John Jones," left Boston for "Providence" with a cargo that included "1 doz. chairs."[12]

Grant also owned shares in several ships, which gave him access to the markets of his co-investors and was cheaper and less financially risky than maintaining his own vessels. Between 1744 and 1748, Grant held shares in the sloop *Willing Mind* and the schooner *Betty.* These vessels made at least eight trips to Philadelphia, four to Virginia, and several to ports in Maryland, Newfoundland, and the West Indies. Cargoes on these voyages included at least three tables, four desks, and over two hundred chairs.[13]

Boston's tremendous venture cargo industry adversely affected some furniture craftsmen in other ports. In 1742, Philadelphia upholsterer Plunkett Fleeson advertised "Several Sorts of good Chair-frames . . . finished cheaper than any . . . imported from Boston, and in Case of any defects, the Byer shall have them made good; an Advantage not to be had in the buying [of] Boston Chairs, besides the Damage they receive by the Sea." Two years later he rebuked "the Master Chair Makers in this City . . . [for] Encouraging the Importation of Boston Chairs."[14]

The appeal of Boston manufactures in other colonies was grounded in the city's own brand of mediated consumerism. During the first quarter of the eighteenth century, Boston merchant-upholsterers established themselves as arbiters of taste in other colonial ports. The material goods that they imported and manufactured were a source of entertainment—"the spark of a new kind of social discourse." In 1735, John Oldmixon (1673–1742) wrote:

> The conversation in Boston is as polite as most of the Cities and Towns of
> England; many of their merchants having traded into Europe and those that

stayed at home having the advantage of society with travelers. . . . a gentleman from London would almost think himself at home in Boston when he observes . . . their houses, their furniture, their tables, their dress and conversation, which, perhaps, is as splendid and showy as that of the most considerable tradesman in London.[15]

Anglicization was the catalyst that enabled Boston tradesmen and their merchant patrons to capitalize on the city's status as the principal source for British goods in the colonies. Many prominent Boston merchants, such as Charles Apthorp, Henry Bromfield, Peter Faneuil, John Fayerweather, and Thomas Hancock, were members of the Church of England and became Loyalists during the Revolution. They wore English-made garments, had themselves immortalized in the manner of minor British royalty by artists such as Robert Feke and John Singleton Copley, and furnished their homes with English imports or locally made interpretations of them. Style became a commodity of personal and public effect. As a result, "Boston-made" became synonymous with "the latest [English] taste," and "Boston chairs" became synonymous with "London chairs."

The Pink of the Mode in Boston Georgian Seating
A set of eight side chairs (fig. 1) that descended from Charles (1698–1758) and Grizzell (Eastwick) (1709–1796) Apthorp was the genesis for many of the stylistic and structural details that became hallmarks of Boston seating furniture during the 1740s and 1750s; however, misinterpretations of the chairs' history, style, and structure resulted in their being attributed to New York. Indeed, the assumption of their New York origin has been so long-standing that the Apthorp chairs became a touchstone for attributing a large group of related Boston seating to that city. The theory that they were purchased in New York by Charles's son, Charles Ward Apthorp (1729–1797), during the 1750s or 1760s and subsequently returned to the Boston branch of the family is refuted by strong historical and physical evidence. Family tradition maintained that the chairs belonged to Charles and Grizzell and that they descended in the female line from their daughter, Susan Apthorp Bulfinch (1734–1815), to Elizabeth Bulfinch Coolidge (1777–1837), to Elizabeth McCalla Miller (b. 1875), and to Elizabeth Symington before being purchased by the New York antiques firm of Ginsburg and Levy.[16]

Charles Apthorp served as the American agent for Thomlinson and Trecothick, the London merchant house that supplied money for the British army in America. His daughter Grizzell married Barlow Trecothick, and his son John moved to London to become a member of the firm. Other Apthorp progeny were conveniently placed in businesses in New York City and Kingston, Jamaica.[17]

Through his connections with London suppliers and his association with Anglophiles such as Thomas Hancock, Apthorp kept abreast of the latest British fashions. In addition to the set of chairs, his household furnishings included a "Mohogony Cabinet with glass doors" valued at £30 and a "Mohogony Beauro with Glass doors" valued at £32. The latter may have referred to the bombé bureau with cabinet illustrated in figure 2. Several scholars have speculated that this piece may have introduced the bombé

Figure 3 Side chair, London, 1725–1735. Walnut and walnut veneer. (Courtesy, Sotheby's.)

Figure 4 John Singleton Copley, *Jeremiah Lee*, Boston, ca. 1770. Oil on canvas. Frame attributed to John Welch, Boston, ca. 1767. White pine, gilded. Portrait dimensions: 95" × 59". (Courtesy, Wadsworth Atheneum, Ella Gallup Sumner and Mary Catlin Sumner Collection Fund.)

Figure 2 Bureau with cabinet, London, 1735–1745. Mahogany with oak, spruce, and an unidentified conifer. H. 97", W. 46³/₄", D. 25¹/₂". (Courtesy, Museum of Fine Arts, Boston; gift of Albert Sack.) This bureau is related to case pieces attributed to the shop of London cabinetmaker Giles Grendy, one of the leading exporters of furniture.

form to Boston. Similarly, London side chairs (see fig. 3) undoubtedly served as the model for the basic design of the Apthorp suite.[18]

Like many London chairs from the late 1720s and early 1730s, Apthorp's have inverted baluster splats with walnut veneer, angular S-shaped stiles, compass seats, shell-carved crests and knees, and tapered rear legs with small squared feet (fig. 1). His estate inventory, taken in 1759, indicates that his "Best Parlour" had "a sett of Yellow damask Window Curtains & Cushions" and "10 Mehogony Chairs Yellow Bottoms" valued at £16. The latter description is significant because several chairs from the Apthorp set retain

fragments of their original, yellow silk damask upholstery. Although the chairs are made of walnut, their brilliantly figured veneers could have been mistaken for mahogany by his estate appraisers. [19]

The carved details on the chairs provide conclusive evidence that they were made in Boston. The carving is attributed to John Welch (1711–1789), the most prolific carver (fl. 1732–1780) in pre-Revolutionary Boston. Among Welch's many commissions were at least twenty-five ornately carved picture frames, many of which were ordered by artist John Singleton Copley (1738–1815) (fig. 4). Several of these frames, including the one on Copley's portrait of Jeremiah Lee, have distinctive, V-shaped shells with scrolls and acanthus leaves that are executed in the same manner as the corresponding elements on the crests of the chairs (figs. 5, 6). The omission of the imbrication (scale motifs) on the frame scrolls may have been to simplify the surface for gilding. In colonial American furniture, this combination of details is unique to Welch. Similar acanthus clusters also occur on a Boston desk-and-bookcase with a scrollboard appliqué attributed to Welch (figs. 7,

Figure 5   Detail of the crest rail carving on the side chair illustrated in fig. 1. (Photo, Gavin Ashworth.)

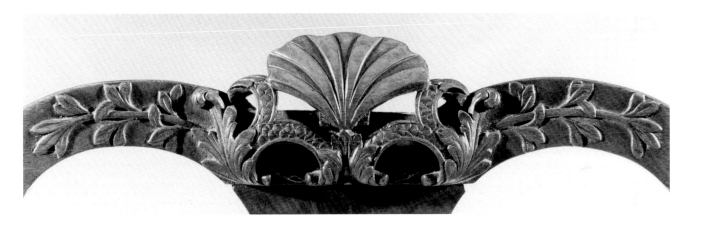

Figure 6   Detail of the shell and acanthus carving on the frame illustrated in fig. 4.

8).[20] The appliqué leaves are accented with cabochons rising from the spines—a detail that occurs on several chairs and case pieces with carving attributed to his shop (see figs. 27, 28, 36, 37).

Figure 7 Desk-and-bookcase with carving attributed to John Welch, Boston, 1750–1755. Mahogany with white pine. H. 95½", W. 40", D. 22". (Courtesy, Saint Louis Art Museum, Museum Shop Fund; photo, Christie's.)

Figure 8 Detail of the scrollboard appliqué of the desk-and-bookcase illustrated in fig. 7. (Photo, Christie's.)

The embryonic feet of the Apthorp chairs are similar to London claw-and-ball feet of the early 1730s (fig. 9). Rather than placing the ball of the foot at the center of the walnut blank (fig. 10*a*), Welch positioned it at the forward corner (fig. 10*b*). This change signals an evolution away from

Figure 9 Detail of the foot of the side chair illustrated in fig. 1. (Photo, Gavin Ashworth.)

(a)

(b)

(c)

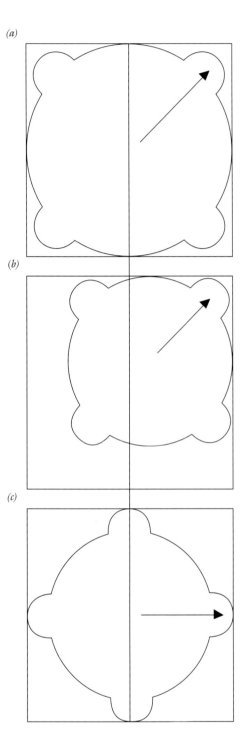

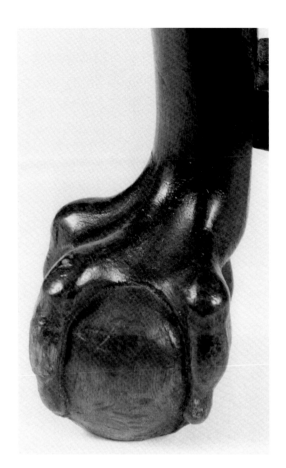

Figure 10 Diagram of (*a*) diagonal orientation with foot placed in center of stock and toes at corners; (*b*) diagonal orientation but with foot placed at front corner; (*c*) frontal orientation with knee blocks on opposite sides (see legs of turret table illustrated in fig. 13). (Drawing, Alan Miller; artwork, Wynne Patterson.)

frontally oriented legs (fig. 10*c*) such as those on compass seat chairs in the late baroque (or "Queen Anne") style. Such chairs probably came into fashion in Boston during the mid to late 1720s. On October 14, 1729, Samuel Grant sold New York ship captain Arnout Schermerhorn a "red Chainey" chair with a "New fashion round seat." Although this chair almost certainly had cabriole legs, the first reference to them occurred the following year when Grant billed Nathaniel Green £2.12 for "1 Couch frame horsebone feet." Later entries for chairs with "horsebone feet" document a progression of cabriole leg/foot forms from sawn and beaded to turned. The Apthorp chairs have the earliest form of claw-and-ball feet and probably date from the early 1730s. On March 8, 1732/33, Grant sold "4 doz: Leathr chairs claw feet" to Peter Faneuil for 27 shillings each.[21]

Boston cabinetmakers and carvers also began using claw-and-ball feet on card tables and tea tables during the 1730s. A card table that descended in the Dalton family of Boston (fig. 11) has feet that are virtually identical to those of the Apthorp chairs (figs. 9, 12). The Dalton table and the concertina-action table illustrated in figure 13 also have escape cuts (saw kerfs made during the removal of the waste stock) on the inner curves of the ankles, like several chairs from the Apthorp set. These cuts reinforce the notion that Welch was initially unfamiliar with the construction of cabriole legs with claw-and-ball feet. On later examples, he and his contemporaries positioned the toes near the side corners of the stock to fully utilize the dimensions of the material (see figs. 10*a*, 16).[22]

Figure 11   Card table with carving attributed to John Welch, Boston, 1730–1740. Mahogany with white pine. H. 28 3/4", W. 31 3/4", D. 16". (Private collection; photo, Wit McKay.) A label in the table reads, "1906 . . . This . . . card table belonged to Peter Roe Dalton, Jnr. . . . Descended to his son Peter Roe, Jnr., was in his house—72 Boylston Street." A Boston bombé chest descended in the same family.

Figure 12   Detail of the foot of the card table illustrated in fig. 11. (Photo, Wit McKay.)

Grant's ledgers document his association with Apthorp and Welch. On May 20, 1738, Grant recorded that Apthorp paid "his order to Jn.º Welch 20—", although he did not specify the nature of the transaction. A year later, Grant noted, "Chas. Apthorp pd ord.ʳ to Jnº Welch end:ᵈ to Gooch 100." Similarly, entries in Grant's account book record several transactions between Welch and merchants such as Thomas and James Perkins. On June 8, 1736, and December 2, 1741, Thomas paid Welch £40 and £60 respectively, and on May 24, 1744, he and James paid Welch £30. Presumably, these payments were for furniture carving, for, like Apthorp, these merchants determined the amount of carved work applied to their purchases.[23]

The materials and construction of the Apthorp chairs (fig. 1) also relate more closely to cabinet- and chairmaking practices in Boston than to those in New York. The splats of the Apthorp chairs are crotch walnut veneered on maple—a sturdy, stable hardwood commonly found in New England furniture. The walnut appears to be from the same flitch used on a slightly later set of chairs that reportedly descended in a Boston family. The cost of the material and the amount of labor involved in producing splats of this quality was substantial, but the visual effect of their matching veneers was stunning.[24]

By the second quarter of the eighteenth century, Boston had a thoroughly established tradition of veneering based upon English precedent.

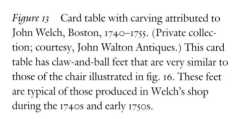

Figure 13 Card table with carving attributed to John Welch, Boston, 1740–1755. (Private collection; courtesy, John Walton Antiques.) This card table has claw-and-ball feet that are very similar to those of the chair illustrated in fig. 16. These feet are typical of those produced in Welch's shop during the 1740s and early 1750s.

Figure 14 Detail of the slip seat of a chair from the Apthorp suite.

Wealthy merchants such as Peter Faneuil purchased veneered furniture made locally and from their agents abroad. In 1738, Thomas Hancock instructed his London factor to "Send with my Spring Goods a Handsome Chiming Clock . . . with a Good black Walnutt Tree Case veneer'd work, with Dark lively branches . . . [and] three handsome Car'd figures Gilt with burnish'd Gold." By contrast, veneered furniture made in New York and Newport during the first half of the eighteenth century is extremely rare.[25]

Like many eighteenth-century Boston chairs, Apthorp's have maple slip seats and triangular white pine glue blocks (blocks may be later additions). The chairs also had yellow silk damask covers that were nailed to the edges of the slip seats (fig. 14)—a distinctive technique that probably evolved from leather chair upholstery. In 1747, Grant sold Jonathan Prescott six walnut compass seat chairs "cov'd over close & nailed."[26] This description could refer to either edge-nailed slip seats or, more likely, over-the-rail upholstery. New York chairmakers were far less regimented in the construction of slip seats and were more likely to use oak, cherry, tulip, or gum than maple. The formulaic approach of Boston's chairmakers may have been in response to the high volume demands of the export trade.

Figure 15   Easy chair with carving attributed to John Welch, Boston, 1730–1740. Walnut and maple. H. 44", W. 31", D. 22". (Courtesy, Winterthur Museum.) The stretchers have a coved outer edge like those on the Apthorp chairs.

Material and documentary evidence indicates that many of the details incorporated in the Apthorp chairs remained fashionable in Boston until the mid-eighteenth century. Were it not for its knee carving, the easy chair illustrated in figure 15 could almost be en suite with the Apthorp chairs. The shells on the easy chair are longer, and they have rounded lower edges and husks (or bellflowers). This design is less naturalistic than the knee carving on the Apthorp chairs, but it is better suited to the shape of cabriole legs.

Grant's accounts refer to numerous chairs with features similar to Apthorp's. He charged Benjamin Dolbeare £6 for "2 Chairs false Seats Flat Strechers" on February 3, 1741, and £10 for "2 Compass ditto" the following day. Later entries record sales and exchanges of chairs with carved crests, legs, and feet. For example, on May 23, 1745, he charged Thomas and James Deskins £13.10 for "9 Wallnutt Chairs Carv'd Tops & Leggs." [27]

Although the Apthorp chairs have an early experimental quality, several

Figure 16 Side chair with carving attributed to John Welch, Boston, 1740–1750. Walnut and walnut veneer with maple and white pine; maple slip seat. H. 38½", W. 22", D. 18⅜". (Courtesy, Brooklyn Museum; photo, Gavin Ashworth.) The veneer on the splats of these chairs appears to be from the same flitch as those of the set including the chair illustrated in fig. 21.

Figure 17 Detail of the knee carving on the side chair illustrated in fig. 16. (Photo, Gavin Ashworth.)

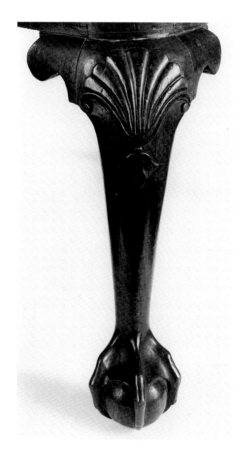

related examples show subtle refinements and modifications. A set of six chairs that descended in the Fayerweather and Bromfield families of Boston are representative (fig. 16). Some of the slip seats are marked "Capn Fayerweather" for merchant John Fayerweather (1685–1760), who, like Apthorp, bought large quantities of chairs and other goods from Samuel Grant. Fayerweather may have given the chairs to his daughter, Margaret (1732–1761), and son-in-law, Henry Bromfield (1727–1820), near the time of their marriage in 1749. Family tradition maintains that Margaret embroidered the covers for the seats.[28]

The carving on the crests (fig. 19) is attributed to Welch, but the design is simpler and required far less labor than that on the Apthorp suite. The small leaves that rise from the scroll volutes are hastily carved versions of those on

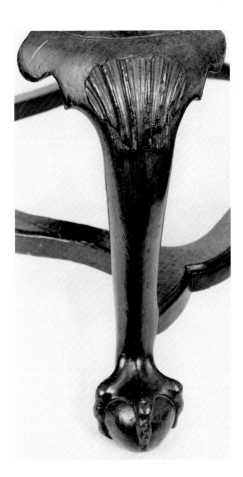

Figure 18   Detail of the knee carving on the side chair illustrated in fig. 1. (Photo, Gavin Ashworth.)

Figure 19   Detail of the crest rail carving on the side chair illustrated in fig. 16. (Photo, Gavin Ashworth.)

several of Welch's simpler frames. Although the knee carving on the Fayerweather chairs is too generic to support an attribution, similar shell and husk designs occur on other chairs in the group (see fig. 21) and on contemporary London chairs (see fig. 3). With their simple convex lobes, these shells required less tools and less time than the more naturalistic ones on the knees of the Apthorp chairs and the easy chair (figs. 17, 18).

The carving on the Fayerweather chairs is also related to that on a desk-and-bookcase that belonged to Boston goldsmith John Allen (1671–1760) (fig. 20), on a very similar set of Boston side chairs that reportedly descended in the Baldwin family of New York (fig. 21), and on the high chest illustrated in figure 22. The acanthus leaves on the crests of both sets of chairs are similar to those at the bottom of the scrollboard appliqué on the Allen desk (figs. 19, 23, 24), and the vine carving on the chairs has flowers, berries, and leaves that nearly quote those on the original (lower) shell drawer of the high chest (figs. 19, 24, 25). The husks and leaves on the crests and shell drawer also match those on the feet of the Allen desk (fig. 26). The feet of the chairs and high chest are, again, very similar. Both sets are derived from the feet on the Apthorp chairs, but their toes were set at the corners of the stock (see fig. 10*a*). [29]

The Fayerweather and Bromfield families patronized Welch both directly and indirectly. An elaborate coat of arms (at the Society for the Preservation of New England Antiquities) that descended in the family of Margaret Fayerweather's brother, Thomas (1724–1806), has acanthus leaves that are virtually identical to corresponding elements on Welch's picture frames. Welch's shop also furnished carving for an extraordinary tall clock case commissioned by Henry Bromfield (figs. 27, 28) and for several related Boston case pieces made between 1735 and 1755. [30]

The Fayerweather chairs are important for their Boston history and their more standardized expressions of the "new fashion" style mentioned by Grant and exemplified by the Apthorp suite; however, several other chairs figure more prominently in the development of venture cargo models. The side chair illustrated in figure 29 is one of the earliest examples with Boston-style block-end stretchers, single-crook styles, and a conforming veneered

Figure 20 Desk-and-bookcase with carving attributed to John Welch, Boston, 1743–1748. Mahogany and sabicu with red cedar and white pine. H. 97¼", W. 42⅞", D. 23¼". (Courtesy, Winterthur Museum.)

Figure 21 Side chair with carving attributed to John Welch, Boston, 1740–1750. Walnut and walnut veneer. H. 38", W. 20½", D. 18⅛". (Courtesy, Bernard & S. Dean Levy, Inc., NYC.)

splat. Except for the veneer, variations of all of these details (or combinations of them) occur on later venture cargo chairs (see fig. 34). The modified trifid feet were less expensive alternatives to claw-and-ball feet, but they, too, were based on early Georgian prototypes. Although somewhat more

Figure 22 High chest with carving attributed
to John Welch, Boston, 1740–1750. Mahogany
with white pine. H. 95¹/8", W. 41¹/4", D. 22¹/8".
(Courtesy, Baltimore Museum of Art; promised
gift of Dorothy McIlvain Scott.)

Figure 23 Detail of the appliqué on the desk-and-bookcase illustrated in fig. 20.

Figure 24 Detail of the crest rail carving on a chair from the same set as the chair illustrated in fig. 21. (Courtesy, Sotheby's.) The acanthus leaves emanate from the scroll volutes like those on the appliqué of the desk-and-bookcase illustrated in fig. 23. Both carvings have chip cuts in the scroll hollows and similar arrangement of the leaf elements.

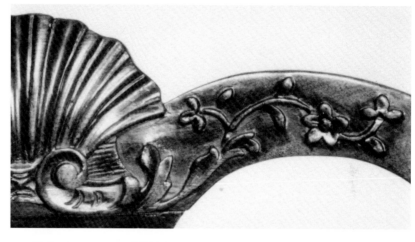

Figure 25 Detail of the lower drawer of the high chest illustrated in fig. 22.

Figure 26 Detail of the foot of the desk-and-bookcase illustrated in fig. 20. The relief-carved husks (one rising from the edge beading and the other hanging from the loop) are products of the same design vocabulary, tool kit, and working style as the corresponding husks on the crest rails of the chairs illustrated in figs. 16 and 21 and the shell drawer illustrated in fig. 25.

Figure 27 Tall clock case with carving attributed to John Welch, Boston, 1750. Mahogany with white pine and courbaril. H. 100". (Courtesy, Art Institute of Chicago, Alyce and Edwin DeCosta and Walter E. Heller Foundation and Harold Stuart Endowments; photo, Sotheby's.)

Figure 28 Detail of a spandrel appliqué on the tall clock case illustrated in fig. 27.

superficial, the carving on the crest and knees is derived from the Fayerweather and Apthorp chairs, respectively. Like many eighteenth-century carvers, Welch could adjust his work to accommodate his patron's pocketbook. This flexibility is most discernible in his frames and his carving for case furniture.[31]

A slightly later Boston side chair features many of the same details, while exhibiting a rear leg form common on Boston late baroque pad foot chairs (fig. 30). The distinctive carved shell on the crest rail is virtually identical to the one Welch carved for John Singleton Copley's portrait of Isaac Smith (figs. 31, 32). Similar shells occur on other Copley frames and on case pieces of obvious Boston-area origin.[32]

Not all of the chairs in this genre exhibit carving attributable to Welch. A side chair (from a set of at least four) that reportedly belonged to New York merchant and ship captain John Aspinwall (1705/6–1774) (fig. 33) is probably from the same chairmaking shop that produced the Apthorp, Fayerweather, and Baldwin suites. All have elaborate walnut veneers and similar splats, stiles, and knee blocks; nevertheless, the shells on the crest rail and knees of the Aspinwall chair resemble those on many venture cargo chairs. These simpler shell forms probably represent the work of several different hands. Aspinwall was a business associate of at least two other New York merchants who purchased Boston furniture—Gerard Beekman and

Figure 29 Side chair with carving attributed to John Welch, Boston, 1735–1745. Walnut and walnut veneer with maple; maple slip seat. H. 39½", W. 21¾". (Courtesy, Museum of the City of New York, gift of Mrs. Screven Lorillard.)

Figure 30 Side chair with carving attributed to John Welch, Boston, 1735–1745. Walnut with white pine; maple slip seat. H. 40", W. 20½", D. 18½". (Courtesy, Metropolitan Museum of Art, Rogers Fund, 1925; photo, Gavin Ashworth.)

Figure 31 Detail of the crest rail carving on the side chair illustrated in fig. 30. The missing tips of the shell resembled those of the shell illustrated in fig. 32. (Photo, Gavin Ashworth.)

Henry Lloyd. Aspinwall probably acquired his chair during one of his frequent voyages to Boston. For example, between March 25, 1739, and September 29, 1740, he made at least five round trips between New York and Boston.[33]

Making Chairs for Export
The carving and veneers on the preceding chairs distinguish them from the basic export model of the 1740s and 1750s. Made of walnut (and in a few instances mahogany), the latter featured a compass seat, single-crook stiles, a conforming, baluster-shaped splat, and claw-and-ball feet (fig. 34). A few structural and ornamental options—stretchers, alternative crest and splat

Figure 32 Detail of the applied shell and upper rail of a picture frame carved by John Welch for John Singleton Copley's portrait of Isaac Smith, Boston, 1769. White pine, gilded. 58½" × 48¼". (Courtesy, Yale University Art Gallery, gift of Maitland Fuller Griggs.)

Figure 33 Side chair, Boston, 1740–1750. Walnut and walnut veneer with maple and white pine. H. 38⅝", W. 21½", D. 21¼". (Courtesy, Diplomatic Reception Rooms, United States Department of State, gift of Mr. and Mrs. Walter M. Phillips.)

shapes, and simple carved shells—were available, but it is unlikely that many venture cargo chairs had veneered splats or intricately carved crests like the Apthorp and Fayerweather examples. Moreover, several tradesmen less accomplished than Welch clearly carved the shells and feet of many export-quality chairs and some of the simpler elements on commissioned work. Venture cargo chairs had to be constructed efficiently and priced accordingly, which eliminated costly carving and veneering. Grant's payments to chairmaker Edmund Perkins suggest tremendous production: £695.5.2 for unspecified work on January 11, 1742; £694.12.7 for "chair frames etc." on February 1, 1745/46; and £790.18.6 for "Chair Frames etc" on February 13, 1746.[34]

As part of this manufacturing process, upholsterers such as Grant frequently supplied raw materials for the craftsmen in their networks. On August 20, 1743, he debited Perkins's account £16.2.7 for 2,304 feet of boards. The following month, Grant recorded the payment of £151.7.6 for "Voyages to Virginia . . . for . . . Walnutt &c." and debited Perkins's account £19.5 for "75 1/2 feet Wallnutt logs."[35] Later entries record similar transactions. Because black walnut grew slowly in the forests of eastern Massachusetts, Boston merchants imported it from the southern colonies. Virginia walnut was especially prized for its grain and figure.

Chairmaker John Perkins's (1723–1776) inventory, taken after Boston's Great Fire of 1760, showed the volume of his shop's manufacture, for it listed "220 wallnot Feet for Chairs" and "500 foot wallnt 2 Inch Plank." Similarly chairmaker, Joseph Putnam (fl. 1750–1767) lost "350 wallnot Feet for Chairs."[36] The mass replication of parts, such as "feet" (chair legs), stretcher components, and loose seats, was essential to increase production and to minimize the cost of manufacturing chairs for export; however, standardization and the economics of venture cargo took a toll upon creativity and limited stylistic developments.

Tracing Fashion's Cargoes: New York
During the late seventeenth and early eighteenth centuries, New York was one of the most important markets for Boston merchants who traded in imported and locally manufactured goods. Several trading firms, such as those of the Faneuils, Wendells, and Deblois, established branches in New

York during the early eighteenth century. Leather chairs were one of the most important commodities exported from Boston to New York during this period. On October 22, 1701, New York merchant Benjamin Faneuil (b. La Rochelle, France 1658, d. New York 1719) imported "12 leather chaires . . . [from] Boston where the above goods were made," and over the next several years he could hardly keep up with the demand. Faneuil acted as a middleman for Boston merchant-upholsterer Thomas Fitch (1668/9–1736). Fitch was an artful promoter of Boston-made products who understood that perceptions of stylishness and desirability could be manipulated for profit. On March 28, 1709, Fitch sold "Abram" Wendell of Albany "Twelve Russhia Chairs & one Arm [chair]." Wendell evidently balked at the price, causing Fitch to cajole: "the chairs are extraordinary Leather & at the lowest price: I refused ready money for them at the same price meerly to sute ye."[37]

The ledgers and letterbooks of Fitch and the account books of his apprentice, Samuel Grant (worked independently, ca. 1728), document the evolution of style and trade patterns in Boston's chairmaking industry during the first half of the eighteenth century. Fitch traded primarily in baroque leather chairs (turned examples, with or without carving, and transitional crook-back chairs), and the vast majority of his patrons were merchants, lawyers, and physicians in Boston, New York, and Newport. Grant maintained and expanded many of the trade channels developed by his master, but his seating forms were in the late baroque and early Georgian styles.[38]

The "red Chainey" chair with a "New fashion round seat" that Grant sold Arnout Schermerhorn, shortly after completing his apprenticeship, signals a departure from the baroque examples marketed by his master; nevertheless, it documents the persistence of earlier trade patterns. Schermerhorn (1686–1749) was a New York shipmaster whose family established a packet service between New York, Boston, and Charleston, South Carolina. On October 4, 1729, the *New-England Weekly Journal* reported that his ship arrived "from New-York." Schermerhorn purchased the chair on that date and probably carried it to New York when his ship departed two weeks later.[39]

Capitalizing on the continued popularity of Boston seating furniture, merchants such as Grant, Peter Faneuil, and Henry Bromfield shipped both commissioned chairs and venture cargo to New York during the 1730s and 1740s. Among the many documented examples are Grant's sale to "Mary Brown of New Y[ork] 1 Easy Chair . . . 20.14.11" on August 9, 1736; Peter Faneuil's shipment of an easy chair "ordered for a lady" to New York in 1737; Joshua Winslow's shipment of "6 Wallnutt Chairs Covered with Crimson Harrateen 40.10.2" to New York on November 28, 1746; and Henry Bromfield's sale of "12 Black Walnut Chair Frames" and "12 Leather Bottoms for Ditto" to Isaac Lattouch of New York on January 8, 1747/48.[40]

Between 1744 and 1748, ships transporting furniture made at least fifty-four trips from Boston to New York. Their cargo included at least twenty-nine desks, four "Great Chairs," twenty-three tables, eight "Chest of Draws," nine couches, three easy chairs, one bookcase, two clock cases, one "scrutoire," one cradle, nine boxes of "Household Furniture," and 1,004 chairs. By contrast, no chairs appear in the cargo manifests of Boston-bound

Figure 34 Side chair, Boston, 1740–1755. Mahogany; maple slip seat. H. 38½", W. 22", D. 21¼". (Chipstone Foundation; photo, Gavin Ashworth.)

Figure 35 Settee, Boston, 1740–1755. Walnut with maple, birch, cherry, and walnut. H. 38", W. 65⅝", D. 28". (Courtesy, Diplomatic Reception Rooms, United States Department of State.)

ships recorded in the New York Shipping Returns for 1731–1738 and 1735–1752 and in the New York Treasurer's Accounts for 1739–1754. These findings are consistent with one New Yorker's comment in 1734 that "our luxury consists . . . [more] of what is imported than what is of [our] own growth manufactories."[41]

The acquisition of luxury was clearly on the mind of New York merchant Henry Lloyd when he arranged for the purchase and delivery of a Boston-made carriage to his home on Long Island. On September 24, 1748, his eldest son (living in Boston) wrote, "[the] chair you'l receive . . . its the very pink of the mode and as good a one as can be procurd." The following year, Henry II sent his father "12 Chair Fraims . . . £72," "1 Ditto round about . . . £9," and "13 seats stuffing & Covering . . . £31.4." Although Massachusetts currency was inflated during the late 1740s, the cost of the chairs was still relatively high.[42]

Many wealthy New York merchants such as Henry Lloyd looked to London and Boston for the latest fashions. As William Smith observed in his *History of the Province of New-York From the First Discovery to the Year 1732* (1757):

> In the city of New-York, through our intercourse with the Europeans, we follow the London fashions; though by the time we adopt them, they become disused in England. Our affluence . . . introduced a degree of luxury in tables, dress, and furniture, with which we were before unacquainted. But we are still not so gay a people, as our neighbors in Boston.

Business associations, friendships, and family connections strengthened ties between the mercantile communities of Boston and New York. For example, Charles Apthorp was the godson of Henry Lloyd and the business associate and friend of Lloyd and his son, Henry II. Following Apthorp's sudden death on December 1, 1758, Henry II wrote his father, "in Mr. Apthorp I have lost my best friend in this place. . . . I could . . . always be sure of his best advice & secrecy. . . . when I had occasion for a sum of money . . . [he] would Cheerfully lend any sum I wanted."[43]

The Lloyds also did business with William Beekman (1684–1770), a New York merchant who purchased leather chairs from Fitch and owned the Boston settee illustrated in figure 35. New York shipping records document Beekman's extensive trade with Boston. Between May 8, 1735, and October 24, 1737, his ship *William and Mary* logged separate departures for Boston (twice), "Boston: N. England," "N. England," "Rhoad Island," and "N. London and R. Island." During the same time frame, this ship returned twice from Boston, twice from Rhode Island, and once from "Boston and Perth Amboy." On May 29, 1736, the *William and Mary* carried "10 Desks" from Boston to New York—a clear indication that Boston goods serviced Beekman's mercantile strategy. By contrast, furniture was never included in the *William and Mary*'s outbound New York cargo.[44]

The overall design of Beekman's settee (fig. 35) is based on London examples like the one shown in Sir Joshua Reynolds's portrait of Warren Hastings (in the National Portrait Gallery, London), but its secondary woods—maple, white pine, birch—are typical of Boston upholstered furniture.[45] The leg profile, shell carving, and basic form of the claw and ball is derived from the Fayerweather chairs. The feet of the settee are the standardized type, with deep webbing and hollows (between the claws) that stop abruptly at the ankle. Similar legs and feet appear on a variety of Boston furniture forms, including desks, high chests, dressing tables, card tables (usually with turrets), tea tables, and pier tables.

A set of side chairs that descended in the Van Cortlandt family provides further evidence of New Yorkers commissioning elaborate Boston seating forms (fig. 36). These objects also reveal that Welch had refined many of the details he had introduced on the crests of the Apthorp chairs, without simplifying them as on the Fayerweather suite. The Apthorp chairs and Van Cortlandt chairs both have crests with high-relief strapwork and acanthus clusters (figs. 5, 37), but the leaves of the Van Cortlandt chairs are accented with curved cabochons like those on the spandrel appliqués of Henry Bromfield's tall clock case (fig. 28) and the scrollboard appliqué of the desk-and-bookcase illustrated in figure 8. Welch also substituted low-relief acanthus leaves for the stiff branches on the crests of the Apthorp chairs and omitted the imbrication on the strapwork.

Another chapter in the history of this suite unfolds with two New York armchairs made to accompany the side chairs shortly after their arrival (fig. 38). The makers of the armchairs enlarged the splat and crest proportionally but copied the dimensions and design of the carving on the Boston prototypes (figs. 37, 39).[46] The New York carver was somewhat less skilled than

Figure 36 Side chair, Boston, 1735–1745. Walnut and walnut veneer with maple. H. 39", W. 20", D. 17¹/₂". (Courtesy, Winterthur Museum.)

Figure 37 Detail of the crest rail carving on the side chair illustrated in fig. 36.

Welch, whose divergent technical repertoire and tool kit produced a much clearer, more naturalistic design. Other variations occur in the carving of the feet. The Boston examples have deeper webbing and high-ridged toes.

Basic construction details also separate the side chairs and armchairs. The side chairs have several "standard" Boston features, including walnut-veneered splats, single-piece shoe/rear rail components, turned rear stretch-

Figure 38 Armchair, New York, 1740–1755. Walnut; red gum slip seat. H. 39½", W. 23", D. 19⅝". (Courtesy, Winterthur Museum.)

Figure 39 Detail of the crest rail carving on the armchair illustrated in fig. 38.

ers, and maple slip seats; whereas the armchairs have solid walnut splats, a separate shoe and rear rail, no rear stretchers, and red gum slip seats, all in keeping with New York chairmaking practices. The eagle head arm supports may also be an Anglo–New York conceit, since they evidently appear there earlier than in Boston. In addition, the sinuous, curved legs of the armchairs have direct parallels in later New York chairs, tables, and case furniture.[47]

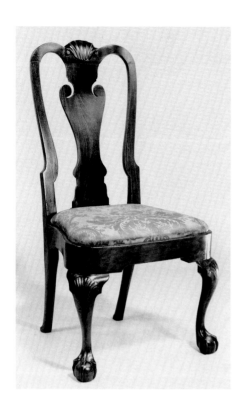

Figure 40 Side chair, New York, 1745–1760. Mahogany; oak slip seat. H. 38³/₄". (Collection of the Albany Institute of History and Art, gift of J. Townsend Lansing.)

New York Chairs in the Boston Style

To compete with imports and to supply the expanding local market, New York chairmakers adapted details from Boston chairs that were either ordered by New Yorkers (see figs. 21, 33) or arrived as venture cargo (see fig. 34). The side chair illustrated in figure 40 is clearly derived from a Boston venture cargo chair; however, the maker replaced the Boston square rear foot with its New York equivalent—a rounded slipper foot. The New York chair also has an oak slip seat and rounded, two-part oak glue blocks like many other locally made examples. The feet appear to be by the same artisan that carved the feet of the Van Cortlandt armchairs.

Another New York side chair (fig. 41) shares details with ornate Boston chairs (see especially figs. 16, 21) as well as with export-grade models (fig. 34). The chairmaker incorporated a standard Boston splat with double-crook stiles and carved details commonly associated with more expensive commissioned chairs. The exaggerated cabriole legs, undercut knees, and nearly webless claw-and-ball feet have no precedent in Boston Georgian seating, but nearly identical details occur on a set of chairs that descended in the Livingston family of New York and a small group of turret-top card tables and china tables with New York histories. Moreover, the shell and highly stylized acanthus carving on the crest rail is by the same hand that executed the knee carving on the aforementioned china tables.[48]

The side chair illustrated in figure 42 departs even further from Boston seating. Although the makers retained the double-serpentine, beaded shoe of the Boston prototype, they modified its double-crook stiles to harmonize with the thin waist and exaggerated volutes of their splat. This distinctive splat and stile shaping appears on several other New York chairs. Other New York details are the gum slip seat and pad rear feet. The knee design, which features broad leaves flanking a cross-hatched reserve, also occurs on numerous tables and chairs from that city.

Tracing Fashion's Cargoes: Newport

During the first half of the eighteenth century, Newport did not have an extensive chairmaking industry. Wendell Garrett's checklist of Newport craftsmen included no chairmakers active between 1730 and 1750, and Jeanne Vibert Sloane's research uncovered only two references to Newport cabinetmakers selling chairs, both after 1760. Shipping records, probate inventories, and correspondence suggest that case forms and tables were the main products of Newport's craftsmen. A survey of harbor records from six Virginia ports reveals that at least 728 chairs arrived on Boston vessels between 1727 and 1755. During the same period, Rhode Island ships regularly transported desks and tables to Virginia, but never chairs. It was not until December 4, 1755, that a Rhode Island cargo included seating forms. Moreover, material evidence strongly suggests that much of the seating used in Rhode Island before 1750 originated in Boston.[49]

Commercial ties between Boston and Newport were particularly strong. For example, at least forty-two of the vessels that entered New York harbor between March 25, 1738, and June 24, 1743, listed Boston and Rhode Island

Figure 41 Side chair, New York, 1745–1760. Mahogany; ash slip seat. H. 38³/₄", W. 21¹/₂", D. 17¹/₂". (Courtesy, Bernard & S. Dean Levy, Inc., NYC.)

Figure 42 Side chair, New York, 1745–1760. Mahogany; red oak slip seat. H. 39", W. 20", D. 17¹/₂". (Courtesy, Winterthur Museum.)

as their previous ports of call. Indeed, in July 1744, Annapolis physician Alexander Hamilton reported hearing "news of a coasting vessel . . . taken by a French privateer in her passage betwixt Boston and Rhode Island."[50]

Because of Newport's close proximity to Boston, land routes were also important in the conveyance of goods. In 1731, Rhode Island Governor Joseph Jencks wrote:

> Directly from Great Britain we have but a Small Quantity of Goods having but two Vessels in a year Trading thither, But by the Way of Boston we receive almost all we use . . . Duck Cordage Broad Cloths Drugges Stuffs Serges

Figure 43   Tall clock case, Boston, 1740–1755. Movement by Thomas Claggett, Newport, 1740–1755. Materials and dimensions not recorded. (Private collection; photo, Gavin Ashworth.)

Shaloons Hollands Garlix thread Laces Seyths Nailes & other Iron Ware Needles Pins tape . . . they being by our Merchants and Shopkeepers mostly imported by land.

By 1736, a regular stage line united the seventy-mile span between Boston and Newport. Bostonian Jonathan Foster initiated a weekly carrier service in 1745 but soon had a rival when Newporter Mathew Pate established a similar service.[51]

A fascinating series of letters between New York City merchant Gerard G. Beekman (1719–1797) (Dr. William Beekman's nephew), Boston merchant Stephen Greenleaf, and Newport ship captain John Channing help personalize the Boston–Newport–New York trade axis. In an August 11, 1746, letter to Greenleaf, Beekman wrote: "I received . . . the Cheirs in good order . . . we Like them much and *so does most that See them* [emphasis added]. . . . If you'd be so good and pay Mr. Johnson for the Clock Case shall reimburse you on first advice." ("Mr. Johnson" may have been Boston cabinetmaker William Johnston [fl. 1741–1756] or japanner and engraver Thomas Johnston [fl. 1732–1767].) The following month, Beekman requested that Channing "pay Mr. Clagget for my Clock Case which may Engage him to keep it till the Case Come which I think is Long." ("Mr. Clagget" was probably William Claggett [1696–1749], a Boston clockmaker who moved to Newport about 1719.) Beekman's frustration over the delay in receiving his clock case persisted. In a December 22, 1746, letter to Greenleaf he griped: "I think Mr. Johnson has make too much diffrence and the Charge of My Clock Case and those sent my Neighbour, having Charged me £10 more than he has them." The New York merchant's luck was no better when it came to the clock's movement. In September 1747, he wrote Channing: "Pray Dont forget forwarding my Clock as soon as possible, I have the Case Which is of as much use as a bell without a Clapper."[52]

A tall clock case with a movement by William Claggett's son, Thomas (fl. Newport ca. 1730–1797), provides material evidence of the strong mercantile and trade connections between Boston and Newport (fig. 43). The case is attributed to the same Boston shop that produced Henry Bromfield's clock case (fig. 27). Both have similar molding profiles and waist doors with integral moldings cut with the same scratch stock that produced the lower element of their arched cornices. Either Claggett or his patrons were importing Boston cases by the 1730s. The earliest Boston cases with his movements have elaborate burl walnut veneers, and one has a history of descent in the Bull family of Rhode Island.[53]

Figure 44 *Abraham Redwood*, attributed to Samuel King (1749–1819), Newport, ca. 1780. Oil on canvas. 42½" × 33½". (Courtesy, Redwood Library and Athenaeum, Newport, Rhode Island.)

Figure 45 Side chair, Boston, 1740–1755. Walnut. H. 38¾", W. 20½". (Private collection; illustrated in The John Brown House Loan Exhibition of Rhode Island Furniture, 1965, pl. 8.)

Samuel Grant's accounts document the direct and indirect shipment of chairs to Rhode Island during the same time frame. For example, on February 1, 1744/45, Grant recorded a transaction with "Samuel Rhodes of Newport." Other customers included "Sarah Leech of Newport" and "Col.º Charles Church of Bristoll." Leech purchased sixteen looking glasses and some fabric valued at £166.5 on May 20, 1737, and Church purchased "8 Wallnutt Chairs Seats Covered with Leather @ 80/ . . . 32.0.0" in 1746. Grant also sold numerous chairs to ship captains who traveled between Boston, Newport, and New York.[54]

Newport merchant Abraham Redwood (1709–1788) purchased Boston chairs through his agent Stephen Greenleaf (also an agent for Gerard Beekman). On May 26, 1749, Greenleaf wrote, "I received yours via friend Proud and have ordered 8 chairs and two roundabouts . . . which will be strong and neat and not high priced." Samuel King's (1748/9–1819) portrait of Redwood depicts the sitter in a roundabout chair that may be one of the two mentioned in Greenleaf's letter (fig. 44).[55]

Newport Chairs in the Boston Style
Most of the Boston chairs with Rhode Island histories are export grade,

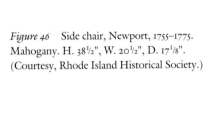

Figure 46   Side chair, Newport, 1755–1775.
Mahogany. H. 38½", W. 20½", D. 17⅛".
(Courtesy, Rhode Island Historical Society.)

such as the set that reportedly belonged to Parson Thomas Smith of Newport (fig. 45). These chairs and late baroque examples made during the 1720s and early 1730s introduced many of the details found in later Newport seating. All of the design features of the chair illustrated in figure 46 are taken from Boston models but stated in a strong Newport accent. The single-crook stiles, baluster-shaped splat, crest shape, and simple carved shell are similar to those on many Boston export-quality chairs (see fig. 34), but the slender stretchers with round shouldered swells and distinctive claw-and-ball feet are typical of Newport work.

Other Newport chairs manifest similar interpretations of Boston designs. A side chair attributed to John Goddard (fig. 47) combines the overall silhouette of the Boston chair with Newport-style knee carving and claw-and-ball feet that relate to those attributed to his master Job Townsend. The Goddards and Townsends were making chairs by the early 1760s.[56]

Figure 47   Side chair, Newport, 1755–1775. Mahogany; maple slip seat. H. 39⁵⁄₈", W. 19⁷⁄₈", D. 16¹⁄₄". (Courtesy, Metropolitan Museum of Art; Rogers Fund, 1955.)

Coastal Shipping and Shopping

From its founding in the 1630s until nearly the mid-eighteenth century, Boston was the principal market for English imports in the colonies. Using canny salesmanship, the city's merchants parlayed their urban mystique into profit. As cities such as New York, Philadelphia, and Newport expanded their commercial enterprises, however, the balance of power began to shift and the gradual diversion of European trade from Boston challenged the long-standing dominance of the city's merchants.

By the late 1740s, the Atlantic marketplace began to change as traders in smaller ports attempted to wean themselves from their Boston suppliers. In every port, colonists endeavored "to carve out profitable niches." In 1750, Providence merchant Obadiah Brown sent the *Smithfield* to London with a "three-folio-page order for British manufactures." As historian James B. Hedges observed, "Brown was in a sense proclaiming the mercantile independence of Providence. He was by-passing the great men of Newport and Boston, from whom Providence shopkeepers had largely purchased their English goods, and he was sending out a ship under his own directions to bring back his own supplies from London and Bristol." Savvy Rhode Island businessmen such as John Banister sought to engage in direct trade with London, being "fully Convinc'd" that such a move presented "the only method to make them selves Independent of the Bay Government, to whom they have a mortal aversion."[57]

As a result of higher taxes, rising inflation, and competition, tradesmen and shopkeepers struggled to maintain their place in Boston's economic structure during the third quarter of the eighteenth century. Historian James A. Henretta noted that, "without increasing returns from the lucrative 'carrying' trade, Boston's merchants could no longer subsidize the work of the shopkeepers, craftsmen, and laborers who supplied and maintained the commercial fleet." The demand for ships, provisions, and arms stimulated the city's economy during the French and Indian War but only temporarily. In 1760, Reverend Andrew Burnaby wrote:

> The province of Massachusets-Bay [sic] has been . . . on the decline. Its inhabitants have lost several branches of trade, which they are not likely to recover again. They formerly supplied . . . other parts of the continent, with dry goods, and received specie in return: but since the introductions of paper-currency they have been deprived of great part of this commerce. Their ship-trade is considerably decreased, owing to their not having been so careful in the construction of vessels as formerly. . . . they have had also a considerable number of provincial troops . . . in pay during the course of the present war, and have been burthened with heavy taxes.

Similarly, Henry Lloyd II remarked, "poor Boston what with loss of Trade & inhabitants & heavy Taxes is reduc'd to a pretty low Ebb." For the first time since its founding, Boston experienced a drop in population as the number of inhabitants declined from 16,382 in 1743 to 15,631 in 1760. At the same time, New York's population rose from 11,000 to 18,000, Philadelphia's rose from 13,000 to 23,750, and Newport's rose from 6,200 to 7,500.[58]

As Boston grappled with these various issues, smaller New England ports, such as Newbury, Salem, Newport, and Portsmouth, expanded their shipping and shipbuilding industries and increased their trade with the West Indies and southern colonies. By 1760, Boston was the only colonial seaport with a stagnant economy. In New York, the total value of British and European imports climbed from £54,957 in 1744 (the start of King George's War) to £267,000 in 1750 and to £480,106 by 1760. Goods that had formerly entered the colonies through Boston were being directed to New York. In fact, when the Anglo-French skirmishes ended in 1760, New York's economic benefits exceeded those of any other colonial city. Having seen the profit potential offered by King George's War, men such as Dr. William Beekman had turned to full-fledged mercantile pursuits during the 1740s. The influx of British troops defending against the French and Indian menace triggered a cottage industry of troop supply. Noted the Reverend

Burnaby, "The present state of this province is flourishing: it has an extensive trade to many parts of the world, particularly to the West Indies. . . . The troops, by having made it the place of their general rendezvous, have also enriched it very much."[59]

As the enterprises of other townships accelerated, Boston's furniture industry stalled. Many immigrant craftsmen were instead drawn to Philadelphia, which was the largest city in North America by midcentury. Philadelphia's rapid growth and ascendance during the 1730s and 1740s stemmed from her economic relationship with the hinterland and the profitability of wheat production for overseas markets. The appeal of cheap land and the development of the interior saw smaller towns mature into "commercial satellites." As Benjamin Franklin observed, "the first drudgery of settling new colonies" was "pretty well over," and urban dwellers had the "leisure to cultivate the finer arts." [60]

By midcentury, Newport had developed industries to compete with Boston's. John Banister boasted to his clients in London that he could fashion a vessel "near 20 p cent" cheaper than those constructed at Boston. Newport's expanding shipping interests made the cabinetmaking trade and venture cargo business even more viable. Jeanne Vibert Sloane estimated that fifty-six cabinetmakers were active in Newport between 1745 and 1775, compared with sixty-four in Boston—a city with a much larger population.[61]

Port of entry records for Annapolis, Maryland, reveal that between April 6, 1756, and December 24, 1775, 128 ships arrived from Boston and sixty-seven arrived from Newport. Although the Boston to Newport ship ratio was nearly two to one, Newport cargoes were stronger in case furniture, tables, and chairs. Sloane estimated that there were approximately nine pieces of furniture per Rhode Island vessel compared to three pieces per Boston vessel. In marked contrast to the situation during the first half of the century, Newport held an advantage over Boston, having shipped 380 chairs, 25 case pieces, and 20 tables.[62]

Such was the changing commercial landscape of the English colonies at midcentury. When Boston lost its position as the preeminent depot of English imports in the colonies, the relevance of its local manufactures as products of a cutting-edge environment simply evaporated. Boston was no longer the cradle of Anglo-aestheticism in America, and Boston chairs were no longer equated with London chairs. As a result, fashionability was no longer Boston's unique marketing tool.

ACKNOWLEDGMENTS For assistance with this article, the authors thank Mark Anderson, Gavin Ashworth, Luke Beckerdite, Kristina Bogojavlensky, Michael K. Brown, Wendy A. Cooper, Bert Denker, Pauline M. de Laszlo, William Voss Elder III, Jonathan L. Fairbanks, Elizabeth D. Garrett, Wendell Garrett, Tamath Groft, Leroy Graves, Clifford Harvard, Morrison H. Heckscher, William N. Hosley, Brock Jobe, Neil Kamil, Peter Kenny, Leslie Keno, Edward Lacy, Deanne Levison, Robert Mottley, Ronald Potvin, Jon Prown, Margaret Reasor, Kevin Stayton, Jeanne Vibert Sloane, Martha H. Willoughby, Carolyn Wilson, Martin E. Wunsch, and Philip Zea. We are especially grateful to Anne Rogers Haley, whose meticulous archival work was integral to this paper.

1. Samuel Maverick, "A Brief Description of New England and the Severall Townes Therein, Together with the Present Government Thereof," *Proceedings of the Massachusetts Historical Society*, 2d series, 1 (1884–1885): 237.

2. Stylistic theories evolved into statements of fact as subsequent surveys repeated and reinforced earlier hypotheses. The authors are grateful for the pioneer observations and archival work of Ralph E. Carpenter, Joseph Downs, Benno M. Forman, Benjamin Ginsberg, Bernard Levy, S. Dean Levy, V. Isabelle Miller, and Joseph Ott. Morrison Heckscher, William Hosley, Jr., Brock Jobe, and Jeanne Vibert Sloane have also been generous with their time and knowledge, and their most recent writings indicate that they were troubled by the history they had inherited. Jobe's research on Thomas Fitch and Samuel Grant laid the foundation for much of the material presented in this article. Alan Miller attributed the carving on the Apthorp chairs and many of the objects illustrated here to Boston and to carver John Welch while working on an article titled "Roman Gusto in New England: An Eighteenth-Century Boston Furniture Designer and His Shop," in *American Furniture,* edited by Luke Beckerdite (Hanover, N.H.: University Press of New England for the Chipstone Foundation, 1993), pp. 161–201. These attributions were the foundation for the arguments presented here.

3. John J. McCusker and Russell R. Menard, *The Economy of British America, 1607–1789* (Chapel Hill: University of North Carolina Press, 1985), as quoted in Timothy H. Breen, "An Empire of Goods: The Anglicization of Colonial America, 1690–1776," *Journal of British Studies* 25, no. 3 (October 1986): 473. Brock Jobe observed that during the mid-1740s Boston exported nearly a thousand chairs per year (Brock Jobe, "Boston Furniture Industry, 1725–1760" [master's thesis, University of Delaware, 1976], p. 105). Lieutenant Governor Gooch letter to the Board of Trade, October 5, 1732, Colonial Office Papers 5.1323, Public Record Office, London (hereinafter cited COP and PRO).

4. Edmund Burke, *An Account of the European Settlements in America,* 2 vols. (1758; reprint ed., New York: Research Reprints, 1970), 2:172–73. Economist Curtis Nettles observed that "Sailings between Boston and England were so much more frequent than sailings from New York that New York carried on a great deal of its correspondence with Europe through Boston." Many New York traders simply endorsed their bills to Bostonians, who then passed them along to London collectors (Curtis Nettles, "The Economic Relations of Boston, Philadelphia, and New York, 1680–1715," *Journal of Economic and Business History* 3, [1930–1931] pp. 187, 195). On April 26, 1708, the *Boston Weekly News-Letter* reported: "Any merchant or others that have any money at New York, and want to remit the same by bills of exchange to Boston, let them apply themselves to Benjamin Faneuil at New York, where they may be supplied."

5. Sir Josiah Child, *A New Discourse of Trade* (London, 1693), as quoted in William M. Fowler, Jr., "Trye All Ports: The Port of Boston 1783-1793," in *Massachusetts and the New Nation,* edited by Conrad Edick Wright, (Boston: Northeastern University Press, 1992), p. 35. James F. Shepherd and Gary M. Walton, *The Economic Rise of Early America* (London: Cambridge University Press, 1979), pp. 47–48. Bernard Bailyn, *The Great Republic: A History of the American People* (Lexington, Mass.: D. C. Heath and Company, 1981), p. 191. The importance of shipping and shipbuilding in New England is further suggested by Massachusetts Governor Jonathan Belcher's (1682–1741) March 2, 1736/37, letter to the Lords Commissions for Trade and Plantations: "The Quantity of shipping cleared last year at the several offices was near thirty Thousand Tuns 12,000 of which may have been built the last year in this Province" (COP, PRO). William Douglass, *A Summary, Historical and Political of the First Planting, Progressive Improvements and Present State of the British Settlements in North America*, 2 vols. (Boston: Rogers and Fowle, 1749–1752), 1:539–40.

6. George Clarke, president and commander-in-chief to the General Assembly of the Province of New York, October 14, 1736, COP 5.1093. Carl Bridenbaugh, *Cities in Revolt: Urban Life in America 1743–1776* (New York: Alfred A. Knopf, 1955), p. 73. As quoted in Bruce MacMillan Bigelow, "The Commerce of Rhode Island with the West Indies, Before the American Revolution" (Ph.D. dissertation, Brown University, 1930), part 1, p. 2.

7. For colonial population figures, see Carl Bridenbaugh, *Cities in the Wilderness: The First Century of Urban Life in America, 1625–1742* (New York: Roland Press, 1938), pp. 6n, 143, 303; and Bridenbaugh, *Cities in Revolt,* pp. 5, 216. Bridenbaugh derived much of his information from Evarts B. Greene and Virginia D. Harrington, *American Population Before the Federal Census of 1790* (1932; reprint ed., Gloucester, Mass.: P. Smith, 1966). The figures for Boston are taken from Myrna Kaye, "Eighteenth-Century Boston Furniture Craftsmen," in *Boston*

Furniture of the Eighteenth Century, edited by Walter Muir Whitehill, Brock Jobe, and Jonathan Fairbanks (Boston: Colonial Society of Massachusetts, 1974), pp. 267–302. The figures for New York are taken from Lois Olcott Price, "Furniture Craftsmen and the Queen Anne Style in Eighteenth Century New York" (master's thesis, University of Delaware, 1977), pp. 145–58. The figures for Newport are taken from Wendell D. Garrett, "The Newport Cabinetmakers: A Corrected Check List," *Antiques* 73, no. 6 (June 1958): 558–61; Joseph K. Ott, "Recent Discoveries Among Rhode Island Cabinetmakers and Their Work," "More Notes on Rhode Island Cabinetmakers," and "Still More Notes of Rhode Island Cabinetmakers and Their Work," *Rhode Island History* 28, nos. 1, 2, 4 (winter, spring, and fall 1969): 18–24, 51–52, 116–21; and Jeanne A. Vibert, "Market Economy and the Furniture Trade of Newport, Rhode Island, The Career of John Cahoone, Cabinetmaker: 1745–1765" (master's thesis, University of Delaware, 1981), pp. 91–93. The figure for Newport is astonishing considering that, by the 1760s, furniture exports were an important part of Newport's economy. Vibert concluded that, during the first half of the eighteenth century, "Newport . . . had a need for imported chairs" (Jeanne A. Vibert, "Rhode Island–Attributed Queen Anne Chairs" [unpublished seminar paper, University of Delaware, 1978], p. 4).

8. For more on Grant, see Brock Jobe, "Boston Furniture Industry, 1720–1740," in Whitehill, Jobe, and Fairbanks, eds., *Boston Furniture,* pp. 26–48. For more on Grant and his family, see W. Henry Grant, *Ancestors and Descendants of Moses Grant and Sarah Pierce* (Lebanon, Pa.: Sowers Printing Company, n.d.), pp. 3, 9, 10, 12. Grant apprenticed with Boston upholsterer Thomas Fitch (1669–1736) and probably took over many of his master's accounts after Fitch's death. Robert Campbell, *The London Tradesman* (1747), as quoted in Audrey Michie, "Charleston Upholstery in All Its Branches, 1725–1820," *Journal of Early Southern Decorative Arts* 11, no. 2 (November 1985): 22. Brock Jobe and Myrna Kaye, *New England Furniture: The Colonial Era* (Boston: Society for the Preservation of New England Antiquities, 1984), p. 11.

9. Samuel Grant's Journal, November 25, 1728 to December 31, 1737. Massachusetts Historical Society (hereinafter cited as MHS).

10. Henry Wilder Foote, *Annals of King's Chapel: From the Puritan Age of New England to the Present Day,* 3 vols. (Boston: Little Brown and Company, 1896), 2:143. Samuel Grant Account Book, 1737–1760, December 26, 1740; May 15, 1749; April 19, 1749; February 5, 1746; October 25, 1736; May 13, 1741; May 18, 1748, American Antiquarian Society, Worcester, Mass. Because the term chair was also applied to riding chairs or chaises, figures listed here and elsewhere do not include references to less than six chairs or "parcels" of chairs. Between April 1, 1744, and April 1, 1745, Grant shipped 809 chairs to other coastal ports and the West Indies (Jobe, "Boston Furniture Industry 1725–1760," p. 123). British Colonies in America, Customs, Boston Clearances 1744–1748, Boston Atheneum.

11. Grant Account Book, April 17, 1744. Boston Clearances 1744–1748, April 21, 1744.

12. For similar arrangements, see merchant Benjamin Bagnall's purchase of "12 Chairs @ 43/Canvas to pack 7/ . . . 26.3.46," on July 29, 1738; merchant Peter Faneuil's purchase of "54 Chairs @ 33/ pack 8 54/ . . . 91.16.0," on September 26, 1738; New York ship captain Robert Griffen's purchase of "12 Chairs @ 32/ozanbrigs 6/ . . . 19.100," on October 17, 1740; and merchant Joshua Winslow's purchase of "12 Wallnutt Chairs 65/ . . . 39.0.0," on April 25, 1745 (Grant Account Book). Ibid., March 6, 1743/44, and April 17, 1744. Boston Clearances 1744–1748. This was probably New Providence in the Bahamas. The harbor clearances listed in the *Boston Weekly News-Letter* of April 26, 1741, confirm that "Power" cleared for "New Providence."

13. Boston Clearances 1744–1748.

14. *Pennsylvania Gazette,* September 23, 1742, and June 14, 1744, as quoted in Alfred Coxe Prime, comp., *The Arts & Crafts in Philadelphia, Maryland and South Carolina 1721–1785,* 2 vols. (Topsfield, Mass.: Wayside Press for the Walpole Society, 1929), 1: 201–2.

15. Breen, "An Empire of Goods," p. 497. For the Oldmixon quote, see Esther Singleton, *Furniture of Our Forefathers* (New York: Doubleday, Page & Company, 1908), pp. 372–73. In his *History of New-England . . . to the Year of Our Lord 1700* (London, 1747), Daniel Neil wrote, Bostonians' "customs and manners are much the same as with the English . . . In the concerns of civil life, as in their dress, tables, and conversations, they affect to be as much English as possible; there is no fashion in London but in three or four months is to be seen in Boston" (as quoted in ibid.). See Neil D. Kamil, "Hidden in Plain Sight: Disappearance and Material Life in Colonial New York," in *American Furniture,* edited by Luke Beckerdite (Hanover, N.H.: University Press of New England for the Chipstone Foundation, 1995), pp. 193–94. Kamil

notes that by 1700, "appraisers in every colony were specifically referring to leather chairs as either *Boston*, *New England*, or *Boston-made*" and that such chairs were considered "novelties of English metropolitan style." The chairs discussed in this article carried the same cultural associations.

16. Morrison H. Heckscher, *American Furniture in The Metropolitan Museum of Art, Vol.I — the Late Colonial Period: Queen Anne and Chippendale Styles* (New York: Metropolitan Museum of Art and Random House, 1985), pp. 63–64.

17. Foote, *Annals of Kings Chapel*, 2:142–44. The colonial credit and barter systems hinged upon a high degree of trust, and family ties reduced risk. In the absence of kinship, bonds of nationalism, religion, politics, or former apprenticeship were tapped with similar expectation.

18. Museum of Fine Arts, Boston, *Paul Revere's Boston, 1735–1818* (Boston: by the Museum, 1975), p. 44, no. 49. Typical was Sir William Pepperell's request of 1737 to a London correspondent for chairs "of ye Newest fashion" (Singleton, *Furniture of Our Forefathers*, p. 332).

19. Inventory of the Estate of Charles Apthorp, January 7, 1759, Suffolk County Probate, no. 11871, p. 1. At least three of the chairs have remnants of their original yellow damask upholstery: Chipstone Foundation, acc. 1993.2; Metropolitan Museum of Art, acc. 1984.21; and private collection. The chair at the Metropolitan Museum of Art is illustrated and discussed in Heckscher, *American Furniture*, pp. 63–64, no. 22.

20. Welch worked for several chairmakers and upholsterers such as Grant. On April 4, 1746, Grant recorded, "To sundry Bills paid etc. . . . Jonathan Welch, carvers 11.10.0" (Grant Account Book). For more on Welch's frame carving, see Barbara M. Ward and Gerald W. R. Ward, "The Makers of Copley's Picture Frames: A Clue," *Old-Time New England* 67 (July–December 1976): 16–20; Luke Beckerdite, "Carving Practices in Eighteenth-Century Boston," in *New England Furniture: Essays in Memory of Benno Forman*, edited by Brock Jobe (Boston: Society for the Preservation of New England Antiquities, 1987), pp. 142–62; Morrison H. Heckscher and Leslie Greene Bowman, *American Rococo, 1750–1775* (New York: Harry N. Abrams, 1992), pp. 137–42; Morrison H. Heckscher, "Copley's Picture Frames," in *John Singleton Copley in America,* edited by Carrie Rebora, Paul Staiti, Erica E. Hirshler, Theodore E. Stebbins, Jr. (New York: Harry N. Abrams, 1995), pp. 143–59. Copley referred to Welch and Boston japanner Stephen Whiting in an October 12, 1771, letter to his stepbrother, Henry Pelham: "I have parted with two small frames, but cannot give orders for more because I would have none come but what are engaged. . . . let me know what you paid Welch for carving and Whiting for Gilding and Give my compts. to Capt. Joy." Copley was working in New York at that time (Beckerdite, "Carving Practices," p. 148). For a discussion of the desk-and-bookcase, see Miller, "Roman Gusto," p. 189.

21. The Grant references are cited in Benno M. Forman, *American Seating Furniture* (New York: W. W. Norton, 1988), p. 286. Grant used the term "feet" for both feet and legs. Evidently "horsebone feet" was synonymous with cabriole legs.

22. The Dalton table is illustrated and discussed in Sotheby's, *Important American Furniture and Folk Art*, New York, October 14, 1989, lot 321. The claw-and-ball feet of the Apthorp chairs and the Dalton table are also related to the winged paw feet of two Boston tall clock cases (Miller, "Roman Gusto," pp. 179–84; see fig. 27 in this article). For more on the concertina-action table, see ibid., p. 195, fig. 51.

23. Grant Account Book, May 20, 1738, and May 25, 1739. Gooch was listed as the owner of the sloop *Eunice,* which departed for the West Indies on February 4, 1745, with "6 Desks, 4 Tables, 2 Easy Chairs." He was also listed as the "file owner" for the *Snow Blackanne*, which departed for the West Indies on May 29, 1746, with "one desk, 5 book cases" (Boston Clearances, 1744–1748). Grant Account Book, June 8, 1736, December 2, 1741, May 24, 1744.

24. The chairs are illustrated in an advertisement by the Caldwell Gallery in *Antiques* 137, no. 1 (January 1990): 177.

25. Faneuil owned "1 English Walnutt Desk" valued at £10 and "12 Carved Fineerd Chairs & a Couch" valued at £105 (Inventory of Peter Faneuil, March 28, 1743, Suffolk County Registry of Probate, no. 7877). Thomas Hancock to Francis Wilkes, Hancock Letterbook, 1735–1740, December 20, 1738, Baker Library, Harvard University.

26. Colonial Williamsburg conservator Leroy Graves was the first to observe this unusual detail. Grant Account Book, August 24, 1747. The high cost of Prescott's chairs (£79.10) probably stemmed from their upholstery. By comparison, the "6 Black Walnut Chairs" that Thomas Hancock purchased the following October cost £37.10 (ibid., October 24, 1747).

27. Grant Account Book, February 3, 1741/2. The authors thank Jeanne Vibert Sloane for this reference. See Grant Account Book, November 2, 1743, May 23, 1745, January 6, 1746, and

passim. On November 2, 1743, a "Mr. Palmer" exchanged "9 Round [probably pad] feet carv'd chairs" for "9 better @ 40."

28. Madam Winthrop's *Old Faces from the Parlor Wall* incorrectly identified Margaret as the daughter of Thomas Fayerweather and Jerusha Groce (1690–1760), New England Historic Genealogical Society (hereinafter cited NEHGS). Thomas was her brother (John B. Carney, "In Search of Fayerweather: The Fayerweather Family of Boston," *New England Historical and Genealogical Register,* vols. 144 (1990), 145 (1991), 146 (1992). This error was perpetuated in subsequent publications. The seat inscription is noted in *Paul Revere's Boston*, p. 89, no. 104. For more on Fayerweather's business, see William B. Weeden, *Economic and Social History of New England*, 2 vols. (Boston: Houghton Mifflin & Company, 1891), 2:588–89. The Fayerweather family papers at the NEHGS contain documents in which John Fayerweather is referred to as "Captain" (John B. Carney to Joan Barzilay Freund, August 24, 1995). On September 8, 1732, Grant charged Fayerweather £11 for "8 Black Wallnutt chairs cushns of Leathr" and £11.2 for "6 Maple Chairs chushn Seats of green cks." (Grant Daybook, September 8, 1732, as quoted in Forman, *Seating Furniture,* p. 287).

29. For more on the Allen desk, see Miller, "Roman Gusto," pp. 170–72. The high chest is illustrated and discussed in William Voss Elder III and Jayne E. Stokes, *American Furniture 1680–1880, From the Collection of the Baltimore Museum of Art* (Baltimore: Baltimore Museum of Art, 1987), pp. 78–79, no. 53. The Baldwin chair is illustrated in Bernard Levy and S. Dean Levy, *"Opulence and Splendor": The New York Chair, 1690–1830* (New York: Bernard & S. Dean Levy, Inc., 1984), p. 4.

30. Another very similar clock case from the same shop also has carving attributed to Welch. It reportedly belonged to Boston merchant Gilbert Deblois (1725–1791). For more on this group, see Miller, "Roman Gusto," pp. 160–200.

31. Ibid. Bernard Levy and S. Dean Levy, *Made in America* (New York: Bernard & S. Dean Levy, Inc., 1988), pp. 50–51, illustrates a Boston chair with single-crook stiles, a compass seat, turned stretchers, and a carved crest rail with imbricated scrollwork similar to that on the Apthorp chairs.

32. See the frames for Copley's portraits of Mr. and Mrs. Isaac Smith (Beckerdite, "Carving Practices," p. 154, fig. 38); the upper shell drawer of the Massachusetts blockfront chest-on-chest illustrated in Israel Sack, Inc., *American Antiques from the Israel Sack Collection*, 9 vols. (Alexandria, Va.: Highland House Publishers, 1974), 4:1056–57; the appliqué of the bookcase illustrated in Miller, "Roman Gusto," pp. 169–70, figs. 10, 11; and the drawer of the dressing table illustrated in Christopher Monkhouse and Thomas S. Michie, *American Furniture in Pendleton House* (Providence: Rhode Island School of Design, 1986), p. 78, fig. 24.

33. Alexandra W. Rollins, ed., *Treasures of State: Fine and Decorative Arts in the Diplomatic Reception Rooms of the U.S. Department of State* (New York: Harry N. Abrams, 1991), p. 92, no. 11. Philip L. White, ed., *The Beekman Mercantile Papers* (New York: New-York Historical Society, 1956), p. 315. Clearances In and Out of New York, COP, 5.1227. For more on the Aspinwall family, see Algernon Aiken Aspinwall, *The Aspinwall Genealogy* (Rutland, Vt.: Tuttle, Co., 1901). Aspinwall amassed a considerable fortune and retired at Flushing, New York (Virginia D. Harrington, *The New York Merchant on the Eve of the Revolution* [1935; reprint, Glouster, Mass.: Peter Smith, 1964], p. 27).

34. Grant Account Book, January 11, 1742, February 1, 1745/46, and February 13, 1746/47. Similarly, Grant credited Edmund Perkins's son Henry £158.3 for "chair frames" on December 28, 1739 (ibid.).

35. Grant Account Book, August 20, 1743, and September 4, 1743. On April 27, 1747, Grant furnished Perkins with "82 1/2 feet Wallnutt" valued at £37.2.6 (ibid.). Virginia walnut appears in the accounts of eighteenth-century London cabinetmakers and carvers such as Samuel Norman (P. A. Kirkham, "Samuel Norman: A Study of an Eighteenth-Century Craftsman," *Burlington*, August 1969, p. 503).

36. Perkins lost a total of £690 in tools and lumber, indicating that his shop was one of the largest in Boston. Jobe, "Boston Furniture Industry, 1725–1760," p. 83.

37. Julius M. Block, Leo Hershkowitz, Kenneth Scott, and Constance D. Sherman, eds., *An Account of Her Majesty's Revenue in the Province of New York, 1701–1709: The Customs Records of Early Colonial New York* (Ridgewood, N. J.: Gregg Press, 1966), p. 35. The letter from Fitch to Wendell is cited in Forman, *Seating Furniture*, p. 284: Forman observed that Boston-made leather chairs owned by New Yorkers "have long been believed to have been of New York origin; [because] they have been there since a week or two after they were made." The same is true of several chairs discussed in this article. Wendell subsequently moved to New York City,

where he established a successful mercantile business. He also opened a branch in Boston, which was managed by his son. The Boston operation became so successful that Wendell eventually moved there (Harrington, *The New York Merchants*, p. 218).

38. Jobe, "The Boston Furniture Industry 1720–1740," p. 28. Jobe counted 141 chairs delivered by Grant to Jacob and John Wendell between 1728 and 1740 (p. 33).

39. Grant Account Book, October 14, 1729. *New-England Weekly Journal* (Boston), October 6, 1729, and October 20, 1729. "Schermerhorn's Wharf" is included in James Lyne's 1728 map of New York. He received the land for the wharf from his father-in-law, Johannes Beekman (Richard Schermerhorn, Jr., *Schermerhorn Genealogy and Family Chronicles* [New York: Tobias A. Wright, 1914], p. 154).

40. Grant Account Book, August 9, 1736. The Faneuil reference is from William B. Weeden, *Economic and Social History of New England, 1620–1789*, 2 vols. (Boston: Houghton, Mifflin & Company, 1891), 2:615–16. Faneuil also had regular business dealings with New York merchant Gulian Verplanck. Grant Account Book, November 28, 1748. Henry Bromfield Account Book, January 8, 1747/48, Bromfield Papers, vol. 16, p. 116, NEHGS. Bromfield seems to have been very familiar with the New York market. On September 26, 1748, he debited Bostonian "Robert Pateshall's New Y^k a/c" £91 and credited the same to "Isaac Lattouch's New Y^k a/c for Cash he paid him at Sundry times." Pateshall's name appears frequently in Bromfield's accounts. Weedon, *History of New England*, 2:616. Under the heading "May 1736," the "Charles Apthorp Ledger Book," vol. 12, 1732 through November 1736, notes, "Benjamin Burroughs pd for a Certificate of a box sent Letouche therin to N. York 5/ pewter 18 0.6.0."

41. New York: Shipping Returns 1731–1738; New York: Shipping Returns 1735–1752; and New York Treasurer's Accounts 1739–1754 in COP 5.1225, COP 5.1226, and COP 5.1227, respectively. Listings of less than six chairs were not included in this tally. As quoted in Esther Singleton, *Social New York Under the Georges, 1714–1776* (New York: D. Appleton, 1902), p. 375.

42. Henry Lloyd II to Henry Lloyd, September 24, 1748, and Henry Lloyd II to Henry Lloyd, May 27, 1749, both in *Papers of the Lloyd Family of Manor of Queens Village, Lloyd's Neck, Long Island, New York 1654–1820*, 2 vols. (New York: New-York Historical Society, 1927), 1:410, 424. Henry II also shipped Boston chairs to other New Yorkers. On May 22, 1752, he asked his father to "take care of a Dozen Chairs for Mr. Welles of Stamford to be deliver'd to you at Queens Village" (ibid., p. 497).

43. William Smith, Jr., *The History of the Province of New-York, Volume One: From the First Discovery to the Year 1732*, 2 vols. (1757; reprint ed., Cambridge: Harvard University Press, 1972), 2:226. Henry Lloyd II to Henry Lloyd, December 1, 1758, in *Papers of the Lloyd Family*, 2:733.

44. Several letters in the Lloyd papers document their association with Beekman. For example, see *Papers of the Lloyd Family*, 1:254, 255, 270. Thomas Fitch Account Books, March 13, 1724, and May 25, 1724 (microfilm), MHS. New York: Shipping Returns 1735–1752 and 1739–1754, COP 5.1226 and COP 5.1227. Beekman's ships made three round trips between March 25, 1739, and September 29, 1740, alone.

45. The portrait is illustrated in Rebora, et al., eds., *Copley in America*, p. 91, fig. 81. This combination of woods is not found in New York upholstered furniture of the same period. A later Boston settee at the Metropolitan Museum in New York has the same secondary woods, and both objects have birch crest rails (See Heckscher, *American Furniture*, pp. 140–41, no. 83). On May 3, 1739, Grant sold John Potwine of Hartford "1 Settee green Harrateen . . . 23.18.0" (Grant Account Book). It cost almost twice as much as similarly upholstered easy chairs.

46. The splat was enlarged by directly quoting the profile of the side chair splat and then broadened along the outer edge by 1/2 inch in width and 3/4 inch in height.

47. See Luke Beckerdite, "Origins of the Rococo Style in New York Furniture and Interior Architecture," in Beckerdite, ed., *American Furniture* (1993), p. 42, for an armchair with eagle head arm terminals attributed to the shop of New York and Charleston, South Carolina, carver Henry Hardcastle. Hardcastle probably moved from New York to Charleston during the summer of 1755.

48. The chairs are thought to commemorate the 1742 marriage of Judge Robert R. Livingston and Margaret Beekman (Levy and Levy, *The New York Chair*, p. 7). A turret-top card table that descended in the Verplanck family is illustrated in Heckscher, *American Furniture*, pp. 174–75, no. 105. A china table that descended in the Halstead family of Milton Neck or Rye, New York, is illustrated in Charles F. Hummel, *A Winterthur Guide to American Chippendale Furniture: Middle Atlantic and Southern Colonies* (New York: Rutledge Books, 1976), p. 45, fig. 37.

49. Garrett, "A Corrected Check List," pp. 558–61. In a 1763 letter to John Goddard, Moses

Brown mentioned "The cherry Table & Leather Chairs I sent ye Money for" (Ralph E. Carpenter, Jr., *The Arts and Crafts of Newport, Rhode Island 1640–1820* [Newport, R.I.: Preservation Society of Newport County, 1954], p. 37). On December 27, 1766, Job Townsend billed Stephen Aryault £180 for "6 chairs made of Black Walnut" (Mabel M. Swan, "The Goddard and Townsend Joiners: Part I," *Antiques* 50 [April 1946]: 230). The aforementioned references are cited in Vibert, "Rhode Island–Attributed Queen Anne Chairs," p. 10. Virginia Shipping Returns, COP 5.1443-47. (The Virginia Returns are fragmentary and deal with six different ports.) Similarly, a survey of shipping returns for Charleston, South Carolina (returns for 1738–1752 missing), revealed that over seventy-five chairs arrived on Boston vessels between 1736 and 1763, but no chairs were listed on Rhode Island ships before 1759 (Shipping Returns: S. Carolina, 1736–1754, COP 5.510).

50. Carl Bridenbaugh, ed., *Gentleman's Progress. The Itinerarium of Dr. Alexander Hamilton, 1744* (Chapel Hill: University of North Carolina Press, 1948), pp. 85, 221.

51. New York Shipping Returns: 1735–1752, COP 5.1226. The Government of Rhode Island Answers to General Inquiries Sent . . . Relating to that Colony, November 9, 1731, COP 5.1268. Bridenbaugh, *Cities in Revolt*, p. 56.

52. Gerard G. Beekman to Stephen Greenleaf, August 11, 1746, and Gerard C. Beekman to John Channing, September 1, 1746, both in White, ed., *Beekman Mercantile Papers,* 1:5. The chairs mentioned in Beekman's letter were shipped with Captain Robert Griffith, a New York mariner who frequently sailed to Boston and Rhode Island and who did business with Samuel Grant. For example, Griffith purchased "1 crimson easie chair & packing . . . 12.18.0" on September 2, 1740, and "1 crimson easie chair [and 1] blew ditto . . . 25.14.0," "1 couch frame squab & pillow . . . 8.11.7," and "12 chairs @32/ 6 oznabrigs 6/ . . . 19.10.0" on October 17, 1740 (Grant Account Book). William Johnston is cited in Kaye, "Boston Furniture Craftsmen," p. 285. Thomas Johnson's label appears on a Boston tall clock case with a movement by Boston clockmaker Benjamin Bagnall (Joseph Downs, "American Japanned Furniture," *Old-Time New England* 28, no. 2 [October 1937]: 65). For more on the Claggetts, see Richard L. Champlin, "High Time: William Claggett and His Clockmaking Family," *Newport History* 47, pt. 3 (summer 1974): 157–90. Gerard C. Beekman to Stephen Greenleaf, December 22, 1747, and Gerard C. Beekman to John Channing, September 4, 1747, both in White, ed., *Beekman Mercantile Papers*, 1:5–28.

53. The authors were not allowed to remove the Thomas Claggett movement from the case to verify its originality. The staggered hood is made of separate, stacked elements like many Boston examples. It seems more experimental because the sides forming the frieze above the cornice are wider than the sides below the cornice, and the step does not return to the more narrowed dimensions of its base. This feature appears to have been an afterthought, perhaps to widen the sides and front of the frieze to accommodate the putti spandrel appliqués. A related clock case (at Cherry-Hill) with the brand of Albany merchant Philip Van Rensselaer (1747–1798) documents the shipment of Boston clock cases to New York during the same period as the chairs discussed in this article. The veneered clocks are illustrated in Helen Comstock, *American Furniture: Seventeenth, Eighteenth, and Nineteenth Century Styles* (New York: Viking Press, 1962), n.p. no. 186; and Oswaldo Rodriguez Roque, *American Furniture at Chipstone* (Madison, Wis.: University of Wisconsin Press, 1984), pp. 87–89. The Chipstone clock reportedly descended in the Bull family of Rhode Island.

54. Grant Account Book, February 1, 1744/45; May 20, 1737. When Dr. Hamilton visited Newport, he "took lodging att one Mrs. Leech's, a Quaker, who keeps an apothecary's shop, a sensible, discreet, and industrious old woman" (Bridenbaugh, ed., *Gentleman's Progress*, pp. 151, 246, no. 341). Grant Account Book, August 30, 1746. Also see Church's purchases of "1 Looking Glass" for £21 on May 29, 1742, and "6 Wallnutt Chairs" for £25.10 on October 23, 1746. Charles Church, son of Benjamin and Alice Church, was born on May 9, 1682, in Bristol, Rhode Island (Church of Jesus Christ of Latter-day Saints, International Genealogical Index 3.05 North America, 1994).

55. Joseph K. Ott, "Abraham Redwood's Chairs?" *Antiques* 119, no. 3 (March 1981); 672. Redwood also purchased fabrics in Boston. On October 20, 1735, "J. Boutineau, Boston" wrote: "Inclosed is severall paterns of floured Damask both silk & worsted with the pryces on the papers. They . . . look much better in the peice than patern if any of them suits you let me know which & the quantity & shall send them to you by first opportunity" (J. Boutineau to Abraham Redwood, October 20, 1735, Redwood Papers, Newport Historical Society). For more on Greenleaf acting as Redwood's agent in Boston, see Bigelow, "The Commerce of Rhode Island," part 1, pp. 14–15. Bigelow noted that "it was customary for Newport merchants

to have their sons educated in Boston and also have them serve business apprenticeships with merchants in that town." The archives at the Newport Historical Society contain numerous letters between Boston merchants, such as Peter Faneuil, James Boudoin, and Jan Boutineau, and Newporters such as Stephen Ayrault and Abraham Redwood.

56. The Smith chairs are illustrated in Joseph K. Ott, *The John Brown House Loan Exhibition of Rhode Island Furniture* (Providence: Rhode Island Historical Society, 1965), p. 8, no. 8. Leigh Keno and Joan Barzilay Freund are preparing an article on the impact of Boston's furniture exports on Newport's furniture industry from the 1720s to the early 1750s for a future volume of *American Furniture*. Vibert, "Rhode Island–Attributed Queen Anne Chairs," p. 10.

57. Breen, "An Empire of Goods," p. 491. James B. Hedges, *The Browns of Providence Plantations*, 2 vols. (Cambridge, Mass., 1952–1968), 1:8. As quoted in Bigelow, "The Commerce of Rhode Island," p. 29. In a May 28, 1739, letter to Thomas and James Hayward of London, Banister wrote, "the people of this Colony being resolved to Brake of their Dependence from Boston therefore have generously purchased the Greatest part of my Cargoe allready" (ibid.).

58. Henretta, "Colonial Boston," p. 81. Andrew Burnaby, *Travels through the Middle Settlements in North-America in the Years 1759 and 1760*, 2d ed. (1775; reprint ed., Ithaca, New York: Cornell University Press, 1960), pp. 103–4. Henry Lloyd II to Henry Lloyd, October 23, 1754, *Papers of the Lloyd Family*, 2:522. Bridenbaugh, *Cities in Revolt*, p. 5.

59. Bridenbaugh, *Cities in Revolt*, pp. 48, 45. Burnaby, *Travels through the Middle Settlements*, p. 81.

60. Bridenbaugh, *Cities in Revolt*, p. 49. Benjamin Franklin, "A Proposal for Promoting Useful Knowledge Among the British Plantations in America" (Philadelphia, 1743), as quoted in ibid., p. 243.

61. Bridenbaugh, *Cities in Revolt*, p. 72. Vibert, "Market Economy of Newport," pp. 91–93.

62. Port of Annapolis Entries, 1756–1775, Maryland, vol. 1 ms. 21, Maryland Historical Society. Vibert, "Market Economy of Newport," p. 23.

William C. Ketchum, Jr., and the Museum of American Folk Art. *American Cabinetmakers: Marked American Furniture, 1640–1940.* New York: Crown Publishers, Inc., 1995. 404 pp.; 350 bw illus., appendixes, bibliography, index. $45.00.

Hyperbole is frequently used on book jackets and promotional literature from publishers, but rarely has it been employed with more temerity than on the jacket for this volume. "*American Cabinetmakers* is one of the most important antiques books ever to be published. The first book to catalog and illustrate all known American wood furniture pieces that bear the signatures, labels, brands, impressions, or ink-stamp marks of their makers, it is an essential volume for serious collectors, antique dealers, auctioneers, museum personnel, researchers, and historical societies. . . . [It] is a classic in the antiques and collectibles field." Rarely has the hype been so ill-deserved.

Books on craftsmen and their marks are popular and extremely useful in studying the decorative arts. Edwin AtLee Barber's *Marks of American Potters* (Philadelphia: Patterson & White Co., 1904); Dorothy T. Rainwater's *Encyclopedia of American Silver Manufacturers* (in various editions of 1966, 1975, and 1986); and Ledlie Irwin Laughlin's *Pewter in America: Its Makers and their Marks* (Barre, Massachusetts: Barre Publishers, 1969) *are* classics in the field. It is comforting to have reliable reference works, such as these and many others that are thoroughly researched and conveniently arranged, on our shelves to answer the most basic questions. Furniture, however, has never been the subject of this sort of basic book on marks and craftsmen, and clearly the authors and publisher hope that collectors, antique dealers, museums, and others will buy this book to fill that void.

According to *American Cabinetmakers's* foreword and introduction, the late director of the Museum of American Folk Art, Robert Bishop, began in the 1970s, with the Henry Ford Museum's associate curator of furniture, Katherine B. Hagler, to accumulate illustrations, clippings, and notes on marked or labeled examples of American furniture. The scope of the project excluded cast- or wrought-iron furniture and examples of wicker, rattan, and "other alien materials." It also excluded clock and musical instrument makers, unless they were known to have manufactured the furniture cases as well as the contents. Only the briefest details of the cabinetmakers' histories were collected to supplement the marks. After Bishop's death in 1991, the next director of the Museum of American Folk Art, Gerard C. Wertkin, discussed the possibility of completing Bishop's compilation with William C. Ketchum, Jr., a prolific writer on various antiques subjects, whose credits include *Hooked Rugs* (1976), *Western Memorabilia* (1980), *Collecting Bottles for Fun and Profit* (1985), *Collecting the 40s and 50s for Fun and Profit* (1985), *Holiday Ornaments and Antiques* (1990), and *Country Wreaths and Baskets* (1991). With the acknowledged assistance of a number of the museum's students in the Folk Art Institute, Ketchum has produced this 404-page book.

I will not waste the reader's time with a detailed criticism or enumeration of the errors of fact in *American Cabinetmakers*. The list would, simply, be much too long. There is no evidence of any original research in this book. It appears to be a cut-and-paste job assembled from secondary sources, books, magazines, and newspapers, with virtually no attempt to confirm details of the individually marked or labeled pieces of furniture or the perfunctory "biographical" information about the craftsmen.

To illustrate this point I mention only the entries on "Silas" Ingals of Vermont and Francis Jackson of Pennsylvania, which appear, not coincidentally, on the same page (182). The mark "S.I." attributed to Silas Ingals was actually used by a Vermont chairmaker named *Samuel* Ingals, who worked in Danville. An accurate biographical entry for Samuel Ingals can be found in Charles A. Robinson's *Vermont Cabinetmakers Before 1855: A Checklist* (Shelburne, Vermont: Shelburne Museum, 1994), an indispensable work that I highly recommend. An arrow-back Windsor armchair labeled by Francis Jackson of Easton, Pennsylvania, and owned by the William Penn Memorial Museum (not the "State Museum of Pennsylvania"), Harrisburg, Pennsylvania, is cited as the basis for the entry on this craftsman. The author claims that "Nothing further is known of Jackson's shop"; however, that very piece of furniture at the museum has a printed paper label with the following text: "FRANCIS JACKSON'S/CHAIR MANUFACTORY,/NORTHAMPTON STREET, EASTON. / Where Windsor and Fancy ___ bot- / tom Chairs are done in the neatest man- / ner; also Spinning wheels, Wool wheels, / Cut reels, and all Kinds of Turning. / The best Copal Varnish, and all Kinds / of colors for graining, for sale. / [and an illegible printer's name in Easton]." Nothing further is known? Indeed!

Bibliographic "sources" at the end of this volume list the secondary works that provided the references to approximately 1,500 craftsmen in the book. Though important volumes such as Ethel Hall Bjerkoe's *The Cabinetmakers of America* (Garden City, N.Y.: Doubleday & Co., Inc., 1957); Charles F. Montgomery's *American Furniture, The Federal Period, 1785–1825* (New York: Viking Press, 1966); and John Bivins, Jr.'s *The Furniture of Coastal North Carolina, 1700–1850* (Winston-Salem, N.C.: Museum of Early Southern Decorative Arts, 1988) are included, the significant omissions are staggering: Charles J. Semowich, *American Furniture Craftsmen Working Prior to 1920: An Annotated Bibliography* (Westport, Conn.: Greenwood Press, 1984); Charles G. Dorman, *Delaware Cabinetmakers and Allied Artisans, 1655–1855* (Wilmington, Del.: Historical Society of Delaware, 1960); Gerald W. R. Ward, *American Case Furniture in the Mabel Brady Garvan and Other Collections at Yale University* (New Haven, Conn.: Yale University Art Gallery, 1988); and Sharon Darling, *Chicago Furniture: Art, Craft, & Industry, 1833–1983* (Chicago: Chicago Historical Society, 1984). A simple look at Beatrice B. Garvan's *Federal Philadelphia, 1785–1825: The Athens of the Western World* (Philadelphia: Philadelphia Museum of Art, 1987) might have revealed to the authors the fine mahogany chest-on-chest illustrated there (p. 72) made and signed by the African-American cabinetmaker, Thomas Gross, Jr., working in Philadelphia in 1807 and later.

Lastly, *American Cabinetmakers* is an affront to me and my colleagues and our predecessors at the Decorative Arts Photographic Collection in the library at Winterthur and at the many other major repositories of documentation on American furniture, such as the marvelous libraries at MESDA and the Metropolitan Museum of Art. Why would a supposed reference book, which boasts a museum as co-author, fail to utilize the most basic, well-known, and public libraries on decorative arts in America?

Bert Denker
Winterthur

Mary E. Lyons. *Master of Mahogany: Tom Day, Free Black Cabinetmaker.* New York: Charles Scribner's Sons, 1994. 42 pp.; color and bw illus., glossary, bibliography, index. $15.95.

Much has been said about the need for finding working-class role models for urban children of color, but little has been written for young readers on the lives and works of African-American artists and artisans who might be such models. As a result, examples of African-American crafts contributions to American history are largely absent from museums, libraries, and curricula. The African-American Artists and Artisans series of juvenile texts published by Charles Scribner's Sons seeks to nurture new generations through lively, well-illustrated, and thoroughly researched biographies, which also add new data to the general literature on American decorative arts.

The series is authored by Mary E. Lyons, a former school librarian in Charlottesville, Virginia, and a winner of the Carter G. Woodson Award of the National Council for Social Studies. Her research and writing have been supported by grants from the National Endowment for the Humanities and the DeWitt Wallace Reader's Digest Fund. The series includes works on twentieth-century artists Horace Pippin and Bill Traylor and on nineteenth-century quilter Harriet Powers. *Master of Mahogany: Tom Day, Free Black Cabinetmaker* is the biography of the best-known, nineteenth-century, African-American cabinetmaker and architectural joiner, Tom Day (1801–ca. 1861).

Day was born a free black at the beginning of the nineteenth century and developed a carpentry and joinery business in rural Milton, North Carolina. By the 1850s, he had become one of the state's largest cabinetmakers, supplying furnishings to state officials, churches, private homes, and the growing tobacco-based economy of the antebellum upper South. Before dying in 1861, Day was one of a small handful of black slaveholders in piedmont North Carolina. His son Devereaux went on to develop lumber and cabinetmaking interests in South America.

Lyons introduces the young reader to antebellum history, cabinetmaking, and nineteenth-century labor practices as she divides Day's early life into his indentured, journeyman, and workshop years up to 1830. Strong historical documentation supports the story of his later, highly public life as a master cabinetmaker. By drawing upon this available research, Lyons builds an objectively comprehensive, although somewhat speculative, text describing the complex life of a financially successful, slave-owning free black in the antebellum South. She also points to southern pre–Civil War racial tensions and the national financial panic of 1857 as causes of Day's economic collapse in 1859. Her focus for Day's business and documented personal activities frees this text of the cloying romanticism that too often characterizes juvenile text descriptions of nineteenth-century southern black life.

Day's work combined late Empire case piece, table, and chair forms with innovative and idiosyncratic surface embellishments, which often project distinctly African sculptural characteristics. His best work is easily distinguishable from contemporary carved mahogany and veneered pieces because of its often anthropomorphic and graceful cyma-curve treatments. Works attributed to him bring a premium in the collector market and are included in the Acacia Collection in Savannah, Georgia, and the Center for African-American Decorative Arts collection in Atlanta, Georgia. Strikingly elegant color photographs by Jim Bridges document Day's church pews, newel posts, and West African mask-like mantel carvings, and ground the text in a graphically rich context of deeply patinated and polished mahogany surfaces and sweeping sculptural forms. The reader yearns to embrace these elegant architectonic embellishments.

An opportunity is lost, however, to link the text more closely to the illustrated objects by showing how the objects were made. Inner-city youths have largely lost touch with the mechanics of crafting handmade objects, and more information could usefully have been provided on tools and techniques associated with woodworking. The absence of even a single image of an African-American actually handcrafting furnishings in a shop could have been corrected by using illustrations drawn from various archival sources. The text, although tantalizing, thus ultimately fails to draw the reader into the magic of actually designing and building such viscerally evocative forms. One sees and senses the textures of the objects without feeling the sensibilities and spirit of their maker.

Similarly, little light is shed on how much Day may have known of, or drawn upon, the Bambara sculptures that today seem so close to his newel-post forms. Nothing is yet known of his understanding of African sculpture, although late 1995 findings suggest that he had a brother who was a missionary to West Africa and with whom he corresponded. Although there was likely a nascent black commerce with former African-American settlements in Liberia and Sierra Leone in the mid-nineteenth century, much research remains to be done to determine how the African diaspora may have tried during this period to trace its roots back into tribal morphologies and symbolic sculptural forms. We learn much here from documented historical records of the life of a free black southern cabinetmaker, but not enough of the spirit of this unique craftsman or of how he might have drawn upon the design components of his African past to develop distinctively African-American decorative references.

Perhaps such questions are beyond the scope of a juvenile text, but Lyons's synthesizing research raises expectations as it extends our knowledge of Day far beyond previously published scholarly texts, with significantly more striking illustrations of Day's work than seen before. To tease but not to satisfy the imagination on questions of how African designs may have influenced African-American decorative arts in the half century before Emancipation only inspires greater curiosity about this generally underdocumented aspect of African-American contributions to the American decorative arts. *Master of Mahogany* transcends its categorization as a juvenile text by introducing us to the life of a unique nineteenth-century cabinetmaking entrepreneur and is a significant contribution to this field of research. Mary E. Lyons's work also adds to the pedagogy of incorporating a wider range of design influences into the broadly assimilationist melange of appropriated forms and embellishments that we now understand the American decorative arts to be.

Ted Landsmark
Boston University

John D. Hamilton. *Material Culture of the American Freemasons.* Lexington, Massachusetts: Museum of Our National Heritage, 1994. Distributed by University Press of New England, Hanover and London. xii + 308 pp.; 36 color and numerous bw illustrations, appendixes, bibliography, index. $75.00.

After decades of largely being ignored by the scholarly community, American fraternalism has been the focus of expanded scrutiny during the last twenty years. Following the publication of Dorothy Ann Lipson's *Freemasonry in Federalist Connecticut, 1789–1835* (1977), studies exploring the sociological, religious, and cultural implications of America's omnipresent, ritual-based, fraternal organizations have appeared with increasing frequency. Volumes such as Christopher J. Kauffman's *Faith & Fraternalism: The History of the Knights of Columbus, 1882–1982* (1982) and Lynn Dumenil's *Freemasonry and American Culture, 1880–1930* (1984) have examined individual groups, whereas Mark Carnes's *Secret Ritual and Manhood in Victorian America* (1989) and Mary Ann Clawson's *Constructing Brotherhood: Class, Gender, and Fraternalism* (1989) have explicated the larger ramifications of the American fraternal movement, which spawned bodies as diverse as the Knights of Labor, the Loyal Order of Moose, and the B'nai Brith. Our understanding of the historical importance of America's oath-bound voluntary organizations, which at their height in the 1890s were estimated to include one of every five American men, also has been enriched in recent years by the work of scholars including John L. Brooke, C. Lance Brockman, Steven C. Bullock, Anthony Fels, Kathleen Smith Kutolowski, and William A. Muraskin. These investigations have been informed by the new perspectives of the last thirty years, which have placed race, class, and gender at the center of historical discourse.

The new literature, however, largely has ignored the importance of material culture as a conduit of meaning within American fraternalism. Artifacts and works of art have been central to American fraternal life from the moment that the first Freemasonry lodge was convened in the colonies in the early eighteenth century. Over the last three centuries fraternalism has manifested itself physically in a vast range of forms and in almost every conceivable medium. The material heritage includes objects as diverse as eighteenth-century silver Masonic jewelry created by Paul Revere, celluloid temperance souvenirs distributed in the 1890s, and buildings such as the twenty-three-story office tower erected by the Supreme Council of the Knights of Columbus in New Haven, Connecticut, in 1969. Although most institutional collections of American decorative arts and historical artifacts contain objects with fraternal associations, this massive body of material has yet to be adequately documented or explicated.

John D. Hamilton's *Material Culture of the American Freemasons* is the fourth publication from the Museum of Our National Heritage in this institution's continuing effort to fill this void in the scholarly literature. Like the first three titles edited by Barbara Franco, *Masonic Symbols in American Decorative Arts* (1976), *Bespangled Painted & Embroidered: Decorated Masonic Aprons in America 1790–1850* (1980), and *Fraternally Yours: A Decade of Collecting* (1986), the present work was produced to accompany an exhibition mounted by the museum in Lexington, Massachusetts—in this instance, a show entitled "The Oblong Square: Lodge Furnishings and Paraphernalia in America Since 1733," held from June 13, 1993, to February 20, 1994. As a series, these four catalogues comprise an invaluable means of entry into the arcane world of fraternal objects and serve as useful tools for investigating American symbolic thought.

Material Culture of the American Freemasons is organized into seven topical chapters, accompanied by six appendixes, a foreword, and a preface. Hamilton, the author, has grouped objects achronologically, according to their function within the fraternity's activities. Lodge room furnishings, for example, are found in chapter three, funereal accoutrements comprise chapter seven, and objects used in dining are gathered in chapter six. Each chapter includes at least one thematic essay, but the bulk of the text is arranged into entries related to individual items from the collections of the Museum of Our National Heritage. These entries are meticulous in documenting the artifacts' provenances and historical associations. The author is to be commended for the extensive research that this undertaking obviously entailed.

The book's greatest strength is the breadth of material illustrated and discussed, ranging from inlaid desks to blindfolds (known within the Masonic fraternity as "hoodwinks") and from casket handles to door knockers. This text will be a useful reference for curators and collectors in their efforts to identify Masonic items and locate related examples. The appendixes listing names, dates, and locations for Masonic artists, regalia manufacturers and dealers, and engravers of Masonic certificates and aprons will also prove invaluable for future scholarship on the subject.

Furniture comprises only a small portion of the volume, but most of the primary Masonic genres of furnishings are represented. Eighteenth-century Chippendale-style side chairs are illustrated and discussed, as are idiosyncratic, nineteenth-century officers' chairs, grain-painted altars, ceremonial candlesticks, stenciled chests, Windsor-style settees, and inlaid desks. The museum's collecting, however, has tended toward early and unique items, and this publication reflects that emphasis. Between 1870 and 1930, vast quantities of Masonic furniture were mass produced in factories by firms such as the American Seating Company, S. Karpen & Bros., and M. C. Lilley & Company. Unfortunately, this major category of Masonic furniture is underrepresented here. An additional appendix documenting these nineteenth- and twentieth-century manufacturers could have filled a significant research void, since many of their products exist today and frequently appear in the marketplace.

Although individuals unfamiliar with Masonic history and culture will find this book helpful as an introductory guide to Masonic artifacts, they also may experience frustration in assimilating the mass of seemingly loosely related information contained here. In spite of its detailed examination of hundreds of individual objects, the structure of this catalogue, which lacks a central historical narrative or explicit thesis, provides insufficient framework for easy digestion of the data presented. Freemasonry is an extraordinarily complex organization that has developed organically over more than three hundred years on six continents and has been shaped by esoteric traditions including hermeticism, Rosicrucianism, numerology, and Martinism. Since each chapter mingles examples from the Scottish Rite, the York Rite, and the Blue Lodge (with a few from the Ancient Arabic Order of Nobles of the Mystic Shrine added to the mix), newcomers to the field may have trouble sorting out the separate Masonic rites, let alone untangling the various traditions influencing them.

Part of the problem may be that Hamilton, a member of the fraternity, has found his scholarship fettered by his own Masonic vows of secrecy. "In describing the significance of items in the collection," he informs us in the preface, "a fine distinction has been made between providing meaningful information for those outside Freemasonry, and in not breaking faith with the confidentiality of ritual" (p. xi). In ensuring that secrets were not revealed, though, the author has unnecessarily denied the reader significant information that would have aided the exegesis of these pieces. Nowhere, for example, does Hamilton inform us that the central ritual of Freemasonry revolves around the reenactment of the murder, burial, and disinterment of Hiram Abif, the architect responsible for constructing Solomon's Temple. This narrative framework, available to the general public in any number of exposés published in the nineteenth century, informs the interpretation of most Masonic objects. All of the brotherhoods' teachings, and thus the significance of the objects used in their inculcation, are based upon the moral lessons inherent in this central narrative, which is enacted in the lodge room during every initiation.

The volume's disregard for recent scholarship on fraternal organizations is also troubling and inexplicable. Hamilton fails to address the insights on Freemasonry and fraternalism presented in the important new studies mentioned previously, and these works are omitted from his bibliography. Rather than entering into the dynamic discourse concerning Freemasonry currently occurring within the academy, the author relies heavily upon the antiquarian publications of Masonic research bodies, Grand Lodges, and other such organizations. By following this conservative course, he documents Masonic individuals, activities, and objects without substantially relating Freemasonry to the social transformations taking place in American society over time. The late eighteenth- and early nineteenth-century rise of the Masonic Knights Templar, for example, who were supposedly successors to the holy warriors of the crusades, is discussed without reference to romanticism and the contemporaneous growth of American interest in things medieval. Similarly, with twentieth-century materials, the reader is shown elaborate theatrical costuming for the presentation of rituals but receives no analysis of the societal forces that motivated men in the 1920s to dress as Biblical patriarchs and Roman centurions.

By presenting materials topically rather than chronologically, and by isolating the fraternity from its cultural context, Hamilton has given us a volume that is rich in factual information but lacking in historical perspective. This work portrays Masonry as unchanging. The Brethren apparently feasted, practiced ritual, and buried each other with little variation from the eighteenth century to the twentieth. This perspective, though, denies the vitality and historical complexity that makes Masonic history worthy of study. Although certain continuities do exist, Masonry is not a monolithic cultural entity existing in isolation from society. Throughout the last three centuries Masonry has both shaped, and been shaped by, transformations in American culture. The fraternity, rather than remaining static, is continually in flux. Over time, Masonic membership repeatedly has boomed and collapsed and experienced changing socioeconomic and ethnic profiles. New technologies have influenced ritual practices. Innovative Masonic organizations, including the Order of the Eastern Star for women and DeMolay for teenage boys, have been invented to meet changing social mores and demands. By focusing tightly upon individual artifacts rather than on larger patterns of object usage, this study provides data for examining the complexity of American Masonic history but does not explore the subject comprehensively.

Although one might wish it were analytically more complex, *The Material Culture of the American Freemasons* is a noteworthy contribution to the study of an overlooked, but significant, facet of American material life. More American Masonic artifacts are illustrated and described between the covers of this volume than have appeared before in a single publication. For the foreseeable future, this text will be the standard reference guide for American Masonic objects.

William D. Moore
Livingston Masonic Library

John A. Fleming. *The Painted Furniture of French Canada, 1700–1840*. Camden East, Ontario: Camden House Publishing; Hull, Quebec: Canadian Museum of Civilization, 1994. Distributed by Firefly Books. 179 pp.; numerous color and bw illus., appendixes, bibliography, index. $34.95.

John Fleming's *The Painted Furniture of French Canada, 1700–1840* is the first major monograph on Canadian furniture since the publication of Jean Palardy's seminal *The Early Furniture of French Canada*. Despite Fleming's long history as a collector and furniture historian, the book is a major disappointment. The publication lacks a scholarly approach, which could have made it an invaluable monograph for Canadian and American collectors, curators, and dealers. Fleming takes a highly personal approach to his study of Canadian furniture, an approach that appears to reflect a poor understanding of furniture history over the past twenty years as well as of current material culture approaches to the field. The reader is presented with an undocumented and unsubstantiated "aesthetic and psychological" analysis that purports to explain why Canadians preferred particular paint colors on furniture. The primary saving grace of the book is that it publishes many heretofore unknown pieces of furniture and that most of the photographs by James A. Chambers are of superb quality.[1]

The monograph is organized with chapters on six specific subjects: "Settlement," "Styles," "Furniture," "Surface, Colour and Decoration," "Conclusion," and "Epilogue." Each of these is further broken down into separate essays. For example, the section titled "Settlement" is further divided into "The Houses" and "Interior Space." Under "Styles," the Louis XIII, Louis XIV, Régence, Louis XV, Chippendale, Adam, Hepplewhite and Sheraton, and Folk traditions are discussed. The "Furniture" section includes essays on woods, construction, hardware, and upholstery. Finally, the section titled "Surface, Colour and Decoration" also includes essays on "Painted Surfaces" and "Sculptural Decoration."

The essays not specifically dealing with the analysis of furniture styles consolidate useful information. In several cases this information is not concisely available to scholars in this country. For instance, in the first essay titled "Settlement," Fleming outlines the history of the French colony, including its settlement patterns, population makeup, and origins, by citing census material as well as contemporary primary sources. A similarly factual presentation of information appears in Fleming's analysis of houses built by French settlers (pp. 28–35) and in his discussion of the interiors of these houses, where he makes a clear connection between house builders and the creators of large, frequently integral case furniture such as armoires. He makes this connection by citing building contracts calling for the creation of both structures and furnishings to go in them (see pp. 43–47). Contemporary travel accounts and inventories are also cited in this section, giving the reader a good understanding of lifestyles and concepts of interior decoration in rural Canada during both the French and British regimes into the nineteenth century.[2]

In the chapter titled "Styles," Fleming's analysis changes tone. Although he outlines the court styles that influenced design in French Canada, he also makes comments that can be interpreted as ethnocentric and are not substantiated by analysis or comparison. For example, when comparing furniture forms made in French Canada with those made in the United States, he makes the following statement: "French furniture, as compared with English and German furniture, the two other major forms in colonial North

America, gave to the early furniture of New France three general characteristics: exuberance of line, harmony of proportion . . . and the integration of decorative features with structure" (p. 52). Not only are such seemingly factual statements purely subjective, they also sound ethnocentric with their implied relegation of non-French furniture forms to a second-best category. Likewise, France is presented as a primary origin of the styles used in the United States and in England through statements such as "English furniture of the 18th century was influenced by French and Dutch designs" (p. 67). Certainly this influence may have been true to an extent, but the statement, like many others throughout the book, is presented glibly, without analysis, examples, or references to back up the author's beliefs.

Fleming's chapter titled "Furniture" includes a discussion of the furniture-making industry in Canada. Beginning with census information identifying occupations by crafts and continuing through apprenticeship records, he cites schools believed to have educated carpenters and cabinet-makers during the seventeenth and eighteenth centuries and mentions a number of extant contracts between joiners and clients for the creation of furniture. Yet this section and a subsequent one titled "Construction" are notably weak in the analysis of the actual furniture under discussion. On page 83, for example, Fleming comments that "many of the surviving examples of French Canadian furniture have been executed with the greatest technical competence and a sure sense of design to the smallest unseen detail." Earlier in the book he notes that the dating of furniture is approximate, "based upon an analysis of construction techniques, other material characteristics (types of wood, thickness of planks, use of pins, nails, glue, paints, colours and combinations of colours, layers of paint, et cetera) or style features that establish a *terminus post* . . ." (p. 21). Sadly, none of these construction details are explained in the appropriate chapter on furniture, or anywhere else in the book, or illustrated in photographic form. Indeed, many of these details are discussed only haphazardly in a small number of the object captions, leaving the reader without any sense of how frequently they occur or what patterns or generalizations might be deduced as a result of them; nor are there *any* photographs of construction details to allow the reader to observe what Fleming is referring to. Though the author's assumptions may well be true, a book that purports to be a source of information on Canadian painted furniture should at least outline criteria with which to judge, date, and attribute furniture.

Some of these comments, furthermore, seem again very protective. By saying that Canadian furniture has been "executed with the greatest of technical competence" one might assume that Canadian furniture of the French period (before 1760, one would assume) is very finely constructed. In fact, Canadian furniture prior to and after 1760 is anything but finely crafted. By comparison to what was contemporaneously made in the United States, it is very crudely constructed. Drawer sides and bottoms and even fronts are planks, sometimes up to two-inches thick, and to describe them as executed with the greatest of technical competence is misleading.[3] Rather than obfuscating this fact, Fleming might better have spent his time by clearly identifying and illustrating this feature and other characteristics of Canadian furniture and explaining them in terms of the technological and historical development of the Canadian colony.

In the following chapters on "Paint" and "Sculptural Decoration," Fleming assigns great importance to the use of certain colors and decorative patterns. He writes: "The colours that predominated in 18th-century French Canada were the blues, green, and reds of 17th-century France. These are colours still identified with the natural world in the symbolic and psychological meanings, both sacred and secular" (p. 138). Throughout the chapter he makes reference to theory with respect to the use of color: For example, "the eye sees the greatest elementary beauty in simple colours: red, yellow, green and blue. . . . Blue, as the colour of the sky and secondarily of water, is associated in European tradition with fidelity and with things spiritual, while green has always been linked to youth, growth and hope" (pp. 119–20). He attempts to identify the use of certain colors with specific values and associations, some unconscious, made by Canadian consumers. Sadly, although Fleming is able to cite a number of sources for the importation of color pigments for the manufacture of paints in Canada before the English occupation of the 1760s, most of his documentation for the use of color postdates the Treaty of Paris and, in fact, appears in English/American publications dating after 1763. Very significantly, this section also lacks any reference to chemical analysis of the painted surfaces of the furniture illustrated in the book. In fact, the only paint analysis to appear in the book is presented in the object captions of the handful of pieces that belong to Canadian museums such as the Royal Ontario Museum, the Canadian Conservation Institute, or the Canadian Museum of Civilization.

In the preface to the book Fleming makes the disclaimer that he has "not tried . . . to lard a lean book 'with the fat of others' works'" (p. 10). Sadly, this is too true. The publication could have been the one scholars have been waiting for. It could have synthesized more than thirty years of Canadian scholarship since Palardy's publication, but instead it is a wasted opportunity. Some attempt could have been made, for instance, to identify bodies of work, either by region or by maker. This identification could have occurred through the analysis of construction techniques, through a scientific analysis of woods used in stylistically related pieces, or with a serious and systematic chemical analysis of pigments used. None of this scholarship appears in the book except in an amateurish and haphazard way.

Francis J. Puig
University of South Florida

1. Jean Palardy, *The Early Furniture of French Canada* (Toronto: Macmillan, 1965). Fleming, incidentally, lists a large number of published articles in his bibliography, which add to the references on early Canadian furniture and technology since the publication of Palardy's book. Fleming is identified as a collector and historian of Canadian furniture in the biographical material on the book's jacket. See especially pages 121 through 124. Unfortunately, the analysis of these pieces is weak at best. Construction analysis is rudimentary, wood analysis is nonexistent, and provenance is generally not given. Detail photographs are also lacking.

2. Notably absent from this essay and elsewhere throughout the book is anything more than a passing mention of the British occupation of Canada after the Treaty of Paris in 1763, which ended the French and Indian Wars. This treaty granted Canada and its territories east of the Mississippi River to Britain. At almost the same moment, the secret Treaty of Fontainbleau of 1762 granted to Spain France's holdings west of the Mississippi River, thus virtually ending France's empire in North America. The same pattern existed in the French settlements of the Mississippi River Valley in the eighteenth century. See Francis J. Puig, "The Early Furniture of the Mississippi River Valley, 1760–1820," in *The American Craftsman and the European Tradition, 1620–1820*, edited by Francis J. Puig and Michael Conforti (Minneapolis: Minneapolis Institute of Arts, 1989), pp. 159–61.

3. I refer the reader to a commode of curly maple and pine illustrated in Puig, "Early Furniture of the Mississippi River Valley," p. 171. This piece of furniture, probably made in the Quebec region after the English occupation of Canada, is remarkably thickly constructed, but by no means unique given the many similarly constructed pieces in Quebec museums that this author has examined. In this instance, the shaped drawer fronts are close to three-inches thick in sections. With respect to the fine detailing referred to by Fleming, this piece, again like many others, has only two large dovetails instead of the four or five more commonly found on contemporaneous pieces made in the United States.

Kenneth Joel Zogry. *"The Best the Country Affords"*: Vermont Furniture, *1765–1850*. Bennington, Vt.: Bennington Museum, 1995, 176 pp.: 56 color and 145 bw illus., bibliography, index. $55.00; $37.00 pb.

Charles A. Robinson, with an introduction by Philip Zea. *Vermont Cabinetmakers and Chairmakers Before 1855: A Checklist*. Shelburne, Vt.: Shelburne Museum, 1995. 126 pp.; 14 color and bw illus., index. $14.95.

"The Best the Country Affords": Vermont Furniture, 1765–1850 provides a striking departure from recent patterns in the design and presentation of furniture exhibition catalogues. The latter usually begin with several essays, followed by a series of detailed, formulaic descriptions and analyses of a body of furniture, frequently grouped chronologically by form. Kenneth Joel Zogry stated a desire to produce a cohesive, "user friendly" publication, which would provide "an important contribution to the field that showcased the furniture and was aesthetically pleasing." His solution was a geographical approach rather than one organized by furniture forms or arranged strictly chronologically; furthermore, "A conscious decision was made not to bog down the narrative or the notes with minute descriptions of construction or condition" (p. 7).

Zogry divides Vermont into five regions (the southeast, northeast, southwest, west central, and northwest). He introduces each region with a short chronological overview and a contextual framework for the furniture. This orientation is followed by a series of catalogue entries of furniture from the region, organized in an approximate chronology. When possible, Zogry "group[s] significant objects together, whether from the same shop tradition, town, or family," when a grouping provides "a particularly interesting comparison" (p. 7).

Having just suggested the need for new approaches in furniture catalogues (see my review of Brock Jobe's *Portsmouth Furniture* in *Studies in the Decorative Arts* 3, no. 2 [Spring-Summer 1996]: 139–40), I was especially intrigued with the approach taken in *"The Best the Country Affords."* There are some major benefits to the design. In both essays and the catalogue entries, the pieces are put into geographic, economic, and social context both locally and regionally. Zogry continuously sought for the sources of the furnitures' design and construction, looking at specific features of the individual pieces and backgrounds of the makers. In the process, he revealed a much more heterogeneous world than has been generally conceived of for Vermont, one that was quite at variance with traditional views regarding its furniture. These notions had generally postulated that there were few local makers and those that did exist created unsophisticated wares that were pale mimics of their urban counterparts—exotic folk art creations or essentially plain products only in part saved by the use of bright paints over local woods. (This same image has also influenced conventional thinking about Maine and New Hampshire furniture, with, of course, the begrudging possibility that Portsmouth might have had something more to offer.) Zogry found pieces ranging from the very plain to the highly sophisticated. Pieces frequently reflected outside influences but quite as often retained local features that emphasized the creativity and design concepts of the local makers. As was true elsewhere, factory practices affected styles and construction techniques, and although paint was often used for decorative purposes, so too were mahogany and rosewood veneers. This world, then, was more complex and sophisticated than has previously been thought.

Despite the diversity, patterns emerge from the text and pictures. In the eighteenth century, settlers moved into southern Vermont in increasing numbers, and clearly many brought with them traditions from Connecticut and New York. The latter would continue significantly to influence patterns in western Vermont. To the east, though, increasing influence came from eastern Massachusetts and New Hampshire, especially as turnpikes and other overland routes opened the area. By mid-century, the railroad further strengthened ties between Vermont and eastern Massachusetts and New Hampshire. That period also saw a rapid expansion of small furniture factories, especially in the central region of the state, which were providing substantial quantities of fairly unpretentious furniture as well as some relatively sophisticated and stylish objects. By that point, much of what was being made in Vermont echoed national patterns and exhibited fewer local characteristics.

There is much to be said for Zogry's approach. It explicitly ties furniture to the overall societal matrix and considers specific construction and design details that illuminate overall themes. He also eliminates the blizzard of marginal data. Happily, one does not have to slog through facts about a replaced stretcher or a chalked number "632" on the back of a chest of drawers; nor is there great detail on whose auction hall or antique establishment the piece has moved through. The absence of such data is refreshing.

There is still room for improvement, however. Because of the fluidity in topics being presented (makers here, styles there, shop traditions further on), one tends to get lost. Complicating the presentation is the strict geographic patterning of the approach, while the information is everywhere bleeding over the rigid boundaries. To absorb fully all of the information, the reader needs to take careful notes and have both state and regional maps at hand. Zogry's presentation is at times rather obscure, suffering from awkward writing and from ideas needing fuller explication. Finally, there are more than a few black and white photographs that are too dark and too small to be of major diagnostic use, and the index is totally inadequate.

Still, this publication is a pioneering work, employing a new approach, and it opens the way for further development. For example, the geographic approach has tremendous potential, but it might have been structured to allow overall analysis of the forces affecting the various parts of the region. For example, the discussion about the roles of turnpikes and other roadways into the region could have been done *once* thoroughly, rather than fragmented among three different sections of the book. Also, several themes could have been more rigorously pursued, such as the geographical and chronological patterns of New York or New England influence or the development of furniture factories throughout the region. This kind of discipline would have clarified the book's purpose and eliminated marginal entries, such as the desk and bookcase on page 138 owned by James Wilson (1763–1855), who made globes, or the secretary on page 168 owned by Alexander Twilight (1795–1857), the first African-American to receive a college degree in America. Important as these men were, their stories add practically nothing to furniture history.

Also, a more concentrated look at the local characteristics of the furniture might have revealed social patterns not yet discerned. The conservative styles of "Northern Kingdom" furniture may tell us much about those peoples' mindsets. Similar styles were apparently expressed in eastern Maine in the early and mid-nineteenth century, a period of serious economic challenge in that region. These features might reveal the views of people on the economic margin who felt they couldn't take big chances, outlooks that were reflected in their very furnishings.

Kenneth Zogry has done much to bring furniture into a more central role in discerning social patternings. His efforts have opened new doors and suggested further ventures. Probably most important, Zogry has presented the *first* major work on Vermont furniture. That is no mean trick.

Charles Robinson's *Vermont Cabinetmakers and Chairmakers Before 1855: A Checklist* provides a major body of information on the craftsmen who produced the furniture analyzed by Zogry. As anyone who has ever attempted such a checklist knows, the work of ferreting out the data and then organizing it into a presentable format is formidable at best. This publication is the type that others are glad to have and equally glad someone else prepared.

Vermont Cabinetmakers and Chairmakers is presented in a straightforward manner. In a preface Robinson describes the major sources he used, and he notes that, although more names could have been teased from sources such as deeds and probate records, it was time to get the material out to those who could use it.

An introductory essay by Philip Zea, curator of Historic Deerfield, follows the preface. Like Zogry, he notes the mismatch between traditional views and actual evidence regarding furniture manufacture in Vermont, stressing a surprising heterogeneity in products of the region due to various heritages, local factors, and so forth. Zea accentuates the importance of Robinson's checklist by evaluating the origin of Vermont makers—the overwhelming body of immigrants came from Massachusetts and New Hampshire—information at variance with traditional suppositions of strong Connecticut and New York influences on Vermont furniture styles. Such findings, as well as implementing some of the suggestions above regarding Zogry's approach, might bring a degree of order to the presently perceived heterogeneity of Vermont furniture patterns.

The checklist, which makes up most of the volume, is alphabetically arranged. The entries provide the pertinent data that has been located about each individual, which varies from a line of text to fairly extended paragraphs. Overall, the information will be of great help to scholars, dealers, and collectors.

The checklist could be improved, however, in a couple of ways. First, there is a need for a more standardized format relaying basic key information such as working dates, location, and the maker's specific occupation (e.g., cabinetmaking, chairmaking, turning, and so forth). Supplementary material could then be added.

Second, the cross-referencing system is quite frustrating. For example, the entry for Harvey E. Babst directs the reader to Goodale and Babst; the Goodale and Babst entry further directs the scholar to "J. W. Goodale," where the reader finally finds out that the firm of Goodale and Babst operated in 1851. Similarly, in the entry on Asahel Barnes, a cabinetmaker from New Haven, Connecticut, George F. Barnes is mentioned as his son. One then checks the biography for George F. Barnes and is directed to Asahel Barnes, Jr. Only then does the reader learn that the two men—George F. and Asahel, Jr.—were partners in the cabinet- and chairmaking business in Burlington during 1843 and 1844. There's got to be a better way!

Nevertheless, the checklist is rich in important information. It will help identify the makers of many pieces of presently unidentified Vermont furniture. Like Zogry's work, it will also provide scholars with important data with which to further research and analyze the furniture industry in Vermont and place it within the larger regional and national scene.

Edwin A. Churchill
Maine State Museum

Compiled by
Gerald W. R. Ward

Recent Writing on
American Furniture:
A Bibliography

▼ U N L I K E T H E lists in previous volumes of *American Furniture,* which have been divided by year of publication, titles in the following bibliography are presented simply in alphabetical order. Dividing the works by year of publication did not seem to be a high priority, and in fact occasionally served to hinder the use of these annual compilations. It is hoped that a single list will help the reader locate material more easily. This year's list consists mainly of works published in 1995 and through May 1996, and also contains citations to material published in 1991 or later that has not been included in the first three volumes of *American Furniture.*

The short title *American Furniture 1995* is used in citations for articles and reviews published in last year's issue of this journal, which is also cited in full under Luke Beckerdite's name.

A new periodical, generated in England and titled *Journal of Material Culture* (ISSN: 1359–1835), is scheduled to be published three times a year beginning in 1996. It "aims to promote and develop a general comparative and international perspective [by] publishing papers on theory and methodology, interpretive strategies and substantive studies of key themes and issues." Despite the journal's theoretical bent, presumably articles on furniture may occasionally appear in its pages. Another English journal, *Things,* published twice a year beginning in 1994 by the Royal College of Art/ Victoria and Albert Museum Course in the History of Design (ISSN 1356– 921X), occasionally publishes articles and book reviews on furniture, written by present and past students in the program.

This year, the list includes a greater than usual number of references to publications about furniture by contemporary craftsmen. Many of these works are unsigned articles or brief gallery catalogues, numbering in the hundreds and often difficult to distinguish from advertising. I've only included a sampling to provide the reader with, hopefully, some useful indications of trends and activity in modern woodworking. In some cases, this sort of material is cited alphabetically under the craftsman's name, but signed articles and catalogues are listed under the author's name in the usual manner.

As always, I would be grateful to receive suggestions for material that should be included in these annual lists. Review copies of significant works would also be appreciated. Copies and citations may be sent to:

Gerald W. R. Ward
Carolyn and Peter Lynch Associate Curator of
American Decorative Arts & Sculpture

Museum of Fine Arts, Boston
465 Huntington Avenue
Boston, Massachusetts 02115

I am grateful to those individuals who have supplied copies or citations of their work, and to the staffs of the library of the Museum of Fine Arts, Boston; the Portsmouth Athenaeum; and the Winterthur Museum. As always, Neville Thompson at Winterthur deserves a special word of thanks for her generous assistance.

Adams, E. Bryding, ed. *Made in Alabama: A State Legacy.* Birmingham, Ala.: Birmingham Museum of Art, 1995. 392 pp.; 363 color and bw illus., exhibition checklist, bibliography, appendixes, index. (See especially E. Bryding Adams, "Mortised, Tenoned, and Screwed Together: A Large Assortment of Alabama Furniture," pp. 190–237.)

Albertson, Karla Klein. "Classical Savannah: Telfair Museum of Art" (book and exhibition review). *Antiques and the Arts Weekly* (August 4, 1995): 1, 68–71. 14 bw illus.

Albertson, Karla Klein. "Made in Alabama: A State Legacy" (book and exhibition review). *Antiques and the Arts Weekly* (March 15, 1996): 1, 68–70. 14 bw illus.

Albertson, Karla Klein. "Made in America: Ten Centuries of American Art" (exhibition review). *Antiques and the Arts Weekly* (July 14, 1995): 1, 68–71. 24 bw illus. (Includes some furniture.)

Alcouffe, Daniel, Anne Dion-Tenenbaum, and Amaury Lefébure. *Furniture Collections in the Louvre.* Dijon, France: Faton, 1993. 2 vols. Vol. 1: 360 pp.; 345 color illus. Vol. 2: 212 pp.; 205 color illus.

Alexander, John D., Jr. *Make a Chair from a Tree: An Introduction to Working Green Wood.* Rev. ed. Mendham, N.J.: Astragal Press, 1994. 133 pp.; bw illus., line drawings, bibliography, index.

Algoud, Henri, Léon Le Clerc, and Paul Banéat. *Authentic French Provincial Furniture from Provence, Normandy, and Brittany: With 179 Photographs.* New York: Dover Publications, 1993. 20 pp.; 179 bw illus. (Contains complete plates from *Le mobilier provençal, Le mobilier normand,* and *Le mobilier breton,* published 1924–1928 by C. Massin, Paris; all part of the series *Collection de l'art regional de France.* Includes an English translation of the original French captions and a new publisher's introduction.)

Ames, Kenneth L. Review of John R. Porter, ed., *Living in Style: Fine Furniture in Victorian Quebec.* In *American Furniture 1995,* pp. 263–69.

Anderson, Henry H., Jr. "To Burr or Not to Burr?" *Maine Antique Digest* 23, no. 11 (November 1995): 6D–7D. 8 bw illus. (Re desk thought to have been owned by Aaron Burr.)

Anderson, Marcia G. Review of Jessica H. Foy and Karal Ann Marling, eds., *The Arts and the American Home.* In *Journal of the Society of Architectural Historians* 54, no. 2 (June 1995): 260.

Anderson, Mark J. "A New Look at Sulfur and Other Composition Inlay." In *Chester County Historical Society Antiques Show [Catalogue] 1995,* pp. 36–40. West Chester, Pa.: Chester County Historical Society, 1995. 9 bw illus.

Anderson, Mark J., Gregory J. Landrey, and Philip D. Zimmerman. *Cadwalader Study.* Winterthur, Del.: Henry Francis du Pont Winterthur Museum, 1995. 60 pp.; color and bw illus., tables, line drawings, bibliography, appendixes.

[Art Institute of Chicago]. "Chicago's Art Institute Lists Recent Acquisitions." *Antiques and the Arts Weekly* (July 21, 1995): 80. 5 bw illus. (Includes card table by Charles-Honoré Lannuier, ca. 1810; center table attributed to Pottier and Stymus, New York, ca. 1862, with marquetry top by Josef Cremer of Paris; Portsmouth chest of drawers, ca. 1800–1810, attributed to Langley Boardman; Boston Empire pier table by Emmons and Archibald; and other examples of furniture.)

Auslander, Leora. *Taste and Power: Furnishing Modern France.* Berkeley: University of California Press, 1996. xv + 495 pp.; 68 bw illus., bibliography, index.

Baca, Elmo. *Rio Grande High Style: Furniture Craftsmen.* Salt Lake City: Gibbs Smith Publisher, 1995. 176 pp.; illus.

Baca, Elmo. *Romance of the Mission: Decorating in the Mission Style.* Salt Lake City: Gibbs Smith Publisher, 1996. 128 pp.; illus.

Backofen, Al. "Bartlett School Desks" (letter to the editor). *Maine Antique Digest* 24, no. 6 (June 1996): 3A–4A. (Re New Hampshire desk ex coll. Hymie Grossman.)

Banks, William Nathaniel. "Newbury and Newburyport, Massachusetts, 1635–1835." *Antiques* 148, no. 1 (July 1995): 70–83. 21 color and 6 bw illus. (Includes some furniture.)

Barker, Marilyn Conover. *The Legacy of Mormon Furniture: The Mormon Material Culture, Undergirded by Faith, Commitment, and Craftsmanship.* Salt Lake City, Utah: Gibbs Smith Publishers, 1995. 144 pp.; numerous color and bw illus., bibliography, index.

Baron, Donna K. "Definition and Diaspora of Regional Style: The Worcester County Model." In *American Furniture 1995,* pp. 167–90. 26 color and bw illus.

Bartinique, A. Patricia. "Kindred Spirits: The Arts and Crafts Furniture of Charles P. Limbert." *Antiques and the Arts Weekly* (October 27, 1995): 1, 68–69. 13 bw illus.

Bartinique, A. Patricia. *Kindred Styles: The Arts and Crafts Furniture of Charles P. Limbert.* New York: Gallery 532 Soho, 1995. 128 pp.; 164 illus.

Beach, Laura. "The Find of a Lifetime: How Connecticut Dealer William Bartley Landed a Philadelphia Hairy-Paw Foot Table." *Antiques and the Arts Weekly* (December 22, 1995): 36E. 2 bw illus.

Beach, Laura. "Masterpieces of Americana Unveiled at Israel Sack, Inc." *Antiques and the Arts Weekly* (January 26, 1996): 88–89. 6 illus. of furniture. (Re exhibition of documented furniture at the dealer's gallery, January 17 to February 3, 1996.)

Beach, Laura. "Philadelphia's Story: How One Museum Is Building Its Collections." *Antiques and the Arts Weekly* (March 22, 1996): 1, 68–72. 19 bw illus. (Includes some furniture.)

Beach, Laura. "Vermont Furniture, 1765–1850: The Best the Country Affords" (book and exhibition review). *Antiques and the Arts Weekly* (June 16, 1995): 1, 68–71. 19 bw illus.

Beach, Laura. "When Modern Design Was Sexy: Edward J. Wormley Estate at Braswell's." *Antiques and the Arts Weekly* (March 29, 1996): 94–95. 16 bw illus.

The Beauty of Huanghuali: An Exhibition of Fine Huanghuali Furniture from the

Late Ming to Early Qing Dynasties. Text by John Kwang-Ming Ang; trans. Jane Fong-Sai Tzen. Taipei, Taiwan: Artasia, 1995. 92 pp.; color illus., bibliography.

Beckerdite, Luke, and William N. Hosley, eds. *American Furniture 1995.* Milwaukee, Wis.: The Chipstone Foundation, 1995. 298 pp.; numerous color and bw illus., bibliography, index. Distributed by University Press of New England, Hanover, N.H., and London.

"Berks Survey Concludes, But Researchers' Work Continues." *Antiques and the Arts Weekly* (March 8, 1996): 46–47. 5 bw illus. (Re study of Berks County clocks by Richard S. and Rosemarie B. Machmer.)

Berliner, Nancy, et al. *Beyond the Screen: Chinese Furniture of the 16th and 17th Centuries.* Boston: Museum of Fine Arts, Boston, 1996. 158 pp.; color illus., index.

Berliner, Nancy, and Sarah Handler. *Friends of the House: Furniture from China's Towns and Villages.* Salem, Mass.: Peabody Essex Museum, 1996. 133 pp.; color and bw illus. (Also published as *Peabody Essex Museum Collections* 131, no. 2 [1995].)

Binzen, Jonathan. "An Artist Masters the Craft of Furniture Making." *Home Furniture,* no. 3 (Summer 1995): 86–91. 12 color illus. (Re contemporary woodworker Duane Paluska.)

Binzen, Jonathan. "A New Perspective on Old Furniture." *Home Furniture,* no. 1 (Winter 1994): 84–89. 7 color illus.

Binzen, Jonathan. "Tage Frid: Woodworking Master and Mentor." *Home Furniture,* no. 4 (Fall 1995): 30–35. 7 color illus.

Bird, Michael S., foreword by Howard Pain, introduction by Claudia Kinmonth. *Canadian Country Furniture, 1675–1950.* Toronto: Stoddart, 1994. 403 pp.; 600+ color and bw illus., bibliography, index.

Bishop, Robert, and Jacqueline M. Atkins, with the assistance of Henry Niemann and Patricia Coblentz. *Folk Art in American Life.* New York: Viking Studio Books in association

with Museum of American Folk Art, 1995. xii + 228 pp.; 272 color and bw illus., bibliography, index. (Includes some furniture.)

Bocola, Sandro, ed., with essays by Ezio Bassani, Sandro Bocolo, Hans Himmelheber, Lorenz Homberger, Piet Meyer, Andrew Knecht Oti-Amoako, and Roy Sieber. *African Seats.* Munich and New York: Prestel, 1995. 200 pp.; 123 color and 291 bw illus., catalogue, bibliography.

Bonson, James, Vivian Bonson, Jeannine Boring, Robert Conrad, Joan Conrad, and William Dancy. *Pennsylvania Folk Art of Samuel L. Plank.* Allensville, Pa.: Kishacoquillas Valley Historical Society, 1994. 67 pp.; 72 color illus., bibliography, index.

Bowe, Nicola Gordon, ed. *Art and the National Dream: The Search for Vernacular Expression in Turn-of-the-Century Design.* Dublin: Irish Academic Press, 1993. 213 pp.; 124 bw illus., index. Distributed by International Specialized Book Services. (See especially Wendy A. Kaplan, "The Vernacular in America, 1880–1920: Ideology and Design.")

Boyd, Virginia T., and Lawrence J. Jacobsen. "Gustav Stickley: The Creation of Art Through Machine Production." *Wisconsin Academy Review* 39, no. 4 (Fall 1993): 4–9. 7 bw illus., bibliography. (Includes Jacobsen's "Notes from an Arts and Crafts Collector" on p. 7.)

Boynton, Lindsay. *Gillow Furniture Designs, 1760–1800.* Royston, England: Bloomfield Press, 1995. 239 pp.; 32 color and 299 bw illus.

Brown, Peter B. *In Praise of Hot Liquors: The Study of Chocolate, Coffee, and Tea-Drinking, 1600–1850: An Exhibition at Fairfax House, York, 1st September to 20th November 1995.* York, England: York Civic Trust, 1995. 104 pp.; color and bw illus. (With some discussion of period use of tea tables and related objects.)

Bruner, Michael. *Advertising Clocks: America's Timeless Heritage.* Atglen, Pa.: Schiffer Publishing Ltd., 1995. 128 pp.; illus.

Buck, Susan. "'Bedsteads Should be

Painted Green': Shaker Paints and Varnishes." *Old-Time New England* 73, no. 260 (Fall 1995): 17–35. 10 bw illus.

Budden, Sophie, and Frances Halahan, eds. *Lacquerwork and Japanning: Postprints of the Conference held by UKIC at the Courtauld Institute of Art in London, May 1994.* London: United Kingdom Institute for Conservation of Historic and Artistic Works, 1994. 50 pp.; bw illus.

Candee, Richard M. Review of Robert B. Gordon and Patrick M. Malone, *The Texture of Industry: An Archaeological View of the Industrialization of North America.* In *Journal of the Society of Architectural Historians* 54, no. 2 (June 1995): 236–39.

[Castle, Wendell]. *Angel Chairs: New Work by Wendell Castle.* New York: Peter Joseph, 1991. 111 pp.; color and bw illus., bibliography. (Essays by Arthur C. Danto, Peter T. Joseph, and Emma T. Cobb.)

[Castle, Wendell]. "New Art Furniture by Wendell Castle Exhibited in 'Starlight' at Peter Joseph." *Antiques and the Arts Weekly* (March 15, 1996): 36.

Cathers, David M. *Furniture of the American Arts and Crafts Movement: Furniture Made by Gustav Stickley, L. and J.G. Stickley, and the Roycroft Shop.* 1981. Rev. ed. Philmont, N.Y.: Turn of the Century Editions, 1996. 256 pp.; illus.

Chilton, Meredith, ed. *The Bedroom from the Renaissance to Art Deco.* Toronto: Decorative Arts Institute, 1995. 207 pp.; 52 bw illus. (Edited lectures from 1993 Decorative Arts Institute presented by University of Toronto School of Continuing Studies, George B. Gardiner Museum of Ceramic Art, and the Royal Ontario Museum. Includes papers on English and American subjects by Jessie Poesch, Cheryl Robertson, and others; see especially Elizabeth Fleming, "Fashion and Function: An Investigation of the English Dressing Table of the Late Eighteenth Century.")

[Christie's]. *Furnishings from Thomas Molesworth's "Old Lodge" for George Sumers, circa 1935: The Property of Dr. and Mrs. George S. Bayoud.* Sale 8180. New York: Christie's, June 7, 1995. 145

pp.; numerous color and bw illus., chronology, bibliography. (See esp. Wally Reber and Paul Fees, "Interior West: The Craft and Style of Thomas Molesworth," pp. 12–15; "Thomas Canada Molesworth [1890–1977]: A Chronology," pp. 16–17; "Western High Style: Thomas Molesworth Comes to Glenwood Springs," pp. 18–21; and Laura Bayoud Hunt, "Life at the Old Lodge," pp. 22–23.)

[Christie's]. *Important American Furniture, Silver, Prints, Folk Art and Decorative Arts.* Sale 8342. New York: Christie's, January 27, 1996. 193 pp.; numerous color and bw illus. (The numerous furniture entries include a Pennsylvania hairy-paw tea table, lot 247.)

[Christie's]. *Pennsylvania German Folk Art and Decorative Arts from the Collection of Mr. and Mrs. Richard Flanders Smith.* Sale 8116. New York: Christie's, June 3, 1995. 164 pp.; numerous color and bw illus., bibliography.

[Christie's]. *Property from the Estate of Mrs. Lansdell K. Christie.* Sale 8360. New York: Christie's, January 27, 1996. 59 pp.; color and bw illus.

Churchill, Edwin F. Review of Brock W. Jobe, ed., *Portsmouth Furniture: Masterworks from the New Hampshire Seacoast.* In *Studies in the Decorative Arts* 3, no. 2 (Spring-Summer 1996): 139–41.

Coleridge, Anthony. "An Addition to Chippendale's *oeuvre.*" *Antiques* 149, no. 6 (June 1996): 862–67. 8 color illus.

[Colonial Williamsburg]. "Colonial Williamsburg Adds Chest, Portrait, Purchased from Sotheby's to Exhibition." *Antiques and the Arts Weekly* (July 21, 1995): 40C. (Re painted chest by Johannes Spitler, ca. 1800, of the Shenandoah Valley, ex coll. Henry P. Deyerle.)

Cook, Clarence. *The House Beautiful: An Unabridged Reprint of the Classic Victorian Stylebook.* 1881. Reprint. New York: Dover Publications, 1995. 336 pp.; 97 bw illus.

Cooke, Edward S., Jr. Review of Katherine S. Howe et al., *Herter Brothers:*

Furniture and Interiors for a Gilded Age. In *American Furniture 1995,* pp. 253–59.

Cooke, Edward S., Jr. "The Social Economy of the Preindustrial Joiner in Western Connecticut, 1750–1800." In *American Furniture 1995,* pp. 113–44. 32 color and bw illus.

Crawford, Alan. *Charles Rennie Mackintosh.* London: Thames and Hudson, 1995. 216 pp.; 25 color and 142 bw illus., bibliography, index.

Crawford, Alan. "Charles Rennie Mackintosh: The Architect as Artist." *Antiques* 149, no. 6 (June 1996): 878–87. 13 color and 3 bw illus.

Crawford, Barbara, and Royster Lyle, Jr. *Rockbridge County Artists and Artisans.* Charlottesville: University Press of Virginia, 1995. 254 pp.; 15 color and 275 bw illus., bibliography, index. (See "Furniture" and "Tall Clocks," pp. 79–137.)

Crispin, Thomas. *The English Windsor Chair.* Wolfeboro Falls, N.H.: Alan Sutton, 1992. xvi + 191 pp.; numerous bw illus., line drawings, chart, glossary, bibliography, index.

Crom, Theodore R. "An American Beauty: The Samuel Mulliken, II, Salem, Mass., Dwarf Clock." *NAWCC Bulletin* 37, no. 6 (December 1995): 756–61. 16 bw illus.

Cromley, Elizabeth. "A History of Beds and Bedrooms." In *Perspectives in Vernacular Architecture,* ed. Thomas Carter and Bernard Herman, pp. 177–86. Columbia: University of Missouri Press, 1991. Illus. (See also an earlier article by the same author, "Sleeping Around," *Journal of Design History* 3 [1990]: 1–17.)

D'Ambrosio, Anna Tobin. "Artistry in Rosewood: Furniture by Elijah Galusha." *Antiques and the Arts Weekly* (September 1, 1995): 1, 68–70. 8 bw illus.

D'Ambrosio, Anna Tobin. "'The Distinction of Being Different': Joseph P. McHugh and the American Arts and Crafts Movement." In *The Substance of Style: Perspectives on the American Arts and Crafts Movement,* ed. Bert Denker, pp. 143–59. Winterthur, Del.: Henry Francis du Pont

Winterthur Museum, 1996. 5 bw illus.

D'Ambrosio, Anna Tobin. Review of Michael L. James, *Drama in Design: The Life and Craft of Charles Rohlfs.* In *American Furniture 1995,* pp. 260–63.

Danby, Miles. *Moorish Style.* London: Phaidon, 1995. 240 pp.; 150+ color and 80 bw illus.

Davidoff, Donald A. "Maturity of Design and Commercial Success: A Critical Reassessment of the Work of L. and J.G. Stickley and Peter Hansen." In *The Substance of Style: Perspectives on the American Arts and Crafts Movement,* ed. Bert Denker, pp. 161–81. Winterthur, Del.: Henry Francis du Pont Winterthur Museum, 1996. 6 bw illus.

Davidoff, Donald A., and Stephen Gray. *Innovation and Derivation: The Contribution of L. and J. G. Stickley to the Arts and Crafts Movement.* Morris Plains, N.J.: Craftsman Farms Foundation, 1995. 128 pp.; numerous bw illus., checklist, chronology.

Davis, John P. S. *Antique Garden Ornament: 300 Years of Creativity: Artists, Manufacturers, and Materials.* Woodbridge, England: Antique Collectors' Club, 1991. 389 pp.; 102 color and 446 bw illus., appendixes, bibliography, index. (Includes garden furniture, but devoted exclusively to English objects.)

"Decorating the American Home, 1850–1900." *Antiques and the Arts Weekly* (June 30, 1995): 1, 68–69. 5 bw illus. (Re exhibition at Metropolitan Museum of Art designed to complement Herter Brothers exhibition.)

Denker, Bert, ed. *The Substance of Style: Perspectives on the American Arts and Crafts Movement.* Winterthur, Del.: Henry Francis du Pont Winterthur Museum, 1996. vii + 469 pp.; 140 bw illus. Distributed by University Press of New England. (See especially essays cited individually by Anna Tobin D'Ambrosio, Donald A. Davidoff, Catherine L. Futter, Michael L. James, and Neville Thompson.)

Design Quarterly 163 (Winter 1995): 1–32. Color illus. (Re Norwest Corporation's collection of modern design.)

"Documented Desk at Wilson Brothers."

Maine Antique Digest 23, no. 11 (November 1995): 9A. 2 bw illus. (Re desk made by William Wayne of Philadelphia in 1770, with original bill of sale.)

Dohrn-van Rossum, Gerhard. *History of the Hour: Clocks and Modern Temporal Orders.* Chicago: University of Chicago Press, 1996. 344 pp.; illus.

Dormer, Peter. *Furniture Today: Its Design and Craft.* London: Crafts Council Gallery, 1995. 100 pp.; color and bw illus. (Re English furniture.)

Duncan, Alastair. *Paris Salons, 1895–1914.* Vol. 3, *Furniture.* Woodbridge, England: Antique Collectors' Club, 1995. 392 pp.; 121 color and 1,150 bw illus.

Dunham, Judith. *Details of Frank Lloyd Wright: The California Work, 1909–1974.* San Francisco: Chronicle Books, 1994. 144 pp.; 175 color illus.

[Dunnigan, John]. *John Dunnigan, Furniture Maker.* New York: Peter Joseph Gallery, 1991. 36 pp.; color and bw illus.

"Early Maryland Life, 1634–1800: Maryland Historical Society." *Antiques and the Arts Weekly* (May 17, 1996): 1, 68–69. 9 bw illus. (Re gallery reinstallation, including furniture.)

Easton, Rita. "Imitation—The Sincerest Form of Flattery?" *Antiques and the Arts Weekly* (October 6, 1995): 120–21. 6 bw illus. (Review of Emyl Jenkins, *Emyl Jenkins' Reproduction Furniture.*)

Edwards, Clive. "British Imports of American Furniture in the Later Nineteenth Century." *Furniture History* 31 (1995): 210–16.

Edwards, Robert, and Robert Aibel. *Wharton Esherick, 1887–1970, American Woodworker, May 3 through July 20, 1996.* Philadelphia: Moderne Gallery, 1996. 36 pp.; bw illus.

Emlen, Robert P. Review of Timothy D. Rieman and Jean M. Burks, *The Complete Book of Shaker Furniture.* In *American Furniture 1995*, pp. 269–73.

The Endowed Chair: Terry Adkins, Fletcher Benton, Wendell Castle, . . . New York: Franklin Parrasch Gallery, 1992. Unpaged; color and bw illus. (Includes essay by Arthur C. Danto, "The Seat of the Soul.")

[Esherick, Wharton]. "Wharton Esherick, American Woodworker, at Moderne Gallery in Philadelphia." *Antiques and the Arts Weekly* (April 26, 1996): 98. 3 bw illus.

Evans, Nancy Goyne. *American Windsor Chairs.* New York: Hudson Hills Press in association with the Henry Francis du Pont Winterthur Museum, 1996. 744 pp.; 25 color and 1,000+ bw illus., 24 maps, checklist of American Windsor craftsmen, 1745–1850, glossary, bibliography, index.

Ewald, Chase Reynolds. *Old Masters of New England.* Castine, Me.: Country Roads Press, 1994. 120 pp.; numerous bw illus. (See essay on Seth Reed, Shaker furniture maker, pp. 89–95.)

Fairbanks, Jonathan L. "Judy Kensley McKie: Symmetry and Rhythmic Complexity." In *Judy Kensley McKie: New Furniture*, unpaged. Boston: Gallery NAGA, 1995. 8 color illus., chronology, bibliography.

Fane, Diana, ed. *Converging Cultures: Art and Identity in Spanish America.* New York: Brooklyn Museum in association with Harry N. Abrams, 1996. 320 pp.; numerous color and bw illus., glossary, bibliography, index.

Fitzgerald, Oscar P. *Four Centuries of American Furniture.* 2d rev. ed. Radnor, Pa.: Wallace-Homestead Book Co., 1995. xiv + 401 pp.; numerous bw illus., bibliography, index. (Originally published in 1982 as *Three Centuries of American Furniture.*)

Fleming, John A. "The Anglo-American Influence on French-Canadian Furniture After 1760." *Antiques* 148, no. 2 (August 1995): 192–97. 16 color illus.

Frankel, Candie. *Encyclopedia of Country Furniture.* 1993. Rev. ed. New York: Freidman/Fairfax Publishers, 1996. 192 pp.; illus.

Freund, Joan Barzilay. *Masterpieces of Americana: The Collection of Mr. and Mrs. Adolph Henry Meyer.* New York: Sotheby's Books, 1995. 96 pp.; 135 color and 15 bw illus.

Furniture History 31 (1995): 1–235. Numerous bw illus. (Eleven articles on English furniture; see also article by Clive Edwards cited separately.)

Futter, Catherine L. "'Color in the

House': Painted Furniture of the American Arts and Crafts Movement." In *The Substance of Style: Perspectives on the American Arts and Crafts Movement*, ed. Bert Denker, pp. 341–57. Winterthur, Del.: Henry Francis du Pont Winterthur Museum, 1996. 6 bw illus.

Garrett, Wendell. *American Colonial: Puritan Simplicity to Georgian Grace.* Edited and designed by David Larkin; principal photography by Paul Rocheleau. New York: Monacelli Press, 1995. 276 pp.; 200+ color illus.

Gaulkin, Zachary. "Production Furniture with a Human Touch." *Home Furniture*, no. 6 (Spring 1996): 90–95. 8 color illus. (Re Shackleton furniture shop in Bridgewater, Vermont.)

Gill, Tracy, and Simeon Lagodich. *One Hundred Years on the Edge: The Frame in America, 1820–1920.* New York: Gill and Lagodich, 1996. 24 pp.; 35 illus.

Gray, Nina, and Suzanne Smeaton. "Within Gilded Borders: The Frames of Stanford White." *American Art* 7, no. 2 (Spring 1993): 33–45. 17 color and bw illus.

"Greene and Greene Ultimate Bungalow." *Maine Antique Digest* 24, no. 5 (May 1996): 6A. 3 bw illus. (Re exhibition at Thorsen House, Berkeley, California.)

Greiff, Constance. *Art Nouveau.* New York: Abbeville Press, 1995. 96 pp.; 55 bw illus., bibliography, index.

Greiff, Constance. *Early Victorian.* New York: Abbeville Press, 1995. 96 pp.; 55 bw illus., bibliography, index.

Griffith, Lee Ellen. "Mrs. J. Amory Haskell: An American Collector." *Antiques and the Arts Weekly* (March 1, 1996): 1, 68–71. 16 bw illus. (Re exhibition, including some furniture, at the Monmouth County [New Jersey] Historical Society.)

Gruber, Alain, ed. *The History of Decorative Arts: Classicism and the Baroque in Europe.* New York: Abbeville Press, 1995. 496 pp.; 477 color illus.

The Guild 9: The Designer's Reference Book of Artists. Madison, Wis.: Kraus Sikes, 1994. 231 pp.; numerous color illus., index. (See "The Studio Furniture Movement," pp. 118–20, and the illustrated listing of furniture makers, pp. 117–64.)

Gustafson, Eleanor H. "Charles Bullard, Ornamental Painter of Boston." *NAWCC Bulletin* 37, no. 5 (October 1995): 624–25. 1 bw illus.

Gustafson, Eleanor H. "Museum Accessions." *Antiques* 148, no. 4 (October 1995): 410. 1 color illus. (Re acquisition by Warner House Association, Portsmouth, N.H., of Portsmouth high chest dated 1733.)

Gustafson, Eleanor H. "Museum Accessions." *Antiques* 149, no. 5 (May 1996): 650, 652. 5 color and 1 bw illus. (Re acquisitions by the High Museum of Art, Brooklyn Museum, MESDA, Minneapolis Institute of Arts, and Concord Museum.)

Haley, Anne Rogers. "Boston Cabinetmakers and Allied Craftsmen, 1780–1799: A New Resource." *Antiques* 149, no. 5 (May 1996): 760–65. 4 color and 4 bw illus. (Re the Boston assessors' taking books.)

Haley, Anne Rogers. "John and Thomas Seymour in England: A New Look at Seymour-Attributed Furniture in the American Museum in Britain." *America in Britain* 33, no. 2 (1995): 5–9. 4 bw illus.

Hall, John, with an essay by Thomas Gordon Smith. *John Hall and the Grecian Style in America*. Acanthus Press Reprint Series, The 19th-Century: Landmarks in Design, Vol. 2. 1840. Reprint. New York: Acanthus Books, 1996. 176 pp.; bw illus., line drawings. (Reprints of *The Cabinet Maker's Assistant; A Series of Select and Original Designs for Modern Dwelling Houses*, and *A New and Correct Method of Hand-Railing*.)

Harper, Douglas. "Some Early West Chester Craftsmen." In *Chester County Historical Society Antiques Show [Catalogue] 1995*, pp. 14–19. West Chester, Pa.: Chester County Historical Society, 1995. 4 bw illus.

Heller, Carl Benno. *Art Nouveau Furniture*. Kirchdorf: Berghaus, 1994. 152 pp.; 106 color illus.

Henshaw, Julia P., ed. *The Detroit Institute of Arts: A Visitor's Guide*. Detroit: Detroit Institute of Arts in association with Wayne State University Press, 1995. 336 pp.; 800+ color and bw illus., glossary, index. (Includes some furniture.)

The Herman Miller Collection 1952: Furniture Designed by George Nelson and Charles Eames, with Occasional Pieces by Isamu Noguchi, Peter Hvidt, and O.M. Nielson. Acanthus Press Reprint Series, The 20th Century: Landmarks in Design, Vol. 5. 1952. Reprint. New York: Acanthus Press, 1995. 128 pp.; illus. (Includes new introduction by Ralph Caplan to reprint of catalogue.)

Hewett, David. "The Best the Country Affords: Vermont Furniture, 1765–1850" (exhibition and book review). *Maine Antique Digest* 23, no. 7 (July 1995): 32D–33D. 9 bw illus.

Hewett, David. "Bourgeault Blowout in Manchester: Bombé Chest Record Explodes!" *Maine Antique Digest* 23, no. 12 (December 1995): 10A. 1 bw illus.

Hewett, David. "An Essential Book" (review of William C. Ketchum, Jr., *American Cabinetmakers: Marked American Furniture, 1640–1940*). In *Maine Antique Digest* 24, no. 2 (February 1996): 34E–35E.

Hewett, David. "Kasten on Parade." *Maine Antique Digest* 24, no. 4 (April 1996): 38D–39D. bw illus.

Hewett, David. "Record Price for David Wood Shelf Clock." *Maine Antique Digest* 24, no. 4 (April 1996): 9A. 1 bw illus.

Home Furniture, no. 1 (Winter 1994), no. 6 (Spring 1996). Various pp.; numerous color and bw illus. (In addition to articles cited elsewhere individually, this popular magazine contains numerous short articles featuring objects made by contemporary woodworkers.)

Horn, Richard. *Fifties Style*. New York: Friedman/Fairfax Publishers, 1993. 175 pp.; numerous color and bw illus., bibliography, index. (See esp. chap. 4 on furniture and furnishings.)

Hosley, William N. "Regional Furniture/Regional Life." In *American Furniture 1995*, pp. 3–38. 35 color and bw illus.

[Hucker, Thomas]. *Thomas Hucker*. New York: Peter Joseph Gallery, 1992. Unpaged; bw illus., bibliography. (Essays by Peter D. Slatin, Peter T. Joseph, and Rose Slivka.)

"Innovation and Derivation: The Contribution of L. and J. G. Stickley to the Arts and Crafts Movement." *Antiques and the Arts Weekly* (September 29, 1995): 1, 68–69. 5 bw illus.

[Jackson, Daniel]. "Daniel Jackson, 1938–1995." *American Craft* 55, no. 5 (October/November 1995): 23. 1 bw illus. (Obituary of contemporary woodworker.)

James, Michael L. "Charles Rohlfs and 'The Dignity of Labor.'" In *The Substance of Style: Perspectives on the American Arts and Crafts Movement*, ed. Bert Denker, pp. 229–41. Winterthur, Del.: Henry Francis du Pont Winterthur Museum, 1996. 5 bw illus.

Jenkins, Emyl. *Emyl Jenkins' Reproduction Furniture: Antiques for the Next Generation*. New York: Crown Publishers, 1995. xix + 204 pp.; numerous bw illus., directory, bibliography, index.

Johnson, Bebe Pritam, and Warren Eames Johnson. *The Furniture Art of Judy Kensley McKie*. Foreword by Jack Lenor Larsen. East Hampton, N.Y.: Pritam & Eames, 1994. Unpaged; color and bw illus.

Kamil, Neil D. "Hidden in Plain Sight: Disappearance and Material Life in Colonial New York." In *American Furniture 1995*, pp. 191–249. 46 color and bw illus.

Kangas, Matthew. *Breaking Barriers: Recent American Craft*. New York: American Craft Museum, 1995. 64 pp.; 19 color and 38 bw illus.

Kaplan, Wendy. "The Inaugural Exhibition at the Wolfsonian in Miami Beach, Florida." *Antiques* 148, no. 4 (October 1995): 482–91. 16 color illus. (Includes some American and European furniture.)

Kaplan, Wendy, ed. *Designing Modernity: The Arts of Reform and Persuasion, 1885–1945: Selections from the Wolfsonian*. New York: Thames and Hudson, 1995. 352 pp.; numerous color and bw illus., checklist, index. (Includes some American and European furniture.)

Kardon, Janet, ed. *Craft in the Machine Age, 1920–1945: The History of Twentieth-Century American Craft*. New York: Harry N. Abrams in association with the American Craft Museum, 1995. 304 pp.; numerous color and bw illus., appendixes, bibliography, index. (See Kate Carmel, "Against the Grain: Modern American Woodwork," pp. 74–87, and illus. on pp. 208–25.)

Kaye, Myrna. "Evidence from Robert Harrold's Hand . . ." *Maine Antique Digest* 23, no. 8 (August 1995): 6B. 3 bw illus. (Re documentation for Portsmouth rococo furniture.)

Kenyon, Gerald A. *The Collection of Irish Furniture at Malahide Castle*. Dublin: by the author, 1994. 144 pp.; illus.

Ketchum, William, and the Museum of American Folk Art. *American Cabinetmakers: Marked American Furniture, 1640–1940*. New York: Crown, 1995. 404 pp.; 350 bw illus., appendixes, bibliography, index.

Kindred Spirits: The Eloquence of Function in American Shaker and Japanese Arts of Daily Life. San Diego: Mingei International, 1995. 166 pp.; color illus.

Kirkham, Pat. *Charles and Ray Eames: Designers of the Twentieth Century*. Cambridge, Mass.: The MIT Press, 1995. x + 486 pp.; numerous color and bw illus., chronology, bibliography, index.

Kisluk-Grosheide, Danielle O. "The Marquand Mansion." *Metropolitan Museum Journal* 29 (1994): 151–81. 49 bw illus. (Includes a few pieces of nineteenth-century American furniture.)

Knoll Celebrates 75 Years of Bauhaus Design, 1919–1994. New York: Knoll, 1994. 99 pp.; illus.

Kogan, Lee, and Barbara Cate. *Treasures of Folk Art, Museum of American Folk Art*. New York: Abbeville Press, 1994. 358 pp.; numerous color illus. (Picture book including some furniture.)

Kotula, Nickolas. "Identification of Historical Cabinetmaking Woods." *Maine Antique Digest* 24, no. 3 (March 1996): 14D–16D. 7 line drawings.

Kramer, Fran. "Shaker: The Art of Craftsmanship" (exhibition and book review). *Antiques and the Arts Weekly* (October 20, 1995): 1, 68–70. 19 bw illus.

Kugelman, Alice K., Thomas P. Kugelman, and Robert Lionetti. "The Connecticut Valley Oxbow Chest." Hartford Case Furniture Survey, Part III. *Maine Antique Digest* 23, no. 10 (October 1995): 1C–4C. 17 bw illus., 3 tables, references.

Kylloe, Ralph. *A History of the Old Hickory Chair Company and the Indiana Hickory Furniture Movement*. Londonderry, N.H.: by the author, 1995. 196 pp.; illus.

Kylloe, Ralph. "A Primer on Rustic Furnishings." *Antiques and the Arts Weekly* (July 21, 1995): S24–S25. 4 bw illus.

Kylloe, Ralph. *Rustic Furniture Makers*. Salt Lake City: Gibbs Smith Publishers, 1995. 115 pp.; color and bw illus.

Larkin, David. *The Essential Book of Shaker: Discovering the Designs, Buildings, and Furniture*. New York: Universe, 1995. 96 pp.; color illus.

Leben, Ulrich. "Bernard Molitor, Cabinetmaker." *Antiques* 148, no. 3 (September 1995): 306–15. 16 color illus. (Re Paris craftsman active 1787–1820.)

Leben, Ulrich. *Molitor: ébéniste from the ancien régime to the Bourbon Restoration*. Trans. William Wheeler. London: P. Wilson, 1992. 248 pp.; color and bw illus., bibliography, index. Distributed by Rizzoli, New York.

Levitties, John. *Rethinking English Arts and Crafts: The Modernist Tradition in Turn-of-the-Century British Design*. Philadelphia: Moderne Gallery, 1995. 36 pp.; color illus.

Levy, Bernard and S. Dean, Inc. *In Search of Excellence*. New York: Bernard & S. Dean Levy, Inc., 1995. 72 pp.; numerous color illus.

Levy, Martin. "Nineteenth-Century English Gothic Revival Decorative Arts in a Private Collection." *Antiques* 147, no. 6 (June 1995): 884–93. 15 color illus. (Includes some furniture.)

Lewis, Michael H. "American Vernacular Furniture and the North Carolina Backcountry." *Journal of Early Southern Decorative Arts* 20, no. 2 (November 1994): 1–37. 23 bw illus.

Lieberman, Richard K. *Steinway & Sons*. New Haven: Yale University Press, 1995. ix + 374 pp.; 70 illus., bibliography, index.

Lindquist, David, and Caroline C. Warren. *Victorian Furniture with Prices*. Radnor, Pa.: Wallace-Homestead, 1995. viii + 200 pp.; color and bw illus., bibliography, index.

Lingard, Ann, ed. *Miller's Pine and Country Furniture Buyer's Guide*. New York: Miller's Publications, 1995. 400 pp.; 1,000 color and 2,700 bw illus.

Loomes, Brian. *Painted Dial Clocks, 1770–1870*. Woodbridge, England: Antique Collectors' Club, 1994. 280 pp.; 44 color and 275 bw illus. (Revised edition of *White Dial Clocks*.)

Lubbock, Jules. *The Tyranny of Taste: The Politics of Architecture and Design in Britain, 1550–1960*. New Haven: Yale University Press, 1995. xv + 415 pp.; 10 color and 74 bw illus., line drawings, index.

MacCarthy, Fiona. *William Morris: A Life for Our Time*. New York: Alfred A. Knopf, 1994. xix + 780 pp.; 34 color and 123 bw illus., bibliography, index.

McClelland, Nancy A. "Whimsey and Delight: The Western Decorative Arts as Practiced by Thomas Molesworth." *Auction News from Christie's, New York* 16, no. 4 (June 1995): 2–3. 7 color and 1 bw illus.

McDannell, Colleen. *Material Christianity: Religion and Popular Culture in America*. New Haven: Yale University Press, 1995. 368 pp.; 24 color and 100 bw illus.

Machmer, Richard S., and Rosemarie B. Machmer. *Berks County Tall-Case Clocks, 1750 to 1850*. Reading, Pa.: Historical Society Press of Berks County, 1995. 104 pp.; illus. (With section on clock cases by John J. Snyder, Jr.)

Mack, Daniel. *The Rustic Furniture Companion: Traditions, Techniques, and Inspirations*. Asheville, N.C.: Lark Books, 1996. 144 pp.; color and bw illus., index.

Makers '93: An Anniversary Exhibition of Maine Crafts, November 20, 1993– January 30, 1994. Deer Isle, Me.: Maine Crafts Association and Portland

Museum of Art, 1993. 48 pp.; 72 bw illus., biographies. (Includes some contemporary furniture.)

"Material Culture in Early America." *William and Mary Quarterly*, 3d ser., 53, no. 1 (January 1996): 1–180. bw illus. (Although furniture is not considered here, these six essays provide an interesting look at traditional historians' concept of material culture.)

Matthews, Nancy Mowll, et al. *The Art of Charles Prendergast from the Collections of the Williams College Museum of Art and Mrs. Charles Prendergast*. Williamstown, Mass.: Williams College Museum of Art, 1993. 120 pp.; color and bw illus., bibliography, index. (Re frame-making.)

"Meadowcroft Museum Researching 19th-Century Chairmaking: James Wilson Chair Shop Object of Study." *Shavings: Newsletter of the Early American Industries Association*, no. 125 (May/June 1995): 11. 1 bw illus., 1 line drawing. (Re restoration of chairmaking shop located in Taylorstown, Washington County, Pa.)

Medlam, Sarah. "The Decorative Arts Approach: Furniture." In *Social History in Museums: A Handbook for Professionals*, ed. David Fleming, Crispin Paine, and John G. Rhodes, pp. 39–41. London: HMSO, 1993.

Mendgen, Eva A., et al. *In Perfect Harmony: Picture and Frame, 1850–1920*. Amsterdam: Van Gogh Museum; Zwolle: Waanders Uitgevers, 1995. 277 pp.; color and bw illus., bibliography, index. Distributed by University of Washington Press.

[Metropolitan Museum of Art]. "Recent Acquisitions: A Selection, 1994–1995." *Metropolitan Museum of Art Bulletin* 53, no. 2 (Fall 1995): 50–51, 54–55. (See entries on Essex County wainscot chair, 1640–1700; Newport dressing table, 1740–1750; armchair by Julius S. Dessoir of New York City, 1853; and side chair designed by A. J. Davis, possibly made by Burns and Bro., ca. 1857.)

Miller, Betsy. "Country Is Like a Box of Chocolates." *Antiques and the Arts Weekly* (September 29, 1995): 46–47. 4 bw illus.

Miller, R. Craig. "Unity and Renewal: Modern Design in American Art Museums." *Neos* 5, no. 1 (1995): 2–8. (Published by Design Council, Denver Art Museum.)

Monroe, Michael W., with an essay by Barbaralee Diamonstein. *The White House Collection of American Crafts*. New York: Harry N. Abrams, 1995. 128 pp.; 92 color illus., exhibition checklist, craftsmen biographies. (Includes some furniture.)

[Museum of Early Southern Decorative Arts]. "New in the Collection." *The Luminary: The Newsletter of the Museum of Early Southern Decorative Arts* 16, no. 1 (Spring 1995): 6–7. 3 bw illus. (Includes notes by Paula Locklair on mahogany tea table, New Bern, N.C., ca. 1770–1780, and mahogany side chair, possibly Baltimore, 1800–1810.)

[Museum of Early Southern Decorative Arts]. "New in the Collection." *The Luminary: The Newsletter of the Museum of Early Southern Decorative Arts* 17, no. 1 (Spring 1996): 7–9. 5 bw illus. (Includes notes by Paula Locklair on mahogany game table, North Carolina, 1790–1810 by "WH" cabinetmaking school; walnut cellarette, Tidewater, Virginia, 1770–1790; walnut sawbuck table, Piedmont North Carolina, ca. 1750; and yellow pine corner cupboard, Accomack Co., Virginia, 1750–1760.)

[Museum of Early Southern Decorative Arts]. "Recent Additions to the Collections." In *Old Salem, Inc.: The Annual Report, Fiscal Year 1994/1995*, pp. 12–13. Winston-Salem, N.C.: Old Salem, Inc., 1995. 3 bw illus. (Re mahogany tea table, 1770–1780, New Bern, N.C., and blanket chest of 1788, with sulfur inlay.)

[Museum of Fine Arts, Boston]. "Acquisitions." In *The Museum Year, 1994–1995: The One Hundred Nineteenth Annual Report of the Museum of Fine Arts, Boston*, p. 12. Boston: by the Museum, 1995. 1 bw illus. (Re Massachusetts "Nathan Low" easy chair, ca. 1765, ex coll. Eddy Nicholson, acquired by the Museum.)

National Museum of American Art.

National Museum of American Art, Smithsonian Institution. Washington, D.C.: by the Museum; Boston: Bulfinch Press/Little, Brown and Co., 1995. 279 pp.; numerous color illus., bibliographical references. (Includes some furniture.)

Nelson, Marion, ed. *Norwegian Folk Art: The Migration of a Tradition*. New York: Abeville Press in association with the Museum of American Folk Art, New York, and the Norwegian Folk Museum, Oslo, 1995. 276 pp.; 210 color and 49 bw illus., appendixes, bibliography, index.

[New Orleans Museum of Art]. *Handbook of the Collection*. New Orleans: by the Museum, 1995. 304 pp.; numerous color and bw illus., index. (Includes three pieces of American eighteenth- and nineteenth-century furniture.)

Nine Decades: The Northern California Craft Movement, 1907 to the Present. San Francisco: San Francisco Craft and Folk Art Museum, 1993. 31 pp.; illus.

[Northeast Auctions]. *Important New Hampshire Auction . . . November 5, 1995 . . . The Collection of Marjorie Doyle Rockwell*. Hampton, N.H.: Northeast Auctions, 1995. 55 pp.; color and bw illus. (Includes some furniture.)

Novak, Victoria M. "The Tale of Two Tables." *Winterthur Magazine* (Fall 1995): 14–15. 3 bw illus. (Re neoclassical Delaware card tables donated to Winterthur Museum.)

Park, William. *The Idea of Rococo*. Newark, Del.: University of Delaware Press, 1992. 138 pp.; color and bw illus., bibliography, index.

Parrasch, Franklin. *John Cederquist*. New York: Franklin Parrasch Gallery, 1995. 14 pp.; 6 color and 1 bw illus.

Petraglia, Patricia P. *Sotheby's Guide to American Furniture*. New York: Simon and Schuster, 1995. 300 pp.; 18 color illus., numerous line drawings, bibliography, glossary, index.

Petrucelli, Steven P., and Kenneth A. Sposato. *American Banjo Clocks*. Cranbury, N.J.: Adams Brown Co., 1995. 204 pp.; illus.

[Philadelphia Museum of Art]. *Philadelphia Museum of Art: Handbook of the Collections*. Philadelphia: by the museum, 1995. 359 pp.; numerous color illus., bibliography, index. (Includes some furniture.)

Plante, Ellen M. *The Victorian Home: The Grandeur and Comforts of the Victorian Era, in Households Past and Present.* Philadelphia: Running Press, 1995. 176 pp.; color illus., index.

Podmaniczky, Michael S. "The Forbes Toolbox: From a Loving Family to a Caring Museum." *Winterthur Magazine* 41, no. 4 (Winter 1995–1996): 10. 4 bw illus. (Re nineteenth-century cabinetmaking tools owned originally by Alexander Forbes [1823–1914] of Cleveland, Ohio, recently acquired by Winterthur Museum.)

"The Prairie School: Design Vision for the Midwest." *Museum Studies* 21, no. 2 (1995): 84–192. Color and bw illus. (See esp. Judith A. Barter, "The Prairie School and Decorative Arts at the Art Institute of Chicago," pp. 113–33.)

[Prickett, C. L., Antiques]. *Fine Authenticated American Antiques from the C.L. Prickett Collection.* Yardley, Pa.: by the firm, 1995. 28 pp.; color illus. (Mostly eighteenth-and early nineteenth-century furniture for sale.)

Princenthal, Nancy. "Focus: John Cederquist, Franklin Parrasch Gallery, New York, New York" (exhibition review). *American Craft* 55, no. 4 (August/ September 1995): 68–69. 2 color illus.

Prown, Jules David. "In Pursuit of Culture: The Formal Language of Objects." *American Art* 9, no. 2 (Summer 1995): 2–3.

Rauschenberg, Bradford L. "New Discoveries in a Piedmont North Carolina Chest-on-Frame Group." *Journal of Early Southern Decorative Arts* 21, no. 1 (Summer 1995): 89–93. 2 bw illus.

Rauschenberg, Bradford L. "Timber Available in Charleston, 1660–1820." *Journal of Early Southern Decorative Arts* 20, no. 2 (November 1994): 39–99. 1 bw illus., 1 map.

Raycraft, Don, and Carol Raycraft. *Country and Folk Antiques.* Atglen, Pa.: Schiffer Publishing, 1995. 160 pp.; color illus. (Includes some furniture.)

Regan, Michael R., ed. *American and European Furniture Price Guide.*

Dubuque, Iowa: Antique Trader Books, 1995. x + 242 pp.; numerous bw illus., bibliography, appendixes.

Regional Furniture 9 (1995): 1–152. bw illus. (Fourteen articles on English furniture.)

Restoring Antiques. The Art of Woodworking. Alexandria, Va.: Time-Life Books; Montreal and New York: St. Remy Press, 1995. 144 pp; numerous color illus., line drawings, glossary, index. (Consultants were Paul McGoldrick, Giles Miller-Mead, and Marc A. Williams.)

Robinson, Tom. *The Longcase Clock.* 1981. Rev. ed. Woodbridge, England: Antique Collectors' Club, 1995. 500 pp.; 38 color and 650 bw illus., glossary, bibliography, index.

Rock, Howard B., Paul A. Gilje, and Robert Asher, eds. *American Artisans: Crafting Social Identity, 1750–1850.* Baltimore: Johns Hopkins University Press, 1995. xx + 251 pp.; bw illus., index.

Rodriquez, Mario. "The American Chair Revolution." *Home Furniture*, no. 4 (Fall 1995): 92–99. 10 color and 6 bw illus., line drawing. (Includes "How to Distinguish Regional Origins" by Nancy Goyne Evans.)

Rosenberg, Margot. "Carving in the Neatest Manner." *Christie's International Magazine* 13, no. 5 (June 1996): 34–35. 2 color illus. (Re Philadelphia rococo furniture in collection of Henry A. Batten.)

Routes: Exploring the British Origins of Newfoundland Outport Furniture Design. St. John's: Newfoundland Museum, [1992]. 32 pp.; illus., bibliography.

Sack, Donald R. *The Process of Examination.* Video-tiques, vol. 2. Buck Hill Falls, Pa.: by the author, 1995. Videotape.

St. Germain, Priscilla. "Vanderbilt Herter Brothers Console Table Brings Record Price." *Maine Antique Digest* 23, no. 8 (August 1995): 1B–3B. Several bw illus.

Sammarco, Anthony Mitchell. *J. Sanger Atwill and His Craftsmen: The Art of Furniture-Making.* Ed. Kathryn Grover. Lynn, Mass.: Lynn Historical

Society, 1995. 36 pp.; 25 bw illus., exhibition checklist.

Savage, J. Thomas, with photographs by N. Jane Iseley. *The Charleston Interior.* Greensboro, N.C.: Legacy Publications, 1995. 120 pp.; numerous color illus.

Schneider, Richard. "The Shaker Chair Industry, Mount Lebanon, New York: An Overview." *Antiques and the Arts Weekly* (July 21, 1995): S6–S7. 5 bw illus.

Schorsch, David A. *Pennsylvania-German Folk Art.* New York: David A. Schorsch Co., 1995. 20 pp.; 11 color illus. (Includes some furniture.)

[Schriber, James]. "Furniture By James Schriber at the Peter Joseph Gallery." *Antiques and the Arts Weekly* (April 19, 1996): 18. (Exhibition of contemporary woodwork.)

Schuyler, David. *Apostle of Taste: Andrew Jackson Downing, 1815–1852.* Baltimore: Johns Hopkins University Press, 1996. xii + 290 pp.; illus., maps, bibliography, index.

Scott, Katie. *The Rococo Interior: Decoration and Social Spaces in Early Eighteenth-Century France.* New Haven: Yale University Press, 1995. ix + 342 pp.; color and bw illus., bibliography, index.

Sewell, Darrel, Ivy L. Barsky, and Kelly Leigh Mitchell. "Contemporary American Crafts." *Bulletin of the Philadelphia Museum of Art* 87, nos. 371–72 (Fall 1991): 1–56. 31 color and 10 bw illus., checklist of exhibition. (Includes some furniture.)

Seymour, Liz. "Eliel Saarinen: Bridge Builder." *Home Furniture*, no. 6 (Spring 1996): 25–29. 8 color illus.

[Simpson, Tommy]. *Tommy Simpson.* New York: Leo Kaplan Modern, 1994. 24 pp.; color illus., bibliography.

Simpson, Tommy, with Lisa Hammel. *Hand and Home: The Homes of American Craftsmen.* Boston: Little, Brown and Co., 1994. 152 pp.; numerous color illus. (Includes pictures of the homes of Sam Maloof, Wendell Castle, and other woodworkers.)

[Skinner, Inc.]. *A Shaker Collection.* Sale 1690. Bolton, Mass.: Skinner, Inc., January 13, 1996. 35 pp.; color and bw illus., bibliography. (Includes furniture.)

Snodin, Michael, and Maurice Howard. *Ornament: A Social History Since 1450*. New Haven and London: Yale University Press in association with the Victoria and Albert Museum, 1996. 232 pp.; 139 color and 102 bw illus., bibliography, index.

Snyder, John J., Jr. "Michael Stoner, Cabinetmaker and Chairmaker." *Antiques* 149, no. 5 (May 1996): 746–49. 7 color illus.

Solis-Cohen, Lita. "*American Furniture 1995*" (book review). *Maine Antique Digest* 24, no. 5 (May 1996): 11B. 1 bw illus.

Solis-Cohen, Lita. "American Masterpieces: Tall-Case Clocks of the 18th Century." *Maine Antique Digest* 24, no. 6 (June 1996): 32B. 4 bw illus.

Solis-Cohen, Lita. "Boston Mixing Table Brings $594,000 at Private Auction." *Maine Antique Digest* 23, no. 7 (July 1995): 9A. 1 bw illus. (Re small marble slab or side table of ca. 1740, mahogany with white pine and black cherry.)

Solis-Cohen, Lita. "Chester County Clock Brings $53,900." *Maine Antique Digest* 24, no. 5 (May 1996): 5F. 4 bw illus. (Re tall clock by Isaac Thomas, ca. 1750–1760.)

Solis-Cohen, Lita. "Chester County Spice Box Sells for $90,200." *Maine Antique Digest* 23, no. 12 (December 1995): 9A. 3 bw illus. (Box attributed to Joel Bailey.)

Solis-Cohen, Lita. "A Desk by John Shearer." *Maine Antique Digest* 24, no. 5 (May 1996): 36E. 2 bw illus.

Solis-Cohen, Lita. "Eye-Opening Show of Herter Presents a Pageant of Fashion in the Gilded Age" (exhibition and book review). *Maine Antique Digest* 23, no. 7 (July 1995): 12F–14F. 12 bw illus.

Solis-Cohen, Lita. "The Gallery Shows." *Maine Antique Digest* 24, no. 4 (April 1996): 8D–12D. bw illus. (Re exhibitions at Israel Sack, Inc., on classicism, and others.)

Solis-Cohen, Lita. "Great Furniture Discovery: Hairy Paw Tea Table." *Maine Antique Digest* 23, no. 12 (December 1995): 7A. 2 bw illus. (Re

Philadelphia mahogany table; see also "More on the Hairy Paw Tea Table," *Maine Antique Digest* 24, no. 1 [January 1996]: 9A, 1 bw illus.)

Solis-Cohen, Lita. "Herter at Auction in New York City." *Maine Antique Digest* 23, no. 12 (December 1995): 1C–3C. 20 bw illus. (See also related article by Priscilla St. Germain, pp. 3C–4C, with 11 bw illus.)

Solis-Cohen, Lita. "Scientific Cadwalader Study." *Maine Antique Digest* 23, no. 11 (November 1995): 15B. (Re: review of study published by Winterthur Museum of eighteenth-century Philadelphia furniture owned by the Cadwalader family.)

Solis-Cohen, Lita. "Scientific Cadwalader Study and Video" (review). *Maine Antique Digest* 23, no. 12 (December 1995): 6A.

[Somerson, Rosanne]. *Rosanne Somerson: Earthly Delights*. New York: Peter Joseph Gallery, 1993. 16 pp.; color illus., bibliography. (Includes essay by Edward S. Cooke, Jr., "Brushing Against a Memory.")

[Sotheby's]. *Important Americana: The Collection of Dr. and Mrs. Henry P. Deyerle of Harrisonburg, Virginia*. Sale 6716. New York: Sotheby's, May 26–27, 1995. Unpaged; numerous color and bw illus., bibliography. (See esp. Wendell D. Garrett, "The Great Valley of Virginia.")

[Sotheby's]. *Important Americana: The Collection of Mr. and Mrs. Adolph Henry Meyer*. Sale 6801. New York: Sotheby's, January 20, 1996. Unpaged; numerous color and bw illus., bibliography. (See essays by Leslie Keno and Jonathan Meyer Thomas.)

"Sotheby's Americana Bonanza: The Collection of Mr. and Mrs. Adolph Henry Meyer." *Maine Antique Digest* 23, no. 12 (December 1995): 8A. 1 bw illus.

"Southern Painted Furniture." *Antiques and the Arts Weekly* (April 5, 1996): 26. 2 bw illus. (Re exhibition at High Museum of Art, Atlanta, Georgia.)

Sperling, David A. "Daniel Porter: Apprentice of Daniel Burnap." *Maine Antique Digest* 24, no. 4 (April 1996): 13F. 1 bw illus.

Stayton, Kevin. "Converging Cultures in Viceregal Peru." *Antiques* 149, no. 4 (April 1996): 584–93. 18 color plates.

[Stickley, Gustav]. *Craftsman Homes: Mission-Style Homes and Furnishings of the American Arts and Crafts Movement, including a Rare Promotional Pamphlet: The Craftsman's Story*. 1905, 1909. Reprint. New York: Gramercy Books, 1995. 227 pp.; numerous bw illus.

Stoltzfus, Louise. *Two Amish Folk Artists: The Story of Henry Lapp and Barbara Ebersol*. Intercourse, Pa.: Good Books, 1995. 116 pp.; illus. (Lapp [1862–1904] made furniture in Lancaster County.)

Striner, Richard. *Art Deco*. New York: Abbeville Press, 1994. 96 pp.; bw illus., bibliography, index.

Sweeney, Kevin M. "Regions and the Study of Material Culture: Explorations Along the Connecticut River." In *American Furniture 1995*, pp. 145–66. 17 bw illus.

Sweeting, Adam. *Reading Houses and Building Books: Andrew Jackson Downing and the Architecture of Popular Antebellum Literature, 1835–1855*. Hanover, N.H.: University Press of New England, 1996. 256 pp.; 26 illus.

Take a Seat: The History of Parker Knoll, 1834–1994. Text by Stephen Bland. n.p.: Baron, 1995. 256 pp.; illus., index. (Re English furniture company.)

Talbott, Page. "Allen and Brother, Philadelphia Furniture Makers." *Antiques* 149, no. 5 (May 1996): 716–25. 13 color and 8 bw illus.

Talbott, Page. *Classical Savannah: Fine and Decorative Arts, 1800–1840*. Savannah, Ga.: Telfair Museum in cooperation with the University of Georgia Press, 1995. 196 pp.; numerous color and bw illus., checklist, bibliography, index.

Talbott, Page. Review of John Morley, *Regency Design*. In *Studies in the Decorative Arts* 3, no. 1 (Fall/Winter 1995–1996): 84–86.

"Tall Case Clock Exhibit Extended Through September in Columbia, Pa." *Antiques and the Arts Weekly* (April 26, 1996): 10. (Re show at Watch and Clock Museum of eighteenth-century American clocks.)

Taylor, Fred, and Gail Taylor. *Identification of Older and Antique Furniture*. Tampa, Fla.: ID Video, 1995. 40 min. videotape. (Re furniture from ca. 1840 to 1950.)

Teahan, John. *Irish Furniture and Woodcraft*. Dublin: Country House in association with National Museum of Ireland, 1994. 46 pp.; illus.

Temin, Christine. "Poet in Wood: John Dunnigan." *American Craft* 55, no. 6 (December 1995/January 1996): 50–53. 6 color illus.

Tennant, M. F. *Longcase Painted Dials: Their History and Restoration*. London: NAG Press, 1995. 256 pp.; 24 color and 163 bw illus. (Re English clocks.)

Thompson, Neville. "Louise Brigham: Developer of Box Furniture." In *The Substance of Style: Perspectives on the American Arts and Crafts Movement*, ed. Bert Denker, pp. 199–211. Winterthur, Del.: Henry Francis du Pont Winterthur Museum, 1996. 6 bw illus.

Thompson, Robert Farris. *Face of the Gods: Art and Altars of Africa and the Africa-Americas*. New York: Museum of African Art; Munich: Prestel, 1993. 334 pp.; color and bw illus., bibliography, index.

Tolpin, Jim. "Designing for Success." *Home Furniture*, no. 1 (Winter 1994): 90–93. 5 color illus. (Re contemporary woodworker Anthony Kahn.)

Tolpin, Jim. *The Toolbox Book*. Newtown, Conn.: Taunton Press, 1995. 199 pp.; numerous color illus., line drawings, index. (Includes some brief references to historical toolboxes.)

Tomes, Patricia A. *American Masterpieces: Tall Case Clocks of the Eighteenth Century*. Columbia, Pa.: NAWCC, 1995. 32 pp.; 18 color and 24 bw illus., bibliography.

Trent, Robert F. "Long-Awaited Windsor Chairs Book Magnificent" (review of Nancy Goyne Evans, *American Windsor Chairs*). *Maine Antique Digest* 24, no. 5 (May 1996): 1E. 1 bw illus.

20th Century American Frames from the Lowy Collection. Intro. by Mark Methner. New York: Julius Lowy Frame and Restoring Company, 1996. 34 pp.; color illus.

Ulrich, Laurel Thatcher. "Furniture as Social History: Gender, Property, and Memory in the Decorative Arts." In *American Furniture 1995*, pp. 39–68. 29 color and bw illus.

[Virginia Museum of Fine Arts]. "Virginia Museum of Fine Arts Buys Deyerle Collection Virginia Side Chairs, Tall Case Clock from Sotheby's." *Antiques and the Arts Weekly* (June 30, 1995): 79. (Re northern Virginia chairs, ca. 1810, and Jacob Danner [1763–1850] clock of ca. 1820 from Middleton, Virginia.)

[Virginia Museum of Fine Arts]. "Woolf Painting, Nakashima Furniture Among . . . Gifts." *Antiques and the Arts Weekly* (January 26, 1996): 21. (Re acquisition of fourteen pieces by George Nakashima [1905–1990] made in the 1960s.)

Wagner, John. *Building Adirondack Furniture: The Art, the History, and the How-to*. Charlotte, Vt.: Williamson Publishing Co., 1995. 127 pp.; illus., index.

Ward, Barbara McLean. Review of James M. Gaynor and Nancy L. Hagedorn, *Tools: Working Wood in Eighteenth-Century America*. In *American Furniture 1995*, pp. 251–53.

Ward, Gerald W. R. Review of John R. Porter, ed., *Living in Style: Fine Furniture in Victorian Quebec*. In *Studies in the Decorative Arts* 3, no. 1 (Fall/Winter 1995–1996): 86–87.

Ward, Gerald W. R., comp. "Recent Writing on American Furniture: A Bibliography." In *American Furniture 1995*, pp. 279–87.

Warren, David B. "Living with Antiques: A Houston Collection." *Antiques* 149, no. 5 (May 1996): 726–35. 17 color illus.

Wilner, Eli, with Mervyn Kaufman. *Antique American Frames: Identification and Price Guide*. New York: Avon Books, 1995. xxvii + 228 pp.; illus., bibliography, index.

Wilson, Kenneth M., and Kirk J. Nelson. "The Role of Glass Knobs in Glassmaking and Furniture." *Antiques* 149, no. 6 (May 1996): 750–59. 16 color illus.

Wissing, Douglas A. "Persistence of

Memory: French Furniture in Indiana." *Traces of Indiana and Midwestern History, A Publication of the Indiana Historical Society* 7, no. 3 (Summer 1995): 40–43. 3 color and 1 bw illus.

Wood, James N., and Teri J. Edelstein, with Sally Ruth May. *The Art Institute of Chicago: The Essential Guide*. Chicago: Art Institute of Chicago, 1993. 288 pp.; numerous color illus., index. (Includes some furniture.)

Wood, Stacy B. C., Jr. *Clockmakers and Watchmakers of Lancaster County, Pennsylvania*. Lancaster, Pa.: Lancaster County Historical Society, 1995. 75 pp.; illus., bibliography.

Wood, Stacy B. C., Jr. "Martin Shreiner: From Clocks to Fire Engines." *NAWCC Bulletin* 37, no. 5 (October 1995): 579–89. 20 bw illus.

[Worcester Art Museum]. *Worcester Art Museum: Selected Works*. Worcester, Mass.: by the museum, 1994. 244 pp.; color illus., bibliography, index. (Includes a Newport high chest, 1760–1780.)

Wu Bruce, Grace. *Chinese Classical Furniture*. Hong Kong: Oxford University Press, 1995. 74 pp.; color and bw illus., chronological table, glossary, bibliography, index.

Zea, Philip. "Diversity and Regionalism in Rural New England Furniture." In *American Furniture 1995*, pp. 69–111. 49 color and bw illus.

Zimmerman, Philip D. "Philadelphia Queen Anne Chairs in Wright's Ferry Mansion." *Antiques* 149, no. 5 (May 1996): 736–45. 16 color illus.

Zimmerman, Philip D. Review of Philip Zea and Donald Dunlap, *The Dunlap Cabinetmakers: A Tradition in Craftsmanship*. In *American Furniture 1995*, pp. 273–77.

Zingman-Leith, Elan, and Susan Zingman-Leith. *Creating Authentic Victorian Rooms*. Washington, D.C.: Elliott & Clark Publishing, 1995. 152 pp.; numerous color and bw illus., bibliography, glossary, index.

Index

Abbot, Daniel, 28(fig.)

Abif, Hiram, 195, 210, 313

Ackermann, Rudolph, 49, 139, 152, 155, 161

Adams, Oliver, 99(n25)

Adams, Thomas, 28

Advertisements, 39, 44(fig. 27), 45(& fig.); in Charleston, 142, 143–46, 152; and immigrant carvers, 246–47; for Phyfe reproductions, 71, 72(figs. 14, 15); trade cards, 42(fig.), 43

Aesop (Barlow), 58–61, 59(fig.)

Aesop fables, 57–61, 62(n5), 136(n21)

Aesop Paraphras'd (Hollar), 57, 58(fig. 2)

Aesop's Fables (Croxall, trans.), 58, 60(fig. 6), 61

Affleck, Thomas, 60

African-American decorative arts, 310–11

Aiken, William, 153, 167–68, 174(n52)

Aiken-Rhett house, 167–68, 167(figs.)

Alden, John, 83

Alden, Priscilla Mullins, 83

Allen, Amos Denison, 19, 22(fig.), 24, 26, 27

Allen, Benjamin, 97(n8), 100

Allen, John, 280

Allen, Joseph, 83, 97(n8)

Allen, Samuel, 81, 100

Allen, Samuel (grandson), 97(n8), 100–101

Alling, David, 27, 28, 29, 34, 39, 40–41, 43, 45, 46, 47, 49

Allston family, 169(n5)

Alvord, Elihu, 26

American Seating Furniture: 1630–1730 (Forman), 175

Analysis of Beauty (Hogarth), 124(fig.)

Anderson, James, 207–8, 207(fig.)

Andrews, Reverend, 228(n5)

Annapolis, Maryland, 299

Antients Grand Lodge, 225, 226, 230(n32)

Apthorp, Charles, 269–70, 271–73, 276, 289

Apthorp, Charles Ward, 271

Apthorp, Grizzell (Eastwick), 271

Architectural Record, 5–6, 14

Architecture: and Freemasonry, 205, 209–13; Tiffany house, 3, 4–5, 7(fig. 7), 15(nn 2, 3)

Armchair(s): attributed to Deming and Bulkley, 163, 164(figs.); common, 17, 18(fig. 1), 19(fig.); English Regency, 140(& figs.); fancy, 40(fig.), 41(fig.), 45–46, 47(figs.); leather, 184, 186, 187(fig. 24), 188(figs. 25, 27), 189(fig. 28), 194(n15); New York Georgian, 289–91, 291(figs.), 304(n46); Phyfe reproductions, 75–78, 75(fig.), 76(figs.); in Tiffany breakfast suite, 3, 4(figs.); Windsor, 20(fig.), 21–24, 21(fig.), 22(fig.), 25(& fig.), 26–27, 26(fig.), 28

Art of Decorative Design, The (Dresser), 8

Ashmole, Elias, 205

Ashton, Dore, 110

Aspinwall, John, 284–85, 303(n33)

Austin, Josiah, 26

Avery, Oliver, 24

Bachelard, Gaston, 117, 123

Bachman, Reverend John, 163, 174(n48)

Bacon, Francis H., 15

Bacot family, 169(n5)

Badger, Daniel W., 37

Bagnall, Benjamin, 301(n12), 305(n52)

Baldwin family, 280

Ball, Hugh Swinton, 153

Ballard, Daniel, 269

Ball-back chairs: fancy, 41–42, 41(fig.); Windsor, 30–31, 31(fig.)

Baltimore chairs, 37, 39, 47–49

Bamboo chairs: fancy, 41(& fig.), 165; Windsor, 26, 27

Bancker, Charles N., 74

Banister, John, 298, 299, 306(n57)

Banister-back chairs, 193(n10); common, 18(fig. 2), 19; Windsor, 37(& fig.)

Barelli, Torre & Co., 142

Barlow, Francis, 58–61, 59(fig.), 61(n4)

Barnes, Ambrose E., 7

Barnes, Elizur, 28, 35, 41

Barnes Brothers, 4(figs.), 7, 15(n6)

Barnet, William, 237, 263(n10)

Baron, Alexander, 169(n5)

Baroque, 119, 287

Barrow, James, 264(n21)

Bass, Anne (Savell), 83, 101

Bass, Benjamin, 29, 43

Bass, John, 83, 101

Bass, Joseph, 101, 104

Bass, Mary (Belcher), 101

Bass, Ruth (Alden), 83, 101

Bass, Samuel (Deacon), 83, 101

Bass, Samuel (grandson), 101

Bateman, John, 103

Battwell, Walter, 196, 228(n2)

Fiddle-back common chair, 19–20, 19(fig.)
Fielding, Henry, 125
Finlay, Hugh, 39, 48, 49
Finlay, John, 39
Firescreen, 264(n24)
Fiske, Jonathan, 99(n25)
Fiske, Sally Flagg, 99(n25)
Fitch, Thomas, 182, 185, 188, 287, 301(n8)
Fithian, Philip Vickers, 217, 218
Fleeson, Plunkett, 270
Fleming, John A., 314
Floyd, Benjamin, 66
Fontaine, Pierre, 139
Foot, Bernard, 28
Forman, Benno M., 175–77, 178, 179, 181, 184, 190–91, 192(n4), 194(n15), 303(n37)
Foster, Jonathan, 294
Fox, Frederick, 37, 51
Fragonard, Jean-Honoré, 108(& fig.), 109–10, 110(fig.), 123(fig. 30), 135(n12)
France: and Charleston market, 139; influence on Canadian furniture, 315–16, 318(n2); rococo and femininity in, 110–11
Franklin, Benjamin, 57, 125, 218, 230(n33), 299
Franklin, Walter, 21, 23
Fraser, Charles, 141, 170(n18)
Fraternalism, 311–13. *See also* Freemasonry
Fredericksburg Lodge, 199(fig.), 232(n54)
Freemasonry: apron/floor cloth, 221(& figs.); books on, 311–14; grand master's jewel, 223(& fig. 39); membership, 196, 205, 231(n35); "operative" versus "speculative," 228(n6); and politics, 208, 226, 232(n55); ritual, 195–96, 195(fig.); symbolism and philosophy, 200, 203, 204–27, 229(nn10, 22, 23), 230(n33), 231(nn 42, 46, 48), 232(n49). *See also* Masonic master's chair
French, Charles Hibbard, 83
French, John, 83
French Empire style, 159
Fret-back fancy chair, 45–47(& figs.), 48(fig. 31), 49(& fig.)
Friends and Amateurs in Musick (Middleton), 138(fig. 2)
Fussell, Solomon, 18

Gaines, John, II, 18–19

Gaines, Thomas, 18–19
Gainsborough, Thomas, 137
Gallup, Caleb, 28
Galt, John Minson, 195
Gansevoort, Peter, 51
Garden, Hugh, 11(fig. 14)
Garrett, Wendell, 292
Garvan, Francis P., 68
Gautier, Andrew, 23, 241
Gender, and rococo symbolism, 112–15, 116–17, 124, 136(n21)
Gentleman and Cabinet-Maker's Director, The (Chippendale), 59, 60(fig. 7), 61, 134(n2), 202(figs. 8, 10), 203(& fig. 11), 236
Gere, James, 35, 46
Gibbs, James, 263(n15)
Gill, Bryson, 47
Gillow, Mr., 142
Gilpin, Thomas, 23
Girard, Stephen, 22, 26, 27
Goddard, John, 296
Godwin, Edward William, 12
Gombrich, E. H., 116
Gonzales, Roger, 193(n5)
Gooch, William, 267–68, 302(n23)
Goodrich, Ansel, 24
"Gospel of Good Taste, The" (Tiffany), 14
Gosse, Sir Edmond, 5
Gouldsmith, Richard, 145, 146, 172(n37)
Gragg, Samuel, 43
Grand Lodge of England, 199, 228(n8)
Grant, Samuel, 192, 269–70, 275, 276, 277, 278, 286, 287, 295, 301(nn 8, 10), 303(nn 28, 34, 35), 304(n45)
Great chair, 12(fig.)
Grecian style, 167; fancy chair in, 50–51, 50(fig.), 141
Greene, Joseph, 208
Greenleaf, Stephen, 294, 295
Grendy, Giles, 272(fig. 2)
Griffen, Robert, 301(n12)
Griffith, Robert, 305(n52)
Groce, Jerusha, 303(n28)
Gross, Thomas, Jr., 308
Grotto, 111–14, 111(fig. 9), 112(fig.), 113(figs.), 132
Groult, André, 117(fig.)
Grusius, Gottlieb, 114(& fig. 13)
Gulliver's Travels (Swift), 128

Hagen, Ernest F., 3, 6, 64–67, 65(fig.),

68, 69(fig.), 80(n17); restorations/reproductions, 67(figs.), 68–70, 70(figs.), 73(fig. 13), 76–79, 76(figs.), 78(fig.), 80(n18). *See also* Meier and Hagen
Hagen, Frederick E., 66, 70
Hagen, Henry A., 66
Hagler, Katherine B., 307
Haley, William P., 33
Hall, Richard, 201(fig.)
Halsey, R. T. Haines, 68, 71
Halstead family, 256
Hamilton, Alexander, 293, 305(n54)
Hamilton, George, 214
Hamilton, John D., 313
Hampton Place, 236(fig. 6), 237–39, 237(figs.)
Hancock, Thomas, 271, 277
Hardcastle, Henry, 233–35, 241(fig.), 262(n6), 265(n26), 304(n47)
Harrison, Peter, 241, 263(n15)
Hasolle, James, 205(fig.)
Haven, David, 19
Hawley, Elisha, 19, 26
Hayden, John, 102
Hayden, Jonathan, 102
Hayden, Nehemiah, 102
Hayden, Samuel, 102
Haydon, William, 33, 51
Hayward, Thomas Cotton, 44(fig. 27), 45
Hedges, James B., 297–98
Helme, James C., 51
Henretta, James A., 298
Henzey, Joseph, 26
Henzey, Joseph, Sr., 24, 25(fig.)
Hepplewhite, George, 39
Hercules and Omphale (Boucher), 109(& fig.)
Hermeticism, 205, 206, 211
Hersey, George, 127
Herter, Gustave, 168
Herter Brothers, 13(fig.), 65
Hewing, 88–89, 98(n17)
Heywood, Benjamin F., 51
High-back Windsor chairs, 20(fig.), 21–23, 21(fig.)
Hill, Sullivan, 30
Hints on Household Taste in Furniture, Upholstery and other Details (Eastlake), 8–11
Hiram, King, 210
History of the Province of New-York From the First Discovery to the Year 1732 (Smith), 233, 288